New York, Washington DC & the Mid-Atlantic
TRIPS

50 THEMED ITINERARIES **1131** LOCAL PLACES TO SEE

Jeff Campbell,
Adam Karlin, Ginger Adams Otis, David Ozanich

NEW YORK, WASHINGTON DC & THE MID-ATLANTIC TRIPS

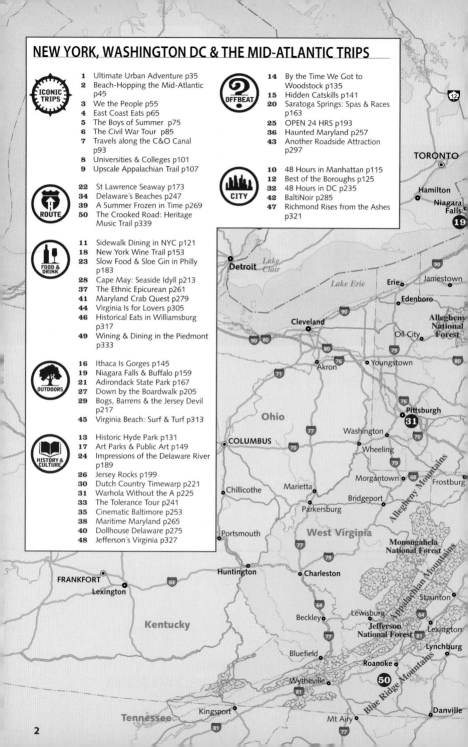

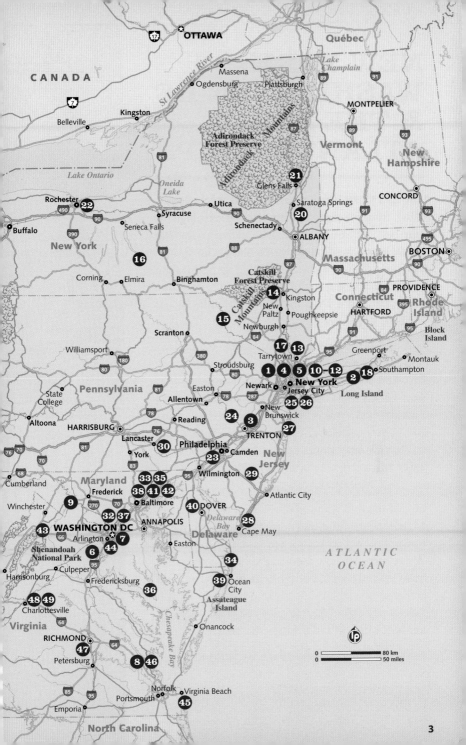

NEW YORK, WASHINGTON DC & THE MID-ATLANTIC TRIPS

The East Coast wears its pride on its sleeve. Everything, from the pizza to the form of government, is "the best." Of course, hyperbolic native boosterism exists everywhere. Usually it's self-acknowledged exaggeration; just a chest-thumping demonstration of hometown love. But folks from Jersey, New York, Philly, Baltimore, DC – they really mean they've got the best. Whatta ya gonna do?

Still, despite this passionate parochial devotion, locals don't always get out and experience what they've got. There are cosmopolitan Manhattanites who've never seen the Catskills. There are die-hard Washington politicos who wouldn't dare mingle with blue-collar Balt'moreans – and vice versa. Virginia's Appalachian trailhounds may dismiss New York's Adirondacks, and nearly everyone skips Jersey's Pine Barrens.

So consider these trips a sort of challenge. We've ranged the mid-Atlantic states from the Thousand Islands to Pittsburgh and down to Richmond. We've traveled its fabled beaches and into its historic past. We've sampled slow food in Philly, steamed crabs in Maryland and shoofly pie in Intercourse, and gathered everything into these adventures so you can too. The East Coast really does have the best, but how much of it do you really know?

Now, what are *you* gonna do?

ST LAWRENCE SEAWAY p173
Boldt Castle, Thousand Islands, NY

"We've ranged the mid-Atlantic states and gathered everything into these adventures so you can too."

THE OTHER 99%

Dubbed the "nation's attic," Washington DC's Smithsonian Institution can only display 1% of its collection. It could solve that by placing the lot on the National Mall (p41) and holding the best yard sale ever.

"We've sampled slow food in Philly, steamed crabs in Maryland and shoofly pie in Intercourse…"

"The East Coast is cities and sand, history and hot dogs..."

Iconic Trips

The East Coast has been *occasionally* known to boast. That's partly because its iconic monuments and scenery verily define iconicness itself. The **Statue of Liberty** (p36), the **Empire State Building** (p35), the **White House** (p41), **Independence Hall** (p58), **Gettysburg** (p88), the **Appalachian Trail** (p107): these things represent the heart of America, and even the soaring nature of the human spirit. What about everyday life? The East Coast is **cities** (p35) and **sand** (p45), **history** (p55 and p85) and **hot dogs** (p65), **Ivy League universities** (p101) and the crack of a **baseball** bat (p75).

"...its iconic monuments and scenery verily define iconicness itself."

IVY LEAGUE SMARTS

The mid-Atlantic states contain four of the original eight Ivy League universities – Columbia (p104), Cornell (p147), Princeton (p231) and the University of Pennsylvania (p103) – plus the continent's second-oldest college, William & Mary (p101).

ULTIMATE URBAN ADVENTURE p35
Statue of Liberty

BEACH-HOPPING THE MID-ATLANTIC p45
Boardwalk, Cape May, NJ

THE BOYS OF SUMMER p75
The New York Yankees – East Coast icons of the national pastime

Routes

See that raggedly coastline? The one rimmed with barrier islands and tattered by enormous bays? Driving that is one of the mid-Atlantic's best, more definitive experiences, and we've provided trips to take you from "The Nation's Summer Capital" of **Rehoboth Beach** (p249), to the small-town charms of tiny **Berlin** (p269) and even tinier **Snow Hill** (p270). Torn between your waterside wanderlust and the desire for a bucolic village vacation? Then take the drive up to the **St Lawrence Seaway** (p173), with its network of a thousand islands, quaint fishing hamlets and old-fashioned farm stands, all set against the aquatic backdrop of Lake Ontario and the St Lawrence River. But for mountain scenery, take the **Crooked Road** (p339) in the foothills of the Appalachians to hear how the fiddle and banjo players pick it. You've come a long way, baby.

"See that raggedly coastline? Driving that is one of the mid-Atlantic's best experiences..."

DELAWARE'S BEACHES p247
Rehoboth Beach

ST LAWRENCE SEAWAY p173
Thousand Island–hopping along the St Lawrence Seaway

A SUMMER FROZEN IN TIME p269
Surf and sand at Ocean City, MD, the East Coast's "OC"

Food & Drink

We're forever hearing from friends and relatives who've moved away and now incessantly pine for the bagels, pizza, deli, hot dogs, crabs, egg creams, cheesesteaks and cheesecake they can't seem to find as good in the rest of the country. Maybe it's the water, or maybe they should just move back.

So, yes, we've devoted several trips to the mid-Atlantic's less expensive, greasier delights, including **New York's pushcart cuisine** (p121) and Chesapeake Bay **crab shacks** (p279). However, that doesn't mean we've neglected the finer things in life. There's a locavore movement emerging in **Philly's restaurants** (p183), a wealth of authentic ethnic cuisine being served in **DC's suburbs** (p261) and Virginia offers both a **winery romp** (p333) and a historic **Colonial feast** (p317).

A ROLLING FEAST

No self-respecting New Yorker eats street hot dogs anymore. No, they seek carts selling vegan lentil soups, handmade tamales with mole, fresh waffles, and marinated kebabs with tzatziki. And, OK, soft pretzels.

SIDEWALK DINING IN NYC p121
Exotic treats at NYC's Chinatown

SLOW FOOD & SLOE GIN IN PHILLY p183
Cheese is one of the many foody delights at Philadelphia's Italian Market

WINING & DINING IN THE PIEDMONT p333
Barboursville Vineyards, VA

PINE BARREN BLUES

While you're eating your pancakes,
consider this: the cultivated blueberry
was developed in the 1910s by 22-year-
old Elizabeth White in the sandy scrub of
New Jersey's Pine Barrens.

Outdoors

The East Coast may contain nothing to equal the sheer heart-stopping drama of a Yosemite or Yellowstone, a Grand Canyon or the Everglades, but we do have an abundance of natural beauty – far more than we're usually credited with.

The older, gentler **Appalachian Mountains** (p107) are the region's most famous highlight, and their blue hills give up nothing in soulful majesty. Then there are the Atlantic Coast's **bays** and **beaches** (p205 and p313), **Niagara Falls** (p159), south Jersey's **Pine Barrens** (p217) and New York's **Adirondack Mountains** (p167) and **gorges** (p145).

But, actually, what the mid-Atlantic has is seasons. And each paints its own ephemeral masterpiece across the land.

History & Culture

Did we mention that the East Coast contains the heart of America? America itself was drafted, born and is still governed here. America nearly tore itself apart here, brother fighting brother across its sloping green fields. The diversity of America is on display here: in New York's historic **Hyde Park** (p131), in Baltimore and DC, in the echoes of the **Underground Railroad** (p241) rumbling through Maryland. Avant-garde culture vultures genuflect at the temples of Waters and Warhol – **Baltimore's** John (p253) and **Pittsburgh's** Andy (p225), that is. **Sinatra** and **Springsteen** rocked the world here (p199), and **Dutch Country** rocks in rocking chairs (p221). Hudson River and New Hope painters changed **American art** here (p189), and **New York** (p149), we hear, still does.

"America nearly tore itself apart here, brother fighting brother across its sloping green fields."

② Offbeat

We'll be the first to admit it – the mid-Atlantic tends to harbor a love for the weird. Between the Jersey grease-bomb **diners** straight out of the '50s (p193), a tie-dyed wonderland in **Woodstock** (p135), a cave with a **Stalacpipe Organ** in Virginia (p299) and all the creepy-crawly, **ghostly happenings** in Maryland (p257), it's hard to imagine that this is the same region that offers such straightlaced sights as the White House and the Smithsonian. But it's true. Just ask the giant gnome permanently residing on Skyline Drive.

ROADSIDE DISTRACTIONS

Life-size Foamhenge (p301)
doesn't need embellishment,
but if you find shining knights,
damsels fluttering around
a maypole, spit-roasted
meats and sheep-tossing,
it's no hallucination. You've
stumbled onto September's
Enchantment Faire.

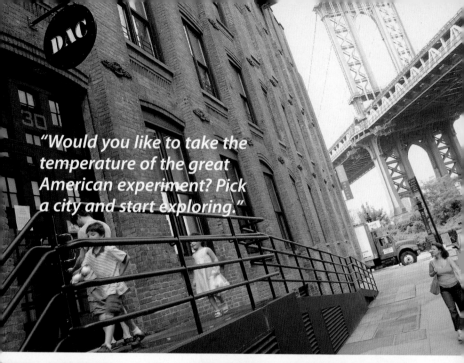

"Would you like to take the temperature of the great American experiment? Pick a city and start exploring."

Cities

Surely, if anything justifies all that East Coast braggadocio, it is its cities, which crowd so closely together they practically rub elbows. **New York** (p115 and p125), **Philadelphia** (p183), **Pittsburgh** (p225), **Baltimore** (p285), **Washington DC** (p235) and **Richmond** (p321) make for colossal urban adventures. Each has its own personality and gravitational pull, whether your interests are art, music, food, history, architecture or nightclubbing. Would you like to take the temperature of the great American experiment, in which a bunch of ethnically and culturally diverse immigrants come together to fashion a singular nation? Pick a city, any city, and start exploring.

THE BEST TRIPS

VIRGINIA IS FOR LOVERS
p305
Old Town Alexandria, VA

THE TOLERANCE TOUR
p241
Thurgood Marshall statue,
Annapolis, MD

Contents

NEW JERSEY & PENNSYLVANIA TRIPS 181

WASHINGTON DC, MARYLAND & DELAWARE TRIPS 233

VIRGINIA TRIPS 295

Trips by Theme

Trips by Season

Expert-Recommended Trips

The Authors

JEFF CAMPBELL

Jeff grew up in central Jersey (exit 8A), moved to San Francisco, married a Jersey girl and now finds himself once again a resident of the Garden State – raising his own Jersey girl and boy! For Lonely Planet, he's been the coordinating author of the award-winning *USA* three times, plus *Hawaii, Florida, Southwest USA* and others. His favorite trip is Slow Food & Sloe Gin in Philly (p183).

ADAM KARLIN

Adam is DC born, Maryland bred and Delaware…well, DC born and Maryland bred, anyways. He's been around the block for Lonely Planet, having worked on seven titles to date, but knows he's in his place when he feels the salt and the fresh of the Chesapeake Bay wrapped around his ankles. His favorite trip is The Civil War Tour (p85).

GINGER ADAMS OTIS
Ginger Adams Otis lives in New York City and has written nine titles for Lonely Planet, including *Brazil*, *Puerto Rico* and *New York City Encounter*. For this book she traveled to *Last of the Mohicans* territory in upstate New York, braved the St Lawrence River to explore the fabled castles of Thousands Islands and enjoyed searching out the best street vendors in New York City. Her favorite trip is Adirondack State Park (p167).

DAVID OZANICH
David Ozanich is a writer living in New York City. He won the GLAAD Media Award, among others, for his play *The Lightning Field,* following its successful runs in New York and London. He is coauthor of the young adult book series *Likely Story*, published by Knopf. His favorite cocktail is a gin and tonic and his favorite trip is Virginia Is for Lovers (p305).

LONELY PLANET AUTHORS
Why is our travel information the best in the world? It's simple: our authors are independent, dedicated travelers. They don't research using just the internet or phone, and they don't take freebies, so you can rely on their advice being well researched and impartial. They travel widely, to all the popular spots and off the beaten track. They personally visit thousands of hotels, restaurants, cafés, bars, galleries, palaces, museums and more – and they take pride in getting all the details right, and telling it how it is. Think you can do it? Find out how at lonelyplanet.com.

CONTRIBUTING EXPERTS

Daniel Aubry is a Manhattan-based photographer who has been traveling in and photographing the Hudson Valley for decades. He offers his recommendations in Art Parks & Public Art (p149).

Steve Politi has worked as the general sports columnist at the *Star-Ledger* for the past three years. The New Jersey native lives in Montclair, NJ, with his wife Nancy and their turtle, Thomas. Steve talks baseball in The Boys of Summer (p75).

Simona Rabinovitch writes about pop culture, travel and entertainment for Canada's national newspaper the *Globe and Mail* and for international magazines. Simona spoke with musician Moby for 48 Hours in Manhattan (p115).

Julie Scharper was born and raised in Lutherville (just outside Baltimore) and works as a reporter for the *Baltimore Sun*. Julie takes us on a tour of Baltimore by night in BaltNoir (p285).

Kip Waide has been tending bar for over two decades and **Sheri Waide** graduated from San Francisco's California Culinary Academy in 1994. In 2004, they opened their own restaurant, Southwark, one of the many featured in Slow Food & Sloe Gin in Philly (p183).

NEW YORK, WASHINGTON DC & THE MID-ATLANTIC ICONIC TRIPS

When does something that is pretty well-known, or relatively famous, or defining of a shared experience or essential idea become truly iconic? We'll tell you. When it becomes the Lincoln Memorial, the National Mall, Times Square, Yankee Stadium, Cooperstown, Columbia University, Ellis Island, the Liberty Bell, a Philly cheesesteak, Harpers Ferry, Antietam, the Appalachian Trail.

In fact, the overwhelmingly iconic nature of many of the mid-Atlantic's biggest attractions can get in the way of seeing them fresh, as if for the first time. It's easy to suffer a psychic dissonance, to see the Statue of Liberty without really seeing that fine lady, instead only seeing the thousands of images you already know from logos, T-shirts and green foam hats, ad infinitum.

 The East Coast has quite a bit of iconic music. Give these tunes a spin, and see the regional chapter playlists for more.

- "Take the 'A' Train," Ella Fitzgerald with the Duke Ellington Orchestra
- "Autumn in New York," Frank Sinatra
- "Summer in the City," The Lovin' Spoonful
- "My Old School," Steely Dan
- "Centerfield," John Fogerty
- "(I've Had) the Time of My Life," Bill Medley & Jennifer Warnes
- "Gonna Fly Now (Theme from *Rocky*)," Nelson Pigford & DeEtta Little
- "My City of Ruins," Bruce Springsteen

So here we're bringing you New York, Washington DC, the American Revolution, the Civil War, a hot dog and pizza, an Ivy League campus, the Blue Ridge Mountains, a major league baseball game and summertime beaches in ways that are fresh. What you see is up to you.

 NEW YORK, WASHINGTON DC & THE MID-ATLANTIC'S BEST TRIPS

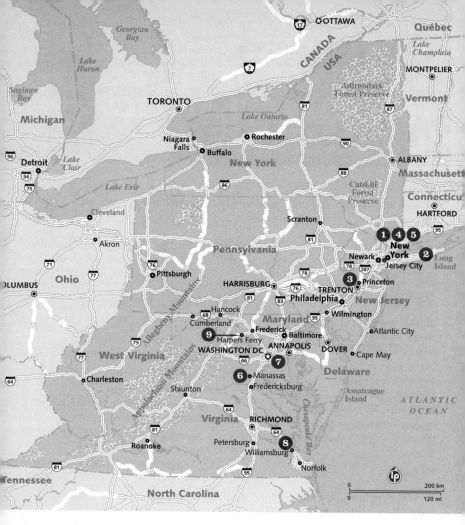

ICONIC TRIPS

Ultimate Urban Adventure

WHY GO Are you ready? In around 3000 words and 250 miles, we're going to visit the iconic highlights and the diverse peoples of four of America's greatest cities: New York, Philadelphia, Baltimore and Washington DC. It's a big trip, so put that coffee in a to-go cup and let's get started.

TIME
7 – 10 days

DISTANCE
250 miles

BEST TIME TO GO
Year-round

START
New York

END
Washington DC

ALSO GOOD FOR

CITY

The thing about ❶ New York is, you can see the world here – all in the time it takes you to cross the street. From Little Italy to Little Korea, Chinatown to uptown, New York City is full of dynamic contrasts and historical firsts. Anchored by wall-to-wall buildings and some nine million people, the city never stops moving – and each neighborhood has its own distinct flavor and personality. You could wear yourself out in just New York, so pace yourself; we've got a lot of sidewalks to cover.

It's easy to float through Manhattan on a wave of sensory delight, getting punch-drunk on the overwhelming nature of it all. At the southern tip of the island, Wall St and Battery Park are filled with huge, hulking skyscrapers crammed into an area built on a colonial scale. Dubbed "the concrete canyon" by locals, it's a neck-wrenching, Gotham-esque architectural cityscape. Among the quirky buildings you'll find the ❷ Cosmopolitan Hotel, just a few blocks from Ground Zero. Travel a few more blocks north and you're in Tribeca, home to cobblestone streets and trendy restaurants like ❸ Thalassa, serving fresh Greek seafood, and ❹ Industria Argentina, with robust dishes straight from Pampas.

Chinatown, Little Italy, and the East and West Villages are stacked next to each other as the city continues northward. In teeming Midtown is the ❺ Empire State Building, on the east side near the UN, and Grand Central Station. To the west is ❻ Times Square and "The Great White Way," aka Broadway, the theater district. Both these neighborhoods stop

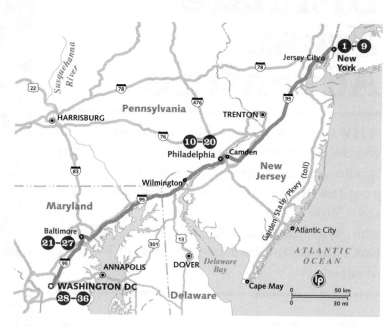

at 59th St, at the foot of a stone wall that signals the start of **7** **Central Park**. This lush, green oasis, full of ponds, brambles and long, meandering walks, covers the heart of New York City, stretching nearly 50 blocks north and into Harlem.

But if we're talking icons, we need to head into New York Harbor, first to greet the **8** **Statue of Liberty**. She is, to be sure, one bright green lady, but it's hard to imagine a more attractive symbol of kinship, freedom and welcome being fashioned out of 31 tons of copper. Her construction, overseen by sculptor Frédéric-Auguste Bartholdi, was a joint effort between America and France to commemorate the centennial of the Declaration of Independence. She was, in keeping with true ladies everywhere, fashionably late: she didn't arrive on her pedestal until 1886. It took another 15 years for her pedestal poem, *The New Colossus*, by Emma Lazarus, to join her: "Give me your tired, your poor, Your huddled masses yearning to breathe free, The wretched refuse of your teeming shore. Send these, the homeless, tempest-tost to me, I lift my lamp beside the golden door!"

Lady Liberty, then, raises her torch not so she can see her way, but so you can find yours. This is why New York contains the world, and why, despite the hustle and hustlers the Big Apple is notorious for, New York is at heart a city of welcome. In every "New York moment," where strangers help strangers and move on without ever exchanging names, is a bit of that light.

Of course, visitors to the Statue of Liberty itself are more restricted in the wake of September 11. You cannot go inside the statue anymore – a sad fact for those who've never experienced the thrill of climbing more than 300 steps to the crown for its incredible view – but you can visit the museum and the pedestal observation deck.

Yet all the sentiment Lady Liberty inspires would be little without that other icon in New York Harbor: **9 Ellis Island**. The island and its large building served as New York's main immigration station from 1892 until 1954, processing a record number of 12,000 individuals daily from nearly every country. Today, Ellis Island represents the mythical gateway to freedom that America has, over the course of her history, represented to many. It is where those huddled masses actually got off the boat.

The greeting immigrants received at Ellis Island was not always one of open arms, however: doctors gave them the once-over, they were given new names if their own was too strange, and any identified as polygamists, criminals, anarchists, or too destitute, were turned around. At times, such as after WWI and during the communist "Red Scare" in America, Ellis Island functioned more like a holding pen than a gateway. The impressive Immigration Museum cleans up but does not erase these aspects of the island's legendary history, and it puts them into context: most immigrants were processed in a day in generally clean and safe conditions.

ASK A LOCAL

"In the summertime I like to head out to Governor's Island. It's a great place to walk around and look at the skyline, or hang out and picnic with your friends, and the ferry is fast and cheap from Lower Manhattan. The best part is it's almost never crowded."
Dylan Butler, Queens

But ultimately, the reason to visit Ellis Island isn't for the place; it's for the people. Oral histories of real Ellis Island immigrants, taped in the 1980s, accompany nearly every exhibit and display. These moving first-person accounts bring to life the names and give voice to the many faces that make up America's family portrait.

Why did those people want to come to America? Hold that thought and let's go to **10 Philadelphia**. To begin to take the measure of this city, let's start at **11 City Hall** in Penn Square, which sits where William Penn originally envisioned it should – in the center of his orderly grid between the Delaware and Schuylkill Rivers. Stand in the center of the building, at the intersection of Market and Broad Sts – from here the avenues shoot out in plumb-straight compass lines. Or perhaps they lead in: Penn founded his Pennsylvania colony in 1681 as a "holy experiment" in religious tolerance, and he designed Philadelphia to be its capital. City Hall wasn't built until over two centuries later, and it's probably far too ornate – festooned with 250 sculptures, in and out, and topped by one of Penn himself – for the sober Quaker. But more interestingly, if Penn ascended City Hall's 548ft tower to its observation deck, what would he make of his City of Brotherly Love today?

Philly is chock-full of anachronistic historic collisions like this, where the past pushes right through the present, like a brick through a gauzy scrim, and you feel the trajectory of America in a jolting flash. The city actively cultivates this, of course. **⓬ Independence National Historical Park**, due east of City Hall along Market St, has been dubbed "America's most historic square mile." It all sounds very grade-school-trip-ish until you actually walk the brick streets and stand where they debated the Declaration of Independence and amble through the worn tilted headstones in the graveyards. Sitting with the costumed role-players and hired storytellers on park benches as they spin ye olde tales in Old City is, we have to admit, kind of fun, but that's not the real juice. It's that moment when the park ranger stops talking and you realize: Washington, Adams, Jefferson and Franklin were real men, and, like William Penn and his colony, they dreamed up America's "holy experiment" in democracy right here. This is why people came.

> **DETOUR**
>
> Go ahead, there's I-95. Bypass New Jersey – many do. But Jersey's **Liberty State Park** (www.liberty statepark.org), just across the Hudson in Jersey City, is an excellent, less-crowded departure point for ferry trips to Ellis Island and the Statue of Liberty. In addition, the park offers its own reason to come here: the sparkling, interactive **Liberty Science Center** (www.lsc.org), which is packed with hands-on experiments and those way-cool IMAX and 3-D movies.

To take in the national park properly takes several days. Try to cram Independence Hall, the Liberty Bell, the National Constitution Center, the Portrait Gallery and all the other Revolutionary rigmarole into one day, and you'll burp tricorner hats and essential freedoms all night. Go more slowly, and truly discover Philly as you do.

"…like a brick through a gauzy scrim, you feel the trajectory of America in a jolting flash."

A delicious place to do that is **⓭ Reading Terminal Market**, on Market St between City Hall and the national park. It's about now that you realize something wonderful: after New York, where sightseeing requires serious strategic planning and time management, Philly seems almost a quaint village. Its central neighborhoods are immanently walkable, and more charming for it.

Reading Terminal Market has existed in the railroad terminal since 1892, and, particularly after its sparkling 1990s renovation, the market remains a centerpiece of Philly's tourist trade and everyday gastronomic life. Everyone comes here – making for great people-watching – because the market has everything: cheesesteaks, restaurants, Amish crafts, regional specialties, and top-quality butchers, produce, cheese, flowers, bakeries, confectioners and so on. It is Philly's cornucopia.

Speaking of gastronomic delights, we should also note that Philly is developing a lively restaurant scene, highlighted by a handful of celebrity-chef destinations. One of these is only blocks from Reading Terminal: **⑭ Morimoto**. This Stephen Starr–themed restaurant combines surreal futuro-modern neon-lit booths with the Japanese-cuisine wizardry of Iron Chef Morimoto.

A bit of a hike post-dinner will take you to the sumptuously cozy boutique B&B, **⑮ Rittenhouse 1715**. It's on a quiet alley a half-block from Rittenhouse Square, one of Penn's original public squares and probably the most beautiful, full of tree-shaded statuary.

Northwest of Penn Square is the Museum District, along Benjamin Franklin Parkway, a boulevard modeled after Paris' Champs-Élysées. At the base is Logan Circle, which collects the Franklin Institute (a fabulous interactive museum), the Academy of Natural Sciences, and the monumental Central Library. At the top is the show-stopper, the **⑯ Philadelphia Museum of Art**, which is Philly's side of capital-C culture to go with its entrée of capital-H history. By all means, make like Rocky Balboa, sprint up the wide entrance steps, turn, and raise your arms to the sky – everyone does (maybe Rocky was cheering the downtown view). The *Rocky* statue is at the base of the steps, to the right (smile!).

The Museum of Art is at the southern edge of **⑰ Fairmount Park**, which hugs the Schuylkill River and is actually bigger than Central Park (take that, New York). The zoo is here, but like Manhattan's green space, this is really Philly's lungs, a grassy head-clearing space to unwind with a jog, bike ride, frisbee and a blanket.

MURALS & MOSAICS

Boasting more public murals than any other American city, with 2400 and counting, Philadelphia truly rewards walkers. Join an official **Mural Arts Walk** (www.muralarts.org) or download the self-guided brochure. One folk artist who is personally responsible for over 100 mosaic marvels is Isaiah Zagar. The real mind-blower is his phantasmagorical **Magic Gardens** (www.philadelphiamagicgardens.org) on South St at 10th. More Zagar murals can be found throughout the South St neighborhood.

Along Philadelphia's other river, the Delaware, is **⑱ Penn's Landing** (www.pennslandingcorp.com). In the summer, this is where Philly loosens up: concerts and festivals pack the waterfront every weekend. Also here is the **⑲ Seaport Museum** (love the working boat-shop) and historic ships: the steel cruiser *Olympia* and the submarine *Becuna* are highlights.

Finally, make time to cruise the stately Ivy League campus of the **⑳ University of Pennsylvania** (www.upenn.edu). To get there, take the subway to the vaulted 30th St Station. Don't miss the stunning Fisher Fine Arts Library or the Museum of Archaeology & Anthropology.

Next up we encounter ㉑ **Baltimore**. Truth be told, New York, Philadelphia and DC can be all too aware of their own importance; they can get a little full of their own bad selves. Baltimore, meanwhile, has often been passed over as the poor ugly stepsister – crime-ridden, artless, and unloved by Northeast sophisticates and Washington politicos. Well, no longer. Today Baltimore serves several roles in the great scheme of the mid-Atlantic Chain of Being.

> *"Baltimore, meanwhile, has often been passed over as the poor ugly stepsister… Well, no longer."*

First: it is a working-class alternative to the yuppie hordes draining the soul out of DC, Philly and New York. Women who drink cosmos and talk about Manolo Blahnik get mugged here, by sexy, smart Baltimore girls.

Second: there are a lot of artists and writers in New York who are more concerned about looking like artists and writers than actually, y'know, writing or making art. While this is to be expected wherever scenesters congregate, Baltimore has been quietly producing a hugely talented crop of creative types, attracted by cheap rents and the social tensions of a city that's not, by a long shot, totally family-friendly.

And yet, Baltimore kind of is friendly. That can be very refreshing when you're traveling through the Eastern urban corridor. There's a real camaraderie to this town, detectable when everyone cheers on the underdog Baltimore Orioles at ㉒ **Camden Yards** (the Os aren't even bad enough to be legendarily bad, like the White Sox), and in the wedding of a mixed-race couple in hip Mount Vernon, or when families enjoy a summer's day under the long shadows cast by Federal Hill. In addition to these beautiful Baltimore moments, the city's Inner Harbor, despite being a bit artificial, is one of the nicest waterfronts in America. It's hard not to be stirred at night by the neon waves of the ㉓ **National Aquarium** – or, for that matter, to not be amazed by its stunning collection of sea life.

SPEAK ENGLISH, HON

Although its rarity has been increased by gentrification, there are still Baltimoreans (particularly in 'burbs like Essex and Dundalk) who proudly speak what's been called the most slurred accent in the English language: Bawlmerese (Baltimorese). It's a combination of Southern drawl and Northeastern hardass, exemplified by the ubiquitous appellate of "hon" to sentences. A small lexicon includes "wooder" (water), "share" (shower), "amblance" (ambulance), "crown" (crayon), "cowny" (county), "aks" (ask) and "Merlin" (Maryland).

The strength of the local arts scene is no real surprise to Baltimore natives, who know their town has long supported some of the best small arts museums in the country, such as the excellent ㉔ **Walters Art Museum**. This penchant for creativity certainly extends to the city's culinary scene, which also draws off the ethnic enclaves that are the bedrock of Baltimore communities. A restaurant like ㉕ **Miss Shirley's** exemplifies these characteristics by combining high-end Southern stylings (this town is as Southern as it is Northern – a unique cultural milieu that's another one of B'more's most attractive features) with a local, eccentric edge: think corn cake and crab-topped eggs Benedict.

But another great thing about this city is that it knows the comfort of being comfortable. Sometimes, you want a big Italian meal served by loud Italian (-American) staff, and these elements come together with predictably delicious results at family, Chianti-over-checkered-tablecloth joints like ㉖ **Amicci's**. You don't want to drive after a night on the town in Baltimore, so book a room at Mt Vernon's ㉗ **Peabody Court**.

BEST OF THE MONUMENTS

The capital is thick with monuments and memorials; these are a few that stand out from the marble competition:

- FDR Memorial – more a 7.5-acre park on the era Roosevelt governed; stunningly beautiful at night.
- Korean War Veterans Memorial – this line of ghostly soldiers seems almost haunted on snowy days.
- Vietnam Memorial – done in low, lovely black granite, hands down the most powerful monument in the city.

At last, we come to ㉘ **Washington DC**, which is saddled with more iconicness than any place really needs.

Pity poor residents. Geopolitics has packed too much city into too small a space, especially a space that's regularly ignored by a federal government it doesn't even get a real voice in. There's a local DC of neighborhoods, friends, families and immigrants all struggling and occasionally achieving the vaunted American dream, but then this town's been thrust into the role of capital of the free world as well. Thus, the great DC dichotomy: the regal seat of American superpower, and the multiculti, crime-ridden entrepot of journalists, politicos, drug dealers, cops, corner boys, teachers, trannies, small-business owners and any public symbol you'd care to name that's meant to encapsulate America to the world.

Encapsulating America is part of what this trip is about, and in many ways everything has simply been a preamble for the ㉙ **National Mall**, which contains within its few miles of grass the Smithsonian Institution, several thousand tourists, dozens of school groups, a flock of ducks and the soul of the country. You can start your exploration at either end: from the ㉚ **Capitol** and its stately sense of importance, open to the public via tours out of its guide services kiosk, or from the ㉛ **Lincoln Memorial**, which looks out over the reflecting pool and the country "Poppa Abraham" preserved through the Civil War. If you're interested in touring the White House, call ahead (☎ 202-456-7041); tours must be arranged in groups of 10 or more and are self-guided.

The founding fathers believed their countrymen needed to immerse themselves in worldly knowledge to take their place among the world's great nations (an attitude depressingly absent in some of their modern descendants) and there is no greater monument to (and working engine of) American intellectual curiosity than the **32** **Library of Congress**, the world's largest library. Have a look at the main reading-room and try not to be stunned by the scope of the thing.

When you're ready to eat, give your taste buds a little pep talk and remind them not to burst with anticipation. DC has evolved from the land of a thousand stodgy power lunches to a little gem of international energies, all competing to wow this dignitary and that official. Yet it's also a city of neighborhoods, and immigrants, and the ethnic options are cheap and plentiful.

Take **33** **Mixtec**, our favorite Mexican spot in town, where the service is friendly and the menu looks as long as a Latin American constitution. Meanwhile, **34** **Cityzen** is an example of just how much the DC power-dinner has evolved: from steak and steak, to a tasting menu of salt-crusted daurade, Yukon potatoes with sea urchin and yellowtail tataki designed by French Laundry–graduate Eric Ziebold, named "Best chef, Mid-Atlantic" in 2008 by the James Beard Foundation.

BEST OF THE MUSEUMS

Our favorite museums from a city packed with 'em:

- Freer & Sackler Galleries – the national galleries of Asian art are wonderfully understated and criminally under-visited (www.asia.si.edu).

- Reynolds Center for American Art – consists of the National Portrait Gallery and American Art Museum; strives to be the best collection of American art in the world (http://americanart.si.edu/reynolds_center).

- US Holocaust Memorial Museum – the most unsettling museum in DC tackles a difficult subject with expertise and sensitivity (www.ushmm.org).

When you're ready to crash out, you have options galore. At the two extremes, there is the hipper-than-thou sharp chic of the **35** **Hotel Palomar**, which, conversely, looks extremely young but feels as important as the most dignified DC digs. Then there is the dorm fun of the **36** **Washington International Student Center**. Clearly this isn't the poshest sleep available, but it attracts a hell of a fun crowd, and it can be very interesting seeing this town through the eyes of new foreign friends.

And that, after all, is the other purpose of this trip: to see with fresh eyes and experience why East Coast cities deserve their iconic status in the first place.

Jeff Campbell, Adam Karlin & Ginger Adams Otis

TRIP INFORMATION

GETTING THERE
Take I-95 to get to all these cities, only not during rush hour.

DO

Camden Yards
The home of the awesome...well, fun-to-watch Baltimore Orioles is a grand ballpark hemmed in by brick walls and populated by rabid Baltimoreans. ☎ 410-547-6277; http://baltimore.orioles.mlb.com; 333 W Camden St, Baltimore; ☒ Apr-Oct

Capitol
Packed with beautiful artwork, inspiring sculptures, semi-baroque federal architecture and, oh yeah, Congress. ☎ tours 202-224-4048; www.aoc.gov/cc/visit/index.cfm; 1st St SW & Independence Ave, Washington; ☒ 9am-4:30pm Mon-Sat (first-come, first-served)

Ellis Island
Ferry tickets include the Statue of Liberty; reserve tickets highly recommended on weekends. ☎ 212-363-3200; www.nps.gov/elis; ferry terminal Battery Park, New York; park admission free, ferry adult/child $12/5; ☒ ferry 9:30am-3pm, park open to 5pm; ⬤

Empire State Building
An art deco wonder stretching so high it sways with the wind, and with views that go on for days. Buy tickets online to avoid the queues. ☎ 212-736-2100; www.esbnyc.com; 350 Fifth Ave, New York; adult/child $19/13; ☒ 8am-2am, last elevator 1:15am

Independence National Historical Park
Get free timed tickets for Independence Hall tours at the visitors center. ☎ 800-537-7676; www.nps.gov/inde; Market & 6th Sts, Philadelphia; national park sites admission free; ☒ visitors center 8:30am-7pm, hours vary for individual sites; ⬤

Library of Congress
This magnificent institution's role is to catalogue all the world's knowledge, and it does a good job of it. ☎ 202-707-4604; www.loc.gov; 101 Independence Ave SE, Washington; ☒ 10am-5:30pm Mon-Sat

National Aquarium
A solid contender for best aquarium in the country – hence the name. ☎ 410-576-3800; www.aqua.org; 501 E Pratt St, Baltimore; adult/child 3-11/under 3 $21.95/12.95/free; ☒ 9am-5pm Sun-Thu, to 8pm Fri & Sat, with seasonal variations

Philadelphia Museum of Art
The museum's 200 galleries contain world-class Asian, US and European art. ☎ 215-763-8100; www.philamuseum.org; 26th St & Benjamin Franklin Pkwy, Philadelphia; adult/child $14/10; ☒ 10am-5pm Tue-Sun; ⬤

Seaport Museum
The museum sells tickets for the historic ships. ☎ 215-413-8655; www.phillyseaport.com; Columbus Blvd & Walnut St, Philadelphia; adult/child $10/7; ☒ 10am-5pm Mon-Sat; ⬤

Statue of Liberty
Ferry tickets include Ellis Island; book a free "monument pass" to access the pedestal observation level. Reserve tickets highly recommended on weekends. ☎ 212-363-3200; www.nps.gov/stli; ferry terminal Battery Park, New York; park admission free, ferry adult/child $12/5; ☒ ferry 9:30am-3pm, park open to 5pm; ⬤

Walters Art Museum
This unexpected slice of joy houses an impressive collection of manuscripts, Asian art and contemporary exhibitions. ☎ 410-547-9000; www.thewalters.org; 600 N Charles St, Baltimore; ☒ 11am-5pm Wed-Sun, to 8pm Fri

EAT

Amicci's
Like the Baltimore locals serving the excellent food, Amicci's likes to look good while packing plenty of attitude. ☎ 410-528-1096; 231 S High St, Baltimore; dinner $14-19; ☒ 11:30am-midnight

Cityzen
The most talked about restaurant in DC in 2008, Cityzen richly deserves all its attention and acclaim. ☎ 202-787-6006; Mandarin Oriental Hotel, 1330 Maryland Ave, Washington; tasting menu $80-110; ☒ dinner Tue-Sat

Industria Argentina
Feels like a Buenos Aires hot spot, with sleek masculine decor and hearty steaks. ☎ 212-965-8560; www.iatribeca.com; 329 Greenwich St, New York; mains $12-25; ⊙ 11am-10pm Mon-Sat

Miss Shirley's
Eggs Benedict will never seem the same after trying it topped with lumped crab meat at Baltimore's best brunch spot. ☎ 410-889-5272; 513 W Cold Spring Lane, Baltimore; dinner $10-16; ⊙ breakfast & lunch

Mixtec
The best hangover cure in the city is this excellent spot's huevos rancheros with hot chocolate. ☎ 202-797-1819; 1792 Columbia Rd NW, Washington; mains $5-10; ⊙ 9am-10pm Sun-Thu, 10am-11pm Fri & Sat

Morimoto
It's the best kind of event dining; put yourself in Morimoto's hands and order the Omakase. ☎ 215-413-9070; wwww.morimoto restaurant.com; 723 Chestnut St, Phila-delphia; mains $23-42; ⊙ 11:30am-2pm Mon-Fri, from 5pm nightly

Reading Terminal Market
Lines at lunchtime are crazy; leave plenty of time to browse. ☎ 215-922-2317; www .readingterminalmarket.org; 12th & Arch Sts, Philadelphia; mains $3-15; ⊙ 8am-6pm Mon-Sat, 9am-4pm Sun; ♿

Thalassa
Ultra-fresh and flavorful fish dishes in a stylish yet breezy warehouse space. ☎ 212-941-7661; http://thalassanyc.com; 179 Franklin St, New York; mains $18-35; ⊙ 11am-11pm

SLEEP

Cosmopolitan Hotel
NYC's oldest hotel is a nondescript but clean cheapy in Tribeca; corner rooms are best. ☎ 212-566-1900; www.cosmohotel.com; 95 W Broadway, New York; r $175

Hotel Palomar
As hip as DC gets, the Palomar is cool and contemporary, one of the best-designed (and priced) midrange sleeps around. ☎ 202-448-1800; www.hotelpalomar-dc.com; 2121 P St NW, Washington; r $143-359

Peabody Court
In the heart of Mount Vernon, the Peabody is old-school ornate while surrounded by one of Baltimore's hipper, but yuppiefying, 'hoods. ☎ 410-727-7101; www.peabodycourthotel .com; 612 Cathedral St, Baltimore; r from $189

Rittenhouse 1715
An old-world feel with luxe stylings, earth tones, fabric headboards, and pampering baths. No parking. ☎ 215-546-6500; www .rittenhouse1715.com; 1715 Rittenhouse Sq, Philadelphia; r $249-700

Washington International Student Center
You couldn't be better placed to engage DC's nightlife, which basically centers on this wild street, along with some great restaurants. ☎ 202-667-7681; www.washingtondc hostel.com; 2451 18th St NW, Washington; dm $23

USEFUL WEBSITES
www.baltimore.org
www.dcvisit.com
www.gophila.com
www.nycvisit.com

LINK YOUR TRIP
www.lonelyplanet.com/trip-planner

TRIP
2 Beach-Hopping the Mid-Atlantic opposite
3 We the People p55
5 The Boys of Summer p75

Beach-Hopping the Mid-Atlantic

WHY GO The East Coast without its beaches would just be the Midwest without its friendliness. Who needs that? Thankfully, we'll never know. With this trip, we've hopped from one sandy natural beauty to another, searching out all the places and ways East Coast city-folk wash their uptight urban blues away.

Mid-Atlantic beaches and their many attractions are covered in several trips in this book. This selection, though it has its share of nightlife and shore towns, emphasizes the places to go when you want to get away from all that and recharge the batteries.

To that end, we begin with ❶ **Fire Island National Seashore** (www .fireisland.com), a skinny barrier island running parallel to Long Island that contains much wonder, beauty and flaming adventure along its scant 32 miles. Fire Island offers sand dunes, forests, white beaches, camping, hiking trails, inns, restaurants, 15 hamlets and two villages. Its scenes range from car-free residential villages of summer mansions and packed nightclubs to stretches of sand where you'll find nothing but pitched tents and deer (overpopulation of deer is a big problem here). ❷ **Robert Moses State Park**, the only part of the island that's accessible by car, lies at the westernmost end and features wide, soft-sand beaches with mellow crowds. It's also home to the ❸ **Fire Island Lighthouse**, which houses a history museum. Walk way east along the shore here and you'll stumble upon a lively nude beach.

The gemlike parts of Fire Island, though, are found further east, in the tranquil, car-free villages. Davis Park, Fair Harbor, Kismet, Ocean Bay Park and Ocean Beach combine small summer homes with tiny towns that have groceries, bars, nightclubs and restaurants. It's all very lively and happening between Memorial Day and Labor Day, the summer

TIME
7 – 10 days

DISTANCE
230 miles

BEST TIME TO GO
Jun – Sep

START
Fire Island, NY

END
Assateague Island, MD

ALSO GOOD FOR

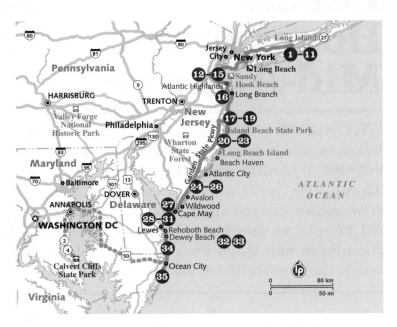

high season, but keep in mind that most small shore-towns, and these in particular, shut down almost completely outside summer. How exactly are you supposed to get to these car-free villages? Why, by using the South Bay Water Taxi, of course.

Perhaps the most infamous villages here are those that have evolved into gay resorts: **4 Cherry Grove** and the **5 Pines**. While day trips are easy to Fire Island, staying on this oasis, where boardwalks serve as pathways between the dunes and homes, is wonderful. Until recently, accommodations meant a stay in someone's summer share-house or beachy basic rooms at the Belvedere (for men only), or the Grove Hotel in Cherry Grove. Now the Pines has jumped in with Fire Island's first "boutique" hotel: the **6 Madison Fire Island,** which rivals anything Manhattan has to offer in terms of amenities, but also has killer views from a rooftop deck and a gorgeous pool (and pool boys). A less-coifed alternative on the Pines is the **7 Pines Bluff Overlook**, right on the water. Still, the Grove Hotel remains the main source of entertainment with its nightclub, and the Grove offers a couple of recommended, popular eateries: **8 Michael's** dishes up fancy pizza and nice Italian dinners, while **9 Rachel's** is the go-to breakfast place for your hangover-curing espresso.

If you want to skip the scene altogether and just get back to nature, enjoy a hike through the 300-year-old **10 Sunken Forest**, where crazy, twisty trees have been misshapen by constant salt-spray and breezes. It's "sunken" because its 40 acres are below sea level; it has its own ferry stop (called Sailor's Haven). At the eastern end of the island, the 1300-acre preserve of ⑪ **Otis Pike Fire Island Wilderness** is a protected oasis of sand dunes that includes a beach campground at Watch Hill (reservations are a must, as sites fill up a year in advance); just beware of the fierce mosquitoes.

Once you're finished on Fire Island, it's time to go to Jersey, and like Fire Island, our first destination is a sliver of land jutting into the Atlantic Ocean. Since we're not in a hurry, we'll take the scenic route. From the Garden State Pkwy, take exit 117 to Rte 36 east. Following signs for Bayshore Waterfront Park, turn left onto Main St to Port Monmouth; bear left onto Wilson Ave.

When this dead ends, turn right and drive a mile to a small wharf containing the ⑫ **Belford Seafood Co-op**. At this little gem, the guy behind the counter promised: "If it doesn't come off those boats, it doesn't come in that door." This is as fresh as fish, lobster and crab get, and you'll want a cooler to take some with you, though an attached restaurant (with Brooklyn views) serves it cooked.

FIRE ISLAND FERRIES

Getting to and around Fire Island villages requires a boat. If you didn't bring yours, no worries. Fire Island ferries can get you there; trips take about half an hour. Most ferries leave the Long Island towns of Bay Shore and Sayville, and they go to far more places than we've had room to mention in this trip. Find out how many, and get boat schedules and rates, at www.fire island.com.

Return to Rte 36 east and take the turnoff for ⑬ **Atlantic Highlands**, following First St into the heart of downtown. Often overlooked by the shore masses, this historic town is a very quaint place to browse and eat (either before or after the beach). At the end of First, near the wharf, turn right onto Ocean Blvd, which meanders through residential neighborhoods to the ⑭ **Mount Mitchell Scenic Overlook**; pull over. Mt Mitchell is all of 266ft high, but that still makes it the highest point on the Atlantic seaboard from Maine to Mexico. The Jersey shore doesn't offer more spectacular views: over the dunes of Sandy Hook and across to Staten Island and Brooklyn. Aaaaah.

In fact, ⑮ **Sandy Hook National Recreation Area** is our true destination. Sandy Hook contains the historic Fort Hancock and the Sandy Hook Lighthouse, and exploring the small exhibits and the old military camp with its gun batteries makes a pleasurable break from the stress of sunning all day on one of its six extremely wide and expansive beaches. North Beach, at the end, has a food-service pavilion with a view deck, and Gunnison Beach is – *honey, look at all the naked people!* Yes, Sandy Hook has Jersey's only legal nude beach; Gunnison Beach went au naturel in the late 1970s, and, not surprisingly, its parking lot fills up first. But note: be prepared to join in. "Get naked or get lost" is pretty much its motto.

Which brings up another important point: Sandy Hook is strictly day-use, and once its parking lots fill up, no more cars are let in. On summer weekends, arrive by 10am or prepare to be turned away. Spring and fall are also nice times to be here, though. Horseshoe crabs mate on the beaches in May (see for yourself), and monarch butterflies arrive in fall. At these times, you could call the peninsula Windy Hook, and on bay side, windsurfers and kiteboarders put on a show.

Beautiful **Long Beach**, 30 miles from New York City, much closer than either Jones Beach or Fire Island, is one of the best stretches of sand you can find. It's easily accessible by train, has clean beaches, a hoppin' main town strip with shops and eateries within walking distance of the ocean, a thriving surfing scene and many city hipsters. **Lincoln Beach**, at the end of Lincoln Blvd, is the main spot for surfing.

South of Sandy Hook, beaches are strung like the crunchy-sweet beads on a candy necklace, and you want to bite off and chew each one. A nice choice, with a big parking lot and a simple food-pavilion, but nothing else to distract from sea and sand, is ⑯ **Seven Presidents Beach**, about 10 minutes south of Sandy Hook.

On this trip, we're driving right past all the sticky, dripping-ice-cream carnival madness of Asbury Park, Point Pleasant and Seaside Heights and heading for Jersey's shining jewel: ⑰ **Island Beach State Park**. The entire Atlantic Coast has only a handful of protected, undeveloped barrier beaches, and this is one. The park is divided into three sections, and only one mile in the central section has lifeguard-protected ocean swimming (and concessions). However, swimming is allowed (but unsupervised) on the other two miles of the central Recreation Area.

These are outstandingly beautiful beaches, but if you want to escape crowds, keep going to the Southern Natural Area. Here, three miles of pristine sand are open for sunbathing, picnicking and strolling, and a handful of very short hikes take you into the sweepingly beautiful dunes and wetlands. You can see nesting osprey and sneak up on wading great blue herons. It's a peaceful, tranquil vision of what the coast used to be like before, you know, all the people showed up.

"...beaches are strung like the crunchy-sweet beads on a candy necklace, and you want to bite off and chew each one."

Island Beach has two interpretive nature centers that lay out the ecology, and there are nature programs and guided Barnegat Bay kayak trips throughout July and August. But remember, as at Sandy Hook, when the parking lots fill up, the entrance is closed. Come midweek or arrive by 10am on summer weekends. The closest place to stay is ⑱ **Island Beach Motor Lodge** in South Seaside Park. This sufficiently well-kept but absolutely no-frills place is the opposite of tranquil in busy summer, but convenience trumps all concerns: it sits essentially at the park entrance. It also has a not-at-all-bad attached restaurant, the **19** **Atlantic Bar & Grill**.

From the southern tip of Island Beach State Park, you can see our next destination: **20** **Long Beach Island**, or LBI as it's called. Since there's no bridge, and it's too far to jump, return to the Garden State Pkwy and access the island via Rte 72. Most people who come to LBI turn right and go south, so turn left and go north.

Much of northern LBI is not exactly welcoming to day-trippers, as Loveladies and Harvey Cedars contain lots of "no beach access" signs stabbed out front of mansion-like summer homes. But where you *can* legally park, you can enjoy any of these beaches. Keep driving, though, to Barnegat Light at the very end.

This low-key town has a handful of diners, restaurants, convenience stores, and motels, and it takes its name from "old Barney" – the **21** **Barnegat Lighthouse**, whose slender maroon-and-white silhouette is arguably the most handsome on the coast. The lighthouse was built in 1857–58 and has 217 steps to the top, where the views, particularly of Island Beach, are just too sweet. The trails, picnic areas and lovely beaches make this a great getaway. A block from the water is the **22** **North Shore Inn**, a friendly place with clean, good-sized rooms. For a fun dinner, cruise back to Harvey Cedars to **23** **Plantation Restaurant**. With its wicker furniture, its spicy, blackened and jerked dishes, and its long list of tropical rum and tequila drinks, it provides an upscale Caribbean atmosphere that stands out among the shore's typical surf-and-turf joints.

DETOUR New Jersey's Long Beach Island is sprinkled with salty beach towns, and its most popular is at the south end: **Beach Haven**. This cutesy place has a teeny-tiny amusement park, tons of restaurants and cafés, seaside kitsch galore, and even a fun musical theater, **Surflight Theatre** (www.surflight.org), which has been presenting Broadway's well-loved chestnuts every summer for almost 60 years. Where should you go when the sun goes down? Go to *Oklahoma!*

Now, we again skip south on the Garden State Pkwy, past the boardwalks of Atlantic City and Ocean City, and take Rte 601/30th St to **24** **Avalon**. This quiet residential community enjoys one of Jersey's more idyllic white-sand beaches, and a huge parking lot at Avalon and 30th Sts makes it easy to reach. It's the perfect alternative to the amusement-crazy areas along the southern Jersey coast. At night, the retail corridor along Dune Dr, between 20th and 30th Sts, glows with twinkling Christmas lights, making it too small-town cozy for words.

For dinner, go to adjacent Stone Harbor to **㉕ Sea Salt**, one of the best restaurants in New Jersey – forget the shore. It's about the size of a beach tag,
and as plain-looking as could be, which only adds to the impact: who expects
such confident, accomplished cuisine served so simply, in such a relaxed
place? The Argentinean chef experiments with ceviches of fish, blueberries,
mango and peppers; mixes quail with chorizo and okra; tosses shrimp and
scallops in his Jersey corn soup; and even deep-fries poisonous blowfish, for
souls brave enough to try it.

We're almost finished with Jersey, but let's make one more stop: Stone
Harbor's **㉖ Wetlands Institute**. This is an excellent place to experience
the nonsandy side of the coast's barrier-island ecology. Like an avian
reality-show, the institute hangs a video camera over an osprey nest, and
from April to September you can watch the ungainly osprey chicks grow up.
Other aaaawesome wildlife exhibits include baby terrapins, and there's a short
wetlands hike and guided kayak trips.

When you're done, drive to Cape May at the very tip of Jersey and book passage on the **㉗ Cape May–Lewes Ferry**. On high-summer weekends, ferries
leave more than hourly from 6:30am to 8pm, and slightly less frequently
in other seasons. It's a pleasant 80-
minute ride to Lewes in Delaware,
and for day-trippers on foot, there's
a bus near the ferry terminal that can
take you to Delaware's beaches.

THE STING OF THE RIVER

Maryland's rivers may look freshwater and, ergo,
jellyfish-free, but many are connected to the
brackish estuary that is Chesapeake Bay. Thus,
while splashing about in a quiet, forested inlet,
you may come skin-to-tentacle with a nasty
jelly. A good remedy for stings is vinegar or a
sprinkling of meat tenderizer (but don't leave
it on more than 15 minutes); rubbing your skin
makes it worse.

But the ferry takes you across more
than a state line. The Maryland and
Delaware shores provide a bit of a
schizophrenic entity, kind of like the
states they service. Whereas New Jersey and New York are firmly of the
Northeast, and Virginia speaks to the
Old South, Delaware and Maryland are caught in between, and their beach
culture is no exception.

Once you get off the ferry, the closest beach option is attractive **㉘ Cape
Henlopen State Park**. On clear days you can see all the way to New Jersey
(some would argue whether this is a good thing or not – just kidding, Jersey),
and there's an intimate gay-and-lesbian scene for those who are tired of the
party going on just south of here.

Exemplifying Delaware's odd cultural mix is the town of **㉙ Rehoboth Beach**,
where you'll find a bumping gay version of a slightly subdued Mardi Gras,

hunter-enthusiasts from central Pennsylvania's Bible Belt, congressional staff from Washington DC on weekend breaks and Confederate flag–waving good old boys. This juxtaposition reaches the height of sureality when you've walked by several Jeff Gordon T-shirt stands (South), bumper stickers bemoaning the Philadelphia Eagles (North) and **30** **La La Land**, a Victorian house decked out in prancing fairies and gold stars, serving a luscious menu of New American mouth-watering joy: mustard-roasted lamb chops, wild-mushroom ravioli and all the artesian goodness good foodies just cry over.

If all that good food is making you keel over into slumber, might we recommend going a little ways off the beach to the **31** **Corner Cupboard Inn?** As practically perfect as the B&B genre gets, this lovely little spot is set back in some attractive woods, and just overwhelms with good service and warm, cozy touches.

This all makes for a seaside culture that's always exciting, if utterly mixed up. If you need to party, head just a few minutes south of here to **32** **Dewey Beach**. This sits just north of the best stretch of sand in this state, **33** **Delaware Seashore State Park (DSSP)**, something of a hidden gem among Atlantic beaches. It's not that DSSP is particularly isolated, but because there's so much tourist activity in Ocean City, MD, and the Delaware beach towns, the park tends to be overlooked. This is a shame, although the traveler absence means you can pretty much have a long, windy sweep of Atlantic seafront to yourself. If you surf, you'll be pleased to know the park is one of the Eastern seaboard's top wave-providers.

If you need more of a family escape, head further south to **34** **Bethany Beach**. Of Delaware's three main beach-towns, Bethany is undoubtedly the most physically attractive, and it is certainly the most family-oriented.

DELAWARE DON'TS

If you're driving north from Ocean City onto the Delaware shore, be extremely wary of the (very sudden) speed limit changes centered around Bethany Beach and several private gated communities that dot the highway up to Dewey Beach. First: it is actually dangerous to drive fast through these areas; kids cross the roads frequently. Second: the Delaware State Police love manning speed traps around here, and your butt will get heavily ticketed if you tempt the traffic gods.

Dewey attracts the frat boys and Rehoboth has its gay nightlife edge, but Bethany is basically a small village of family diners, cute cafés and beachfront bookshops.

Heading south again, we have to battle through the intense scrum of developments and same-same hotels that is Ocean City, MD. There are all the usual activities in "the OC" to partake in – Skee-Ball, boardwalk-hopping, pizza-gnoshing etc, but don't linger too long, because you need to be off to one of the best wild-animal preserves in Maryland, and the dream come true of many a pony-lover. The contrasting environments show Maryland–Delaware at its most confusing: Northeastern enough to seem mean, but friendly enough past the surface, and either well-developed beachside madness or perfectly preserved rural oceanfront escape.

The isolated **35** **Assateague Island National Seashore** is as windblown and sand strewn as you want, but the real attraction here is a herd of wild horses whose origin remains a mystery – some say they are the descendants of horses lost in a shipwreck (whose ruins are being excavated as of 2008). Although the breezes here are probably too high for a picnic, if you can duck behind a dune you'll be out of the way of the sand. If you come here, there's a good chance you'll spot the horses, so don't look silly searching everywhere, expecting a mare to be hiding somewhere behind the bushes!

In Calvert County, MD, off the long speed trap that is Rte 4, **Calvert Cliffs State Park** (www.dnr.state .md.us/publiclands/southern/calvertcliffs.ht), the nicest beach we can think of near a nuclear reactor, awaits. The cliffs aren't exactly Big Sur, but they front a good stretch of wetlands, are studded with shark teeth (kids love shark teeth!) and look out on a gorgeous panorama of Chesapeake tidelands. To get here, take HG Truman Pkwy from Rte 4 to the park entrance.

And really, once you've seen wild horses, gotten a tan where the sun don't normally shine, spied on osprey, climbed lighthouses, kayaked wetlands, eaten your gourmet heart out, and flown your freak flag, don't you feel better?

Jeff Campbell, Adam Karlin & Ginger Adams Otis

TRIP INFORMATION

GETTING THERE
On Long Island, Hwy 27 leads to towns that access Fire Island; in New Jersey, all shore points are accessed from the Garden State Pkwy.

DO

Assateague Island National Seashore
Feel the ocean move in utter isolation, just miles from Ocean City. ☎ 757-336-5956; www.assateagueisland.com; 7206 National Seashore Lane (off Rte 611), MD; individual/vehicle $3/10; ⊙ 5am-10pm summer, with seasonal variations

Barnegat Lighthouse
The lighthouse is surrounded by a nice picnic area and dramatic causeway. ☎ 609-494-2016; Broadway, Long Beach Island, NJ; admission $1; ⊙ 10am-4:30pm; 🔽

Belford Seafood Co-op
Look for the faded green-shingled building; the co-op is owned by the harbor boats. ☎ 732-787-6508; Monmouth Rd, Belford, NJ; restaurant mains $12-25; ⊙ 8:30am-4:40pm Mon-Sat, 8:30-noon Sun, restaurant 11am-9pm Tue-Sun; 🔽

Cape Henlopen State Park
The north shore of this charming stretch of beach attracts gay-trippers looking for an attractive slice of seafront. ☎ 302-645-8983; www.destateparks.com/chsp/chsp.htm; 42 Cape Henlopen Dr, DE; ⊙ 8am-sunset

Cape May–Lewes Ferry
Reservations aren't required, but they are essential at peak times. ☎ 800-643-3779; www.cmlf.com; Hwy 9, Cape May, NJ; car & driver $34, adult/child $9.50/4.75; ⊙ daily, hours vary; 🔽

Delaware Seashore State Park (DSSP)
You wouldn't think a small state like Delaware could conceal a long swathe of untouched, undeveloped beach, but here you go. ☎ 302-227-2800; www.destateparks.com/dssp/dssp.asp; 39415 Inlet Rd, DE; ⊙ 8am-sunset

Fire Island Lighthouse
Sweeping Long Island Sound views, and even glimpses of the Empire State Building on a clear day. ☎ 631-681-4876; www.fireisland lighthouse.com; Robert Moses Causeway, Fire Island, NY; admission free; ⊙ 9:30am-5pm; 🔽

Fire Island National Seashore
Access Fire Island by ferry from Long Island towns Sayville and Bay Shore. ☎ 631-289-4810; www.nps.gov/fiis; NY; admission free; 🔽

Island Beach State Park
This is a great place to bike; no rentals. Beach fires are allowed in designated areas. ☎ 732-793-0506, kayak tours 732-793-1698; www.njparksandforests.org; Seaside Park, NJ; Memorial Day to Labor Day parking $10; ⊙ 8am-dusk; 🔽

Otis Pike Fire Island Wilderness
Arrange camping permits far in advance. ☎ 631-281-3010; www.nps.gov; Watch Hill, Fire Island, NY; admission free, campsites $25; 🔽

Robert Moses State Park
The only park on Fire Island you can drive to. ☎ 631-669-0449; www.nysparks.state.ny.us; Fire Island, NY; admission free; 🔽

Sandy Hook National Recreation Area
Sandy Hook is another great place to unpack the bike; no rentals. ☎ 732-872-5900; www.nps.gov/gate; Hwy 36, NJ; Memorial Day to Labor Day parking $10; ⊙ sunrise-sunset; 🔽

Sunken Forest
Enjoy great hikes through this strange forest. ☎ 631-289-4810; www.nps.gov; Fire Island, NY; admission free; ⊙ 9:30am-5pm; 🔽

Wetlands Institute
The institute conducts active research; time your visit for a full-moon kayak. ☎ 609-368-1211; www.wetlandsinstitute.org; 1075 Stone Harbor Blvd, Stone Harbor, NJ; adult/child $7/5; ⊙ 9:30am-4:30pm Mon & Sat, to 8pm Tue-Thu, 10am-4pm Sun; 🔽

EAT

Atlantic Bar & Grill
A trusty surf and turf with a raw bar and gently Asian preparations. ☎ 732-854-1588; 24th & Central Ave, South Seaside Park, NJ; mains $26-42; ⊙ from 5pm; 🔽

La La Land

If you need a gorgeous, fine-dining treat to offset the grease of standard boardwalk eats, you'll love this La La. ☎ 302-227-3887; 22 Wilmington Ave, Rehoboth Beach, DE; mains $26-33; ❂ dinner

Michael's

Serves gourmet pizzas with fresh toppings like basil, pineapple and more, and traditional Italian dinners. ☎ 631-597-6555; Cherry Grove, Fire Island, NY; mains $12-20; ❂ 11am-10pm

Plantation Restaurant

As many specialty drinks as entrées, and both are interesting and above average. ☎ 609-494-8191; www.plantationrestaurant.com; 7908 Long Beach Blvd, Harvey Cedars, NJ; mains $12-36; ❂ 11:30am-10pm Sun-Thu, to 11pm Fri & Sat; ♿

Rachel's

A low-maintenance diner with delicious coffee, burgers, fries and sandwiches. ☎ 631-597-4174; Cherry Grove, Fire Island, NY; mains $12-18; ❂ 8am-9pm; ♿

Sea Salt

It's reservation only and a BYOB; so don't forget to bring some wine. ☎ 609-368-3302; www.seasaltstoneharbor.com; 8307 3rd Ave, Stone Harbor, NJ; mains $22-45; ❂ from 5:30pm Wed-Mon

SLEEP

Corner Cupboard Inn

You can take a shady, sylvan break from the beach here, even though you're never too far from the ocean. ☎ 302-227-8553; www.cornercupboardinn.com; 50 Park Ave, Rehoboth Beach, DE; r $175-240

Island Beach Motor Lodge

A full range of motel rooms, efficiencies and apartments; weekly rates. ☎ 732-793-5400; 24th & Central Ave, South Seaside Park, NJ; r $95-225; ♿

Madison Fire Island

Boutique accommodations on the beach; Madison has airy suites, a beautiful pool and waterfront access. ☎ 631-597-6061; www.themadisonfi.com; The Pines, Fire Island, NY; r $200-775

North Shore Inn

Efficiencies are only $10 more; rates drop outside July and August. ☎ 609-494-5001; www.northshoreinn.com; 806 Central Ave, Barnegat Light, NJ; r $145-165; ♿

Pines Bluff Overlook

A weathered beach guesthouse with big suites, just steps from the ocean. ☎ 631-597-3064; www.pinesbluffoverlook.com; The Pines, Fire Island, NY; r $250-300

USEFUL WEBSITES

www.beach-net.com
www.nps.gov/neje

LINK YOUR TRIP

www.lonelyplanet.com/trip-planner

We the People

WHY GO America is a product of its difficult birth. Who we are today is a result of what happened then. And what happened then, happened here – across these mid-Atlantic states. Hitch up your knee-length breeches; grab your tricorner hat. This trip is about how "we the people" were born.

TIME
5 – 8 days

DISTANCE
240 miles

BEST TIME TO GO
May – Sep

START
Princeton, NJ

END
La Plata, MD

ALSO GOOD FOR

HISTORY &
CULTURE

On the East Coast, we walk every day in colonial footsteps. And yet, when those who made us, who made America – through the bloodshed of war, through the eloquence of their thoughts, through the force of sheer charisma – have their names slapped on every middle school and their profiles engraved on every coin, one's sense of living history flatlines into a cold marble whatever.

So we're not looking for statues. We're looking for a pulse. After all, the founding fathers were just people trying to do their best in difficult times.

Let's begin in ❶ **Princeton**, since it makes a good starting point, travel-wise. Princeton's big Revolutionary War moment is commemorated at ❷ **Princeton Battlefield State Park**. There isn't much to see. What we have is a grassy field, a historic house, some plaques, and a leap of the imagination. It was here, on January 3, 1777, that George Washington and his untrained, ill-equipped troops won their first victory against British regulars, then the world's most powerful army. The British had been relatively unimpressed by the colonists' Declaration of Independence, and up until this moment they'd been shoving the Continental Army around like a schoolyard bully.

Princeton saw, apparently, one of the war's fiercest battles. Stand here in the fading light of a brittle January afternoon and the desperation

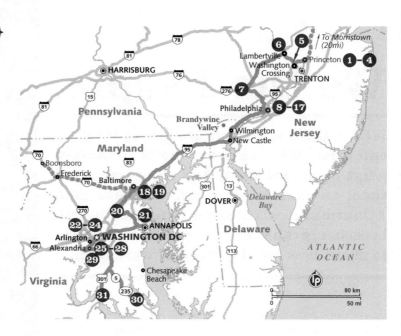

of the colonists becomes as clear as the puff of your own breath: if they lose, it's pretty much over.

This emotional turning point, however, isn't what Norman Rockwell decided to commemorate in 1937, when the colonial-era **3 Nassau Inn** asked him for a painting. No, he went the other way. Below the Nassau Inn, over the bar in the **4 Yankee Doodle Tap Room**, hangs Rockwell's 13ft-wide artwork, which portrays a haughty "Yankee Doodle" prancing on his pony pasts the jeers and catcalls of a bunch of drunken British redcoats. It's silly and it's also clever, because it skewers both the self-serious patriots and the slovenly arrogance of the British. Which, in its roundabout way, partly explains why the war turned out the way it did.

 **DETOUR**   In 1776, after crossing the Delaware and before his victory in Princeton, Washington won another surprising battle: in Trenton on December 26 over mostly Hessian troops. Altogether, these "ten crucial days," as they are called, shifted everyone's perception of the Continental Army. Trenton's battle is remembered at the **Old Barracks Museum** (www.barracks.org), and every December the region's parks coordinate a series of reenactments (www.tencrucialdays.com). And yes, you can join them to cross the Delaware and defeat the British all over again.

This portrait contrasts nicely with another: that of *Washington Crossing the Delaware*. About 20 minutes from Princeton is **5 Washington Crossing State Park**, where 10 days before the battle at Princeton, on Christmas night 1776,

Washington led his army across the ice-packed Delaware River in a raging snowstorm. How desperate must you be to do that? Washington had retreated across the same river about a week before, and he knew if he didn't win *something* before winter closed in, his army might desert him entirely come spring, since very few give their life for a lost cause.

The park itself offers an overstuffed exhibit in the visitors center, historic buildings, and nice trails through pretty woods. It's a great place for a picnic, but not terribly evocative. The copy of the painting in question is on the Pennsylvania side (Washington Crossing Historic Park). According to historians, the artist, Emanuel Leutze, got almost none of the details right: the boats, the light, the river, Washington himself – all wrong. Like Rockwell's, the scene is a caricature, one that captures not the moment itself but how everyone felt about it afterward.

As an aside, if you're here, call to see if the **6** **Black Bass Hotel**, north of the park along the Delaware River, has reopened. During the Revolution, the inn remained loyal to the British, so Washington definitely did not sleep here; in 2007, it was damaged by floods. Once renovations are complete, it should once again be a fun, historic spot for an ale, a meal, and a night's stay.

> **DETOUR** The coldest winter in a century hit during 1779–80, and Washington and his troops didn't spend it shivering at Valley Forge, but in Jockey Hollow in Morristown, New Jersey. By spring the soldiers were so sick and tired they threatened to mutiny. Washington forestalled this, but the next year the Continental Army *did* march on Philadelphia – threatening to quit over lack of pay and supplies. Learn more at **Morristown National Historical Park** (www.nps.gov/morr), about an hour north of Princeton.

Our next stop is **7** **Valley Forge National Historical Park**, northwest of Philadelphia, which commemorates not a battle but the "birthplace of the Continental Army." It was here, over the famously devastating winter of 1777–78, that the rag-tag short-term militia Washington had whipped together was reconstituted and trained into a cohesive force. Marching and drills aside, Washington changed his recruitment strategy: he offered land and more money for those who'd commit to fight to the end. Men (and women) across the range of colonial society responded: most were English, but they were joined by Dutch, French, Germans, Irish, Spaniards, Swedes, enslaved Africans seeking freedom and even some Native Americans. Two-thirds of the troops were foreign-born, and regiments were integrated. In this way, the army came to reflect the society it was fighting for. It was the war's ideals made flesh.

Valley Forge is one of the better places that evoke the war experience, its wide fields dotted with soldiers' huts and light-blue cannons. Despite the occasional statue of a horse-mounted general, the park has an egalitarian focus, exemplified by Washington's quote chiseled onto the National Arch: "Naked and starving as they are, we cannot enough admire the incomparable patience and fidelity of the soldiery."

We know what drove these citizen-soldiers to face England's dauntingly equipped professional army. It was the promise of liberty, and the self-evident truth of equality, that emerged out of the contentious political debates in **8** Philadelphia. If the last time you visited **9** Independence National Historical Park was your high-school field trip, it deserves to be given another shot.

The centerpiece is the same, **10** Independence Hall, where both the Declaration of Independence and the Constitution were signed. Inside the hall, the experience is largely the same as well: a green-clad park ranger walks you through the building and the history. Still, to occupy the same space where the colonists' "high treason" took place, to look up at the "rising sun" chair (where Washington sat when he presided over the Constitutional Convention), is goose-bump-inducing without any interactive folderol. Yes, it takes a leap of imagination to mentally fill the Assembly Room and conjure America's ideological moment of birth, but it has become more like a small step.

This is mostly due to all the sites now around Independence Hall. Historic buildings like Congress Hall and Old City Hall are fine, but make sure not to miss the west wing's Great Essentials exhibit, which displays draft pages of the big documents. To book geeks like us, nothing is cooler or more immediate than seeing the Constitution with inked deletions and revisions.

Then check out the **11** Liberty Bell in its new house. With thoughtful consideration for a million snapshots, the bell is now perfectly framed with Independence Hall in view behind it through tall glass windows. Take your digital phone picture, then pause over the exhibit, which is a disquisition on what makes an icon. For two centuries, people have invoked the Liberty Bell whenever the definition or meaning of freedom is in question, making the cracked bronze relic a perfect example of the whole universal ideals vs practical application debate that, we're just guessing, isn't likely to ever end in this country.

The new **12** National Constitution Center is the ideal companion to Independence Hall, providing the opposite yet complementary experience: nothing of historical importance happened here, but the center vividly provokes the emotions. Your ticket includes the 17-minute live performance of "Freedom Rising." Instead of playing dress up, the show sends a narrator in a blue suit alone onto a bare stage to address you and speak directly and emotionally about what those high-fallutin' ideas mean. To hear those words spoken in earnest, accompanied by a little music and video, is a smart reminder of theater's simple power to move the heart.

The rest of the center is devoted to translating the Constitution's laws and amendments into personal terms using every socket wrench in the interactive toolbox. With a cacophony of video and voices and real people and buttons and artifacts and live presentations, the center works hard to make anything even slightly abstract easily "relatable." Slavery, September 11, Nixon, Florida's 2000 presidential vote fiasco – we might actually have paid attention in class if we'd had this when we were in school. Then there's the Hall of Signers, in which are gathered life-size statues of the Constitution's 39 delegates (and three dissenters). Stand among them, rub their heads, see how short John Adams really was: it's goofy fun.

Other Philadelphia highlights include the **13** **Portrait Gallery at the Second Bank**. What did "we" used to look like? Charles Wilson Peale painted hundreds of portraits of 18th-century politicians, soldiers, businessmen and Philadelphia matrons, and a great many of his works are on display in this curiously pink building.

When the National Constitution Center was built in 2000–03, they unearthed over a million archaeological artifacts from a single city block dating from 1760 to 1840. All those cracked vases and broken plates are now being painstakingly reassembled in the **14** **Independence Living History Center**, which offers a first-hand look at the raw evidence of us and the detective work that's required to piece our story together.

Finally, across the street, is **15** **Harmony Lane**. Here, reenactors in colonial costumes play games, sew things, and tell bad Revolutionary War jokes. It's a bit of harmless cornball historical amusement. But a less self-

ONCE UPON A NATION

From Memorial Day to Labor Day, 13 storytelling benches are staffed in Old City. These are run by **Once Upon a Nation** (http://historicphila delphia.org/once-upon-a-nation), which also places costumed actors around town – a mad Quaker, Ben Franklin, colonial townsfolk – who'll give you a piece of their mind (for free!). The Colonial Army also hands kids (wooden) rifles and musters them into shape daily. For a fee, Once Upon a Nation offers guided tours with costumed docents and presents "evenings with" Franklin, Washington and Jefferson.

conscious encounter can be had at the storytelling benches dotted around Old City; at these, people dress normally and simply discuss the times. They are a memorable reminder that a good conversation is often the best interactivity.

If you're in Philly to experience the American Revolution, the only place to consider staying is **16** **Thomas Bond House**. Three curators were called in to get the period details exact – so that the furnishings reflect the original occupants, rather than a luxurious, faux interpretation of colonial style. The 1st floor, where the wealthy Bond family slept, has larger rooms, Chippendale reproduction furniture, and ornate bedspreads. On the 4th floor, where the slaves slept, the rooms are smaller, with plain pine furnishings and wrought-iron bed frames. You will of course take your meals across the street at **17** **City Tavern**, where they've painstakingly re-created the building *and* the menu – so that you're served Thomas Jefferson's favorite sweet-potato biscuits when you sit down and can drink George Washington's recipe for ale in your pewter goblet. In both places, we're thankful they drew the line at historical accuracy with the utilities, but they do allow you to dabble in a colonial lifestyle without, of course, having to defeat the British.

> *"…they allow you to dabble in a colonial lifestyle without, of course, having to defeat the British."*

Eventually the colonists did defeat the British – in 1783, so the history books tell us. And though France and Spain helped, afterward the disciplined, regal Washington was given the lion's share of the credit as the mother of all founding fathers; he was pressed into becoming America's first president and enjoyed what today would be called "cult status." Continuing our journey south into **18** **Baltimore**, to the neighborhood (as opposed to house) of Mount Vernon, we find the first **19** **Washington Monument** is, in the vein of the genre, a large, none-too-subtle column jutting into the sky. A more interesting site is just south of Baltimore, in the city of Laurel, Prince George's County, MD. Here, the five-part **20** **Montpelier Mansion** and its 70-acre grounds are all that remains of what was once a 9000-acre plantation that hosted George Washington, his wife, Abigail Adams and (a bit later) Franklin Roosevelt, among others. When he wasn't at home, where *did* George Washington sleep? For one, in the **21** **Middleton Tavern** in Annapolis, which is now a somewhat rowdy surf-and-turf joint, directly overlooking the city's cobblestoned harbor.

DETOUR

Although Baltimore may claim to have the oldest Washington Monument in the country, the tiny town of Boonsboro, MD, can proudly say it has the oldest *completed* monument. While construction of this **monument** (www.dnr.state.md.us/publiclands/western/washington.html), which looks like a rough cylinder of stones, began after Baltimore began work on its monument, the Boonsboro structure was finished first, in 1827. The DC monument, for the record, wasn't completed until 1885. Take I-70 west from Baltimore to US 40 towards Braddock Heights.

Now let's see, the nation's capital is named after… oh yes, *him*. In **22** **Washington DC**, the well-known **23** **Washington Monument** is the centerpiece of the National Mall, its two-toned sandstone (the construction was done in two phases) is visible from across the city. To what degree Washington would have appreciated these monuments, we'll never know; he was not immune to adulation and celebrity. Yet there is no question that he would have prized most the evidence of his legacy on display on Constitution Ave in the **24** **National Archives**: the Declaration of Independence, whose promises he secured, the Constitution he helped shape, and the Bill of Rights that followed, ensuring the US government respected the common freedoms that define democracy. Washington helped here too when he became the nation's first *ex-president*, setting an example for the graceful abdication of power upon which America's quadrennial presidential elections have been predicated ever since.

These and other suitably awe-inspiring original documents are on display in the National Archives' Rotunda for the Charters of Freedom. Awe-inspiring, that is, until you read the Constitution's preamble and get that *Schoolhouse Rock!* song stuck in your head. However, don't leave without touring the Public Vaults, which displays but a snippet of the archives' vast holdings. It's a fascinating stroll through our national attic – like opening a dusty trunk and finding grandpa's letters, if your gramps was Abraham Lincoln.

We'll wrap this tour with a couple more worthwhile George Washington stops. High above ㉕ **Alexandria**, with a spectacular view of Washington DC, is the ㉖ **George Washington Masonic Memorial**. A towering monument from the Masons to one of their most famous members, it comes replete with Doric columns and a breathtaking Memorial Hall. A collection of former presidents' Mason aprons and a series of stained-glass-window portraits of Revolutionary icons, like Ben Franklin, are particularly unique. Several portraits of Washington's family members are especially interesting for history buffs. It will be impossible to miss the 17ft bronze statue of George that is the focal point of the Memorial Hall. To top it all off, there's a Shriner's exhibit on one of the lower floors with oodles of vintage Shriner hats. Totally wild and worth a look.

An offbeat place to hang your hat is the ㉗ **216 Bed and Breakfast**. This unusual B&B is an 1890 row house with only three rooms. It's newly renovated with a skylight, kitchen and garden and an antique vibe nicely juxtaposed with modern amenities. A group could rent the whole shebang

ASK A LOCAL

"Just north of Mount Vernon and off the tourist-beaten path is **River Farm**. In 1773 George Washington gave the lease to the property as a wedding present to Tobias Lear, whose bride was Martha Washington's niece. Today River Farm is the headquarters of the American Horticultural Society. The estate is beautifully landscaped…three venerable old black walnut trees still stand, reminders of the 18th-century landscape that Lear and Washington knew. A pleasant step into the past."
Mark Drummond, Alexandria, VA

and get a feel for what it would be like to actually live in Old Town Alexandria. Similarly, for a meal not served by colonial-costumed waiters, try the ㉘ **Majestic**. This rustic American café is both low-key and high-end, with food ranging from succulent scallops to liver and onions. On Sundays they offer "Nana's" special: a $78 prix fixe that feeds four and changes monthly. Expect fried chicken, strawberry shortcake and more, served family style.

Finally, ㉙ **Mount Vernon** is the ultimate pilgrimage for enthusiasts of George Washington. He lived here, high atop Chesapeake Bay, from 1759, when he married Martha, until his death in 1799. Over the years, Washington expanded it from six to 21 rooms, and in his gardens he grew cherry trees (forget the apocryphal cherry-tree story – old George would lie through his wooden teeth if it suited him). The gardens are immaculately maintained today, and are among the finest colonial gardens you'll ever see. Recently, they have added a very impressive education center and museum, with hands-on activities for kids and more instructive exhibits for adults (perhaps a display of presidential china?). Down the road you can view Washington's reconstructed Whiskey Distillery and Gristmill. You can take home some grist, and make hoecakes, but sadly there is no colonial whiskey for sampling.

Mount Vernon hosts several special events throughout the year, like "Breakfast with George" on his birthday. July 4th hosts the First Virginia Regiment encampment with period-clad reenactors. Exercise your second amendment rights and buy a wooden rifle from the gift shop and join the militia.

True Washington buffs should keep going towards the tip of the state, along Rte 235, to the **30** **Sotterley Plantation**, a beautiful old house many believe served as a model for Washington's eventual Mount Vernon home. To finish off your journey, head to nearby La Plata, MD, former home of Washington's good friend, Dr James Craik, and host of the **31** **Crossing at Casey Jones**. This is the sort of aristocratic small-town place that serves artful takes on local recipes (in this case the bounty of the tidewater) while resting secure in its knowledge that it's the best restaurant for miles. Washington would approve.

Jeff Campbell, Adam Karlin & David Ozanich

TRIP INFORMATION

GETTING THERE
From Philadelphia, take I-95 north to Rte 206 north to Princeton.

DO
George Washington Masonic Memorial
Grand Masonic temple in tribute to America's first president. ☎ 703-683-2007; www.gw memorial.org; 101 Callahan Dr, Alexandria, VA; admission free; 🕙 10am-4pm

Independence Hall
To see inside, get a free timed ticket from the visitors center for the 40-minute tour; book by 10am on busy weekends. No tickets needed from 5pm to 7pm. ☎ 800-537-7676; www .nps.gov/inde; Chestnut & 6th Sts, Philadelphia; admission free; 🕙 9am-7pm; 👤

Independence Living History Center
A refreshingly low-key place full of working archaeologists. ☎ 215-629-4026; 3rd & Chestnut Sts, Philadelphia; admission free; 🕙 9am-5pm, to 6pm Thu-Sat

Independence National Historical Park
A large parking lot right underneath the visitors center is very convenient. ☎ 800-537-7676; www.nps.gov/inde; Market & 6th Sts, Philadelphia; national park sites free; 🕙 8:30am-7pm, hours vary for individual sites; 👤

Liberty Bell
As at Independence Hall, you'll go faster through security if you carry less. ☎ 800-537-7676; 6th St at Chestnut St, Philadelphia; admission free; 🕙 9am-7pm; 👤

Montpelier Mansion
A fine example of Georgian architecture, which has hosted presidents and dignitaries for three centuries. ☎ 301-953-1376; 9650 Muirkird Rd, Laurel, MD; adult/child $3/1; 🕙 11am-3pm, reduced hours Sun & winter

Mount Vernon
The main man's main house – all you ever wanted to know about George Washington. ☎ 703-708-2000; www.mountvernon.org; southern end of GW Pkwy, Mount Vernon, VA; admission $6-13; 🕙 9am-4pm

National Archives
The website also has a wealth of information about the founding documents. ☎ 202-501-5000; www.archives.gov; 700 Constitution Ave, Washington DC; 🕙 10am-5:30pm, to 9pm summer

National Constitution Center
The center is walkable to Independence Hall, the Liberty Bell, and most Old City sites. ☎ 215-409-6700; www.constitutioncenter .org; 525 Arch St, Philadelphia; adult/child $12/8; 🕙 9:30am-5pm Mon-Fri, to 6pm Sat, noon-5pm Sun; 👤

Portrait Gallery at the Second Bank
Peale himself was quite a character, and you get his life too. ☎ 800-537-7676; 420 Chestnut St, Philadelphia; admission free; 🕙 11am-5pm; 👤

Princeton Battlefield State Park
The 1772 Thomas Clarke House has exhibits and has more limited hours than the park. ☎ 609-921-0074; http://www.state.nj.us /dep/parksandforests/parks/princeton.html; 500 Mercer Rd, Princeton, NJ; admission free; 🕙 park dawn-dusk, house 10am-noon & 1-4pm Wed-Sat, 1-4pm Sun; 👤

Sotterley Plantation
This period plantation and mansion occupies a perfect perch over the Potomac River. ☎ 301-373-2280; www.sotterley.com; 44300 Sotterley Lane, off Rte 235, Holly-wood, MD; tour/self-guided $10/3; 🕙 10am-4pm Tue-Sat, from noon Sun

Valley Forge National Historical Park
There's a cell-phone tour while driving, a trolley tour (for a fee), and storytelling benches. ☎ 610-783-1077; www.nps .gov/vafo; 1400 N Outer Line Dr, King of Prussia, PA; admission free; 🕙 park 6am-10pm, visitors center 10am-5pm; 👤

Washington Crossing State Park
PA's Washington Crossing Historic Park, across the Delaware, has different hours and fees; check the website (www.ushistory.org /washingtoncrossing) for details. ☎ 609-737-9303; www.njparksandforests.org; 355 Washington Crossing-Pennington Rd, Titusville, NJ; admission $5 summer weekends only; 🕙 park dawn-dusk, visitors center 9am-4pm; 👤

Washington Monument (Baltimore)
Yet more proof that nothing says, "Way to go George" like a big, phallic landmark. ☎ 410-396-0929; 699 Washington Pl; suggested donation $1; ☾ dawn-dusk Wed-Sun

Washington Monument (Washington DC)
This obelisk, the tallest structure in Washington DC, stands at exactly 555ft and 5 inches. ☎ 202-426-6841; National Mall; ☾ 9am-4:45pm

EAT & DRINK

City Tavern
"The most genteel tavern in America" once again serves Martha Washington's potpie, among other tasty period dishes. ☎ 215-413-1443; www.citytavern.com; 138 S Second St, Philadelphia; mains $18-33; ☾ 11:30am-9pm; ♿

Crossing at Casey Jones
A no-nonsense Maryland menu of crab cakes and broiled steak. ☎ 202-787-6006; 417 E Charles St, La Plata, MD; mains $20-26; ☾ lunch & dinner Mon-Sat

Majestic
A family-friendly upscale diner with lots of comfort food served 21st-century style. ☎ 703-837-9117; www.majesticcafe.com; 911 King St, Alexandria, VA; mains $12-26; ☾ 11:30am-2:30pm & 5:30pm-10pm Mon-Sat, 1-9pm Sun

Middleton Tavern
You can't decide between the lobster ravioli and a juicy T-bone? Fine; just hit up the excellent oyster bar. ☎ 410-263-3323; 2 Market Space, Annapolis, MD; mains $12-25; ☾ 11:30am-1:30am

Yankee Doodle Tap Room
Princeton professors, students and out-of-towners gather in this friendly atmospheric pub, serving local brews and hearty meals. ☎ 609-688-2600; www.yankeedoodletaproom.com; 10 Palmer Sq, Princeton, NJ; mains $13-36; ☾ 7am-11pm; ♿

SLEEP

216 Bed and Breakfast
Intimate, private B&B in the heart of Old Town Alexandria. ☎ 703-548-8118; www.216bandb.com; 216 S Fayette St, Alexandria, VA; r $225

Black Bass Hotel
Only 270 years old and should look better than ever in 2009; call for current information on both the restaurant and rooms. ☎ 267-293-0265; www.blackbasshotel.com; 3774 River Rd, Lumberville, PA; ♿

Nassau Inn
A Princeton favorite, evoking 18th-century elegance with 21st-century comforts, like wi-fi. ☎ 609-921-7500; www.nassauinn.com; 10 Palmer Sq, Princeton, NJ; r $250-280; ♿

Thomas Bond House
Fosters a social atmosphere for those visiting the national park. ☎ 215-923-8523; www.thomasbondhousebandb.com; 129 S Second St, Philadelphia; r $135-190; ♿

USEFUL WEBSITES
www.independencevisitorcenter.com
www.ushistory.org

LINK YOUR TRIP
www.lonelyplanet.com/trip-planner

East Coast Eats

WHY GO Philly cheesesteaks. New York pizza. Maryland crabs. It may not all be haute cuisine, but this is the true soul of the mid-Atlantic, and any trip here just wouldn't be complete without sampling the greats. Pack your Alka-Seltzer and loosen your belt. We're goin' in.

TIME
7 days

DISTANCE
650 miles

BEST TIME TO GO
May – Sep

START
New York

END
Prince Frederick, MD

ALSO GOOD FOR

FOOD & DRINK

Unlike California or the South or even the Southwest, New York is never described as having one defining cuisine. Try asking for some "New York food," for example, and you could wind up getting anything from a hot dog to a South Indian feast or a $500 Japanese-sushi smorgasbord. Cuisine here is global by definition, constantly evolving by its very nature.

That said, it's the food items with the longest histories that folks usually have in mind when they refer to New York specialties. And those at the top of the list are those introduced by Italians and East European Jews, because these groups were among the earliest wave of immigrants here. Bagels (Jewish) and slices of pizza (Italian) are integral parts of the local food scene. But egg creams, cheesecake and said hot dogs, just to name a few, are also uncontested staples of New York eats.

A derivative of sausage and one of the oldest forms of processed food, the hot dog goes back thousands of years, making its way to New York via European butchers in the 1800s. One, Charles Feltman of Germany, was apparently the first to sell them from pushcarts along the Coney Island seashore. But Nathan Handwerker, originally an employee of Feltman's, opened his own shop across the street, offering hot dogs at half the price of those at Feltman's and putting his former employer out of business. The original, legendary ❶ **Nathan's Famous hot dogs** still stands in Coney Island, while its empire has expanded nationally. And there is barely a New York neighborhood

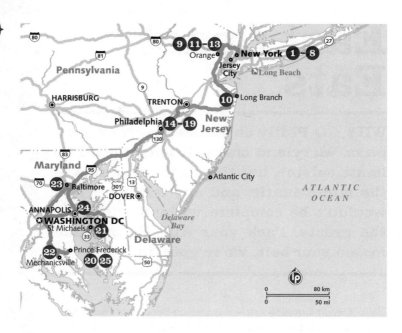

in existence that does not have at least a few hot-dog vendors on its street corners – though some locals would never touch one of those "dirty-water dogs," preferring the new wave of chichi hot-dog shops that can be found all over town. Enjoy yours, wherever it's from, with "the works": plenty of spicy brown mustard, relish, sauerkraut and onions.

Like the ubiquitous hot dog, bagels were a European invention. But they were perfected during the turn of the 19th century in New York City – and once you've had one here, you'll have a hard time enjoying one anywhere else. Basically, it's a ring of plain-yeast dough that's first boiled and then baked, either left plain or topped with various finishing touches, from sesame seeds to chocolate chips. "Bagels" made in other parts of the country are often just baked and not boiled, which makes them nothing more than a roll with a hole. And even if they do get boiled elsewhere, bagel-makers here claim that it's the New York water that adds an elusive sweetness not found anywhere else.

The most traditionally New York way to order your bagel is by asking for a "bagel and a schmear," which will yield you said bagel with a small but thick swipe of cream cheese. Or splurge and add some lox – thinly sliced smoked salmon, just like that originally sold from pushcarts on the Lower East Side by Jewish immigrants back in the early 1900s. Quite possibly the best place to get your bagel fix is ❷ H&H Bagels, a New York institution that's been boiling bagels since 1972. Its award-winning options include sesame, pumpernickel, blueberry, poppyseed, garlic, sourdough and more, all served with thick dabs of sour cream or whatever topping you wish.

There's more to do with your dough in New York than boil it into bagels – pizza is another wheaty treat to be had here. Pizza is not indigenous to Gotham (and as you'll see in Jersey, each region has its own take on it), but New York–style pizza is a very particular item, and the first pizzeria in the country was ❸ **Lombardi's**, which opened here in 1905 and is still serving up slices. Pizza made its way over to New York in the 1900s through Italian immigrants, and its regional style soon developed. While Chicago-style is "deep dish" and Californian tends to be light and doughy, New York prides itself on having pizza with a thin crust and an even thinner layer of sauce. Standard slices in the city are triangular, but Sicilian-style joints serve them square.

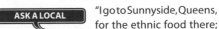

"I go to Sunnyside, Queens, for the ethnic food there; it has all sorts: markets, restaurants, bakeries, a great park to eat outdoors, and a wonderful place to get cholados. It has a Turkish restaurant, an Irish market, two Romanian bakeries as well as one Romanian restaurant and one Romanian nightclub, a great Armenian market across the street from a great Lebanese market and lots more stuff. Just a wonderful place to visit, and where I bring a lot of my tours."
Myra Alperson, Manhattan, leader of Noshwalk Tours

Today there are pizza parlors about every 10 blocks, especially in Manhattan and most of Brooklyn, where you'll find standard slices for $2. The style at each place varies slightly – some places touting cracker-thin crust, others offering slightly thicker and chewier versions, and plenty of nouveau styles throwing everything from shrimp to cherries on top. A Manhattan-must is ❹ **Two Boots**, which, thanks in part to the traditional brick-oven baking, serves up what many New Yorkers feel is the best pie in town.

It would be easy to spend your day weighing up the virtues of thin crust vs thick, or seeking out the city's best hot dog, but be sure to leave enough room for some New York dessert. And what better one to start with (just to start, of course) than an egg cream?

People hear the words "egg cream" and tend to get suspicious. Well fear not. The frothy, old-fashioned beverage contains no eggs or cream – just milk, seltzer water and plenty of chocolate syrup (preferably the classic Fox's U-Bet brand, made in Brooklyn). But when Louis Auster of Brooklyn, who owned soda fountains on the Lower East Side, invented the treat back in 1890, the syrup he used was made with eggs, and he added cream to thicken the concoction. The name stuck, even though the ingredients were modified, and soon egg creams were a standard at every soda fountain in New York. For the complete egg-cream experience, ask for a seat at the counter at **5** **Lexington Candy Shop**, a hole-in-the-wall Upper East Side luncheonette that has retained its original vintage charm – and, of course, its soda fountain.

After a starter of egg cream, it's time to indulge in a little slice of heaven going by the name of "cheesecake." Sure, cheesecake, in one form or another, has been baked and eaten in Europe since the 1400s. But New Yorkers, as they do with many things, have appropriated its history in the form of the New York–style cheesecake. Immortalized by Leo Lindemann in 1921, the particular type of confection he served in his Midtown restaurant **6** **Lindy's** – made of cream cheese, heavy cream, a dash of vanilla and a cookie crust – became wildly popular in the '40s. Today, you'll find Lindy's cheesecake on menus across the country, but somehow it just tastes better when eaten at the source.

It wasn't until 1950 that another cheesecake challenger rose to the heights of Lindy's – and this family bakery was, and still is, based in Brooklyn. **7** **Junior's**, named after the owner's two sons, concocted cheesecakes that were baked on top of crispy, graham-cracker crusts and airy sponge cakes. It used to be that you had to travel to Flatbush Ave to sample these creamy delights, not to mention the plate-sized burgers and deep-fried onion rings, but now you can just swing by the family's Midtown shop.

Chewing your way through the Big Apple can be food-coma inducing. Before heading out on the next leg of this culinary tour, rest your weary head and expanding waistline at the **8** **Hotel Giraffe**. A swank hotel with a distinctive deco-gone-modern vibe, Giraffe also offers a rooftop bar that's great for grabbing a cocktail to wash down the day's eats. If New York City hasn't filled you up yet, tuck into some tapas, served at the rooftop bar.

THE MUNCHMOBILE

Look! Driving the Parkway! Is it a van with a hot dog on top? Is it a balding caped crusader of culinary justice? Yes, it's the Munchmobile!

Every summer, New Jersey's *Star-Ledger* gives writer Pete Genovese a spandex suit and the keys to the van. Each week he takes a band of volunteer "Munchers" to find New Jersey's best pizza, chili, Chinese, subs, doughnuts, milkshakes and oh so much more. Read all about it at www.nj.com/munchmobile.

Having rested, and moved that belt buckle along a couple of notches, you'll be ready for the next stop: New Jersey. Here the most mundane foods are discussed and debated with the seriousness of Michelin food guides. Take pizza. All the elements must be dissected – the dough, the cheese, the sauce, the texture. Whole dissertations could be written on just the grease: are we talking bland greasy grease or good, flavorful, bright orange grease? And how much is there: once you fold, do you get a few measly drops or a flood? These things matter, and loyalty, once won, is rarely cast aside.

So it is with some trepidation that we offer a few recommendations. New Jersey is a big state, and these are passionate issues, and, in truth, there is *so much* good stuff. With that out of the way, quite a bit of passion is inspired by the pies at **9 Reservoir Restaurant** in South Orange. As one local humbly put it, "it's the best pizza place in the world." These are high-quality pizzas with a bold, unique flavor, and this three-generation, family-run restaurant consistently dusts the competition. Then, if you're down the shore, make sure to stop at **10 Ferraro's Famous Tomato Pies** in Bradley Beach. From the outside, it looks like nothing – just another average pizza-shack. But the owner, Aldo Ferraro,

THE RESTAURANT GUYS

When we tell you that two Jersey guys get on the radio every weekday at 11am to discuss food, you figure, what, it's just pizza talk.

And you'd be right. Francis Schott and Mark Pascal talk pizza, but they also talk shad, sustainable farming and terrines, with food-celebrity guests like Ruth Reichl. If they're not careful, the **Restaurant Guys** (www.restaurantguysradio .com) are going to become the Click and Clack of the culinary arts. Tune in to New Brunswick's WCTC 1450AM.

puts his heart and soul into the place, and into his pies, which have a crispier, thin crust and are topped with Naples tomatoes and fresh mozzarella. Not your typical greasy pizza.

Can we talk dogs? The Garden State is quite proud of the fact that it can claim to have created not one but two types of hot dogs. According to legend, Jimmy Buff's of Newark created the first Italian dog over 75 years ago. Today, that epochal moment lives on at **11 Jimmy Buff's** in West Orange. What is an Italian dog? It's a hot dog smothered in grilled peppers and onions and french fries, slathered in mustard and ketchup, and stuffed into crusty Italian bread. You can get the same thing with Italian sausage and – oh man, is it lunchtime yet? The Texas wiener, or chili dog, is also said to have been born in the state, though whether it was in Plainfield or Paterson – who knows? We'll let them argue about that. There is no dispute, however, over where to find the best one today: ramshackle **12 Hiram's**, in Fort Lee. Their chili has a majestic, sinus-clearing piquancy, and they toast their buns.

But one of the most famous, or perhaps infamous, hot dogs in New Jersey is the Ripper, which is the devious brainchild of **13 Rutt's Hut** in Clifton. The name alone lets you know you're in for something very, very special. Indeed, the Ripper is a hot dog deep-fried till its skin rips apart. In other words, these are not pretty dogs, but something happens in that oil that's akin to magic. If there were seats, you'd have to sit down, but there aren't, so you'll have to handle it standing up. The timid can order an "in and outer," while the seriously twisted could order a "cremator" – but we've really only ever *heard* of someone eating these blackened monstrosities.

In Philadelphia, most of the boasting centers on its namesake gastronomic pleasure: the Philly cheesesteak. This is, of course, a soft white roll filled with grilled, thinly sliced beef and onions and covered with a gooey mess of melted cheese. Like hot dogs or pizza, the elements are simple, but difficult to master. Get a bland cheesesteak, and you think: it's just a sandwich. Get a good cheesesteak, and all thinking stops as your synaptic pleasure centers are overwhelmed by aromatic oniony goodness.

"Get a good cheesesteak, and all thinking stops as your pleasure centers are overwhelmed by oniony goodness."

While it's a bit put on at this point, a good place to begin is in the crosshairs of the cheesesteak's greatest rivalry: between ⑭ **Pat's King of Steaks** and ⑮ **Geno's**. Truth be told, there's not a lot of difference between them, but they keep the quality high because, well, because they've been bragging to the world for decades. You can sample more cheesesteaks at Philadelphia's ⑯ **Reading Terminal Market**, which is a one-stop-shop for good eats that presents the gamut of Pennsylvania specialties. In particular, search out the Dutch Country or Amish stalls and butchers. The Pennsylvania Dutch love their meats, and you should definitely sample some scrapple. It's really just a sort of pork terrine cut into slices, but like electoral politics, it's best to focus your attention on the results, not on the process.

Finally, don't leave Philly without a visit to the rambling, outdoor ⑰ **Italian Market**. It's one of the world's oldest markets, and it retains a scruffy flea-market feel. There's fresh produce, bakeries, cheese shops, spice shops, and a tremendous number of butchers: you're in luck if you're looking for some fresh game, rabbit, duck, grouse or peacock to take home. However, the real reward for coming is the chance to experience the epitome of an Italian deli: ⑱ **Di Bruno Bros**, which has commanded the attention and respect of several generations of the city's restaurateurs and Italian-Americans. Before heading south for more grub (if you can stomach it), sleep off your salami sandwich at the charming ⑲ **Alexander Inn**. Smack dab in the middle of Center City, this boutique hotel is surrounded by plenty of stores that are perfect for window shopping – another way to work off that last meal if you're still too full to hit the sack.

After a good night's sleep, you're hopefully ready to refuel with some authentic Maryland eats. Grab some of the free breakfast buffet at the Alexander Inn, then hop on the I-95 heading south – it'll probably take you about three hours, so make sure you leave yourself enough time to arrive before lunch.

As in the rest of the country, Maryland, Delaware and DC residents specialize in eating their local bounty – in this case, chicken and crabs. While Southern states will make a justifiable claim to frying the best chicken in the country, the Eastern Shore's huge poultry-farming industry has led to some pretty tasty variations on cooked bird in this part of the country. With that said, folks here generally prefer their chicken fried, and our favorite – to be served with sweet white corn, of course – is sold at the tiny, bare bones ⓴ **Golden Chicken** in Prince Frederick, in Calvert County. The chicken itself is excellent, but what really sets this place apart are the biscuits, which we have never had as good anywhere else: buttery, soft, like little clouds of puffy baked yumminess.

HOW TO PICK CRABS

Rip off the claws and legs, except for the back flippers. Discard the legs (not the claws). Use a fork or finger to pry off the "flap" (shaped like the Washington Monument on males) and insert your thumb into the space between the top and back shell. Pry the top shell off and break the crab in half to dig out the body meat, then use your mallet to crack the claws and have at it.

Crabs, of course, specifically blue crabs, are what this region is best known for. We've dedicated an entire trip to the best crab shacks in Maryland, places where buckets of steamed blue crabs are served on newspaper with pitchers of beer, ears of corn and clouds of Old Bay seasoning. Two excellent institutions that we weren't able to fit into our crab quest include the ㉑ **Crab Claw**, in St Michaels, which scores points for the crowds of day-trippers it regularly pulls in from across the Bay Bridge, and the ㉒ **Sandgates Inn** in Mechanicsville, a Southern Maryland favorite that exemplifies all the best of the genre: casual attitude, fresh crabs and stunningly scenic waterfront location.

They don't do diner and deli with as much passion as the folks in New Jersey and New York do, but the above two genres are well-loved here, and we have included two exemplars of the class. In Baltimore, ㉓ **Jimmy's Restaurant** is one of the only greasy spoons we've been in that retains a liquor license and scrapple, a fried hash of all the pork products you didn't want to ask about. It's a dockside legend, as much for its friendly Baltimore attitude as its food, loved by locals and tourists alike. In Annapolis, ㉔ **Chick & Ruth's Delly** is the watering hole to the wildebeests of the Maryland State Legislature. While the Jewish-deli experience isn't as pronounced here as it is up north, there are plenty of Jewish residents in this state who've turned corned beef and schmaltz (chicken fat, mmm) into beloved favorites of the state's bickering politicians.

HALF-SMOKED

Wander around Washington DC and you'll notice a certain type of sausage for sale at local hot dog stands: the vaunted "half-smoke." No one really knows where the title comes from – some say it stems from the sausage being half beef, half pork, but it has nothing to do with smoking, since the meat is grilled. What's for sure is a half-smoke is coarser, spicier, bigger and, frankly, better than a normal hot dog.

This region is at its best when it comes off as laid back and languid, but that doesn't mean local cuisine doesn't have its high-end variations. To this end, plenty of fancy restaurants, especially in smaller towns that are off the fusion radar, have developed haute versions of local recipes, bringing out the most rarified flavors of fresh seafood and local livestock. The firelit, dark and intimate **25 Old Field Inn** is a good example; its essentially French takes on local field-and-stream is heavy, creamy and usually leaves you feeling like you've devoured the most delicious brick on the Bay.

While this is by no means the end of the gourmet road for this part of the country, you've probably gained several pounds by now and are ready to travel it off. With a full belly and, if you can afford it, a full tank of gas, you're ready to hit the highway for your next adventure. Just remember your Alka-Seltzer.

Jeff Campbell, Jennye Garibaldi, Adam Karlin & Ginger Adams Otis

TRIP INFORMATION

GETTING THERE
These cities can be accessed via the I-95.

EAT
Chick & Ruth's Delly
The original Annapolis deli does a mean chopped liver beloved by loyal regulars. ☎ 410-269-6737; www.chickandruths .com; 165 Main St, Annapolis, MD; mains $6-10; 🕑 6:30am-10pm Sun-Thu, later on weekends

Crab Claw
Deck dining, steamed blue crabs, fried chicken and cold beer: basically, the essence of Maryland happiness. ☎ 410-745-2900; 304 Mill St off Rte 33, St Michaels, MD; mains $11-30; 🕑 11am-10pm Mar-Nov

Di Bruno Bros
The cheeses are phenomenal. ☎ 215-922-2876; www.dibruno.com; 930 S 9th St, Philadelphia; mains $5-8; 🕑 9am-5pm Mon, 8am-6pm Tue-Sat, 8am-2pm Sun; 🚹

Ferraro's Famous Tomato Pies
House salads are tasty, and Italian dishes are huge. ☎ 732-775-1117; www.ferraros famous.com; 400 Main St, Bradley Beach, NJ; mains $9-16; 🕑 from 11am; 🚹

Geno's
Figure out your order and your cheese before you step up; they hate indecision. ☎ 215-389-0659; www.genosteaks.com; S 9th St & Passyunk Ave, Philadelphia; mains $6-8; 🕑 24hr; 🚹

Golden Chicken
The amassed powers of Land O' Lakes corporation couldn't make biscuits this buttery. ☎ 410-535-5984; Fox Run Shopping Center, off Rte 4, Prince Frederick, MD; mains under $10; 🕑 lunch & dinner

H&H Bagels
Who creates the "best" bagel in New York is a matter of opinion; most agree that H&H ranks high up there. ☎ 212-595-8000; www .hhbagels.net; 639 W 46th St, New York City; bagels $2-5; 🕑 24hr

Hiram's
Lean way over the picnic tables to catch the drips. ☎ 201-592-9602; 1345 Palisades Ave, Fort Lee, NJ; mains $2-2.50; 🕑 10:30am-9pm or so, hours vary; 🚹

Italian Market
The main action is along 9th St between Christian and Washington Aves. www.philly italianmarket.com; 9th St btwn Fitzwater & Wharton Sts, Philadelphia; 🕑 9am-5pm Tue-Sat, to 2pm Sun; 🚹

Jimmy Buff's
They say the cheesesteaks are good too, but we never get to them. ☎ 973-325-9897; www.jimmybuff.com; 60 Washington St, West Orange, NJ; mains $2-5; 🕑 10:30am-8:30pm Mon-Thu, to 10:30pm Fri & Sat, 11am-7pm Sun; 🚹

Jimmy's Restaurant
If you appreciate diners, you'll find no better in Baltimore than this excellent institution on Fell's Point. ☎ 410-327-3273; 801 S Broadway St, Baltimore; under $10; 🕑 5am-8pm

Junior's
Junior's makes its own famous version of cheesecake with a graham-cracker crust. ☎ 212-302-2000; www.juniorscheesecake .com; 1515 Broadway, New York City; mains $16-25; 🕑 6am-11pm

Lexington Candy Shop
Small, narrow and with a 1920s zinc-topped bar, Lexington is the place for egg creams and root-beer floats. ☎ 212-288-0057; www .lexingtoncandyshop.com; 1226 Lexington Ave, New York City; mains $8-15; 🕑 7am-7pm Mon-Sat, 9am-6pm Sun

Lindy's
Immortalized as "Mindy's" in the musical *Guys and Dolls*; their creamy, cheesy confection is world famous. ☎ 212-767-8343; www .lindysnyc.com; 825 Seventh Ave at 53rd St, New York City; cakes $40; 🕑 9am-8pm

Lombardi's
A Little Italy landmark, this family-run establishment does thin-crust pizza with homemade sauce and crazy toppings. ☎ 212-941-7994; www.firstpizza.com; 32 Spring St at Mott St, New York City; mains $12-20; 🕑 11:30am-11pm

Nathan's Famous hot dogs
You might not be able to match competitive eater Kobayashi, but you can still eat like a champ at this Coney Island institution. ☎ 718-946-2705; www.nathansfamous.com; 1310 Surf Ave, Brooklyn; ☾ 8am-1am Mon-Thu, 8am-2am Fri-Sun; ♿

Old Field Inn
Filet mignon topped with crab imperial is the epitome of high-end Chesapeake Bay surf and turf. ☎ 410-535-1054; 485 Main St, Prince Frederick, MD; meals $17-30; ☾ lunch & dinner Mon-Fri, dinner only Sat & Sun

Pat's King of Steaks
Same as Geno's but across the street; get one from each and settle this once and for all! ☎ 214-468-1546; www.patskingofsteaks.com; S 9th St & Passyunk Ave, Philadelphia; mains $6-8; ☾ 24hr; ♿

Reading Terminal Market
The restored train station is the perfect setting for the bustling stalls. ☎ 215-922-2317; www.readingterminalmarket.org; 12th & Arch Sts, Philadelphia; mains $3-15; ☾ 8am-6pm Mon-Sat, 9am-4pm Sun; ♿

Reservoir Restaurant
It's cash only, and the pastas and Italian dishes are great, too. ☎ 973-762-9795; www.reservoir.qpg.com; 106 W South Orange Ave (Rte 510), South Orange, NJ; mains $10-18; ☾ 11:30am-10pm Mon & Wed-Fri, 4:30-10:30pm Sat, 3-10pm Sun; ♿

Rutt's Hut
Rutt's brick hut is about as pretty as its dogs, but step up anyway. ☎ 973-779-8615; 417 River Rd, Clifton, NJ; mains $1.70-3; ☾ 10am-11pm, to 1am Fri & Sat; ♿

Sandgates Inn
Another Maryland crab house overlooking the water, overflowing with good times. Their version of Old Bay is legendary. ☎ 301-373-5100; 27525 N Sandgates Rd, Mechanicsville, MD; mains $12-28; ☾ lunch & dinner

Two Boots
Many contend the pizza here is the best in the city. ☎ 212-777-1033; www.twoboots.com; 74 Bleecker St, New York City; mains $12-18; ☾ 11am-11pm; ♿

SLEEP

Alexander Inn
Modern rooms with a deco twist. What you save on your room here, you can spend on your next meal. ☎ 215-923-3535, 877-253-9466; www.alexanderinn.com; 301 S 12th St, Philadelphia; r $120-170

Hotel Giraffe
The 12-floor Giraffe earns its stripes, or dots, with sleek, modern rooms and a sunny rooftop area. ☎ 212-685-7700, 877-296-0009; www.hotelgiraffe.com; 365 Park Ave South at 26th St, New York City; r $339

USEFUL WEBSITES
www.chowhound.com
www.urbanspoon.com

LINK YOUR TRIP
www.lonelyplanet.com/trip-planner

The Boys of Summer

WHY GO Across the East Coast, a wave of new stadiums is transforming both major- and minor-league baseball. We decided to check them out, and we asked New Jersey's Star-Ledger sports columnist Steve Politi to join us and share his thoughts on ballpark food, fandom, the end of Yankee Stadium and interviewing A-Rod.

Steve Politi has been a sports writer for the *Ledger* for 10 years, the last three as a columnist, and he says that today "is the golden age of baseball." Considering that since 2001, Pittsburgh, Philadelphia and Washington have new stadiums; that the Yankees and Mets open new stadiums in 2009; and that New Jersey had no professional baseball before 1994 and now has eight minor-league teams in new stadiums – we'd have to agree. Ignore any honeyed nostalgia over the national pastime: right now is the best time to be a baseball fan.

The place to begin is obviously ➊ **New York**. This is where Alexander Cartwright and the New York Knickerbockers developed the modern game, and it's where the most hallowed field in baseball history is (as we write) about to be demolished: ➋ **Yankee Stadium**. In his column, Politi went public with his dismay, and it still gets him hopping mad: "Why tear down Yankee Stadium? Why would we do this to the greatest place in the world? Sure, it's not the same as it was 20 years ago, but you walk through the tunnel and it takes your breath away."

Since 1923, Yankee Stadium has been a repository of cherished memories, and Politi has his: "My dad took me to my first baseball game to see the Yankees. I'll always remember the traffic and that my friend threw up in the car. My dad hated sports and didn't even care about the game. It was just what parents think they have to do for their kids."

TIME
2 – 7 days

DISTANCE
350 miles

BEST TIME TO GO
May – Oct

START
New York

END
Norfolk, VA

ALSO GOOD FOR

OUTDOORS

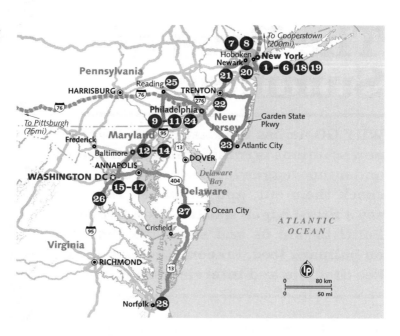

In his case, Politi's father put him on the path to becoming a sportswriter. Politi's first assignment for the *Ledger* was the 1998 World Series, Yankees vs Padres. "It was the Yankees' historic 125-win season. My first week on the job and it doesn't get any bigger." But sometimes it does. Politi was covering the final game of the 2003 American League Division Series and polishing his story on the Yankees' loss, when Aaron Boone's home run shocked everyone and won the game. Politi quips, "The best moment in Yankees' history ruined my column. Yankee Stadium shakes in these moments."

> "...for a billion and change, you'd hope the Yankees are getting something bigger and better."

Yeah but, Steve, what about **3** Shea Stadium? "It's the worst pit in the world out of all the stadiums I've covered. And I've seen maybe 40 arenas around the globe. It sucks the good out of the weather. On a beautiful spring day, it's too hot, sweaty; wind blowing from all directions. You think to yourself – what's wrong with this place? Mr Met is only smiling cause it's painted on his face."

OK, weeelll…that's why the Mets are building a new one. Politi shrugs: "The new stadium is gonna be nice. But this is the way it always is with the Mets – it's gonna be overshadowed by the Yankees," who are building, he says, "a great facility." According to what he's seen, it will be overall grander but more intimate, with fewer seats, and for a billion and change, you'd hope the Yankees are getting something bigger and better.

We'll find out, of course, when new eras officially start for both teams. When you come, make sure to make a pilgrimage to the place where baseball started: ❹ **Madison Square Park.** This is where, in the 1840s, the Knickerbockers set the rules for balls and strikes, marked out the base paths, and stopped throwing at the runner to make an out. Meanwhile, New York's new-in-2008 ❺ **Sports Museum of America** honors baseball's modern heroes (as well as those in 17 other sports), and a convenient place to stay nearby is the ❻ **Ramada Eastside Hotel** – a few blocks from Madison Square Park and the subway's 4 train, direct to Yankee Stadium (and an easy transfer to Shea).

Crossing the Hudson River into New Jersey, we find two other important baseball stops: the first is Hoboken, to remember ❼ **Elysian Fields.** As the shiny brass plaque at 11th and Washington Sts says: "On June 19, 1846, the first match game of baseball was played here on the Elysian Fields between the Knickerbockers and the New Yorks. It is generally conceded that until this time the game was not seriously regarded." What the plaque doesn't say is that the New Yorks, a

No baseball tour would be complete without a visit to Cooperstown in upstate New York and its **National Baseball Hall of Fame** (http://web.baseball halloffame.org). The appropriately stately, red-brick building contains an orgy of artifacts and memorabilia, plus a new multimedia theater presentation, but the most moving experience is still the hushed Plaque Gallery, where all 278 hall-of-famers get their due. Cooperstown is on Rte 80 between I-90 and I-88, west of Albany, New York.

team of former cricket players, kicked the vaunted Knickerbockers in the patootie, 23 to 1. Unfortunately, nothing remains of the ballfield today; there's just a small park with swing sets and amazing Manhattan views.

The next Jersey stop is the ❽ **Yogi Berra Museum** in Montclair. This mini-Cooperstown is an overlooked gem of Yankee history and baseball memorabilia. Politi has interviewed Yogi several times, and says, "Yogi lives in Montclair, and he's there at the museum all the time. The guy has 12 million stories." He also has 10 World Series rings, the most of any player, and they are all on display here, along with three of the Yankees' World Championship trophies, the mitt Yogi used when he caught Don Larson's perfect game in the '56 World Series, and much more. The museum also has box seats where you can watch the minor-league New Jersey Jackals play in the attached stadium.

But we're touring the majors right now, and we're going to ❾ **Philadelphia.** In 2004, the Phillies inaugurated their attractive new yard, ❿ **Citizens Bank Park.** Like all the new "classic style" stadiums, it's got quirks that get you close to the action: grab a cheesesteak in Ashburn Alley, a food promenade behind centerfield, and you can eat it over the visitor's bullpen and shout encouragement. If they moved the Philadelphia skyline a bit closer, the park views would be improved, but Citizens Bank does have the Liberty Bell – one that lights up and "rings" when the Phillies hit a home run. For a place to stay, try the ⑪ **Best Western Independence Park Hotel**; it's well-placed in Old City, and a quick subway ride to the park.

Now, let's visit the home of the Orioles, ⑫ **Camden Yards** in ⑬ **Baltimore**. Built in 1992, "Camden Yards is the model," Politi says, "the one that all new ballparks strive to be. It's still great – accessible, comfortable, good sight-lines and good food." Indeed, notwithstanding the brickful beauty of Camden Yards and the other parks, one of the most welcome improvements is the food. It still ain't cheap, but it's a whole lot nicer to skip the hockey-puck hamburgers for roasted pork sandwiches, crab cakes, fajitas, empanadas, barbecue, gyros, even sushi.

DETOUR

It's a little out of the way for this trip, but don't miss the home of the Pittsburgh Pirates, **PNC Park** (pittsburgh.pirates.mlb.com). This fantastic stadium sits right on the Allegheny River with an unobstructed view of Pittsburgh's downtown and the city's magnificent steel bridges. Plus, how's this for history: Pittsburgh played in the first World Series in 1903, losing to Boston and Cy Young. Statues of Willie Stargell and Roberto Clemente recall Pittsburgh's glory days. Pittsburgh is about six hours' drive from Philadelphia via I-76.

So, Steve, what do you like? "I'm pretty much a hot dog guy. I don't need tuna rolls when I go to a ballpark. If the roving vendor can't throw it at you, I don't need it." We'll have to agree to disagree on this one, because at Camden Yards the fat Boardwalk Fries with malt vinegar are awesome. And we don't want them thrown at us.

Our recommendation for a place to stay in Baltimore is the ⑭ **Sheraton Inner Harbor Hotel**, which is, in fact, the official hotel of the Orioles. You may not see ballplayers in the lobby, but you'll be steps from the yard.

The last major-league stadium on our tour is the newest (for now). ⑮ **Washington DC** inaugurated ⑯ **Nationals Park** in 2008 to rave reviews – unlike the Washington Nationals themselves. Since the former Expos moved from Montreal and changed their name in 2004, the team has lived in the cellar of the standings. Does that matter? Politi says he's been to most of the major-league parks, and "my measure of a stadium is: is it a destination? Would you go even if you weren't a fan of the teams?" Nationals Park passes that test: the main entrance offers an immediate, dramatic view of the green diamond, cherry blossoms grace an area near left field, and the Washington skyline poses in the distance. One day they'll have a team to match it. For an attractive place to stay in DC, try the ⑰ **L'Enfant Plaza Hotel**.

However, over the last decade, an even more striking development in baseball has been the resurgence of the minor leagues. As Politi says, "Gone are the days when you wake up and say, 'Let's go to the ballpark.' Prices are too high, it's too crowded. Close to 8 million people go to those two New York ballparks in a year." Politi adds, "A minor-league game is a completely different experience, and I would argue a better one."

It starts with the stadiums themselves. Most seat about 6000 people, and they rarely fill up, so you can sit virtually anywhere – behind home plate, over the dugout, on a grassy slope past the outfield. The same seats in Yankee Stadium are $100, $200, $400, depending on the game; in the minors, tickets are usually no more than $10. In the minors, whatever you may lose in pro excitement, you gain in intimacy and the joy of affordable baseball.

"A minor-league game is a completely different experience, and I would argue a better one."

Plus, did we mention that the minor-league parks are brand-spanking new, too? Let's start our trip through the minors back in New York, with the Brooklyn Cyclones. This single-A Mets affiliate opened ⑱ **KeySpan Park** in 2001 right next to the Coney Island amusement park. Coney Island's old parachute jump practically sits in right field, and the amusement park's roller-coaster and Ferris wheel make for one screaming, brightly lit "skyline." That not intimate enough? Foul balls often land in the parking lot to the sound of broken glass (courtesy of the PA system).

Brooklyn has a long and storied baseball history, but it's had nothing since the Brooklyn Dodgers moved to Los Angeles 45 years ago and Ebbets Field was razed for apartments. Now, a tiny museum and park statues honor Jackie Robinson, Pee Wee Reese, Gil Hodges and other greats.

Just across New York Harbor, the single-A Staten Island Yankees were founded in 1999. The "Baby Bombers" play in ⑲ **Richmond County Bank Ballpark** at St George, next to the Staten Island ferry (which is free, folks). You want a skyline? Try all of Lower Manhattan. Even another billion couldn't buy that view for Steinbrenner's Bronx Bombers.

In New Jersey, the Newark Bears were also founded in 1999, bringing pro-fessional baseball back to a city where it once thrived. The original Bears were a Yankees farm-team who, in 1946, fielded a young catcher named Yogi Berra. Newark was also host to the Eagles, an extremely successful Negro League club. Today, the ⑳ **Bears & Eagles Riverfront Stadium** honors both, as trains rumble over the gun-metal-gray bridge and the New York skyline shimmers hazily in the twilight.

The Bears, however, are an independent minor-league team playing in the independent Atlantic League; neither is affiliated with major-league baseball. This means the ballplayers aren't signed prospects, but a combination of young players who hope to be signed and older players who can no longer keep a job in the majors. As Politi says, "The Newark Bears had Rickey Henderson when no major-league team would take him."

Does this make for bad baseball, or a disappointing afternoon at the park? To answer that, let's visit the Somerset Patriots, who opened **㉑ Commerce Bank Ball Park** in Bridgewater in 1999. The Patriots are also an independent team in the Atlantic League, and they've been managed by former All-Star Sparky Lyle to three Atlantic League championships, so the boys can play. The stadium itself is as red-brick gorgeous as any modern pro stadium, just smaller – a clean, bright, snappy park in what are essentially the Jersey suburbs.

But minor-league teams know that's not enough, so they pile on the promotions and entertainment. Giveaways include batting helmets, hats, gloves, T-shirts, mugs, coolers and more, plus they frequently have fireworks after games. During the game, free-roaming mascots keep things loose and very silly: the Patriots have a uniformed soldier – "General Admission." The Staten Island Yankees have "Scooter 'the holy' Cow" and his buddies, "Red" and "Huckleberry," pratfalling over the field. At Newark, between-inning contests include the "What Exit?" game and the "Big Hair Challenge," which gives three women from the stands a can of hairspray to see what they can do. That, right there, is worth $10.

A LOT OF BULL & MILLIONAIRES

The resurgence of the minor leagues started in 1988, when *Bull Durham* made the minors seem cool and fun. Then the 1994 baseball strike, which canceled the regular season and the World Series, made major-league ballplayers seem like whiny millionaires. Then, a renegotiated agreement with major-league baseball forced minor-league teams to build professional-quality stadiums. Now, fans who don't want to be fleeced by major-league concessions and ticket prices can attend minor-league games and still enjoy pro ball.

Still, one of the greatest thrills of minor-league ball is seeing tomorrow's All-Stars today. One of the better teams for that is the Trenton Thunder, a double-A Yankees affiliate in beautiful **㉒ Mercer County Waterfront Park** in Trenton. Joba Chamberlain, currently the Yankees' ace-in-the-making, pitched for the Thunder in 2007. When Roger Clemens made his comeback, he played here. For these, Politi says, "the stadium was overflowing with fans."

Politi has his own stories of covering minor-league ball when he was a cub reporter in North Carolina. He followed Michael Jordan when he dabbled in the minors, and he saw Derek Jeter and Alex Rodriguez come up. How great is minor-league baseball? Politi still shakes his head, remembering: "One day A-Rod was hitting off a T and the guy putting balls on the T was Ken Griffey Sr." Politi chatted with Griffey about the rising star. "You could tell just by watching A-Rod play he would be great, but you don't know he'll be the home-run king."

How different are the majors? Flash forward, and Politi describes being in the Yankees' clubhouse a few years ago. A-Rod had consented to be interviewed, but he kept putting Politi off for "just a few more minutes." This stretched for three hours, until Politi (no shrinking violet himself) got A-Rod's publicist to intervene, and A-Rod finally sat for the interview. "It's challenging sometimes," Politi says of dealing with major leaguers. "There are a lot more of us than there are of them. Not every player is" – here Politi pauses for a long time, searching the sky for a word that won't get him into trouble once it lands in print – "cooperative," he finishes with a smile.

But it's getting late, and there are still dozens of minor-league stadiums we could visit, so we'll stick to the highlights. If you're down the Jersey shore, make sure to catch a night game at the independent Atlantic City Surf. Dubbed the "sandcastle," **㉓ Bernie Robbins Stadium** is perfectly positioned to frame the AC casinos in all their neon glory. At the other end of the Atlantic City Expressway are the independent Camden Riversharks, whose **㉔ Campbell's Field** has one of the best views in all of baseball: at the foot of the dramatic Ben Franklin Bridge, with Philadelphia skyscrapers looming just across the Delaware River.

A LEAGUE OF THEIR OWN

With both affiliated and independent minor leagues, it can get a bit confusing, so here's the skinny: "Minor league baseball" is the official name for major league–affiliated teams and leagues. Teams mentioned in this trip play in the New York–Penn, Eastern, South Atlantic or Carolina Leagues. Independent baseball is an independent product. However, they coordinate with major-league baseball, since it's a source for new players. The independent teams in this trip play in either the full-season Atlantic League or the short-season Can-Am League.

In contrast to the Jersey clubs, the double-A Reading Phillies (in Reading, PA) have been around a long time, since 1933, and **㉕ FirstEnergy Stadium**, built in 1951, is one of the oldest parks. However, it's had numerous renovations, and its signature exploding train is great fun: the whistle blows when men get on base and fireworks shoot out when they score. Reading, dubbed "Baseballtown," is also rich in baseball history (see www.baseballtown.org).

Just outside DC, the single-A Potomac Nationals play in **㉖ Pfitzner Stadium** in Woodbridge, Virginia. Their hall of fame isn't too shabby, including Barry Bonds, Albert Pujols, Bernie Williams and Andy Pettite. Meanwhile, the Delmarva Shorebirds, the Orioles' single-A affiliate, have a nice little museum devoted to pro ball on the Delaware, Maryland, and Virginia (Delmarva) peninsula, at their **㉗ Arthur Perdue Stadium**. Both facilities are pretty, though lacking spectacular views.

Finally, the Norfolk Tides, a triple-A Orioles affiliate, represent the top level of the minors, and their stadium is tops too: **㉘ Harbor Park** was built in

1993 by HOK Sport Facilities, who built Camden Yards, Citizen Bank Park, Nationals Park and many others. It's larger, holding about 12,000, and very scenically situated in downtown Norfolk, Virginia, on the Elizabeth River.

But after all this baseball talk, we still don't know one essential fact: who does Steve Politi root for when he goes to a ballgame?

BASEBALL PILGRIMAGES

No matter how hard you tried, you could never do this trip in one shot. Plus, maybe you want to see Fenway Park or Wrigley Field as well. How do you figure it all out? Check out **Ballgame Travel** (http://ballgametravel.com), a website devoted to just that; it even offers some discounted hotel rates in the bargain.

Politi smiles that A-Rod smile again: "I don't have one team anymore. I root for stories. You can't really root for one team when you cover them all." That's very nice, very political, but, come on, Steve, who *did* you root for, when you were just a fan and not a big-shot sportswriter?

Politi keeps fouling off our best fastballs until finally he leans in and says, almost sotto voce: "My brother was a big Yankees fan. And just to piss off my brother, I would root for the Blue Jays."

So there you have it: fans are always defined by their passion, no matter where that passion comes from.

Jeff Campbell

TRIP INFORMATION

GETTING THERE
The four major cities are connected via I-95.

DO & EAT

Arthur Perdue Stadium (Delmarva Shorebirds)
A single-A minor-league Orioles affiliate in the South Atlantic League. ☎ 410-219-3112; www.theshorebirds.com; 6400 Hobbs Rd, Salisbury, MD; admission $6-12; ☼ 70 home games Apr-Aug; ♿

Bears & Eagles Riverfront Stadium (Newark Bears)
An independent team in the Atlantic League. ☎ 866-554-2327; www.newarkbears.com; 450 Broad St, Newark, NJ; tickets $8-10; ☼ 70 home games Apr-Aug; ♿

Bernie Robbins Stadium (Atlantic City Surf)
An independent team in the Can-Am League. ☎ 609-344-7873; www.acsurf.com; 545 N Albany Ave, Atlantic City, NJ; tickets $5-11; ☼ 47 home games May-Sep; ♿

Camden Yards (Baltimore Orioles)
The stadium is near Inner Harbor, and Baltimore's light-rail line has a Camden Yards stop. ☎ 888-848-2473; www.orioles.com; 333 West Camden St, Baltimore, MD; tickets $8-80; ♿

Campbell's Field (Camden Riversharks)
An independent team in the Atlantic League. ☎ 866-742-7579; www.riversharks.com; 401 N Delaware Ave, Camden, NJ; tickets $5-13; ☼ 70 home games Apr-Sep; ♿

Citizens Bank Park (Philadelphia Phillies)
To come by train, take the Broad St Line to the Pattison stop. ☎ 215-463-1000; www.phillies.com; 1 Citizens Bank Way, Philadelphia, PA; tickets $15-50; ♿

Commerce Bank Ball Park (Somerset Patriots)
An independent team in the Atlantic League. ☎ 908-252-0700; www.somersetpatriots.com; 1 Patriots Park, Bridgewater, NJ; tickets $5-12.50; ☼ 70 home games Apr-Sep; ♿

FirstEnergy Stadium (Reading Phillies)
A double-A minor-league Phillies affiliate in the Eastern League. ☎ 601-375-8469, tickets 610-370-2255; www.readingphillies.com; 1900 Centre Ave (Rte 61 South), Reading, PA; tickets $7-10, all-you-can-eat $19-21; ☼ 71 home games Apr-Aug; ♿

Harbor Park (Norfolk Tides)
A triple-A minor-league Orioles affiliate in the International League. ☎ 757-622-2222; www.norfolktides.com; 150 Park Ave, Norfolk, VA; tickets $9.50-11; ☼ 72 home games Apr-Aug; ♿

Hoboken Museum
Get a map of Hoboken sights; exhibits change and don't always address baseball history. ☎ 201-656-2240; www.hobokenmuseum.org; 1301 Hudson St; admission by donation; ☼ 2-9pm Tue-Thu, 1-5pm Fri, noon-5pm Sat & Sun; ♿

KeySpan Park (Brooklyn Cyclones)
A single-A minor-league Mets affiliate that plays in the New York–Penn League. ☎ 718-449-8497, tickets 718-507-8499; www.brooklyncyclones.com; 1904 Surf Ave, Brooklyn, NY; tickets $7-14; ☼ 38 home games Jun-Aug; ♿

Mercer County Waterfront Park (Trenton Thunder)
A double-A minor-league Yankees affiliate in the Eastern League. ☎ 609-394-3300; www.trentonthunder.com; 1 Thunder Rd, Trenton, NJ; tickets $6-10; ☼ 71 home games Apr-Aug; ♿

Nationals Park (Washington Nationals)
Take the DC Metro Green Line to the Navy Yard. ☎ 888-632-6287; www.nationals.com; 1500 South Capitol St SE, Washington DC; tickets $10-67; ♿

Pfitzner Stadium (Potomac Nationals)
A single-A minor-league Nationals affiliate in the Carolina League. ☎ 703-590-2311; www.potomacnationals.com; 7 County Complex Ct, Woodbridge, VA; tickets $8-13; ☼ 70 home games Apr-Aug; ♿

Richmond County Bank Ballpark (Staten Island Yankees)
A single-A minor-league Yankees affiliate that plays in the New York–Penn League.

☎ 718-720-9265; www.siyanks.com; 75 Richmond Terrace, Staten Island, NY; tickets $5-13; ⊗ 38 home games Jun-Aug; ♿

Shea Stadium (New York Mets)

The new stadium is right next to the old one, so it's on the same subway line: 7. ☎ 718-507-TIXX; www.mets.com; 123-01 Roosevelt Ave, Flushing, NY; tickets $5-117; ♿

Sports Museum of America

Not just baseball, but over two dozen sports in 19 galleries with fully interactive razzle-dazzle. ☎ 212-747-0900; www .sportsmuseum.com; 26 Broadway, New York; adult/child $27/20; ⊗ 9am-7pm, last entry 5:30pm; ♿

Yankee Stadium (New York Yankees)

As with Shea, the new stadium is next door to the old, so take the same trains: B, D or 4. ☎ 718-293-4300; www.yankees.com; 161 St & River Ave, the Bronx, NY; tickets $14-400; ♿

Yogi Berra Museum

The museum is attached to the New Jersey Jackals stadium (www.jackals.com) on the Montclair State University campus. ☎ 973-655-2378; www.yogiberramuseum.org; 8 Quarry Rd, Little Falls, NJ; adult/child $6/4; ⊗ noon-5pm Wed-Sun, to 7pm during Jackals home games; ♿

SLEEP

Best Western Independence Park Hotel

This historic, Victorian-flavored hotel has a great central location, giving you direct access to subway lines to the park. ☎ 800-624-2988; www.independenceparkinn.com; 235 Chestnut St, Philadelphia; r $140-256; ♿

L'Enfant Plaza Hotel

A huge, stylish hotel right on Metro Green Line to the park, with lots of amenities. ☎ 800-635-5065; www.lenfantplazahotel .com; 480 L'Enfant Plaza, SW Washington DC; r $280-340; ♿

Ramada Eastside Hotel

This standard, moderately priced hotel is well-located for the subway to the stadiums . ☎ 212-545-1800; www.ramada.com; 161 Lexington Ave, New York; r $250-270; ♿

Sheraton Inner Harbor Hotel

The Orioles' "Official Headquarters Hotel" is a large, dependable choice, conveniently within walking distance to the stadium. ☎ 410-962-8300; www.starwoodhotels .com/sheraton; 300 S Charles St, Baltimore, MD; r $209-274; ♿

USEFUL WEBSITES

www.ballparkdigest.com
www.minorleaguebaseball.com

SUGGESTED READS

• *No Minor Accomplishment*, Bob Golon

LINK YOUR TRIP

www.lonelyplanet.com/trip-planner

TRIP
1 Ultimate Urban Adventure p35
4 East Coast Eats p65

The Civil War Tour

WHY GO Millions of Americans have blood ties to the Civil War. The intensity of the Civil Rights movement was fed by proximity to the physical spaces of the nation's other great Civil conflict. Physically retracing this phase of American history gives unparalleled insight into other chapters of that narrative.

The Civil War defines America. No other conflict of such scale and significance has been fought in, literally, American backyards. Walk or drive by its associated geography, through suburban interchanges and picture-book towns and rolling hills, farmland, forest, swamps and grassy fields, and you are on graves, graves, graves. There are 100,000 American combat dead in a 10 sq mile area near Fredericksburg, VA; that's a grim math that evokes spirits of Western Europe and Central Africa, yet within easy access to the mid-Atlantic urban corridor.

The impact of visiting these spaces in the right mindset can't be overstated. With the right light and the right soundtrack – a low, soft-creeping sunset and the purple chorus of thousands of crickets against an old split-rail fence – a one-two punch of history and physical landscape induces a sort of "stoned by history" afterglow. The effect is followed by a jarring juxtaposition of bloody legacy and bucolic scenery, the latter a happy aftereffect of the decision to keep battlefields untouched and pristine.

These sites are scattered over huge swathes of the American South, but Virginia, in many ways the epicenter of the war, packages some of the conflict's seminal events in a space that includes areas of the prettiest countryside on the Eastern seaboard. So head off, from Georgetown, Washington DC, to time travel as best you can into the war that Oliver Wendell Holmes Jr said "touched with fire" the hearts of those who passed through it.

TIME
2 days

DISTANCE
320 miles

BEST TIME TO GO
Aug – Dec

START
Georgetown, Washington DC

END
Appomattox, VA

ALSO GOOD FOR

HISTORY &
CULTURE

BEST TRIP

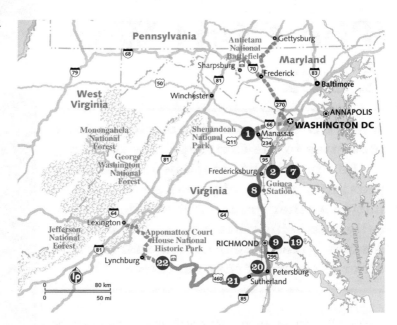

It takes about an hour driving through the tangled knots of suburban sprawl that scar Northern Virginia to reach your first destination: Manassas. Over-developed in the mid-1990s, today it is still glutted with gas stations, but the forces of conservation have occasionally prevailed. In the early 1990s, the Walt Disney Company proposed an American history–themed park in Haymarket, but, to the satisfaction preservationists, Disney's America did not take over the site of the Battle – actually, battles – of Bull Run. What did assault this area were 35,000 men of the Union Army, in 1861, and what they saw then approximates the view of ❶ **Manassas National Battlefield Park**, today a stretch of gorgeous countryside that has miraculously survived the predations of the Army of Northern Virginia real-estate developers.

"Some 32,500 Confederate soldiers were thrust into this backdrop of pastoral North America."

This is as close as any of us will come to 19th-century rural America. From the visitors center, you look out onto green, redefined; in waving hills, dark, brooding tree-lines, the low curve of fields and the soft hump of overgrown trench works.

Some 32,500 Confederate soldiers, as untested and fresh as their enemies, were thrust into this quintessential backdrop of pastoral North America. After a series of charges and countercharges, the Southern line was held by troops under Thomas J "Stonewall" Jackson, an evangelist Virginian who sucked on lemons and rode into battle with one arm above his head to balance his bodily "humors."

Both sides realized a long, hard war was at hand and called up thousands of troops. Europe watched nervously; in a matter of weeks, the largest army in the world was the Union Army of the Potomac. The second biggest was the Confederate States of America Army. A year later, at the Battle of Shiloh, 24,000 men were listed as casualties – more than all the accumulated casualties of every previous American war combined.

Your next stop south on I-95 is ❷ **Fredericksburg**; if battlefields preserve rural, agricultural America, Fredericksburg is an excellent example of what the nation's main streets once looked like: orderly grids, touches of green and friendly storefronts.

Assuming you're hungry, you're a bit spoiled for choice here. ❸ **Bistro Bethem** is an excellent main-street corner spot and bustling restaurant in which to perch over period dishes, like quail with cornbread cherry stuffing, on a perfect sunny day. If you need lighter "faire," ❹ **Olde Town Wine & Cheese Deli** serves up delicious sandwiches and enough gourmet meats and cheeses to keep the average picnic-goer in lunch-basket heaven; mark your entrance to the South by washing your meal down with some sweet iced tea.

DETOUR The Battle of Antietam, fought in Sharpsburg, MD, on September 17, 1862, has the dubious distinction of marking the bloodiest day in American history. The battlesite is preserved at **Antietam National Battlefield** (www.nps.org/anti) in the corn-and-hill country of north-central Maryland. Even geographic nomenclature became violent; the Sunken Road turned into "Bloody Lane" after bodies were stacked there. In the park's cemetery, many of the Union gravestones bear the names of immigrants who died in a country they had only recently adopted.

You don't have to sleep here if you want to power through the tour, but Fredericksburg is defintely worth a linger, and the ❺ **Richard Johnston Inn**, with its colonially cozy ambience and old-stone air, is an excellent place to rest thy head. Should you just need a caffeine jolt and a bit of soft-folk-music-accented culture, ❻ **Griffin Bookshop and Coffee Bar** awaits with some mocha-latte infused rocket fuel.

Still, all of this yuppie joy can't hide what put this town on the map: one of the worst blunders in American military history. In 1862, when the Northern Army attempted a massed charge across open terrain at local entrenched Confederate position, a Southern artilleryman looked at the field and uphill slope the Union forces had to cross and told a commanding officer, "A chicken could not live on that field when we open on it." Sixteen charges resulted in an estimated 6000 to 8000 Union casualties.

7 **Fredericksburg & Spotsylvania National Military Park** is not as immediately compelling as Manassas because of the thick forest that still covers these battlefields, but the woods themselves are a sylvan wonder. Again, the pretty nature of…well, nature, grows over graves; the nearby Battle of the Wilderness was named for these thick woods, which caught fire and killed hundreds of wounded soldiers after the shooting was finished.

In nearby Chancellorsville, Robert E Lee pulled off his greatest victory when, outnumbered two to one, he *split* his forces and attacked both flanks of the Union army. The audacity of the move caused the Northern force to crumble and flee across the Potomac yet again, but the victory was a costly one; in the course of the fighting, Stonewall Jackson had his arm shot off by a nervous Confederate sentry (the arm, by the way, is buried near the Fredericksburg National Park visitor center; ask a ranger for directions).

The wound was patched, but Jackson went on to contract a fatal dose of pneumonia. He was taken to what is now the next stop on this tour: the **8** **Stonewall Jackson Shrine** in nearby Guinea Station. Here Stonewall lay surrounded by his family, in a small white cabin set against attractive Virginia horse-country, overrun with hanging sprays of purple flowers, daisy fields and trees tied up in the thick strands of gypsy moth nests. After a series of prolonged ramblings, Jackson fell silent, then looked up with a smile, whispered, "Let us cross over the river and rest in the shade of the trees," and died.

 The Battle of Gettysburg, fought in Gettysburg, PA, in July of 1863, marked the turning point of the war. **Gettysburg National Battlefield** (www.nps.gov/gett) does an excellent job of explaining the course of the combat. Look for Little Round Top, where a Union unit checked a Southern flanking maneuver, and the field of Pickett's Charge, where the Confederacy suffered its most crushing defeat up to July 1863. Abraham Lincoln gave his Gettysburg Address here to mark the victory and the "new birth of the nation" on said country's birthday: July 4.

From here it's not too far along I-95 to **9** **Richmond**, former capital of the Confederacy and modern multicultural tail end of the Northeast urban corridor. The South truly begins here, and the **10** **Virginia Historical Society**, an excellent repository of archival records and creative exhibits, explains just how this invisible line is drawn.

Richmond is a rainbow city, but reports continue of serious income disparities and a divided public memory, both with direct antecedents from the war. **11** **Monument Ave**, south of W Broad St, which runs through the city's most aristocratic neighborhood, mixes shaggy-bearded Confederate statuary with a sculpture of African American tennis-star Arthur Ashe, a nod to diversity in a state that wanted to combine celebrations for Martin Luther King Jr Day with a commemoration of Confederate generals. **12** **Hollywood Cemetery**, just west of Belvidere St, isn't as controversial as much as elegiac, a mood brought on by the graves of, among others, some 18,000 southern soldiers.

There are two Civil War museums in Richmond, and they make for an interesting study in contrasts. The ⑬ **Museum of the Confederacy (MOC)** was once a shrine to the Southern "Lost Cause," and still attracts a fair degree of neo-Confederates and their ilk. But the MOC has also graduated into a respected educational institution, and its collection of Confederate artifacts is probably the best in the country. The optional tour of the ⑭ **Confederate White House** is highly recommended for its quirky insights into one of the most fascinating chapters of American history (did you know the second-most powerful man in the Confederacy may have been a gay Jew?).

On the other hand, the ⑮ **American Civil War Center**, located in the old Tredegar ironworks (the main armament producer for the Confederacy), makes an admirable, ultimately successful, effort to present the war from three perspectives: Northern, Southern and African American. The exhibits are lovely and the effect is clearly powerful, reflected in the wall of sticky notes the museum leaves for visitors to jot impressions on.

Richmond has one of the most vibrant African American communities in America, and in a nod to that legacy, we dine in Jackson Ward on a "fish boat" at ⑯ **Croaker's Spot**, soul food's answer to fish and chips: a plate of fried whiting fillets smothered in hot sauce, onions and peppers, with cheese grits and cornbread on the side. For a more refined take on the theme, ⑰ **Julep's** is widely recognized as the cutting edge of Richmond's slew of refined takes on New Southern cuisine.

Out of many contenders, there are two excellent sleeping options in Virginia's capital: the ⑱ **Massad House Hotel**, a cozy, centrally located study in Tudor-style budget bliss, and one of the poshest palaces of Dixie patricians: the ⑲ **Jefferson Hotel**, a modern execution of the moonlight-and-magnolia cliché.

WHAT'S IN A NAME, PART 1?

Although the Civil War is the widely accepted label for the conflict covered in this trip, you'll still hear die-hard Southern boosters refer to the period as the "War Between the States." What's the difference? Well, a Civil War implies an armed insurrection against a ruling power that never lost its privilege to govern, whereas the name "War Between the States" suggests said states always had (and still have) a right to secession from the Republic.

WHAT'S IN A NAME, PART 2?

One of the more annoying naming conventions of the war goes thus: while the North preferred to name battles for defining geographic terms (Bull Run, Antietam), Southern officers named them for nearby towns (Manassas, Sharpsburg). Although most Americans refer to battles by their Northern names, in some areas folks simply know Manassas as the Battle Of, not as the strip town with a good Waffle House.

Petersburg, just south of Richmond, is the blue-collar sibling city to the Virginia capital, its center gutted by white flight following desegregation. ㉚ **Petersburg National Battlefield Park** marks the spot where Northern and Southern soldiers spent almost a quarter of the war in a protracted, trench-induced stand-off. The Battle of the Crater, made well-known in Charles Frazier's *Cold Mountain*, was an attempt by Union soldiers to break this stalemate by tunneling under the Confederate lines and blowing up their fortifications; the end result was Union soldiers caught in the hole wrought by their own sabotage, killed like fish in a barrel.

Drive south of Petersburg, then west through a skein of back roads to follow Lee's last retreat. It's best to do this drive near sunset, when the trees that line the road burn in brilliant flaming reds and purples; crickets call between the cool spaces in the grass; insects hop against the parachute seedlings of dead dandelions; and the flora and fauna bursts into white clouds, hovering just over the fields that stretch to the indigo-dark crests of the Shenandoah Mountains. This is classic rural America, and for a taste of its weirdness, plus a visit to one of the most hospitable eccentrics you're likely to meet, say hello to Jimmy Olgers and ㉑ **Olger's Store**, a sort of museum/temple/attic of all-things eccentric in Dinwiddie, VA.

DETOUR Located in one of the prettiest valleys of the Virginia Shenandoahs, **Lexington** deserves your time, especially if you're coming from Appomattox Courthouse. The town's two major universities both have ties to the war. The Virginia Military Institute sent an entire graduating class into combat for the Confederacy and houses the carcass of Stonewall Jackson's horse, Little Sorrel. Washington and Lee has the body of Robert E Lee and his horse, Traveler (who got the dignity of a burial).

About 85 miles west of here is ㉒ **Appomattox Court House National Park**, where the Confederacy (and Olgers' own forebear) finally surrendered. The park itself is wide and lovely, and the ranger staff are extremely helpful, but you may want to head back to Richmond for the night; the town of Appomattox is pretty plain.

There are several marker stones dedicated to the surrendering Confederates, and the most touching one marks the spot where Robert E Lee rode back from Appomattox after surrendering to Grant. His soldiers stood on either side of the field waiting for the return of their commander. When Lee road into sight he doffed his hat; the troops surged towards him, some saying goodbye while others, too overcome with emotion to speak, passed their hands over the white flanks of Lee's horse, Traveler. It's a spot that's dedicated to defeat, and humility, and reconciliation, and the imperfect realization of all those qualities is the character of the America you've been driving through.
Adam Karlin

TRIP INFORMATION

GETTING THERE
From Georgetown in Washington DC, take the Key Bridge across the Potomac to Rte 66 west to get to Manassas.

DO

American Civil War Center
The triple-viewpoint perspective at this institution makes it one of the country's best Civil War museums. ☎ 804-780-1865; www .tredegar.org; 490 Tredegar St, Richmond; adults/students/children 7-12 $8/6/2; ⏲ 9am-5pm; ♿

Appomattox Court House National Park
The site of the beginning of America's long, painful process of national reconciliation is gorgeously preserved in southside Virginia. ☎ 434-352-8987; www.nps.gov/apco; 5 Main St, off Hwy 24, Appomattox Court House; admission $4; ⏲ 8:30am-5pm Tue-Sun

Confederate White House
We highly recommend taking a guided tour of Jefferson Davis' old digs at the Museum of the Confederacy; there are quirky tales aplenty hidden in these walls. ☎ 804-649-1861; www.moc.org; 1201 E Clay St, Richmond; admission $3 plus MOC admission; ⏲ 10am-5pm Mon-Sat, from noon Sun

Fredericksburg & Spotsylvania National Military Park
This thickly wooded area is perfect for shady walks. The rangers are incredibly helpful and knowledgeable. ☎ 540-371-0802; www.nps .gov/frsp; 120 Chatham Lane, Fredericksburg; ⏲ 8.30am-6.30pm

Hollywood Cemetery
No matter what your feelings are on the many Confederate soldiers that are buried here, Hollywood Cemetery is supremely elegant and sad. ☎ 804-648-8501; 412 S Cherry St, Richmond; ⏲ 8am-5pm

Manassas National Battlefield Park
Perhaps the prettiest battlefield covered on this tour; simply one of the best preserved spaces on the East Coast. ☎ 706-361-1339; www.nps.gov/mana; 6511 Sudley Rd, Manassas; admission $3; ⏲ 8:30am-5pm

Museum of the Confederacy (MOC)
One of the best museums in the country for viewing actual uniforms, weapons and associated accoutrements from the war. ☎ 804-649-1861; www.moc.org; 1201 E Clay St, Richmond; admission $8; ⏲ 10am-5pm Mon-Sat, from noon Sun

Olger's Store
This old general store has been converted into an excellent museum of wacky local paraphernalia by true Southern gentleman and host, Jimmy Olgers. www.craterroad .com/olgersstore.html; Hwy 460, Dinwiddie; ⏲ whenever Jimmy says

Petersburg National Battlefield Park
Local rangers provide good insight into the ennui and horror of the first incident of trench warfare in military history. ☎ 804-458-9504; www.nps.gov/pete; 1001 Pecan Ave, Hopewell; ⏲ 9am-5pm

Stonewall Jackson Shrine
This small cabin is set against one of Virginia's prettiest backdrops of field and forest, and catches the light beautifully at sunset. ☎ 804-633-6076; 12019 Stonewall Jackson Rd, Woodford; ⏲ 9am-5pm

Virginia Historical Society
This rather excellent museum explains why Virginia lies at the center of everything. ☎ 804-358-4901; www.vahistorical.org; 428 North Blvd, Richmond; adult/child & on Sun $5/free; ⏲ 10am-5pm Mon-Sat, from 1pm Sun; ♿

EAT

Bistro Bethem
The New American menu, seasonal ingredients and down-to-earth but dedicated foodie vibe here all equal gastronomic bliss. ☎ 540-371-9999; 309 William St, Fredericksburg; mains $15-34; ⏲ lunch & dinner, closed Mon

Croaker's Spot
Richmond's most famous rendition of refined soul food is comforting, delicious and sits in your stomach like a brick pile.

☎ 804-421-0560; 119 E Leigh St, Richmond; mains $9-19; ◷ lunch & dinner

Julep's
Where classy, old-school Southern aristocrats like to meet and eat, balanced out by the fresh experimentation of an innovative kitchen. ☎ 804-377-3968; 1719 E Franklin St, Richmond; mains $15-30; ◷ dinner Mon-Sat

Olde Town Wine & Cheese Deli
Damn us as yuppies, but this shop's turkey Reubens are delicious. Oops, our Blackberries are beeping. ☎ 540-373-7877; 707 Caroline St, Fredericksburg; mains $4-7; ◷ lunch Mon-Sat

DRINK

Griffin Bookshop and Coffee Bar
While it's not technically a café, Griffin is great for sitting and sipping lattes in recumbent intellectual bliss. ☎ 540-899-8041; 723 Caroline St, Fredericksburg; ◷ 9am-9pm, 12-5pm Sun

SLEEP

Jefferson Hotel
They've maintained the almost imperial sense of tradition at this most famed of Richmond hotels. ☎ 804-788-8000; www .jeffersonhotel.com; 101 W Franklin St, Richmond; r $300-800

Massad House Hotel
Massad's great by any standard, but excellent rates and supreme location give it a special place in our hearts. ☎ 804-648-2893; www .massadhousehotel.com; 11 North 4th St, Richmond; r $75-110

Richard Johnston Inn
Well thank goodness: someone made a B&B that's pretty much as cute, friendly and historically evocative as surrounding Fredericksburg itself. ☎ 540-899-7606; www .therichardjohsntoninn.com; 711 Caroline St, Fredericksburg; r $98-210

USEFUL WEBSITES
www.civilwartrails.org
www.pbs.org/civilwar

LINK YOUR TRIP
www.lonelyplanet.com/trip-planner

Travels along the C&O Canal

WHY GO In its day, the Chesapeake and Ohio Canal was both an engineering marvel and commercial disaster; today, it's one of the nicest national parks in the mid-Atlantic. Bike or hike the former canal path from Washington DC to West Virginia and experience the lush scenery of the Potomac watershed.

Georgetown is hot in the summer.

Not in a cute, "Oh man, it's warm" kinda way. No, DC's version of the house on the hill is sweltering: humid and heavy. People don't move, but to cross from one air-con store to the next.

But in one corner of this 'hood folks are all about being active. Down on Thomas Jefferson St, enthusiastic college students in scratchy, 19th-century costumes mumble "dude" to each other before selling visitors tickets to a canal ride. Across the street from brand-name, consumerist America, mules are hitched to a wooden boat. And families, friends and couples are beating feet and mounting bicycles on one of the country's great rights-of-way.

This is the beginning of the C&O Canal and, specifically, the ❶ **Chesapeake & Ohio Canal National Historical Park**. This lovingly preserved stretch of waterfront pathway runs from here, on Washington DC's southwestern shores, 184.5 miles up the Potomac River to Cumberland, MD, over 74 elevation-changing locks and under the 3120ft Paw Paw Tunnel.

We'll start here, in Georgetown, where the canal path runs along a verdant, willow and broadleaf-shaded tunnel of dark green and smooth brick pathways. There's a convincing reconstruction of the first leg of

TIME
3 – 4 days

DISTANCE
185 miles

BEST TIME TO GO
**May – Jun,
Oct – Nov**

START
**Georgetown,
Washington
DC**

END
**Cumberland,
MD**

ALSO GOOD FOR

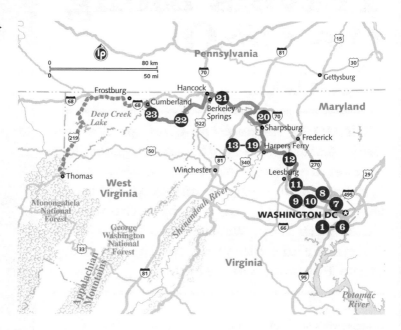

the canal path, staffed by the aforementioned costumed interpreters working out of the friendly ❷ **Georgetown Visitor Center**. From here you can pick up maps of the park and book onto a ❸ **Canal Boat Ride**, a favorite activity of the kids. The one-hour trips are a leisurely way of lazing into the rhythms of the waterway, and the accompanying tour and lectures are well worth the $5 price tag.

We should add here that no one is using the canal today for its original purpose. Originally plotted as a transportation line between the Eastern seaboard and the industrial heartland west of the Appalachian Mountains, the "Grand Old Ditch" was completed in 1850, but by this time it was like an Atari 2600 had arrived in a store full of PS2s. The Baltimore and Ohio Railway was already trucking cargo west of the Alleghenies; in a stroke of alphabetical justice, the B&O had supplanted the C&O.

A series of floods, coupled with the canal's own lack of profitability, equaled the death of the C&O in 1924, and for some 30 years plans for the land were thrown back and forth: should the canal towpath become a park or a parkway? US Supreme Court Justice William O Douglas firmly believed the latter, and hiked the full length of the path with 58 companions (only nine made it to the end) to prove his point. Public opinion was swayed, and the C&O was saved. Today, a similar conservation fight is being waged for ❹ **Georgetown Waterfront Park** (www.georgetownwaterfrontpark.org). When finished, this space will replace long stretches of riverside parking lots and urban scarification with an interactive fountain, river stairs, pathways and a labyrinth.

Thousands of people in the DC area, all the way to the western spur of the Maryland Appalachians, use the C&O towpath: as a recreation base, nature gateway or just a jogging path. You can set out at whatever pace you find most comfortable; we prefer to attempt the canal as a series of day trips.

In that vein, it's nice to get a good meal before attempting a 184.5-mile walk (or bike ride), and one of the best, most romantic places for a quiet dinner is on the Georgetown end: **5** **Ristorante Piccolo**, which fairly screams "candle-lit, romantic Italian evenings." Indulge in all of the above and get going already; if you're biking, you may want to stick to the 11-mile-long **6** **Capital Crescent Trail** for a while. It has nicely hard-packed concrete for riding and runs parallel to the canal for much of its length.

RIDING ON LOCK DOWN

There are 75 locks on the C&O, and every one of them helps regulates the height of the Potomac River, making each a little engineering stroke of genius. There's no lock 65, and locks 63 and 64 are fractional – not because anyone wanted to confuse future visitors, but because the water level at these spots can be raised or lowered incrementally. Each lock makes a pleasant picnic spot for those needing biking or hiking breaks.

If you stick to the sandy canal path, you'll soon be out of the pedestrian shopping promenades of Georgetown and amidst a quiet, tree-shaded 'scape of flat, algae-green canal water, berry bushes, thick woods and squawking, somewhat aggressive geese. If you're lucky, you may spot some deer, or a great blue heron haughtily surveying its domain.

About three miles up this way you'll run into **7** **Fletcher's Boat House**, a good spot for a picnic or, if you're looking to boat around, organizing gear rental. Be careful as you go, though; while the Potomac is undoubtedly a beautiful river for kayaking, pollution has clogged these waterways with rubbish, fridges, mysterious blue barrels and yes, the occasional body (but don't let that put you off).

You'll follow the curvy canal path for 15 miles to Cabin John, MD, and the **8** **Great Falls Tavern Visitor Center**, another spot from where you can book canal rides. From here you'd do well to explore **9** **Great Falls National Park**, with its miles of river-cliff rock climbing, forested trailways and impressive lookouts over Potomac gorges. One of our favorite paths in this area is the aptly named 4.7-mile **10** **Billy Goat Trail**, which takes you on a tight and enjoyable scramble over some rugged, boulder-strewn terrain. The trail begins near Great Falls Tavern Visitor Center.

Heading north, at Mile 35 you can cross into Virginia (if you're so inclined) on **11** **White's Ferry**, the last remaining ferry-crossing on the Potomac River. Roughly 20 miles north of here are a glut of sites that can break up any monotony you may be feeling (which you shouldn't be – we're not even halfway through!). Watch out, as you bike or hike, for the aqueducts which once dotted the entire towpath. It may not be Rome, but these systems were still engineering marvels for their time and are well worth a pause in the shade. The biggest one of all is the impressively elegant ⑫ **Monocacy Aqueduct**, a great work of 19th-century American civil engineering, located at Mile 42 of the canal trail.

At Mile 58, a trailhead links to the ⑬ **Appalachian Trail**; if you're thinking of attempting a portion of this challenging trail, this is a good spot to head out from. Why? Well, two miles north of here is ⑭ **Harpers Ferry**, West Virginia, the headquarters of the trail itself. But you don't have to approach this town as a hardcore trekking base. The Ferry is a fine place for dawdling of a historic nature; in point of fact that's pretty much what the town has been built for and marketed as for generations.

In its day, Harpers Ferry, sitting as it does in the West Virginia panhandle, was the gateway to the American West (which was, back then, what we consider today the eastern Midwest. Confused?). The trickle down impacts of this geographic importance turned the town into a center of industry, transportation, and, in sociohistorical terms, often uneasy but occasionally progressive race relations. Today you'd hardly know the Ferry was once one of the most important towns in the country, but it does make for a bucolic, calculatedly cute day trip.

If you'd like to pause here for a break from the towpath you'll want to first get a pass from the ⑮ **Harpers Ferry visitors center**, which opens the town's small public museums, located within walking distance of each other, for your perusal. All of these little gems are worth their own small stop; one deals with the area's importance to the development of modern firearms (rifling was essentially invented here), another's exhibits focus on the nature of the local landscape, and one is dedicated to the town's African American history. A particularly good way of killing time is by climbing up to the Harpers Ferry graveyard, a quiet, green place that is just above a hiking trail and has gorgeous views over the gorge.

> *"A particularly good way of killing time is by climbing up to the Harpers Ferry graveyard..."*

For those of you who appreciate kitsch (and if you don't, what's up, dude?), the ultimate, if overpriced, attraction to seek out in these parts is the ⑯ **John Brown Wax Museum**. A somewhat imbalanced albeit brave zealot, Brown led an ill-conceived slave rebellion here that helped spark the Civil War. The museum dedicated to his life and the event is sort of laughably old-school, and well worth a visit for all that; nothing says historical accuracy like scratchy vocals, jerky animatronics and a light-and-sound show that sounds like it was recorded some time around the late Cretaceous.

If you're getting tired of trail food, it might be in your interest to head up the road to nearby Bolivar and dine on high-end mountain cuisine of the fresh field-and-stream variety, done up in mouth-watering ways at ⑰ **Anvil**. And if you need a place to sleep off miles of bike-riding soreness and wash away towpath mud and dust, consider staying here – it's a great spot for a luxurious crash.

⑱ **Hilltop House Hotel** is the most famous lodging in Harpers Ferry, and justifiably so. Fashioned from the mountain stone that is towering all around you, the hotel is comfortably traditional, in keeping with the town's spirit, but modern enough when it comes to amenities. The real attraction here is the view; the Hilltop lives up to its name, and provides stunning vistas around the ridge and rivers of this corner of the Appalachians.

Smaller, cozier, and a bit more contemporary, ⑲ **Town's Inn** is centrally located and friendly. If the Hilltop feels as if it were carved from the stone, the Inn feels as if it was carved into it. It's a better base for exploring Harpers Ferry the town, although it lacks the Hilltop's signature views and storied history.

WILLIAM O DOUGLAS: C&O HERO

William O Douglas, defender of the C&O Canal, goes down as a favorite supreme court justice. The longest-serving justice in history was an environmentalist who argued rivers could be party to litigation, was the lone dissenter on over half of his 300 dissenting opinions, wrote the most speeches and books as a justice, and had the most marriages (four) and divorces (three – his last marriage, to a 23-year-old law student, lasted till his death) on the bench.

When you're ready to get back on the towpath, you're looking at over 100 miles more hiking and biking trail to cover. Still, the nice thing about the towpath is that it is, essentially, flat; with the exception of the canal locks and their shifts in elevation you're going along at a level plain, even if you're surrounded by some of the Eastern seaboard's most rugged terrain. And to be fair, while it may not be the Rockies (indeed, a lot of the Appalachians seem more pleasant than imposing), these hills can be a royal pain to walk over and around – another reason the canal towpath is so popular.

Thirteen miles north of Harpers Ferry is Sharpsburg, MD, site of the 1862 Battle of Antietam and the single bloodiest day in American history. ⑳ **Antietam National Battlefield** preserves a beautiful stretch of Maryland countryside, although it can be hard getting your head around the fact that all these waving fields of corn, whispering tree-lines and sunken roads – including "the" Sunken Road, where the bodies of dead soldiers became a terrible new element of the landscape – mark the site of a battle that claimed 23,000 casualties.

As the towpath snakes north you start escaping the historical tracks of the 19th century and come close to the contours of the 18th. At Mile 124 in Hancock, MD, you can make a side trip over the Rte 522 bridge to Berkeley Springs, WV, America's original resort town. How original? When George Washington needed a spa, he lit out for the Springs and their…well, springs.

Although this town is still best known for its spas (and there's plenty of high-end pampering goodness to be had), one of the more enjoyable activities here is strolling around and soaking up the odd New-Age-crystal-therapy-meets-the-Hatfields-and-the-McCoys vibe. If you do need a pamper, ignore the gym-room ambience and immerse yourself in the relaxation that is Berkeley Springs State Park's **㉑ Roman Bath House** and its enchanting, spring-fed pools.

DETOUR

The town of Thomas, WV, isn't more than a blip on the…where'd it go? Oh, there it is. The big business of note for travelers here is **The Purple Fiddle** (www.purplefiddle.com), one of those great mountain stores where bluegrass culture and artsy day-trippers from the urban South and Northeast mash up into a stomping good time. Thomas is about 80 miles past Cumberland, so it's a bit of a jog to get here, but its well worth the effort.

Back on the canal, if you've stuck it out to Mile 151, you'll be rewarded with one of the most impressive engineering accomplishments of a towpath that is, in and of itself, a pretty impressive engineering accomplishment. **㉒ Paw Paw Tunnel**, in Paw Paw, WV, runs directly into the mountains and out of them again; the edifice speaks to both the will of the canal's builders and the somewhat quixotic nature of their enterprise, as all of this (literal) moving of mountains did nothing to save their investment. Oh well – still makes a nice walk.

If you've pushed all the way to Mile 184.5 and **㉓ Cumberland**, MD, we tip our hats to you, as does, we're sure, old William O Douglas. You've managed to trace one of the great innovations in American engineering, the route of much of the nation's westward trade and history, and, you know, almost 200 miles of hiking and biking trail. Have a well-deserved beer, and have someone pick you up so you don't have to do the whole damn thing back the other way.
Adam Karlin

TRIP INFORMATION

GETTING THERE
Thomas Jefferson Rd is between 30th and 31st St NW in Georgetown; Cumberland is on Rte 68 in Western Maryland.

DO
Antietam National Battlefield
This battlefield overlooks a gorgeously appointed stretch of Maryland farmland and hill country. ☎ 301-432-5124; www.nps.gov /anti; 5831 Dunker Church Rd, Sharpsburg, MD; ☼ 8:30am-around 6pm

Appalachian Trail Conservancy
The ATC headquarters, dedicated to maintaining the trail, are located here along with a visitors center. ☎ 304-535-6331; www .appalachiantrail.org; Washington St & Storer College Pl, Harpers Ferry, WV; ☼ 9am-5pm, to 4pm Sat & Sun

Canal Boat Ride
What better way to spend the day than a relaxing, mule-fueled chug up the canal. www.nps.gov/choh; from Georgetown & Great Falls Visitor Center; rides $5; ☼ 11am, 1:30pm & 3pm; ♿

Capital Crescent Trail
One of the capital's best biking trails runs from Georgetown to Silver Spring, MD, often paralleling the C&O. ☎ 202-234-4874; www .cctrail.org; access near Water St, Georgetown; ☼ daylight hours

Chesapeake & Ohio Canal National Historical Park
The administrative body of the 184.5-mile path that runs from Washington DC to the Western Maryland panhandle. www.nps .gov/choh; ☼ daylight hours; ♿

Fletcher's Boat House
The best (well, only) place on the trail within walking distance of Georgetown to rent boats and bikes. ☎ 202-244-0461; www.fletchers boathouse.com; 4940 Canal Rd NW, Washington DC; per hr canoe/kayak/bike $11/8/6

Georgetown Visitor Center
Most people start the C&O towpath trail from this quaint historically preserved slice of the Georgetown waterfront. Say hi to the mules.

☎ 202-653-5190; 1057 Thomas Jefferson Rd, Georgetown

Great Falls National Park
Probably the most rugged landscape to be found within DC day-tripping distance are these river-carved gorges. ☎ 705-285-2965; www.nps.gov/grfa; 9200 Old Dominion Dr, McLean, VA; admission $3; ☼ 7am-dark

Great Falls Tavern Visitor Center
Located in a wealthy DC suburb, this center is a natural launching-point for exploring Great Falls National Park. ☎ 301-767-3714; 11710 MacArthur Blvd, Potomac, MD

Harpers Ferry visitors center
This visitors center sells tickets for the small museums scattered throughout Harpers Ferry. ☎ 304-535-6298; Filmore St, off US Rte 340; tickets $5; ☼ 8am-5pm

John Brown Wax Museum
One of the last, great, ridiculous animatronics wax museums in America. Long may it and its kitschy corniness reign. ☎ 304-535-6342; http://johnbrownwaxmuseum.com; 168 High St, Harpers Ferry, WV; adult/child 6-12/under 6 $7/5/free; ☼ 9am-5pm mid-Mar to mid-Dec

Roman Bath House
These naturally heated mineral-water springs make for a pretty perfect muscle-relaxant after spending a long day of trail beating. ☎ 304-258-2711; Berkeley Springs State Park, 2 S Washington St, Berkeley Springs, WV; baths & treatments $10-80; ☼ 10am-5pm

White's Ferry
If the coast guard hasn't shut these guys down by the time you arrive, have a ride on the last trans-Potomac ferry. ☎ 301-349-5200; White's Ferry Rd (Rte 107); one-way/roundtrip $4/6; ☼ 5am-11pm

EAT
Anvil
If crab, country ham and a rurally pleasant dining setting doesn't get you to the door, what will? ☎ 304-535-2582; 1290 W Washington St, Bolivar, WV; mains $13-25; ☼ lunch & dinner Wed-Sun

Ristorante Piccolo
This bouncy, bright Italian joint is popular with both the Georgetown upper crust and romance-seeking students. ☎ 202-342-7414; 1068 31st St NW, Georgetown; mains $13-23; ☽ lunch & dinner Mon-Sat

SLEEP
Hilltop House Hotel
Closed for renovation at press time, the Hilltop is one of the most beautiful and storied grand old hotels of the Appalachians. ☎ 703-771-6301; www.hilltophousehotel

.com; 400 E Ridge St, Harpers Ferry, WV; call for current rates

Town's Inn
This lovely B&B consists of two pre–Civil War residences (Heritage and Mountain house) smack dab in the heart of historic Harpers Ferry. ☎ 877-489-2447; www.thetownsinn .com; 179 High St, Harpers Ferry, WV; r $30-140

USEFUL WEBSITES
www.bikewashington.org/canal
www.candocanal.org

LINK YOUR TRIP
www.lonelyplanet.com/trip-planner

Universities & Colleges

WHY GO The hallowed halls of higher ed are among America's most famous institutions. Journey from Williamsburg to New York to peer behind the ivy-covered walls at some of the East Coast's big guns, and imagine life as a student or professor. You might just enroll all over again.

TIME
4 – 5 days

DISTANCE
380 miles

BEST TIME TO GO
Year-round

START
Williamsburg, VA

END
New York

ALSO GOOD FOR

HISTORY & CULTURE

The history of colleges in this country goes back a long way, since well before the colonies became the United States. Let's start as close to the very beginning as possible at the ❶ **College of William & Mary**, in Williamsburg. Only Harvard has seniority over this classic Virginia college which was founded in 1693 with a grant from King William III and his wife, Queen Mary II.

Visitors will be primarily interested in the ❷ **William & Mary Historic Campus**. The Sir Christopher Wren Building is the oldest school building in continuous use in the US. It was completed in 1699 and was restored, along with the other historic buildings on campus, by John D Rockefeller, Jr when he was also busy buying up and preserving Colonial Williamsburg. The Wren Building's graceful design, with large brick archways, will fascinate. Originally, the entire college was contained within this building. Thomas Jefferson was in residence when he matriculated through William & Mary in 1760. Sit down on the lawn and imagine yourself as a young scholar in a tricorner hat drinking ale. Afterwards, head to the romantic ❸ **Crim Dell** and its ornate wooden bridge spanning this pond on the heavily forested campus.

Williamsburg has a variety of eating and sleeping options, many of which are located in and around Merchants Square. Here you can shop for little trinkets, visit the large Barnes & Noble, or pick up some seersucker shorts. If you're planning to spend the night in Williamsburg, you should make reservations at the ❹ **Fife and Drum Inn**, a B&B

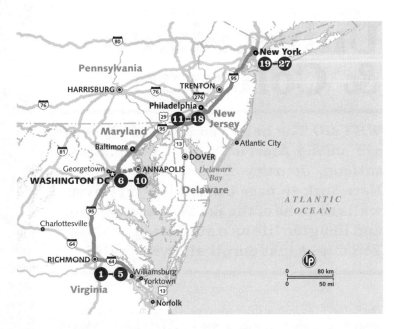

right in the square. From there you'll be able to hear real fifes and drums as the regiments march through nearby historic Williamsburg. You might choose the William and Mary room, which looks out onto the college's Sorority Court. This sunny room has a four-poster bed, a hand-painted floor, and is decorated with a picture of the Wren Building.

Want to mix it up with the kids? Head to nearby Yorktown and stop in at the **Yorktown Pub** (☎ 757-886-9964) on Water St. It's popular with students and locals for its inexpensive, tasty food and the relaxed, friendly atmosphere. Hop onto a stool by the front windows and enjoy the view of Yorktown Beach (site of a decisive victory against the British in 1781 that led to the end of the Revolutionary War). Try the St George Golden Ale on tap.

To dine, just step out into the Square and you'll find many remarkably good options. The **5** **Blue Talon Bistro** is an appealing choice. Inside the quaint brick building you'll find a menu with hearty French fare like chicken and mushroom crepes, or salad nicoise. Order the butcher's tasting-board to start, with the chef's selection of cured meats, sausages and pâtés. Sip a nice Bordeaux while, through the large paned windows, you watch kids in rented period costumes trailing behind their parents and fiddling with wooden guns or paper fans.

Continuing up the coast, it's time to get all Northeast corridor about things and head to Washington DC. Specifically, head to **6** **Georgetown University**. For all intents and purposes, Georgetown is part of DC, but it maintains a unique identity. Besides the University, the area is known for its high-end shops, cafés, as well as for being chronically difficult to park in. Georgetown is an urban campus in many ways, and is divided into three main sections. Hulking **7** **Healy Hall**, a Flemish Romanesque building is an imposing, but beautiful, National Historic Landmark. Inside you can visit the cast-iron Riggs Library or the grand Gaston Hall auditorium. The Healy clock tower stands grimly over the area like a disapproving headmaster.

One of the snazziest places to sit down for a meal is the **8** **Café Milano**. This beautiful restaurant has an impressive roster of guests, as even Pope Benedict XVI has been in to sample their homemade pasta. Don't be surprised to see politicos chomping ravioli and gulping wine while they work out some trade

DETOUR Don't miss a trip to Annapolis for a look at the **United States Naval Academy** (www.navy online.com). The highlight of any trip to "the Yard" is watching the plebes march in lockstep around Bancroft Hall. Security is tight though so you'll need a photo ID to get on campus. Book a tour through the Armel-Leftwich Visitor Center (☎ 410-293-8687).

deal with lobbyists. The ceilings are covered in murals and the restaurant's mood is fairly casual considering its spectacular food. As a bonus, the restaurant is just down the street from the famous **9** **"Exorcist" Steps**, where Father Karras tumbles to his death after being tossed out the window by the possessed Regan. The character of Father Karras is a priest at Georgetown University.

Unfortunately, Georgetown doesn't have a ton of great options for spending the night; best to head to the Northwest (NW) section of DC proper and check into the **10** **Hotel Palomar**. This boutique hotel has a trendy restaurant, big spacious rooms with gorgeous bathrooms, and decor with a sort of urban jungle flair – lots of zebra-skin throws and snakeskin-esque carpeting. It's also within walking distance of DuPont Circle and lots of bars.

Moving on north up the corridor, you'll pass through Maryland, Delaware and New Jersey on the way to our next stop. The **11** **University of Pennsylvania**, or UPenn, was founded by Benjamin Franklin. Ever a student himself, in 1749 he decided young men needed an academy of higher learning and, in 1755, Franklin's school became the College of Philadelphia, the first secular university in British North America. Then in 1779, after the American Revolution, the school was renamed and reborn as the University of the State of Pennsylvania.

The campus is as Ivy League gorgeous its genesis suggests. The expansive **12** **Perelman Quad** is studded with modern art (like the classic 1960s "Love" logo) and anchored by several architectural jewels. The monumental **13** **College Hall**, made of green stone and with a gray-slate roof, became forever famous when cartoonist Charles Addams used it as the model for the Addams Family mansion. In turn, the college honored Addams (who studied at UPenn) by naming the **14** **Fine Arts Building** after him and placing a silhouette of Addams' kooky, creepy family out front. By all means, enter the Fine Arts Building, whose interior lead-glass aphorisms and ornate balconies are stunning.

UPenn's **15** **Museum of Archaeology and Anthropology** deserves several hours; the rambling 115-year-old structure is as dramatic as the antiquities it contains. In particular, the ancient China and Egyptian collections – including enormous grinning dragons and numerous dehydrated mummies in various stages of undress – are memorably awesome. Off campus, jump to the other end of the human timeline with a visit to the dazzling **16** **Institute of Contemporary Art**, which has an urbanely, artfully futuristic vision.

ASK A LOCAL

"Penn really is beautiful; I especially love walking along Locust Walk. I never get the feeling there are significant town/gown tensions. It has everything you would expect of a major research university – excellent library (the rare-books collection is outstanding), great speakers, performing arts venues. And then there are gems like the Shakespeare Garden outside the Fine Arts Library. For travelers, it's a must-see!"
Jen Dickman, Morristown, NJ

Sansom St is the prime restaurant corridor, and it's hard to go wrong with any of the eateries here. For more futurama, visit **17** **Pod**, which is a Steven Starr "theme" restaurant that conjures a neo-Tokyo *Blade Runner* vibe, with cellophane-red booths, molded white plastic chairs and tables, concrete floor and servers in gun-metal gray. Oh, and the sushi and Japanese meals are excellent, too. If you're staying the night in Philadelphia, try the adjacent, perfectly-situated **18** **Inn at Penn**, where the stylish wood furnishings evoke a Craftsman feel.

"…the ancient collections – including enormous grinning dragons and dehydrated mummies in various stages of undress – are memorably awesome."

A couple of hour's drive north, there's a place called New York and it has enough universities to rival Boston for the college-town crown. But the roost is ruled by two dueling divas, one from uptown and the other downtown: **19** **Columbia University** and **20** **New York University**. Only one of them is Ivy League (Columbia, if you didn't know) and that forever rains on NYU's parades. To its constant chagrin, no matter how many Olsen twins enroll, NYU will never have the same golden luster as fancy-schmancy Columbia. But both are pretty cool schools, all things considered.

Columbia is another of the colonial colleges (founded in 1754 as King's College) and counts both presidents Roosevelt among its alumni. The central campus, in Morningside Heights (Upper Manhattan, near Harlem), can be viewed by strolling **21** **Campus Walk**, a public path that cuts between Broadway and Amsterdam through the quad. From here you can admire the ornate beaux arts–style surrounds, designed by the legendary architecture firm McKim, Mead and White in the late 19th century. **㉒ Low Memorial Library**, with domed roof and span of columns, is the centerpiece.

Downtown in Greenwich Village, you can find the urban campus of New York University. It has no defined quad, but is centered on **㉓ Washington Square Park**, with its famous arch that you've seen in every rerun of *Friends*. Founded later than the other universities, in 1831, NYU is known for its art, business and law schools. NYU (masquerading as UNY) is also where Keri Russell as "Felicity" matriculated. Walk down West 4th St and admire the brick **㉔ NYU School of Law** where JFK Jr got his degree. Further east on 4th St is **㉕ Bobst Library**, a severe orangey-red brutalist cube of a building, designed by Phillip Johnson, which houses one of New York's largest libraries.

If you're near NYU, unpack your bag at the basic but comfortable **㉖ Washington Square Hotel**. From here you'll easily be able to go carous-ing up and down Bleecker St with the NYUers into the wee hours. And if the next morning's hangover isn't enough to convince you to hightail it home, then drop by the **㉗ NYU Office of Admissions** right down the street – surely they'd be happy to hand you an application. Got your transcripts ready?

David Ozanich

ASK A LOCAL

"Unlike a lot of places, **Souen** (☎ 212-627-7150; 28 East 13th St) is more than a crowded co-ed hangout. The food is macrobiotic, so it's all un-refined, unprocessed, and seasonal, but I swear it tastes great. The decor is subdued, the music quiet enough to carry on a conversation. Come for the kuzu stew and stay for the New York tofu cheesecake and homemade soy ice cream!"

Liz Ureneck, NYU, New York

TRIP INFORMATION

GETTING THERE
Williamsburg is 50 miles east of Richmond via the I-64.

DO

College of William & Mary
Tours leave from the Office of Undergraduate Admissions. ☎ 757-221-4423; www.wm .edu; 116 Jamestown Rd, Williamsburg; ⏰ tours 10am & 2:30pm daily

Columbia University
The visitors center is in Room 213 of Low Library. ☎ 212-854-4900; www.columbia .edu; 116th St & Broadway, New York; ⏰ tour 1pm daily

Georgetown University
Book an official campus tour through the office of admissions. ☎ 202-687-3600; www.georgetown.edu; 37th St at O St, NW, Washington DC; ⏰ tour hours vary

Institute of Contemporary Art
ICA honors icons like Ant Farm and R Crumb, while also presenting the artists of tomorrow. ☎ 215-898-5911; www.icaphila.org; 118 S 36th St, Philadelphia; admission free; ⏰ noon-8pm Wed-Fri, 11am-5pm Sat & Sun; ♿

Museum of Archaeology and Anthropology
Exhibits include the Americas, Southwest Native Americans, and Native Alaskans. ☎ 215-898-4000; www.museum.upenn.edu; 3260 South St, Philadelphia; adult/child $8/5; ⏰ 10am-4:30pm Tue-Sat, 1-5pm Sun; ♿

New York University
The ultimate urban campus. ☎ 212-998-7200; www.nyu.edu; 50 W 4th St, New York; ⏰ tour hours vary

University of Pennsylvania
No reservations necessary for the one-hour student-led campus tours. ☎ 215-898-7507; www.upenn.edu; Walnut St btwn 34th & 38th Sts, Philadelphia; ⏰ tours 2pm weekdays & noon on fall weekends; ♿

EAT

Blue Talon Bistro
Quaint French restaurant in Merchants Square, near William & Mary. ☎ 757-476-2583; www.bluetalonbistro.com; 420 Prince George St, Williamsburg; ⏰ 8am-9pm

Café Milano
Super-chic Italian restaurant where even the pope has dined. Holy Roller! ☎ 202-333-6183; 3251 Prospect St, Georgetown; mains $17-26; ⏰ 11:30am-11pm

Pod
All we'll say is make sure to visit the restroom, and if you want a "pod," make reservations. ☎ 215-387-1803; www.pod restaurant.com; 3636 Sansom St, Philadelphia; mains $10-16; ⏰ 11:30am-11pm Mon-Thu, to midnight Fri, 5pm-midnight Sat, 5pm-10pm Sun; ♿

SLEEP

Fife and Drum Inn
Charming B&B in Merchants Square. ☎ 888-838-1713; www.fifeanddruminn.com; 441 Prince George St, Williamsburg; r $125-250

Hotel Palomar
Boutique hotel near fancy Embassy Row. ☎ 202-448-1800; www.hotelpalomar-dc .com; 2121 P St NW, Washington DC; r $150-500

Inn at Penn
Families should ask about "Bounce Back" packages, which include breakfast. ☎ 215-222-0200; www.theinnatpenn.com; 3600 Sansom St, Philadelphia; r $249-289; ♿

Washington Square Hotel
Cute little hotel just off of Washington Square. ☎ 212-777-9515; www.wshotel .com; 103 Waverly Pl, New York; r $200-450

LINK YOUR TRIP
www.lonelyplanet.com/trip-planner

Upscale Appalachian Trail

WHY GO Who doesn't love a good nature hike? But too often such outings are bogged down with tents, backpacks and dehydrated foodstuffs. You can spend your days getting earthy on this stunningly beautiful trail, but that's no reason you can't indulge in luxury hotels, exquisite dining and high culture.

TIME
5 days

DISTANCE
250 miles

BEST TIME TO GO
May – Oct

START
Harpers Ferry, WV

END
Pembroke, VA

ALSO GOOD FOR

Arguably the most famous trail in America, the Appalachian Trail runs for 2175 miles of sun-dappled national forests, through quaint trailtowns, and atop many a majestic mountain range between Springer Mountain in Georgia and Mt Katahdin in Maine. Those who tackle the entire journey are known as "thru-hikers." The unofficial speed record was set in 2005 at a mere 47.5 days. The average time to complete is five to seven months. That's a rather large commitment, so this trip focuses on parts of the 550 miles of trail that wind through West Virginia and Virginia.

Start your journey at the "psychological midpoint" of the trail: ❶ **Harpers Ferry**, West Virginia. Harpers Ferry, a postcard-perfect little town nestled between the Shenandoah and Potomac Rivers, is also home to some of the most beautiful scenery along the trail. Conveniently, this is also the headquarters for the ❷ **Appalachian Trail Conservancy**. Their visitors center is located in the heart of town on Washington St and is a great place to ask for advice about how best to tackle the trail.

West Virginia is home to a scant four miles of the trail (which is marked with white blazes along the path). However, the scenery is so awe-inspiring that it would be a shame to miss it. Your hike will be framed by the wild rushing rapids of the Potomac River below, and the craggy, tree-covered mountain peaks above. If you're hiking from Maryland you'll cross the Potomac River on a footbridge and then the

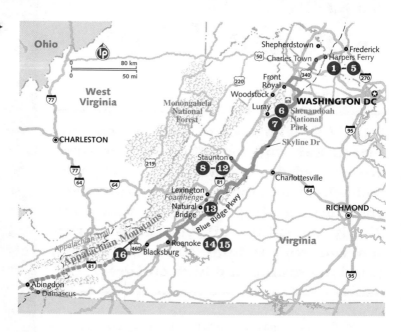

Shenandoah River to pass into Virginia. While in West Virginia proper, stop at the famed **③ Jefferson Rock**, an ideal place for a picnic.

A great accommodations option in Harpers Ferry is the gorgeous brick mansion **④ Jackson Rose Bed and Breakfast,** built in 1795 and listed on the National Register of Historic Places. It also served briefly as Stonewall Jackson's headquarters during the Civil War. The rooms are the most luxurious in town and come decorated with antique furniture and four-poster beds. The Jackson Rose's gardens are quite pleasant and offer an ideal place to relax while reading up on a bit of Harpers Ferry history. Learn about John Brown's antislavery antics or Jackson's military campaigns. A fine place for any gentleman soldier to grab a bite is the **⑤ Secret Six Tavern,** down the hill from the Jackson Rose, open seven days a week for lunch and dinner and it offers entertainment.

Head south from Harpers Ferry towards Front Royal, Virginia (keep your eyes peeled for Dinosaur Land, an educational prehistoric forest, along the way). The highlight of Virginia's Appalachian Trail and, frankly, a highlight of Virginia, is Skyline Drive, which zigzags atop the Blue Ridge Mountains for about 100 miles. The Appalachian Trail parallels this road and crisscrosses it 32 times in **⑥ Shenandoah National Park**. The scenery in this area seems fit for a Hollywood movie like *Legend* – one wouldn't be surprised to find fairies flitting about between the rhododendron and azaleas growing all along the trail. At the many gaps, you'll find spectacular views of Virginia's valleys and plains below. Several information and ranger stations dot Skyline Drive so it's easy to find hiking advice for any skill level.

An ideal location to stay the night on the Drive is ❼ **Skyland**, which sits on the highest peak of the Shenandoah NP. Skyland was founded as an upscale resort in 1888, but the current form was built in the 1920s and it still retains some of those design elements, if showing a little wear and tear. The rooms are comfortable and large, but the decor is a bit dated. An important request to make is for a "room with a view" of the Shenandoah Valley below, so you can sit and gaze at the lights of little towns and farms in the distance. All

things considered, Skyland just can't be beat for easy access to the Appalachian Trail. The concierge and rangers here can point you in the right direction for the trail or its tributaries (sometimes marked with blue blazes), and staff will even pack boxed lunches for those planning a hike. Have your breakfast, lunch or dinner in the great big sleek dining room with spectacular views of the Shenandoah Valley. Drinkers will be happy to know they have a taproom featuring nightly en-

 DETOUR

In nearby Charles Town, WV, you can play the slots or bet on the races at the **Charles Town Races**. It's home to the West Virginia Breeders' Classic, but they run races Wednesday through Sunday. Ladies should bring an oversized hat and men should smoke their fat cigars in the grandstand or the Skyline Terrace while watching the ponies dash round and round the big track. Charles Town is 8 miles west of Harpers Ferry via the US Rte 340.

tertainment and a bar menu available all day. Try the Prohibition Punch, which is sweet and fruity and sure to refresh your tired soul.

At the southern terminus of Skyline Drive is the wonderfully revitalized town of ❽ **Staunton**. Its beautifully restored and maintained downtown has plenty of boutiques and restaurants. A highlight is Gothic Revival ❾ **Trinity Church**, with its 12 Tiffany Studios stained-glass windows. Check into the newly renovated ❿ **Stonewall Jackson Hotel**. Oh, Stonewall Jackson – you just can't ditch his shadow in this area of the world. Originally built in 1924, the hotel retains its gorgeous Colonial Revival–style exterior, but the rooms are brand-spanking new. Go up the marble staircase to the mezzanine and admire the one-of-a-kind 1924 Wurlitzer organ. You can also sample delicious foie gras with a glass of wine in the sophisticated 24 Market restaurant.

All the sightseeing is sure to work up an appetite and Staunton offers a surprising amount of high-end, contemporary dining options. The most exciting and urban is the ⓫ **Staunton Grocery**. The sleek decor offers a lovely counterpoint to the vagaries of the Appalachian Trail. Sample the Southern fried quail or perhaps the crispy pork belly to start. Dinner entrées include sea scallops wrapped in a house-cured pancetta or the house-made gnocchi with morels, ramps, and aged sheeps-milk cheese.

After dinner, get tickets for some Shakespeare at the marvelously out-of-place ⑫ **Blackfriars Playhouse**, a gem not to be missed by any theater lover. The specialty here is Elizabethan and Jacobean drama, sprinkled with a few more modern plays, like Tom Stoppard's *Rosencrantz & Guildenstern Are Dead*. The theater is a painstakingly authentic re-creation of the original London Blackfriars Playhouse. Shows are presented as they were in Shakespeare's day, with the lights from chandeliers kept on, and traditional seating on benches, Lord's chairs, or gallants' stools directly onstage. Since the theater is right next door to the Stonewall Jackson Hotel, you can be in your robe and slippers before the actors are done wiping the greasepaint off their faces.

"...you can be in your robe and slippers before the actors are done wiping the greasepaint off their faces."

The next day head down the Blue Ridge Parkway from Staunton to nearby Roanoke. This portion of the BRP has gentle, rolling hills and not too many overly sharp curves. A good resource for hikers in this area is the Roanoke Appalachian Trail Club and a fine place to pick up your hike is ⑬ **Blackhorse Gap**, where the trail crosses the Blue Ridge Parkway. Oak and hickory trees rise up in Jefferson National Forest to create great green walls of foliage on either side of the road. Dogwood blossoms and tulip trees add splashes of color in the spring and summer while the trees themselves provide the technicolor aesthetic to autumn drives.

After a long day on the trail, you can check into the Tudor-style ⑭ **Hotel Roanoke**. This grand dame has presided over this city at the base of the Blue Ridge Mountains for the better part of a century and provides a welcome respite – with all the modern amenities a business traveler (or a hiker) would need. Downstairs is the Pine Room for those desiring a stiff drink, and a formal restaurant, the Regency Room.

Roanoke is the biggest city in this area of Virginia, so it might be more interesting to sneak out across the train tracks into their downtown market square. Here you'll find the very urban, yet easy-going, ⑮ **Table 50** restaurant with dark, red-and-black romantic decor and a pressed-tin ceiling. Try the tender duck confit for supper or one of the nightly specials like cod or lobster ravioli. For those seeking a night out

HIT THE CIRCUIT

If you're looking for a quick hike, head a few miles south of Skyland to Big Meadows and the **Dark Hollow Falls circuit trail**. It has a slightly different ecosystem than other areas of the trail, so you can see alpine grasses and plenty of deer grazing. It's a relatively short hike – only a couple of miles – and could be completed by even novice hikers in a couple of hours.

on the town, instead of a night out on the trail, seek out some of the various other restaurants and bars scattered about Roanoke.

If you're looking to have the time of your life, you'll find this final stop on the upscale trail perhaps the most fabulous, or at least the most kitschy. The ⑯ **Mountain Lake Hotel** is an old stalwart of Southwest Virginia just north of Blacksburg on Mountain Lake. It also doubled as the Catskills resort "Kellerman's" in a little old movie called *Dirty Dancing*. If you're tired of hiking, you might be interested in taking part in one of the theme weekends, where you can take dance lessons and finally learn to nail that impossible lift. Sadly, Jennifer Grey, Patrick Swayze and Jerry Orbach are not included. There are a variety of accommodations at the resort: some

 **Damascus** is the southernmost "trail town" in Virginia. It abuts Mt Rogers, the highest peak in the state. This little town has a couple of restaurants, and stores to rent equipment for your outdoor adventures. Surrounded by protected and beautiful forest, Damascus is one of the most popular places from which to stage hikes on the Appalachian Trail. The town is accessible via Hwy 58, off the I-81.

will prefer the massive, historic flagstone main building with traditional hotel rooms; others seeking the full *Dirty Dancing* experience might enjoy the rustic lakeside cabins (comfortably modern inside) where Baby and her family stayed. Appalachian Trail purists who just can't wait to hit the trail again, will find it just north of this 2600-acre resort. The Mountain Lake Hotel offers all sorts of other entertainments as well. Got a talent for the talent show? Nobody puts Baby in a corner!

If you've succeeded in meeting your new partner through a series of impromptu, yet still intricately choreographed dirty dances, you can return home. But if for some reason you didn't connect, you can always set off on the trail again and maybe find that mountain man or woman of your dreams. If they have their own rickety cabin, you're in luck – you'll never have to leave.

David Ozanich & Jeff Campbell

TRIP INFORMATION

GETTING THERE
From Washington DC take the I-270 north to US 340 west, which takes you to Harpers Ferry.

DO

Appalachian Trail Conservancy
The headquarters for the Appalachian Trail offers advice, maps and gear. ☎ 304-535-6331; www.appalachiantrail.org; 799 Washington St, Harpers Ferry; ⏰ 9am-5pm, to 4pm Sat & Sun

Blackfriars Playhouse
Don't miss this stunning reproduction of a 17th-century English theater, with performances of Shakespeare and the like. ☎ 540-851-1733; www.ascstaunton.com; 10 S Market St, Staunton; tickets $20-40; ⏰ showtimes vary; ♿

Trinity Church
A gorgeous Gothic Revival church with Tiffany windows. ☎ 540-886-9132; www.trinity staunton.org; 214 W Beverley St, Staunton

EAT

Secret Six Tavern
Tavern food in a historic atmosphere. ☎ 304-535-1159; 186 High St, Harpers Ferry; mains $7-18; ⏰ 11am-9pm

Staunton Grocery
Sleek, modern restaurant with the best food in Staunton. ☎ 540-886-6880; www .stauntongrocery.com; 105 W Beverley St, Staunton; mains $24-29; ⏰ 5:30-10pm Tue-Sat, 5-8:30pm Sun

Table 50
Sultry bistro in downtown Roanoke. ☎ 540-904-2350; 309 Market St, Roanoke;

mains $15-28; ⏰ lunch & dinner Tue-Sat

SLEEP

Hotel Roanoke
Large, full-service Tudor-style hotel in the heart of Roanoke. ☎ 540-985-5900; www .hotelroanoke.com; 110 Shenandoah Ave, Roanoke; r $150-300

Jackson Rose Bed and Breakfast
B&B on the National Register of Historic Places. ☎ 304-535-1528; www.thejackson rose.com; 1167 W Washington St, Harpers Ferry; r $110-200

Mountain Lake Hotel
Perfect that lift at this Virginia resort, home to the film *Dirty Dancing*. ☎ 540-626-7172; www.mountainlakehotel.com; 115 Hotel Circle, Pembroke; r $195-500

Skyland
Resort located high atop Shenandoah National Park off Skyline Drive. ☎ 800-999-4714; www.visitshenandoah.com; Mile 41 Skyline Drive; ; r $89-200

Stonewall Jackson Hotel
A newly restored and renovated Staunton classic. ☎ 540-885-4848; www.stonewall jacksonhotel.com; 24 S Market St, Staunton; r $139-300

USEFUL WEBSITES
www.patc.net
www.ratc.org

SUGGESTED READS
- *Walking the Appalachian Trail*, Larry Luxenberg
- *A Season on the Appalachian Trail*, Lynn Setzer

LINK YOUR TRIP
www.lonelyplanet.com/trip-planner

NEW YORK TRIPS

New York is most famous for its eponymous city, but beyond the borders of Manhattan are deep, sweeping mountain ravines and crags, swiftly moving rivers, and quaint villages slowly being turned into weekend arts and crafts retreats. Upstate New York is a living canvas of lush forests, crystal-clear lakes and stormy dark hills.

Generations of artists have immersed themselves in the solitude of the Catskills, the fragrant vineyards of the Finger Lakes, the soaring heights of the Adirondack Mountains and the roaring thunder of Niagara Falls, which flow into island-studded St Lawrence River.

Anchoring this abundance of natural delights is New York City: five boroughs of culture, art and commerce, all sharing space and competing for attention. The heroes of arts and media, sports and business are worshiped, while the up-and-coming generation plots its revolution in the shadow of Wall St and the Empire State Building.

It's unique, it's eclectic, it's New York.

PLAYLIST 🎵🎵 It's almost impossible to pick a playlist from the plethora of greats written about, in, or just inspired by, New York. Here is a mere taster of standouts.

- "Niagara Falls," Sara Evans
- "I Love New York," Steve Karmen
- "My Dirty Stream (The Hudson River Song)," Pete Seeger
- "Mountain Air," Dan Berggren
- "The 59th Street Bridge Song (Feelin' Groovy)," Simon & Garfunkel
- "New York State of Mind," Billy Joel
- "Walk on the Wild Side," Lou Reed
- "Desolation Row," Bob Dylan

NEW YORK'S BEST TRIPS

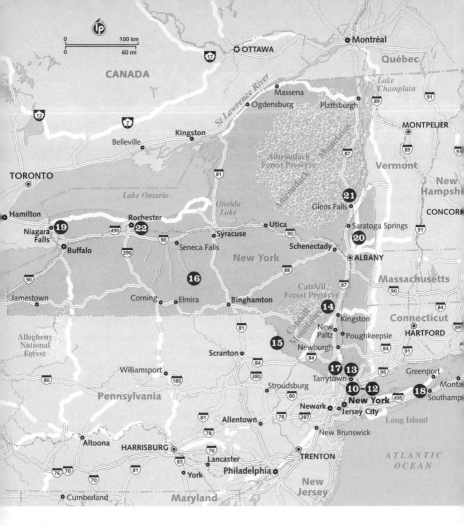

NEW YORK TRIPS

48 Hours in Manhattan

WHY GO Bold and brash New York is a city in flux, moving from one extreme to another in a few short blocks. In 48 hours get a feel for the unique pockets of the city, and do it like a local: on the run, riding the subways, immersed in Manhattan's electric diversity and energy.

Start your morning with a jolt in **❶ Lower Manhattan**, where thousands of hard-charging finance types come streaming into Wall St every day, determined to make their millions. Dozens of major subway and bus lines converge here, along with the Staten Island and New Jersey ferries. Harried businesspeople with swinging briefcases will bump you along as the moribund streets come alive. Take in the morning rush over a foamy cappuccino at **❷ Financier Patisserie**, a Parisian-style bakery hidden inside the historic triangle at Pearl and Mill Lane, near Hanover Sq.

This is the heart of Old New York, where George Washington once slept, ate and worshiped – and was sworn in as the nation's first president. The tiny byways below Wall St are crooked and cobbled, small pathways through a dizzying maze of soaring skyscrapers that eventually lead you to the main thoroughfare of Broadway.

North on Broadway you'll pass two more remnants of pre-Revolutionary New York, **❸ Trinity Church** and **❹ St Paul's Chapel**, where Washington had his family pew; ahead is the teeming chaos of Chinatown.

Merchants line busy **❺ Canal St**, pushing their fake Rolex watches and Louis Vuitton on jostling passersby. Follow the foot traffic east as Canal turns slightly uphill, turning north onto Elizabeth St. The din and excitement of Chinatown will gradually fade as you move

TIME
2 days

BEST TIME TO GO
Mar – Dec

START
Manhattan

END
Manhattan

ALSO GOOD FOR

HISTORY & CULTURE

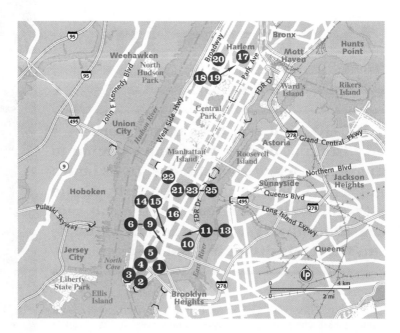

into artsy **6** **Nolita**, a tiny quadrant of streets north of Little Italy. Martin Scorsese grew up on these not-so-mean streets, serving as an altar boy at the ornate marble church on the corner of Prince and Mott Sts. Long before the massive Catholic church was built in midtown, this Irish-Italian structure – the original **7** **St Patrick's Cathedral** – was the seat of the Catholic diocese.

"It used to be the flophouse for bums and prostitutes but now it's home to the avant-garde…"

Following Prince St to the east brings you to the Bowery, one of New York's most infamous streets. It used to be the flophouse for bums and prostitutes – you'll see the signs of wear and tear in pockmarked graffiti buildings next to brand-new condos – but now it's home to the avant-garde **8** **New Museum of Contemporary Art**. Constructed out of seven white boxes stacked unevenly atop each other, the light-filled museum constantly rotates exhibits, bringing emerging artists and established names and mixing them together for a cutting-edge effect.

The main byway of Nolita, leafy, residential Elizabeth St, is a polyglot of languages and cultures, and has one ancient Italian butcher shop Robert De Niro fans will recognize right away. You'll get a taste of the diversity if you stop for lunch at **9** **Café Colonial**, a French-Brazilian fusion joint with a big, tropical mural on the outside wall and the classic Parisian tin-ceiling inside.

Across Houston St and heading east, you are walking the border between the funky Lower East Side on your right and the iconic East Village on your left. When you come across Ave C, head north, into what used to be called ⑩ **Alphabet City**. Comprising Aves A, B, C and D, these four streets entered pop culture lore as the backdrop to the Broadway smash, *Rent,* the story of young creative types struggling to make art (and the rent) in pre-gentrification New York. Formerly a drug ghetto full of tenement squats, there are new signs of life along these prettied-up avenues, like the bluesy bar ⑪ **Louis 649**, on the 1st floor of a restored townhouse, with hardwood floors, a resident pit bull and a louche, speakeasy feel. The ⑫ **6th & B community garden** is a green space that the city let founder in the 1990s, but which was reclaimed by local residents who turned it into the glowing, fragrant urban oasis it is now. It's fronted by a wrought-iron gate with a half-dozen handprints in it – signifying the "hands on" attitude of the garden keepers – and inside has fruit trees, flowering shrubs, small vegetable plots and a towering, 37ft sculpture of recycled "street treasures" found around the city.

Ave B also leads into ⑬ **Tompkins Square Park**, the center of '60s rebellion where Jimi Hendrix once gave an outdoor concert and birth-control advocate Margaret Sanger roiled crowds with fiery feminist rhetoric in the 1900s. Now the park's known more for its graceful weeping willows, park benches where neighborhood elders sit, and strong community vibe.

St Marks Pl W passes tattoo parlors and the few remaining punk-rock record stores to 4th St. South along Second Ave, to 2nd St, and one block east, take note of the name – you're on Joey Ramone Pl, named after the legendary rocker from The Ramones.

At the intersection of Bowery and Bleecker, you can stop for the night at the ⑭ **Bowery Hotel,** where red-tasseled gold keys unlock doors leading to Moroccan-inspired rooms with king-size beds, ornate gold fixtures, swirling ceiling fans and floor-to-ceiling windows. For a bite, slip into the rustic ⑮ **Gemma**, an Italian trattoria with rough-edged wooden tables and wicker baskets hanging from wide brown beams in the ceiling.

Wake up to a brisk walk uptown to ⑯ **Union Square**, a buzzing public meeting place marked by a statue of Gandhi on the southeast corner, and an open-air greenmarket most mornings. Then it's onto the subway and up to the historic neighborhood of Harlem for some shopping along 125th St. If you exit the subway at Lexington Ave and 125th St you can work your way west along the busy commercial street, flanked by big-name chain stores and street vendors selling incense, shea butter and perfumes imported from Africa.

South down Lenox Ave you'll pass the famous ⑰ **Lenox Lounge** on your left – James Baldwin, Malcolm X and Fidel Castro are just a few of the celebrated patrons who've tossed back a few while listening to jazz in the back room. Lenox Ave is a wide, breezy boulevard flanked by glorious brownstones and several churches, most of which have fallen on hard times. At the intersection of 116th, at the ⑱ **Malcolm Shabazz Market**, African merchants sell dashikis and wooden carvings. Across Lenox to the west is ⑲ **Amy Ruth's**, the reigning queen of soul food, and a top spot for lunch. Amy Ruth's most famous culinary contribution is fried chicken on waffles (with syrup); it goes perfectly with the small restaurant's Southern charm and checkerboard floors and tablecloths.

You can continue exploring Harlem by heading west to Amsterdam Ave, then south into Morningside Heights, a quiet neighborhood full of Spanish families and Columbia students. The tall Byzantine arches of the ⑳ **Cathedral of St John the Divine** rise above the squat apartment buildings, inviting you to step inside the Romanesque-style granite and limestone structure. It's a century old, but still not complete – blame those pesky spires, almost impossible to get up. Inside you'll find several rose-colored stained-glass windows and the little-visited Poets Corner, a section of wall dedicated to American writers including Robert Frost, Walt Whitman and Edna St Vincent Millay.

MOBY'S NYC

He's a musician, DJ, producer, activist, vegan – and New Yorker. Moby takes us on tour of his favorite hometown haunts.

Tompkins Square Park is a tiny, sun-drenched park that is a microcosm of New York's diversity. "You'll see punk rockers sleeping off their hangovers, hippies playing guitar, Russian immigrants playing chess, Puerto Rican guys on percussion, corporate lawyers pushing $800 strollers," says Moby of his favorite spot to hang out and listen to his iPod. Monday nights, **Arlene's Grocery**, a dive bar near Moby's Lower East Side home, showcases rock 'n' roll karaoke. "I'm a very provincial person," says Moby, who was drafted to play guitar in the karaoke band. "The appeal of a place is largely determined by its distance from my apartment." As such, Moby's rock side project The Little Deaths made its debut at Arlene's. When working on music at 3am, Moby often heads to the oldest part of **Chinatown** (Mott St, south of Canal St) and literally loses himself in his city. "Most of the city is built on a grid system, so this is one of the only places you can do that. All the signs are in Cantonese or Mandarin and the streets are narrow and winding…I'll listen to my headphones, walk around and just get totally lost."

Unpredictability is the secret weapon of the **Slipper Room**, a delectably gaudy East Village cabaret. "You never know what you're going to get there, it might be some terrible band or a bizarre, fantastic burlesque show," says Moby, who is routinely dragged on stage to perform. "Get a couple of drinks in me and I'm shameless."
Simona Rabinovitch

At 96th St you can hop back on the subway and skip down to **㉑ Little Korea**, conveniently next to **㉒ Macy's** department store, in case you had a hankering to ride its old, wooden escalators. Little Korea is centered on 32nd St between Fifth Ave and Broadway, and its noisy, frantic activity goes 24-7. While you walk the street, watching fast-moving chefs preparing the day's meals in open windows, stop at **㉓ Hun Gallery**, a light-filled 2nd-floor space that fills its 2000 sq ft with delicate water paintings, eclectic installations and all manner of modern art. Nearby is the small **㉔ Lee Young Hee Korea Museum**, displaying a collection of Korean clothing, with special emphasis on the brightly colored silks of the ceremonial *hanbok*.

There's no leaving Little Korea without indulging in the preferred local pastime: it's time to loosen up the pipes at **㉕ Grammy Karaoke**. On the floor above Wonjo, itself a crowded and popular 24-hour Korean BBQ spot, Grammy has private rooms for the vocally challenged and liquor readily available to get the party started. If you don't want to sing but like to watch, sit in the main room where the action is – in Korean, of course.

An all-night songfest is a fitting end to a whirlwind visit to the city that never sleeps – an old cliché that's certainly true in K-town.
Ginger Adams Otis

CITY

TRIP INFORMATION

GETTING THERE
Airports JFK, LaGuardia and Newark all feed into Manhattan, as does the subway.

DO

Cathedral of St John the Divine
Highlights include the Great Rose Window and the Great Organ. ☎ 212-316-7540; www.stjohndivine.org; Amsterdam Ave at 112th St; admission free; 🕑 7:30am-6pm

Hun Gallery
More than 2000 sq ft of light-filled space showcasing modern art and more. ☎ 212-594-1312; www.hungallery.org; 12 W 32nd St; admission free; 🕑 11am-6pm Tue-Sat

Lee Young Hee Korea Museum
Brightly colored ceremonial silk *hanboks* and other traditional garb are on display. ☎ 212-560-0722; www.lyhkm.org; 2 W 32nd St; admission free; 🕑 11am-6pm Mon-Sat

Macy's
An old-fashioned department store stocked with modern designs. ☎ 212-695-4400; www.macys.com; 151 W 34th St; 🕑 10am-9:30pm Mon-Sat, 11am-8pm Sun

New Museum of Contemporary Art
The city's sole museum dedicated to contemporary art. ☎ 212-219-1222; www.new museum.org; 235 Bowery St; admission $12; 🕑 noon-6pm Wed-Sun

St Paul's Chapel
George Washington worshiped here, as did hundreds after 9/11. ☎ 212-602-0800; www.saintpaulschapel.org; Broadway at Fulton St; 🕑 10am-6pm

EAT

Amy Ruth's
Classic soul food in central Harlem. ☎ 212-280-8779; 114 W 116th St; mains $12-18; 🕑 8am-9pm

Café Colonial
Green palms painted on the wall and big wooden tables make this café fresh and fun. ☎ 212-274-0044; www.cafecolonialny.com; 73 W Houston St; mains $10-28; 🕑 11am-10pm; ♿

Financier Patisserie
A bit of the West Bank on Wall St. ☎ 212-344-5600; www.financierpastries.com; 62 Stone St; mains $4-12; 🕑 7am-8pm Mon-Fri, 8:30am-6pm Sat; ♿

Gemma
A lovely trattoria with late-night hours, serving seafood, pasta and antipasto. ☎ 212-505-9100; www.theboweryhotel.com; 335 Bowery; mains $15; 🕑 11am-midnight

DRINK

Grammy Karaoke
Take the tiny elevator up to this Korean karaoke hideaway that never closes. ☎ 212-629-7171; 23 W 32nd St; 🕑 24hr

Lenox Lounge
The red facade with silver lettering is an iconic image in Harlem, and the back-room jazz worth the $15 cover. ☎ 212-427-0253; www.lenoxlounge.com; 288 Lenox Ave; 🕑 noon-3:30am

Louis 649
No cover to see the jazz, but the musicians expect tips at this couch-filled, cream-walled hangout. ☎ 212-673-1190; www.louis649.com; 649 E 9th St; 🕑 6pm-4am

SLEEP

Bowery Hotel
Done up like a sultan's modern palace, the Bowery attracts celebrity crowds. ☎ 212-505-9100; www.theboweryhotel.com; 335 Bowery; r $550

USEFUL WEBSITES
www.nyc.gov
www.nycvisit.com

www.lonelyplanet.com/trip-planner

LINK YOUR TRIP

Sidewalk Dining in NYC

WHY GO Walking New York's streets is the best way to see the city and work up an appetite. New York's vibrant street culture has given rise to a new kind of food that fits the city's hectic pace: fast food with flair and haute-cuisine flavor, eaten on the move.

There's no place like ❶ **Chinatown** to get a feel for the city's most interesting and exotic types of cooking. Swing by the colorful hole-in-the-wall ❷ **Lung Moon Bakery** for sweet almond cookies, fluffy cakes, doughy pork buns, sesame buns or some mango balls with your morning coffee. As the early morning hustle-and-bustle takes over, street markets start hawking their wares: fresh, flopping fish spill onto the sidewalk, live lobsters, oysters and urchins bump along their glass enclosures. Even the big plastic tubs in front of some stores hold edibles: in most cases, mute and terrified frogs, packed inside and no doubt wondering about their fate.

Along chaotic ❸ **Canal St**, fresh fruit and produce are the norm. You can pick up a refreshing coconut drink as you walk – just look for the vendors selling whole coconuts. They'll lop off the rough outside, bore a hole for you, hand you a straw, and you're off, slurping up the clear, sticky coconut sap.

At the intersection of Grand St and Bowery, keep an eye out for the noodle cart – ❹ **Huan Ji Rice Noodles**, to be precise. At the nearby Hester St playground you can sit and enjoy the salty goodness of steamed rice noodles topped with curried fish or pork belly, and doused liberally with secret sauce. Or walk a little further off the beaten path and track down ❺ **Xinjiang Kebabs**, usually on Forsyth St. These spicy, tangy, fire-grilled bits of meat are revved up with cumin, coriander and more exotic herbs. Xinjiang even manages to make chicken hearts, lamb kidneys and tongue taste good.

TIME
1 – 2 days

DISTANCE
1 – 2 miles

BEST TIME TO GO
Apr – Dec

START
Manhattan

END
Jackson Heights

ALSO GOOD FOR

CITY

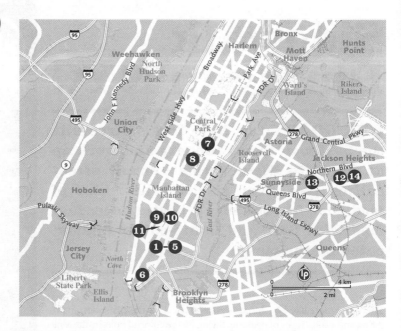

A brisk walk around the South St Seaport and Lower Manhattan area, full of shoppers, history buffs and Staten Islanders streaming off ferries, is a good way to work off your lunch, while building up an appetite for later. If you feel peckish, seek out any of the Jamaican carts selling roti off the commuter-heavy walkway along Water St.

Now that Wall St is as much for sightseeing and shopping as it is for business and high finance, you might consider spending the night at **6** **Gild Hall**, just down the street from the Stock Exchange. The champagne tastes of its regular clientele translate into sleek designer rooms, first-rate room service and a lobby bar/library that pours out free bubbly to all its guests.

AND THE VENDY GOES TO...

Hardworking New Yorkers like to recognize anyone who does their job exceptionally well, and that includes the thousands of nimble-fingered food cart vendors who populate the streets 24-7, selling delicious snacks, often specialties from the chef's native land. Every year the non-profit Street Vendors Project organizes a cookoff among top-nominated food carts. Check out the winners at www.streetvendor.org.

Uptown at Madison Ave and 62nd St is the home of **7** **Tony "the Dragon" Dragonas'** acclaimed food cart. It's Greek treats for everyone, as Tony ladles out his grilled chicken, kebabs, sausages and steaks, all marinated in a special blend of herbs and spices, or carefully puts together a prosciutto-mozzarella sandwich. Everything comes with a salad and hearty dose of tzatziki. Now you're all set for a Broadway show or to hit the nightclubs – and you didn't even need a pre-theater dinner reservation.

When that seductive Manhattan nightlife keeps you going into the wee hours, don't despair for food. It's a 24-7 city, after all. The line for ❽ **Halal Chicken and Gyro** on Sixth Ave and 53rd St starts as soon as the cart arrives at about 7pm, and it stays busy with post-Broadway and nightclub crowds well into the next day, or whenever the owners decide to pack it in.

Repair some of last night's damage with a gentle morning walking around Greenwich Village, a neighborhood of brownstones, crooked colonial roads and high-end shops, and stop by

"Most weekends in the summer I'll find a reason to go out to Red Hook in Brooklyn to visit the Red Hook Food Stalls that usually hang out around Clinton and Bay Sts. There's nowhere else to get such great, tasty Latin food, and they've got everything covered: tacos, burritos, quesadillas, ceviche, *arepas*. You name it, they'll make it."

Kathianne Boniello, College Point, Queens

❾ **Bean Coffee and Tea** for a cup of java and a fresh waffle. These waffles aren't frozen – they're made by the ❿ **Waffle Guy**, aka Thomas DeGeest, who sells them from his traveling truck around Manhattan, but you have to check his website (www.wafelsanddinges.com) to find out where he'll be on any given day.

Head south through Washington Square Park, full of amateur chess players, students, buskers and canine-happy New Yorkers communing in the park's dog-run, and you'll stumble across a famous icon: ⓫ **Thiru "Dosa Man" Kumar**, who runs NY Dosas. His vegan cart produces to-die-for lentil soups, chutneys and, of course, *dosas* (savory pancakes).

From there it's time to head to the mecca of street food: Jackson Heights, Queens. In this immigrant-heavy enclave you could easily spend an afternoon shopping and walking amid the Latin, Middle Eastern and South Asian shops, bars and restaurants. Keep your eyes peeled for a few fabulous faces, starting with Maria Piedad Cano, the ⓬ **Arepa Lady**. A native of Colombia, Maria dishes up from her stall light-as-a-feather cheese-and-meat stuffed *arepas* wrapped in corn husks. Also known to work the area is ⓭ **Antojitos Mexicanos**, a group of Mexican chefs who have a cult following for their spicy Oaxaqueno tamales, imbued with a deep mole and hot jalapeño flavor, and ⓮ **Tacos Guichos**, a neighborhood hangout for chorizo tacos, deep-dish *carnitas* (braised or roasted pork), *chalupas* and much more.

There's plenty more to discover in Jackson Heights, especially around the corner on Broadway. As long as your appetite holds up, New York's street vendors are more than happy to provide you a moving feast.

Ginger Adams Otis

TRIP INFORMATION

GETTING THERE
Accessible from the major three airports as well as the subway.

EAT
Antojitos Mexicanos
Delicious tacos, chalupas, burritos and more, with the flavor and heat of Oaxaca in every bite. **Roosevelt Ave at 61st St, Jackson Heights; mains $3-9; ⏰ 7am-7pm; ♿**

Arepa Lady
Arepas filled with spicy meat, melted cheese and fresh herbs, but the hours are sporadic. **Roosevelt Ave at 78th St, Jackson Heights; mains $4; ⏰ hours vary**

Bean Coffee and Tea
A far West Village hangout serving fresh waffles from Liège, Belgium, provided by the "Waffle Guy." ☎ 212-777-0402; http://the beancoffeeandtea.com; 446 6th Ave; mains $5; ⏰ 7am-11pm; ♿

Halal Chicken and Gyro
Fans line up around the block for the famous rice and chicken, covered with special white sauce. http://53rdand6th.com; 53rd St & Sixth Ave; mains $6; ⏰ 7pm-4am; ♿

Huan Ji Rice Noodles
Delicious balls of rice noodles topped with curried fish, pork belly, or a beef or chicken broth. ☎ 212-966-6232; Grand St at Bowery; mains $1-3; ⏰ 7am-8pm; ♿

Lung Moon Bakery
Squeeze inside this barebones Chinese bakery for freshly made, hot-from-the-oven cookies, pork buns and fluffy cakes. ☎ 212-349-4945; 83 Mulberry St; mains $1-4; ⏰ 8am-2pm; ♿

Tacos Guichos
These friendly cooks like to spice up the fish, chicken, beef and veggie tacos with citrus flavors. ☎ 646-209-7462; Roosevelt Ave at Gleane St, Jackson Heights; mains $2-8; ⏰ 8am-1am; ♿

Thiru "Dosa Man" Kumar
Made on the spot with fresh, vegan ingredients, these *dosas* are legendary. ☎ 917-710-2092; W 4th St at Sullivan St & Washington Sq; mains $4-8; ⏰ 11am-4pm Mon-Sat; ♿

Tony Dragonas
This food stall does a brisk business in grilled platters with homemade Greek sides. ☎ 917-299-1550; 62nd St at Madison Ave; mains $6; ⏰ 10:30am-6pm Mon-Fri, 11am-5pm Sat; ♿

Xinjiang Kebabs
Perfectly seasoned and fire-grilled kebabs, with meats ranging from chicken to lamb kidneys. **Division St at Forsyth St; mains $1; ⏰ 10am-9pm; ♿**

SLEEP
Gild Hall
A business hotel with a boutique feel, designer rooms, a sleek glass and wood lobby, a champagne library and high-end amenities. ☎ 212-232-7700; www.wallstreetdistrict .com; 15 Gold St; r $400

USEFUL WEBSITES
www.jhfff.org

LINK YOUR TRIP
www.lonelyplanet.com/trip-planner

Best of the Boroughs

WHY GO There's a different New York City outside of Manhattan, full of family restaurants, tree-lined streets, old country traditions and avant-garde art. It only takes a subway pass and a little exploration to find the cobblestone byways of Brooklyn, the bucolic wonders of the Bronx and hidden culinary delights of Queens.

TIME
3 days

DISTANCE
15 miles

BEST TIME TO GO
Mar – Nov

START
Brooklyn

END
Queens

ALSO GOOD FOR

HISTORY &
CULTURE

The day begins with a jaunt across the **❶ Brooklyn Bridge**, an iconic structure in Lower Manhattan that spans the East River and helped meld what were once two entirely different cities into one municipal unit more than 100 years ago. As you pass the first arched tower, marked "1875," (mind the bike traffic zipping past), a glance to the right reveals New York's gaping harbor, home to the **❷ Statue of Liberty**, **❸ Governor's Island** and **❹ Staten Island**. Over your left shoulder, if you're gazing northwest, you'll see midtown Manhattan. The silver point is the **❺ Chrysler Building**.

As the bridge's wooden planks turn to concrete, follow the staircase exit on the left to Washington St, under an overpass. Welcome to Brooklyn. If you head left on Washington St, you'll reach **❻ Dumbo** (aka Down Under the Manhattan Bridge Overpass), a former industrial wasteland that's been taken over by artists and turned into a gallery- and loft-heavy residential space – with a few rough edges.

On Front St is **❼ Front St Galleries**, an orange-colored warehouse of about 10 or so artist studios and display spaces. Forward from here will take you under the **❽ Manhattan Bridge** (be sure to look up to catch the latest bits of graffiti art on the track's underside). Make a left onto Jay St, lined with offbeat bars and galleries, then another left on Plymouth St, also shabby, but equally welcoming. As you head under the bridge for a second time, it's worth wandering

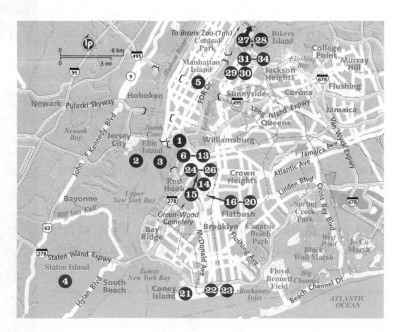

through the two green parks facing the water: **9** **Brooklyn Bridge Park** and **10** **Empire Fulton Ferry State Park**, where Manhattan ferries whisked passengers between the two boroughs for nearly 300 years (stopping in 1924).

Now's a good time to stop at **11** **Bubby's**, a former warehouse that's now a luxury loft building. Bubby's is bright and airy, with vaulted ceilings, twirling fans, wood floors, an old-fashioned bar with faux-green-leather bar stools, and stellar East River views that will distract you from the mac-n-cheese, meat loaf, barbecue ribs and Bubby's famous homemade pies. Or, for a coffee fix, turn right onto Water St and stroll to **12** **Jacques Torres Chocolate**. The buttery, flaky croissants here come stuffed with deep, dark chocolate, which you can eat sitting at one of the three outdoor tables that overlook the waterfront.

An entertaining afternoon lies ahead, so turn uphill and follow the 10-block stretch of leafy **13** **Brooklyn Heights Promenade**, which overlooks the nabe's gorgeous brownstones. Detour down Willow St to No 70 – that's where Truman Capote wrote *Breakfast at Tiffany's*.

No visit to Brooklyn would be complete without stopping by one of the borough's knockout landmarks: the **14** **Brooklyn Museum of Art**. To get there, hop on the subway and head for Eastern Parkway. A short walk from the subway exit you'll find the white pillared beaux-arts museum. It's packed with an extensive Egyptian collection, African arts displays, art-deco masterpieces, and a 5th floor bursting with 58 fabulous Rodin sculptures. Don't forget to leave time for the glass-paned entry and esplanade that features a 1900 replica of the Statue of Liberty.

Around the museum is the gentrified Park Slope neighborhood. The family-oriented Seventh Ave is packed with kid-happy pizza joints and familiar chains. Youthful Fifth Ave is dotted with jazzy bars and trendy restaurants. You might want to step into ⑮ **Convivium-Osteria**, a romantic, candle-filled boîte with flavors from Italy and the Iberian peninsula, and a well-stocked, old stone wine room. On any given night a soulful singer may be strumming a guitar in the small front room, which has tiny tables barely able to hold the big plates of seafood tapas, braised artichokes and tender octopus salad served up here.

Get the full local experience by staying in the cozy ⑯ **Bed and Breakfast on the Park**. The homey Victorian has handsome furnishings and wood floors (underneath pricey Oriental rugs), a flower-filled backyard garden and large, four-poster beds. It's right across the street from Prospect Park.

DETOUR A truly beautiful stretch of land set on Brooklyn's highest point is **Green-Wood Cemetery**, its leafy hills interconnecting with looping roads and trails. Founded in 1838, the cemetery remains one of New York's premier spots for life eternal. Some 600,000 are buried here, including Leonard Bernstein, mobster Joey Gallo and 9/11 victims. Battle Hill – the highest point – is where the "Continental" troops fought off the British during the 1776 Battle of Brooklyn.

Continue your exploration of Brooklyn on day two with an early morning stroll around Park Slope and its famous centerpiece: ⑰ **Prospect Park**. Begin at ⑱ **Grand Army Plaza**, which is dominated by the Soldiers' and Sailors' Monument. The great marble arch directs traffic and serves as a memorial for Civil War Union soldiers. Reliefs are dedicated to the army and navy (left and right as you look from the park).

Inside the park veer left, passing under the Endale Arch to reach the mile-long, 90-acre ⑲ **Long Meadow**. Halfway down the narrow meadow you'll see a Picnic House on the left. Follow the sidewalk on a woodsy walk that follows Lullwater Creek for a good 10 minutes before reaching a lovely white terra-cotta boathouse, built in 1904. Here you can walk across the Lullwater Bridge or hop on the *Independence,* a replica early-20th-century electric boat that will gently tote you around the park's 60-acre lake, which in summer becomes covered with a carpet of green and yellow (pollen from the surrounding trees).

If you exit at the park's north end at 9th St, near the Lafayette Monument, a life-size homage to Marquis de Lafayette, who played a critical role in the

Revolutionary War, you can turn right to walk past Romanesque revival and neo-Jacobean mansions built to impress more than two centuries ago. Turn left into Park Slope on shady one-block Montgomery Pl – named for a British veteran who fought in the Revolutionary War – and navigate your way to Fifth Ave between 3rd and 4th Sts to the **㉒ Old Stone House**, a restored Dutch farmhouse built by original settlers – it's a rare legacy from the days when Brooklyn was actually Breukelen.

It's time to change the Brooklyn vibe from pastoral to offbeat – and that means **㉑ Coney Island**. Grab a train to the Brooklyn coast and step off into the brisk sea air. Right away that works up an appetite, which is why New York invented **㉒ Nathan's Famous hot dogs**, heaping stomach-busters laden with mustard, sauerkraut and as many onions as you can stand.

Stretch your legs along the famous 3-mile **㉓ Coney Island Boardwalk**, buffeted even in the summer by stiff Atlantic breezes, and check out the crazy Wonder Wheel and other 1940s freak show attractions that once made Coney Island the premier location for family fun.

Some intriguing changes start to appear as you move further east along the boardwalk toward Brighton Ave – an area known as Little Odessa, a nod to the Russian immigrants who started flocking here decades ago. Smoked sausage and herring replace the burgers and hot dogs at food kiosks, and Russian-language newspapers compete alongside New York's dailies. Brush up on your Russian as you navigate food shops, delicatessens, bookstores and more, all selling trinkets and items from the homeland, from samovars to sturgeon.

> *"Brush up on your Russian as you navigate shops selling everything from samovars to sturgeon."*

When you've had your fill of trying to decipher Cyrillic, jump back on the train to the hip Brooklyn nabe of Carroll Gardens for a night of fine dining and pub crawling along Smith and Court Sts. **㉔ Cubana Café**, with French doors casually thrown open, is a breezy nook easily spotted by its bright blue exterior. Inside this retro hangout is a tiny, tiled bar and small rickety tables with wildly colored tablecloths and authentic Cuban dishes like pulled pork, garlicky shrimp, *ropa vieja* (beef stew) and sweet plantains.

For a more gourmet experience, squeeze into shoebox **㉕ Grocery** and try to snag a seat under the white awnings and tiki-bar lights in the backyard garden. Nearby you'll find an oddity in low-rise Brooklyn. **㉖ Hotel Le Bleu** has moved into the neighborhood, bringing a touch of Manhattan luxury with its striking skyscraper design. The boutique hotel is made from glass – alternately clear and bright blue – allowing guests to watch twinkling city lights clear across Brooklyn.

CITY

On day three, it's time to switch from Brooklyn to the bustle and grit of **27** **the Bronx**. It's a feast for the senses along **28** **Arthur Ave**, New York's *real* Little Italy, full of old-school bodegas selling gourmet-cured meats, specialty cheeses, imported olive oils, pastas, sauces and homemade focaccia and other breads. The street contains every cliché you can imagine, brought to vivid life: shouting children playing stickball, black-clad thick-ankled *nonnas* heading to mass and singing butchers carving meat.

From Arthur Ave, it's time to pick up the flavor of Japan by heading to **29** **Queens** and one of its most delightful – and hard to find – museums. The works of Isamu Noguchi are on display in the indoor/outdoor **30** **Noguchi Museum** he designed for himself, with granite and basalt installations delicately placed in contemplative locations around the gardens. The museum has 13 galleries inside a converted factory building that circles the inner garden.

The heart and soul of Queens is still in nearby **31** **Astoria**, the old Greek neighborhood that's bursting with energy and activity. Spend the rest of your day in this enclave (Thirtieth Ave and Ditmars Blvd are home to large Greek and Cypriot communities), which is studded with outstanding tavernas and gyro shops.

Along Broadway, the center of hipster Queens, you'll find the restaurants, bars and clubs have a decidedly Latin tone. Steinway, another main drag, has recently been dubbed Little Egypt for all its hookah-friendly cafés and shops.

> **DETOUR** ➤ Ten blocks east of Arthur Ave, off Southern Blvd, is the **Bronx Zoo** (www.bronxzoo.com), renowned for its wide open spaces where the visitors are expected to keep out of the way of the free, roaming animals. Trolleys and gondolas bring you through the Congo Gorilla Forest and around the massive, junglelike zoo that dedicates a large portion of its funds to conservation efforts worldwide.

An old Central European throwback that's become the de facto neighborhood UN is the **32** **Bohemian Beer Garden**. The massive garden out back – with big communal beer tables – is a cross-section of cultures on a sunny afternoon. Enjoy a few dark BrouCzech beers before searching out some of the local Greek delights.

On busy Ditmars, **33** **Mezzo Mezzo** is an Aegean hideaway, full of fresh calamari, spanakopita, moussaka and crisp white wines to go with delicate bream or baked red snapper. Nearby **34** **Ovelia** on Thirtieth Ave serves everything with a twist: the feta is mashed with spices and served warm on pita, while the meat platter goes beyond the usual lamb to include sweetbreads and pork.

There's one more "best" to experience in New York's boroughs: don't leave Queens without sampling Astoria's baklava, sold in every neighborhood restaurant and coffee shop. It's better than anything you'll find in Manhattan.
Ginger Adams Otis

TRIP INFORMATION

GETTING THERE

Brooklyn, the Bronx and Queens are easily accessible from the airports, and via the subway.

DO

Brooklyn Museum of Art

Five stories of African, Egyptian and French art in a massive building on Prospect Park. ☎ 718-638-5000; www.brooklynmuseum .org; 200 Eastern Pkwy; adult/child $8/4; 🕑 11am-5pm Wed-Sun; 🕭

Front St Galleries

The best of the Dumbo art scene spread out over several floors in an old warehouse/gallery. www.frontstreetgalleries.com; 111 Front St; admission free; 🕑 11am-5pm Wed-Sun

Noguchi Museum

Noguchi's earth-friendly art is displayed to perfection at this garden museum. ☎ 718-204-7088; www.noguchi.org; 9-01 33rd Rd at Vernon Blvd; admission $10; 🕑 10am-5pm Wed-Sun; 🕭

Old Stone House

A sturdy Dutch home offering a rare glimpse into homesteading hardships. ☎ 718-768-3195; www.theoldstonehouse.org; 336 Fifth Ave; admission free; 🕑 tours 11am-5pm Sat & Sun; 🕭

EAT & DRINK

Bohemian Beer Garden

Communal tables, thick cigarette smoke and hefty steins of ale, lager and dark brews. ☎ 718-274-4925; www.bohemianhall.com; 29-19 24th Ave; mains $10; 🕑 5-11pm Mon-Fri, noon-11pm Sat & Sun

Bubby's

Comfort food for the ages in a spacious location on the Brooklyn waterfront. ☎ 718-222-0666; http://bubbys.com; 1 Main St; mains $12-24; 🕑 11:30am-10pm Thu-Sun; 🕭

Convivium-Osteria

An Italian eatery with hardwood floors, candles and rickety tables. ☎ 718-857-1833; www.convivium-osteria.com; 68 Fifth Ave; mains $12-22; 🕑 6-11pm

Cubana Café

Heaping plates of shredded beef, roast chicken and spicy rice keep this fave packed. ☎ 718-858-3980; 272 Smith St; mains $8-18; 🕑 11am-11pm; 🕭

Grocery

Make reservations to squeeze into Grocery or its garden for local organic comfort food. ☎ 718-596-3335; http://thegrocery restaurant.com; 288 Smith St; mains $10-22; 🕑 5:30-11pm Tue-Sat

Jacques Torres Chocolate

Three tables share space with baked goods, coffee and oodles of rich, dark chocolate. ☎ 212-414-2462; www.mrchocolate.com; 66 Water St; mains $7; 🕑 9am-7pm Mon-Sat, 10am-6pm Sun

Mezzo Mezzo

Fresh fish from the Greek Isles, with all the usual Hellenic fixings. ☎ 718-278-0444; 29 Ditmars Blvd; mains $10-24; 🕑 11am-11pm

Ovelia

The Athens-born owners bring modern flare to this nightclub-style spot. ☎ 718-721-7217; http://ovelia-ny.com; 34-01 30th Ave; mains $11-25; 🕑 11:30am-11pm

SLEEP

Bed and Breakfast on the Park

A handsome Victorian with a backyard garden. ☎ 718-499-6115; www.bbnyc .com; 113 Prospect Park West; r $235-350

Hotel Le Bleu

Sleek Le Bleu wouldn't be out of place in trendy Manhattan. ☎ 718-625-1500; www.hotellebleu.com; 370 Fourth Ave; r $289-559

www.lonelyplanet.com/trip-planner

LINK YOUR TRIP

TRIP
10 48 Hours in Manhattan p115
13 Historic Hyde Park opposite

Historic Hyde Park

WHY GO Explore the rich Hudson Valley that gave birth to two of America's greatest political dynasties: the Rockefellers and the Roosevelts. Both families have left behind an historic legacy of great homes and gorgeous gardens, full of Old World treasures and flowering beauty.

The Hudson Valley has been fertile ground for creative types for over 200 years, so why not start your trip in one of its most famous towns: ❶ **Sleepy Hollow**. Technically its name is North Tarrytown, but once longtime resident Washington Irving – staring out over the same deep forests and ravines that you see today – dreamed up the Headless Horseman and Ichabod Crane in his famously spooky tale, "The Legend of Sleepy Hollow," well, the name just stuck.

It's not quite on the scale of the grand historic mansions that line the Hudson River, but in its day Irving's home, ❷ **Sunnyside**, denoted a family of means. The quaint, cozy Dutch cottage – which Irving said had more nooks and crannies than a cocked hat – has been left pretty much the way it was when the author lived there. The wisteria he planted 100 years ago still climbs the walls, and the spindly piano inside – probably the locus of the family's nightlife – still carries a tune.

Not far north on Rte 9 is another old home, ❸ **Philipsburg Manor**, a working farm in 17th-century Dutch style. Wealthy Dutchman Frederick Philips brought his family here around 1680 and meticulously built his new farm. Step inside the rickety gristmill and all you'll hear is gushing water and creaky wood; inside the rough-hewn clapboard barns and three-story, whitewashed fieldstone manor, it's all sighs and clanks as old fireplaces and strained beams do their work.

Across the road is the ❹ **Old Dutch Church**, built in 1865 as part of the original Philipsburg Manor, and Sleepy Hollow Cemetery. The

TIME
2 days

DISTANCE
85 miles

BEST TIME TO GO
Apr – Nov

START
Sleepy Hollow

END
Rhinebeck

ALSO GOOD FOR

OUTDOORS

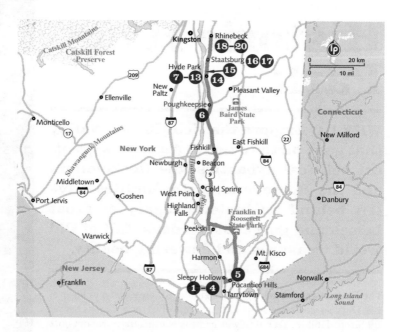

latter is a suitably mysterious place to be the final resting ground of Irving – you can get lost walking the long, curving lanes trying to find his grave in the section called Beekman Mound.

From Philipsburg Manor, art-and-history buffs can grab a shuttle to the sprawling splendor of ⑤ **Kykuit**, the Rockefeller family mansion perched on a bluff high atop the Hudson River. Looking for all the world like an old European estate, the massive and stately neoclassical revival exterior definitely doesn't come off as cozy. Inside it's more fine art gallery than summer home: fine porcelain and famous paintings are everywhere. Outside, the carefully sculpted gardens, dotted with modern art installations from the likes of Giacometti and Picasso, are a delight to wander through.

> "...the carefully sculpted gardens, dotted with modern art installations, are a delight to wander through."

North into the Mid-Hudson Valley along Rte 9 you'll pass through ⑥ **Poughkeepsie** to the several presidential palaces left behind by the Roosevelt family. Their former estates line up along Hyde Park, adding a rich layer of history to Dutchess County. Along the way you'll pass plenty of farm stands offering fresh pies, fruits and veggies. Come in the fall, and you can add pumpkins to that list.

Tuck in for a good night's sleep at ⑦ **Journey Inn**, a six-room B&B – including a Roosevelt Room, of course – right in the middle of Hyde Park's big estates.

You won't go hungry in this town – it's home to the **8** **Culinary Institute of America**, an upstate branch of the city's most famous cooking school. The chefs might all be students, but they know what they're doing, and you can judge their efforts at any of the CIA restaurants, including these four: **9** **American Bounty** for an experiment in local, organic cooking; **10** **Escoffier** for classic French dining; **11** **St Andrew's Café** if you fancy Asian-inspired soups, plus panini and wood-fired pizza; and the **12** **Apple Pie Bakery Café** for desserts.

You'll be in prime position on day two to explore the birthplace of Franklin Delano Roosevelt, known as **13** **Springwood**, a surprisingly down-to-earth home with intimate details – the desk left as it was the day before FDR died, the hand-pulled elevator he used to hoist his polio-stricken body to the 2nd floor, even his private memoirs and musings are accessible in the presidential library. Two miles east of Springwood is **14** **Val-Kill**,

 Not all the old abodes of America's first families sit fallow but revered in the Hudson Valley. **Blue Hill at Stone Barns** (www.bluehillstonebarns.com) in Pocantico Hills is now an organic, sustainable farm that opens its wide doors to visitors, and you can sample the fresh-from-the-earth products at the on-site café and fancy restaurant. If you visit Kykuit via Philipsburg Manor and book the Estate Life Tour, it will include a stop at Blue Hill at Stone Barns, or swing by on your own.

Eleanor Roosevelt's private hideaway. Not at all stately, it really is little more than a cottage, albeit one that hosted many dignitaries and heads of state.

Push north along Rte 9 to **15** **Vanderbilt Mansion**, a marble wonder built by the fabulously wealthy Frederick Vanderbilt, grandson of Cornelius Vanderbilt, once a Staten Island farmer who made millions buying up railroads. It's worth visiting this palatial estate for the beautiful Italian rose garden alone.

Further north is **16** **Staatsburg**, a hot spot for antiquing. If you prefer to look rather than buy, duck into the 100-year-old **17** **Staatsburg State Historic Site**, a beaux-arts mansion boasting 79 luxurious rooms filled with brocaded Flemish tapestries, gilded plasterwork, period paintings and Oriental art.

Fill up on tavern fare at historic **18** **Beekman Arms** in Rhinebeck, a scenic 11 miles north of Mills Mansion, and revel in the fact that you are dining in one of George Washington's old haunts – and yes, he really did sleep here, in one of the original spacious, whitewashed rooms upstairs. Out back, in a large red barn, is the **19** **Beekman Arms Antique Market**, where 30 local antique dealers offer up their best Americana. If you fancy sleeping in a bed that wasn't around when Washington was president, try the **20** **Olde Rhinebeck Inn**, 3 miles out of town. There's reportedly a friendly ghost who likes to pop up in the lobby, but that's the only antique that's likely to move in this beautifully restored 18th-century home.

Ginger Adams Otis

TRIP INFORMATION

GETTING THERE
After leaving the Tarrytown area, cross the Hudson River and follow signs north to Hyde Park's historic old homes.

DO
Kykuit
Buses depart from Philipsburg Manor to this splendid summer home, but book a tour in advance to ensure entry. ☎ Mon-Fri 914-631-8200, Sat & Sun 914-631-3992; www.historichudsonvalley.com; 200 Lake Rd, Pocantico Hills; adult/child $23/21

Old Dutch Church
Formerly part of Philipsburg Manor, this little Dutch church and cemetery are as quaint as they come. ☎ Mon-Fri 914-631-8200, Sat & Sun 914-631-3992; www.historichudsonvalley.com; 450 N Broadway, Sleepy Hollow; 🕑 9am-4pm

Philipsburg Manor
A creaky old Dutch farm, bursting with surprising revelations about the region's slave labor. ☎ Mon-Fri 914-631-8200, Sat & Sun 914-631-3992; www.historichudsonvalley.com; 381 N Broadway, Sleepy Hollow; adult/senior/child $12/10/6; 🕑 10am-5pm Wed-Mon Apr-Oct, 10am-4pm Nov-Dec; ♿

Springwood
The spirit of FDR lingers at his beloved Hudson River mansion, full of his old books, papers and dapper clothes. ☎ 845-229-9115; www.nps.gov/hofr; Rte 9, Hyde Park; admission $14; 🕑 9am-5pm; ♿

Staatsburg State Historic Site
A lavish private 1880s home now open to the public via guided tours. ☎ 845-889-8851; www.nysparks.state.ny.us; Old Post Rd, Staatsburg; admission free; 🕑 10am-5pm Wed-Sat, noon-5pm Sun Apr-Sep; ♿

Sunnyside
Washington Irving's handsome cottage still has the ivy vines planted by the author. ☎ 914-591-8763, Mon-Fri 914-631-8200; 89 W Sunnyside Lane, Sleepy Hollow; adult/senior/child $12/10/6; 🕑 10am-5pm Wed-Mon Apr-Oct, 10am-4pm Nov-Dec; ♿

Vanderbilt Mansion
Built to soothe Cornelius Vanderbilt's bruised ego when Manhattan society rejected him, this Gilded Age beauty is an opulent delight. ☎ 845-229-9115; www.nps.gov/vama; Rte 9, Hyde Park; admission $8; 🕑 9am-5pm; ♿

EAT
Culinary Institute of America
Reserve to eat in any of the school's fantastic restaurants. ☎ 845-452-9600; www.ciachef.edu; 1946 Campus Dr, Poughkeepsie; mains $4-28, tours $5; 🕑 call for details

SLEEP
Beekman Arms
Original 1776-era rooms are cheery; a Beekman add-on and the sister Delamater Inn have more modern options. ☎ 845-876-7077; www.beekmanarms.com; 6387 Mill St, Rhinebeck; r $110-250; ♿ ✦

Journey Inn
Take your pick of the Tuscany Room, the Tokyo Room or others at this elegant inn. ☎ 845-229-8972; www.journeyinn.com; One Sherwood Pl, Poughkeepsie; r $130-190

Olde Rhinebeck Inn
Built by German settlers three decades before the Revolutionary War, this oak-beamed, cozy inn oozes comfort and authenticity. ☎ 845-871-1745; www.rhinebeckinn.com; 340 Wurtemberg Rd, Rhinebeck; r $275-295

USEFUL WEBSITES
www.hudsonvalley.org
www.hydeparkny.us
www.lonelyplanet.com/trip-planner

LINK YOUR TRIP

By the Time We Got to Woodstock

WHY GO Revisit the 1960s counter-culture in the Catskills, where a handful of unspoiled, rustic towns still embrace the free-wheeling and art-focused lifestyle that put this section of upstate New York on the map and inspired a generation.

Get to know woodsy **❶ Woodstock** – famous for the 1969 concert that didn't actually happen here but in Bethel, where you'll be headed later – by walking its two main thoroughfares: Tinker St and Mill Rd. Start at the **❷ town commons**, a nice slice of green at the intersection of Tinker St and Rock City Rd. Most of the town's seasonal festivals, holiday celebrations, craft fairs and flea markets are held here.

The **❸ Woodstock Artists Association Gallery**, adjacent to the commons, is where you're most likely to bump into a local creative type or a visiting Byrdcliffe Arts Colony resident hanging their latest work. The permanent collection features a wide range of Woodstock artists in all sorts of mediums, from gentle charcoal drawings to complex abstract paintings and sculptures, and it has frequent exhibitions.

As you wander along Tinker St, past shops with groovy '60s names – Pegasus Footwear, Modern Mythology, Wild & Sweet – keep an eye out for the **❹ Woodstock Guild**, a collective of more than 600 artisans and artists. It houses the Fleur de Lis Gallery and the Kleinert/James Arts Center, both first-rate spaces showing works ranging from traditional wood carvings to cutting-edge performance pieces.

If you feel a frisson upon entering the neighboring **❺ Woodstock Center for Photography**, that's because it was formerly the Espresso Café, hallowed ground for counter-culture types. Bob Dylan once had a writing studio above the now-defunct Espresso – that's where he typed up the liner notes for *Another Side of Bob Dylan* in 1964 – and Janis Joplin was a regular performer. Now the space is hung with contemporary

TIME
2 days

DISTANCE
70 miles

BEST TIME TO GO
Apr – Oct

START
Woodstock

END
Bethel

ALSO GOOD FOR

OUTDOORS

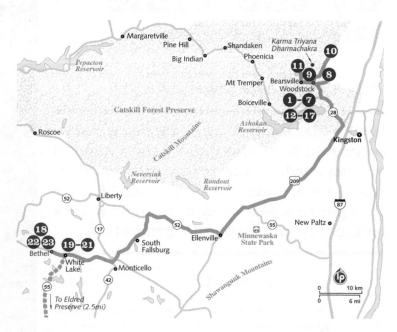

and historical photography exhibits that cover far-flung events from around the globe, as well as introspective nature shots of the rugged Catskills.

At Tannery Brook Bridge is **6 Tinker Village**, a series of shops dedicated to local-made pottery and delicate, hand-wrought jewelry. Tannery Brook's a favorite spot for a dip, too, in the deep swimming hole carved out of the Catskills stone. Fuel up at **7 Taco Juan's**, a colorful fast-food restaurant that's been around Woodstock for ages. Under the aged beams, where pony-tailed hippies mix with big-city weekenders, you'll find homemade tortillas wrapped around tofu, and beans and/or meat for all types of burritos.

Spend time in the afternoon exploring Woodstock's outer edges, starting with **8 Opus 40**, a startling collection of pathways, pools and obelisks spread over 6.5 acres of a former quarry. Creator Harvey Fite, who painstakingly carved and set all the bluestone pieces, thought it would take him 40 years to complete: it took his entire life. His tools are on display at the Quarryman's Museum at Opus 40, a short drive east of Woodstock on County Rd 32.

If you head to Glasco Turnpike you can follow the signs for **9 Byrdcliffe Arts Colony & Theater**, a utopian musicians' colony started in 1902. For decades before "Woodstock the Concert," this site fed artists like Pete Seeger, Leadbelly, and Peter, Paul and Mary. Its 300 acres are open for exploring; pick up a tour map at the entrance mailbox, or time your arrival for one of the frequent stage, dance or musical performances held at the on-site Colony Theater. Not far away, down Bach Rd, is the ❿ **Woodstock Museum**, a cornucopia of '60s avant-garde art run as a nonprofit venture to educate people about the various artist colonies in the area. The hours are hard to pin down – the moon might have to be in the House of Aquarius for it to open.

For a look at modern-day artists' work, follow Rte 212 west to Cooper Lake, where you'll find ⓫ **Elena Zang Gallery**, home to Elena Zang and Alan Hoffman, minimalist pottery makers who also host showings of their friends' art. Their studio is surrounded by delightful "outsider art" they've picked up or created, and placed for maximum effect in the carefully sculpted garden.

Back in downtown Woodstock for the night, the ⓬ **Woodstock Inn on the Millstream** – with its own swimming hole in the backyard – is gated by a phalanx of brushy pine trees, which provide a feeling of privacy while you sit on the comfy front porch, even though you're just a short walk from town. Real nature lovers might prefer the ⓭ **Woodstock Country Inn**, 2 miles out of town in the former home of artist Jo Cantine, and backed by steep ravines and deep woods. Don't go to sleep without checking what's going on at ⓮ **Colony Café**, a former hotel that's been around for a century, transforming from lodge to antique center and then into a burned-out shell after a fire ripped through it. After careful restoration the small, white-walled and brown-beamed building reopened a few years back as an arts center, café and performance house.

⓯ **Woodstock Playhouse** is the local theater, built up from nothing after yet another fire reduced it to smoldering rubble in the late '80s. Now the small, circular playhouse is back in action, thanks to community donations. It's home to the Bird on a Cliff theater company, but also routinely hosts folk singers, bluegrass bands and children's shows. In downtown Woodstock, ⓰ **Joshua's Café** is a plain brick building jazzed up with twinkling lights hanging from the door and windows. The homey restaurant downstairs is a favorite vegan hangout; the casual coffee bar upstairs, full of couches and chairs, hosts local bands and singers on weekend nights.

> **DETOUR** ➤ Get your karma and chakras checked at the blissful **Karma Triyana Dharmachakra** (www.kagyu.org), a Buddhist monastery in the Catskill Mountains, about 3 miles from Woodstock. This '60s leftover is a popular treat for stressed-out New Yorkers and anyone needing a spiritual break. Soak up the serenity in the carefully tended grounds. Inside the shrine room is a giant golden Buddha statue; as long as you take off your shoes, you're welcome to sit down and meditate with him for a while.

Grab a fruit-filled turnover and coffee at ⓱ **Bread Alone**, an organic bakery on Mill Hill Rd. The tiny shop makes all its organic, kosher loaves, croissants and pastries by hand, using brick ovens from France. Stock up and get an early start toward **18** **Bethel**, another artsy village about 40 miles southwest of Woodstock. Bethel was the site of the former pig farm that for three rainy summer days in 1969 hosted a concert that came to symbolize the dreams and aspirations of an entire generation. A visit to the famous field – then owned by Bethel farmer Max Yasgur – is a must-do, but first, you have to get there.

A twisting, scenic drive will take you along the southern border of the protected Catskill Forest Preserve, and through tiny towns including South Fallsburg and Monticello, now just bereft shadows of their former bustling selves as summer megaresorts 40 years ago. The farmhouses are cozier looking and the bright green pastures better tended as you approach Bethel.

Stop on the town outskirts for a lakeshore lunch – two local standouts along Rte 17B are right on the cusp of White Lake. Choose **19** **Bubba's BBQ** and you can fill up on collard greens, mashed 'taters, fried catfish and ribs while overlooking the water. Or take note of **20** **Front Porch**, right across the street, where locals head for a stiff drink in the upstairs martini bar and dinner in the quaint dining room on performance nights. In the evening you can enjoy food and live jazz on the water's edge with a short drive around to the **21** **Fat Lady Café**.

 Find your inner fly-fisher at the year-round **Eldred Preserve** (www.eldredpreserve.com), a favorite of local hunters and outdoor enthusiasts. Eldred is a self-sufficient nature preserve with an on-site motel and restaurant – guess what's heavy on the menu? – and guests can sign up to fish in the trout ponds or rent boats to go hunting for bass. It's near White Lake on Rte 55, about 8 miles from Bethel.

For now, press onward into town until you come to Hurd Rd, following the signs to the famous Woodstock field – it will pop up before you as a rolling field of green. The low-level wood and stone buildings that dot the area are part of this town's major attraction. The **22** **Bethel Woods Center for the Arts**, a state-of-the-art performance and recital center, is designed to be perfectly in harmony with the deep green terrain. As you walk the stone pathways, you can get a bird's-eye view of the gorgeous Pavilion Stage, which has about 50,000 seats set into a sloping lawn, and the outdoor Terrace Stage (where the Arts Under the Stars series takes place), which is like a Greek amphitheater set down in a mossy field.

The jewel of Bethel Woods is the **23** **Woodstock Museum** at the center's entrance, a groovy look back at the tumultuous, spontaneous concert that's come to define the Summer of Love. The captivating multimedia displays use a combination of stock footage, documentaries, retrospectives, letters, books and – above all else – music to tell the story of the '60s and Woodstock, and capture the period's all-embracing spirit.

Ginger Adams Otis

TRIP INFORMATION

GETTING THERE
Head north on I-87, take exit 19 to Rte 28W and then follow Rte 375 north into Woodstock.

DO
Bethel Woods Center for the Arts
A state-of-the-art performance center on a Woodstock field that includes the fantastic Woodstock Museum. ☎ 866-781-2922; www.bethelwoodscenter.org; 200 Hurd Rd, Bethel; adult/senior/child $13/11/9; ⏱ 10am-7pm May-Jan; ♿ 🐕

Byrdcliffe Arts Colony & Theater
One of the area's oldest collectives, with gorgeous grounds to stroll and performances to catch. ☎ 845-679-2079; www.woodstockguild.org; Upper Byrdcliffe Rd, Woodstock; admission free; ⏱ call for performance schedule

Elena Zang Gallery
An outdoor atelier and gallery for local Woodstock artists. ☎ 845-679-5432; www.elenazang.com; 3671 Rte 212, Woodstock; admission free; ⏱ 11am-5pm; ♿

Opus 40
Harvey Fite's quiet and peaceful quarry took him years of painstaking work to create. ☎ 845-246-3400; www.opus40.org; 50 Fite Rd, Woodstock; adult/child $10/3; ⏱ 11:30am-5pm May 25-Oct 12; ♿ 🐕

Woodstock Artists Association Gallery
The "local Louvre," this collective has been inspiring and supporting artists, and showcasing their talent, since 1920. ☎ 845-679-2940; www.woodstockart.org; 28 Tinker St, Woodstock; admission free; ⏱ noon-5pm Thu-Mon; ♿

Woodstock Center for Photography
Permanent photos and rotating exhibits of all kinds of photography – black and white, editorial, multimedia – from local and international artists. ☎ 845-679-9957; www.cpw.org; 59 Tinker St, Woodstock; admission free; ⏱ noon-5pm Wed-Sun; ♿

Woodstock Guild
Run by the Byrdcliffe Arts Colony, the guild and its associated galleries run shows, performances and educational classes. ☎ 845-679-2079; www.woodstockguild.org; 34 Tinker St, Woodstock; admission free; ⏱ 11am-6pm Tue-Sat; ♿

Woodstock Museum
Exhibits 1960s artifacts, archival footage and pictures curated by three local artists. ☎ 845-246-0600; www.woodstockmuseum.com; Bach Rd, off Glasco Turnpike & W Saugerties Rd; admission free; ⏱ noon-7pm Sat & Sun Jul-Sep

Woodstock Playhouse
The outdoor pavilion burned down years ago and is only partially restored, but it still puts on fantastic music and theater shows. ☎ 845-679-4101; www.woodstockplayhouse.org; Rtes 212 & 375, Woodstock; per event $15-25; ⏱ summer performances

EAT
Bread Alone
A legendary bakery dishing up wholegrain, handmade organic fare. ☎ 845-679-2108; www.breadalone.com; 22 Mill Hill Rd, Woodstock; mains $3-12; ⏱ 8am-4pm; ♿

Bubba's BBQ
Finger-lickin'-good Southern cooking, from collard greens to baby-back ribs, on an outdoor patio overlooking the water. ☎ 845-469-4900; 1568 Rte 17B, Bethel; mains $6-14; ⏱ 11am-9pm Wed-Mon; ♿ 🐕

Joshua's Café
Live music, a java lounge and hearty, mostly vegan eats served fresh and grown locally. ☎ 845-679-5533; www.joshuascafe.com; 51 Tinker St, Woodstock; mains $4-22; ⏱ 8am-9pm; ♿

Taco Juan's
There's no missing this popular Mexican organic eatery, thanks to the vivid yellow and blue facade and flamboyant window art. ☎ 845-679-9673; 31 Tinker St, Woodstock; mains $4-12; ⏱ 11am-8pm; ♿

DRINK

Colony Café
Live music in an old, whitewashed building recently rehabbed and reborn. ☎ 845-679-5342; www.colonycafe.com; 22 Rock City Rd, Woodstock; cover $10; ☾ daily, check website for performance schedule

Fat Lady Café
Across the lake from Bethel, this lively spot is perfect for cocktails as the sun goes down. ☎ 845-583-7133; 13 Horseshoe Lake Rd, Kauneonga Lake; ☾ nightly

Front Porch
An old home turned café that opens when there's a performance at Bethel Woods. ☎ 845-583-4838; 1577 Rte 17B, Bethel; mains $12-22; ☾ hours vary

SLEEP

Woodstock Country Inn
This 19th-century farmhouse, built as an artist's retreat, is now an environmentally friendly, rustic-luxe B&B. ☎ 845-679-9380; www.woodstockcountryinn.com; 185 Cooper Lake Rd, Woodstock; r $145-275

Woodstock Inn on the Millstream
Beautifully decorated rooms with flat-screen TVs, quiet pastels and electric fireplaces Also has serene, flower-filled grounds. ☎ 845-679-8211; www.woodstock-inn-ny.com; 48 Tannery Brook Rd, Woodstock; r $140-250

USEFUL WEBSITES
www.bethelwoodscenter.org
www.woodstockny.org

LINK YOUR TRIP   www.lonelyplanet.com/trip-planner

Hidden Catskills

WHY GO Jutting sharply above the northern Hudson Valley, the rocky Catskill Mountains are full of hidden mossy gorges and waterfalls, and quirky, cozy villages that flourished as summer destinations during the heyday of rail travel. Dominated by the sharply peaked Catskills, the area is a magnet for hikers, campers and climbers.

TIME
2 days

DISTANCE
200 miles

BEST TIME TO GO
Apr – Nov

START
Narrowsburg

END
Haines Falls

ALSO GOOD FOR

OUTDOORS

The small town of ❶ **Narrowsburg** (population 414 last time anyone counted), nestled between the Catskill and Pocono Mountains, is a good place to start your trip. From the town, wend your way down Rte 97 to experience river life c 1770 at the ❷ **Museum of Living Colonial History**. Inside the historic fort is a splintery log stockade – a remnant of colonial justice – and in the summer months costumed guides will walk you around the log cabins, a candle-maker and blacksmith, and an 18th-century armory.

Not far away, on Narrowsburg's Main St, you'll find the ❸ **Delaware Valley Arts Alliance**, sitting in a huge, ramshackle structure filled with the sculptures, carvings and paintings of local artists.

There are some spooky haunts to be found in the Catskills. North from Narrowsburg, on Rte 52 at ❹ **Kenoza Lake**, you'll cross ❺ **Three Stone Bridge**. This National Register of Historic Places bridge was built by German and Swiss stonemasons around 1880 and has a lurid tale of murder and witchcraft attached to it – the exact details are fuzzy, but the plaques around the bridge suggest one villager suspected another of putting a curse on him. One night as the suspect walked home, he was ambushed on the bridge by a friend of the cursed man, who bashed his head with a cane and tossed him into the icy waters. For the 100-plus years since, a lone, ghostly male figure can sometimes be spotted crossing the bridge, according to local lore.

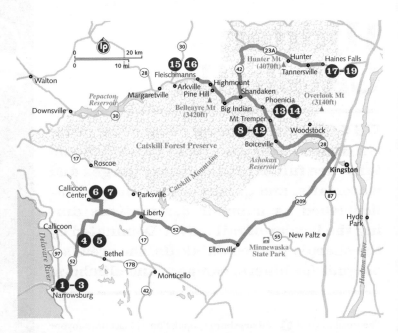

Don't let the scary tales stop you from exploring the surrounding 9 acres of untouched woods and fields that are perfect for hiking and fishing, and maybe even some ghost-spotting. Or you can continue straight across, and head for **6 Callicoon Center**. In the spring, numerous stands selling fresh maple syrup dot these roads; in the summer and fall you'll likely encounter stalls with fresh berries, corn, squash and other farm-grown veggies.

"…untouched woods and fields that are perfect for hiking and fishing, and maybe even some ghost-spotting."

Just outside Callicoon is the organic, equine-powered **7 Apple Pond Farming Center**, run by two dedicated environmentalists. Guests are invited to tour the farm, in use since 1865, and lend a hand with the goat farming, wool-spinning and stall cleaning. Or kick back and take in the mountain views, musing on the farm's innovative use of renewable energy.

Gallop northeast to the whimsical mountain village of **8 Mt Tremper** for the night, in the foothills of the **9 Belleayre Ski Resort**. If an afternoon of lifting hay bales has left you sore, try the **10 Emerson Resort & Spa**, a restored 1870s Victorian that greets guests with champagne flutes. Lovers of kitsch will prefer **11 Kate's Lazy Meadow Motel** (owned and run by Kate Pierson of B-52s fame), a modest, one-story ranch on the outside, but a treasure trove of vintage mid-20th-century decor on the inside. Plus, there's an outside fire pit for toasting marshmallows while gazing across babbling Esopus Creek.

Coffee can be had the next morning at the Emerson Resort's restored 1841 dairy barn, the ⑫ **Country Store**. Sure, the coffee's good, but also check out the real attraction here – the world's largest kaleidoscope. Housed inside a pitch-black, 60ft silo, the gigantic optical instrument spins its bright colors in mesmerizing patterns. A walk through the shops and craft stores that surround the kaleidoscope at Emerson Resort is pleasant, before heading north into ⑬ **Phoenicia**, a cheery, upbeat hamlet dedicated to outdoor fun.

Get a glimpse of early railroad life in the historic ⑭ **Delaware & Ulster Station**, built around 1899, containing the Empire State Railway Museum. Travel in style (or pretend you did) in a 1913 luxury Pullman, go coach in a steam locomotive, and enjoy the displays detailing how the old train tracks turned this corner of the Catskills into a tourist center.

If you follow the slim, winding road around a few hills and through a mountain overpass, you'll soon come to the forgotten factory town of ⑮ **Fleischmanns**, once home to the famous yeast company of the same name. Now little more than a tiny main street surrounded by the second homes of wealthy New Yorkers up in

> **ASK A LOCAL**
>
> "Nothing gets you in touch with local life faster than a lazy day inner-tubing down Esopus Creek. Downtown Phoenicia is the place to go for a day's jaunt – companies there offer beginner tube rentals, an expert trail for those who like it rough, and even kayaks if an old tire's too low-tech for you. No walking required; you'll be picked up at day's end and driven back to your car."
>
> *Rita Carroll, Poughkeepsie*

the hills, Fleischmanns is an offbeat location for lunch. In the summer months it fills up with Orthodox Jewish families who've adopted it as their weekend retreat. On Saturday evenings after Sabbath the families stroll the streets, not doffing their customary clothes or hats even in August heat. ⑯ **Griffin's Corners Café** on Main St is where the modern and Orthodox worlds meet.

Continue north and east about 20 miles into the heights of ⑰ **Haines Falls**. The mountaintop perch of ⑱ **Rosehaven Inn**, at the cleft of Kaaterskill Clove Pass, is ideally situated for a few days of hiking, swimming and kayaking. The house has mammoth bedrooms with gas fireplaces and whirlpool tubs.

You're in the perfect spot to hike around gorgeous ⑲ **Kaaterskill Falls**, a 260ft, cascading delight that's inspired generations of New York artists. The most traveled trail starts at the overlook site on Rte 23A, past Bastion Falls and then up a half-mile incline. There are other delights that are a bit more off the beaten track: consider hiking to Devil's Kitchen Falls, or trekking up the overlooked Kaaterskill High Peak trail. It's lonely, but you'll be rewarded with up-close views of Wildcat, Buttermilk and Santa Cruz waterfalls.

Ginger Adams Otis

TRIP INFORMATION

GETTING THERE
Follow Rte 28 from Kingston into the northern part of the Catskills; Rte 17 hugs the preserve's western edge.

DO
Apple Pond Farming Center
Call ahead to book a tour of this horse-powered farm, or reserve the guesthouse for the night. ☎ 845-482-4764; www.applepondfarm.com; 80 Hahn Rd, Callicoon Center; admission free; ☾ hours vary

Belleayre Ski Resort
A family-friendly ski resort in winter, Belleayre has a swimming pond and hiking trails in summer. ☎ 800-942-6904; www.belleayre.com; 181 Galli Curci Rd, Highmount; admission varies; ☾ year-round; ♿

Delaware & Ulster Station
Revisit the glory days of train travel at this old station and its Empire State Railway Museum. ☎ 845-688-7501; www.esrm.com; Station Rd, Phoenicia; admission free; ☾ 11am-4pm Sat & Sun; ♿

Delaware Valley Arts Alliance
A local artists collective housed in an old hotel that's on the National Historic Register. ☎ 845-252-7576; www.artsalliance.org; 37 Main St, Narrowsburg; admission free; ☾ 10am-4pm Tue-Sat; ♿

Museum of Living Colonial History
Historic Fort Delaware is a bit of living history, with friendly guides in colonial garb. ☎ 845-252-6660; http://co.sullivan.ny.us; Rte 97, Narrowsburg; adult/child $4.50/2.50; ☾ 10am-5pm Fri-Mon; ♿ ⚑

EAT
Country Store
A mini-outlet with a mix of local products, chain stores, a cozy café and the renowned kaleidoscope. ☎ 877-688-2828; www.emersonplace.com; 5340 Rte 28, Mt Tremper; kaleidoscope $5.40; ☾ 10am-6pm; ♿

Griffin's Corners Café
A sunny corner diner with big country breakfasts, hearty yeoman's lunches and dinners and occasional live music. ☎ 845-254-6300; www.griffinscornerscafe.com; Main St, Fleischmanns; mains $3-12; ☾ 7am-9pm; ♿

SLEEP
Emerson Resort & Spa
A premier Catskills resort and spa with several first-class restaurants, set among pine-covered mountains and behind a babbling river. ☎ 877-688-2828; www.emersonplace.com; 5340 Rte 28, Mt Tremper; s/d $190/220

Kate's Lazy Meadow Motel
A kitschy, upbeat and comfortable mountain motel with 1950s-style decor and mini-kitchenettes. ☎ 845-688-7200; www.lazymeadow.com; 5191 Rte 28, Mt Tremper; r $150-180

Rosehaven Inn
Deep in the mountains, this romantic Victorian B&B is surrounded by fantastic hiking trails and swimming holes. ☎ 518-589-5636; www.rosehaveninn.com; 147 Sunset Park Rd, Haines Falls; r Mon-Fri $125, Sat & Sun $175

USEFUL WEBSITES
www.catskillguide.com
www.catskills.com

LINK YOUR TRIP
www.lonelyplanet.com/trip-planner

OUTDOORS

Ithaca Is Gorges

WHY GO New York's splendid upstate towns are perfectly represented in Ithaca, a handsome village built around the Ivy League ambience of Cornell University. Its culturally rich center is perfect for antique and art shopping, while the surrounding natural beauty – steep hills, rocky gorges and tempestuous waterfalls – is ripe for exploring.

Wake up in leafy Ithaca and enjoy the sunrise over this sleepy college town. Then hit the trail early and drive 2 miles south on Rte 13 to ❶ **Buttermilk Falls State Park**, a sprawling swath of wilderness that has something for everyone – a beach, cabins, fishing, hiking, recreational fields and camping.

The big draw, however, is the waterfalls – more than 10 – some sending water tumbling as far as 500ft below into clear pools. Hikers like the raggedy ❷ **Gorge Trail** that brings them up to all the best cliffs. It parallels Buttermilk Creek, winding up about 500ft. On the other side of the falls is the equally popular ❸ **Rim Trail**, a loop of about 1.5 miles around the waterfalls from a different vantage point. Both paths feed into Bear Trail, which will take you to neighboring ❹ **Treman Falls**.

It's a trek of about 3 miles to Treman, but you can also pop back in the car after exploring Buttermilk and drive the 3 miles south to ❺ **Robert J Treman State Park**, still on bucolic Rte 13. Treman is also renowned for cascading falls. Its gorge trail passes a stunning 12 waterfalls in under 3 miles. The two biggies that you don't want to miss are Devil's Kitchen and Lucifer Falls, a multi-tiered wonder that spills Enfield Creek over rocks for about 100ft. At the bottom of yet another watery gorge – Lower Falls – there's a natural swimming hole; it's a deep, dark refreshing pool of river water that's impossible to resist on hot summer days.

TIME
3 days

DISTANCE
30 miles

BEST TIME TO GO
Mar – Nov

START
Ithaca

END
Ithaca

ALSO GOOD FOR

HISTORY & CULTURE

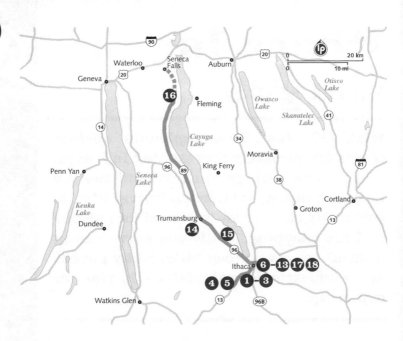

Ease your footsore self into the ⑥ **Moosewood Restaurant** at the downtown ⑦ **DeWitt Mall** in ⑧ **Ithaca** proper when you get hungry – that's the famous Moosewood Restaurant behind the vegetarian cookbook series of the same name. College students, graybeard professors and paint-dabbled artists all call this rustic eatery, with its lounge sofas and wood chairs and tables, their spot.

ARTSY ITHACA

If you're in the mood for a different kind of hiking, check out the **Greater Ithaca Art Trail**. Created by a collective of about 50 local artists, this wandering path takes you on a self-guided tour through working studios belonging to photographers, sculptors, jewelers and more. Call ahead to set up a date, and download the map and participant bios at www.arttrail.com.

There's a more pastoral option 2 miles south, right on ⑨ **Cayuga Lake**. Sitting on huge grounds that hold two fish-filled ponds you'll find ⑩ **La Tourelle Country Inn**, a vine-covered, three-story B&B. Adjacent is the ⑪ **John Thomas Steakhouse**, a family-style farmhouse that has been around since the 1900s. Between its wide, woody beams and creaky old floors, you'll feel like you're back in the days of yore.

Don't miss a stroll down ⑫ **Ithaca Commons** – a pedestrian-only stretch along State St that's packed with bars, shop and clubs. ⑬ **Simeon's** is a Victorian-era bar with long, gilded mirrors and a curving, ornate oak bar.

Devote your next day to ⑭ **Trumansburg**, a one-street town about 15 miles north of Ithaca on Rte 96. It's the gateway to the 215ft-high ⑮ **Taughannock Falls State Park** (for context, that's 30ft higher than New York's Niagara Falls). Taughannock has the highest cascade east of the Rockies – and the towering thunder is a sight not soon forgotten.

"...sit outside on the wide, ample lawn surrounded by gnarly roots and rioting wildflowers..."

Mist from the falls' spray seems to reach all the way through this park's 5 miles of hiking trails, most of which wind their way around the slipperiest parts to bring you safely to the lookout spots at the top. One trail follows the streambed to the falls. You'll be ready to kick back after such a strenuous start, so settle down for lunch at the ⑯ **Knapp Restaurant & Winery** on Cayuga Lake. On a nice day you can sit outside on the wide, ample lawn surrounded by gnarly roots and rioting wildflowers, and look out over the trellis-covered vineyards while you sample the homegrown wines, grappas and limoncellos.

On the return trip, pop into ⑰ **Cornell University's Sapsucker Woods Sanctuary**, a bird-feeding garden and 10-acre pond full of ducks, geese and other wildlife. The 4 miles of trails, open from dawn to dusk, are teeming with birds and butterflies. Also look out for *Stone Egg*, a huge cairn built from local stone by internationally acclaimed environmental artist Andy Goldsworthy and students from Cornell. Wind your way back to Ithaca for the night.

If you have time before you head off on your next trip in the morning, swing by Ithaca's most famous institution, ⑱ **Cornell College**. The lovely, inviting campus mixes old and new architecture and welcomes you down its shaded, arcadian walkways. Panoramic views of Cayuga Lake are available from the 5th floor of the campus's Herbert F Johnson Museum of Art. Designed by IM Pei, the structure's called "the sewing machine building" by irreverent students. You might also get a kick out of Cornell's Wilder Brain Collection, started by the school's first zoologist, Brian Wilder. Once there were as many as 1600 specimens; today only eight brains remain. Wilder originated his creepy collection in the late 1800s, trying to prove old-fashioned notions about brain size and intelli-

DETOUR Bone up on feminist and American history at the **Women's Rights National Historical Park**, just 31 miles north of Trumansburg at Seneca Falls. The park celebrates the suffragist movement, and you can visit the meticulously restored Elizabeth Cady Stanton house, where Stanton raised her seven children and often hosted fellow suffragette Susan B Anthony.

gence as it related to gender and race; after decades of measuring minds, Wilder shocked the world by announcing there was no difference between the brains of whites and blacks.

Ginger Adams Otis

TRIP INFORMATION

GETTING THERE
Head north on Hwy 81 from New York City, via Binghamton, to arrive in Ithaca in about four hours.

DO
Buttermilk Falls State Park
Gushing waterfalls and plenty of those famous Ithaca gorges surrounded by well-tended paths. ☎ 607-273-5761/3440; Rte 13; admission free; ☒ hiking Mar-Nov, park year-round; 🚻 ♿

Cornell University's Sapsucker Woods Sanctuary
Search for the elusive ivory-billed woodpecker and other feathered friends over 4 woody miles. ☎ 607-254-2473, 800-843-2473; cornellbirds@cornell.edu; 159 Sapsucker Woods Rd, Ithaca; admission free; ☒ 9:30am-4pm; 🚻 ♿

DeWitt Mall
A downtown hangout full of funky artists' shops, bars and restaurants, indie bookstores and some big-name chains. ☎ 607-273-8213; 215 N Cayuga St, Ithaca; ☒ 9am-9pm; 🚻 ♿

Robert J Treman State Park
Nine miles of hiking, swimming and fishing in ice-cold rivers and pools. ☎ 607-273-5761/3440; Rte 327; admission free; ☒ hiking Mar-Nov, park year-round; 🚻 ♿

Taughannock Falls State Park
Ithaca's most impressive gorges, cliffs and shale-covered precipices are on stunning display in this park of endless hiking. ☎ 607-387-6739; Rte 89; admission free; ☒ year-round

EAT & SLEEP
John Thomas Steakhouse
Thick and juicy porterhouses, fillets and all the classic steak sides – potatoes, asparagus and creamy spinach – served in a cozy old farmhouse. ☎ 607-273-3464; www.john thomassteakhouse.com; 1152 Danby Rd, Ithaca; mains $12-30; ☒ 5:30-10pm Mon-Fri, 5:30-11pm Sat & Sun

Knapp Restaurant & Winery
Soak up the sunshine and match your portobello sandwich with a lively white wine, or your penne pasta with a rustic red. ☎ 800-869-9271; www.knappwine.com; 2770 County Rd 128, Cayuga Lake; mains $8-16; ☒ 11am-5pm Apr-Nov

La Tourelle Country Inn
A truly sensuous mountain retreat with handsome, antique-filled rooms and an on-site spa. ☎ 800-765-1492; www.latourelle.com; 1150 Danby Rd, Ithaca; r $180-300

Moosewood Restaurant
Chunky veggie soups, buckwheat pancakes and hearty vegetarian pastas, wraps and salads keep this brick and blond-wood eatery packed. ☎ 607-273-9610; www.moose woodrestaurant.com; 215 N Cayuga St, Ithaca; mains $4-15; ☒ 11:30am-9pm Mon-Sat, 5:30-9pm Sun

Simeon's
Paint-stained fingers abound at arty Simeon's, a bistro bar and restaurant that attracts local creative types. ☎ 607-272-2212; www .simeonsithaca.com; 224 E State St, Ithaca; mains $9-25; ☒ 11am-midnight

USEFUL WEBSITES
http://nysparks.state.ny.us/parks
www.visitithaca.com

LINK YOUR TRIP
www.lonelyplanet.com/trip-planner

Art Parks & Public Art

WHY GO The Hudson Valley has inspired artists to live and work amid its abundant nature for generations, creating a rich history of art parks and museums that continues to draw visitors into the Hudson Highlands and offers endless discoveries for the artistically adventurous, like photographer Daniel Aubry.

Art and nature go hand-in-hand in New York, from the famous Hudson River paintings of Thomas Cole to the folksy musings of balladeer Pete Seeger. Start to get a feel for the deep, rich green forests that inspired generations by following the Palisades Parkway north into **1** **Harriman State Park**, the largest in the state. Amid its rocky and tree-lined hiking paths are more than 20 mountain-fed streams and lakes, giving sustenance to shy, white-tailed deer, stately blue herons, and – in the remotest regions – even a big cat or two. Harriman Park connects to the smaller but equally untrammeled **2** **Bear Mountain Park**. Just north of Manhattan, these two forests signal that you have left the city and are now entering the lush Hudson Valley.

Bear Mountain's most picturesque trails wind up steep hills and end at the area's many mountain lakes. Many hikes are long and fairly vigorous. Get a taste of the rampant nature with a drive to **3** **Fort Montgomery State Historic Site** in Bear Mountain Park, off Rte 9W. It offers a picture-perfect view from its cliffside perch overlooking the Hudson River. It's hard to believe the pastoral site was once host to a fierce skirmish with the British. The old foundations still traced in the red earth are the original fortresses American soldiers hunkered behind while they tried to hold off the enemy. A newly opened museum at the entrance has artifacts and more details on the bloody battle.

Stop to drink in more of the scenery at the **4** **Silver Mine** exit off Palisades Parkway. The lakeside picnic grounds are dotted with yellow

TIME
2 days

DISTANCE
95 miles

BEST TIME TO GO
Mar – Nov

START
Harriman State Park

END
Beacon

ALSO GOOD FOR

OUTDOORS

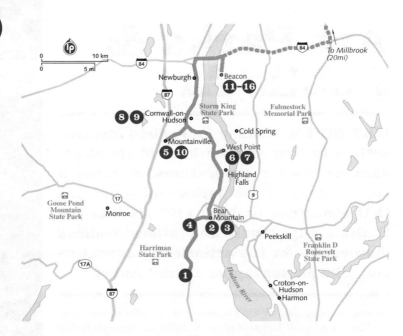

dandelions and red and orange Indian paintbrush flowers. There's an easy hike around the site – pick up a map at the visitors center just off the main road. Or enjoy a quiet picnic while you listen to the calls of the mallard ducks that populate the big pond.

ASK A LOCAL

"Don't miss Andy Goldsworthy's whimsical stone structure installation, *A Wall That Took a Walk*, at Storm King Art Center. The wall meanders through the woods, then enters a pond and comes out on the other side. Its hump-backed spine grows and shrinks and juts off in surprising directions, playing tricks on your eyes while you walk."

Daniel Aubry, New York City & Beacon

As you travel north from the state parks, you'll arrive at a little hamlet known as Mountainville, famous for its outdoor sculpture park, **5 Storm King Art Center**. Local photographer, Daniel Aubry, describes this 500-acre tract of lovingly landscaped lawns, fields and woodlands as a one-of-a-kind outdoor installation. Placed carefully among the flowing grasses, rocky paths and brash thickets of pine trees are huge abstracted steel works by the likes of Richard Serra, Alexander Calder, Isamu Noguchi and Mark di Suvero. Each of these massive works is intended to be seen in relation to the ever-changing nature around it. At any moment, your perception of a piece can change, altered by the moving skyline and gyrating grasses teased by the wind. The sculptures can appear as harsh and intrusive hunks of metal in the sharp morning sun, strange and curious visitors in the lowering twilight or bedeviled creations when a summer storm strikes.

Leave your artistic side behind for a moment and stop in to visit Storm King's neighbor, the burg of ❻ **West Point**. It's home to the famous military academy – an incongruous cohabitant for arty Mountainville. ❼ **West Point Academy's** 16,000 acres occupy one of the most breathtaking bends of the Hudson River, definitely worth a stroll, and contain many fine examples of American military art – all on display on the manicured fragrant lawns.

West Point's strange mix of military and bohemian cultures continues a 10-minute drive away in Cornwall-on-Hudson at ❽ **Inn at Painter's**. This offbeat but entertaining place to spend the night, or at least grab a bite and a drink, has seven rambling rooms filled with local artwork and splashy murals. Visiting Admirals tend to prefer the more formal ❾ **Cromwell Manor Inn**, a Greek Revival mansion that looks like something from *Gone With the Wind* but set down in the rugged Hudson Valley. If the art at Storm King beguiled you into wanting more, then stay at the ❿ **Storm King Lodge**, a white clapboard B&B with a massive back porch that overlooks the art center's massive meadows.

Next day it's off to bucolic ⓫ **Beacon**, a riverside town, home to Daniel Aubry's studio, as well as ⓬ **Dia: Beacon**, a former factory that's now a major museum, stuffed full of large-scale installations. This 3000-sq-ft offshoot of the Dia Gallery in New York is a short walk from the center of town. Inside its industrial walls are big names on a big scale, including an entire room of Andy Warhol shadow paintings, and a hanger-sized space to house Richard Serra's *Torqued Ellipses*. Aubry describes stepping inside as a strange sensation: "the abundant energy and nature that permeate the Hudson Valley are oddly absent in this larger-than-life museum, its huge pieces, shorn of any context, hanging like carcasses on the thick and rough metal walls."

DETOUR A wealthy couple in Millbrook, north of Beacon, donated **Innisfree** (www.innisfreegarden.com), their private garden, to the public in 1960, revealing several carefully cultivated acres done in the Eastern style – "cup" gardens and berms in lieu of large, sprawling, geometric patterns. Stones, lakes and natural growths are incorporated "as is," creating a lovely tranquility that seems spontaneous, but with the same impact as a great work of art.

Once you're ready to come back to human scale and reconnect with humankind, head to Main St and swing by ⓭ **Cup & Saucer Tea Room**, a Victorian sandwich shop that uses thick and crunchy homemade bread and makes delicious scones and quiches. For an especially hearty meal, stop at the ⓮ **Piggy Bank**, a Southern-style Beacon favorite with meaty pulled pork and ribs.

Wind up with a stroll down Main St for a look at the gallery scene. Aubry recommends ⓯ **Fovea**, a nonprofit gallery devoted entirely to photojournalism, while ⓰ **Van Brunt**, attracting top-shelf talent, is another standout.
Ginger Adams Otis

HISTORY & CULTURE

TRIP INFORMATION

GETTING THERE
Rte 9W brings you into Mountainville and Storm King. Cross to the Hudson River's east side to get to Beacon and the Dia center.

DO
Dia: Beacon
Huge pieces of art hang in this former factory, which still has a gritty, industrial feel. ☎ 845-440-0100; www.diabeacon.org; 3 Beekman St, Beacon; adult/senior/child under 12 $10/7/free; ☷ 11am-6pm Mon-Thu May-Oct, 11am-4pm Fri-Mon Oct-May; ♿

Fort Montgomery State Historic Site
Gorgeously located former Revolutionary fort. ☎ 845-446-2134; http://nysparks.state .ny.us; Rte 9W, Bear Mountain Park; adult/ senior $3/2; ☷ museum 9am-5pm Wed-Sun, grounds daily; ♿ ⛰

Fovea
The best photojournalism from around the world is the focus of this collectively run gallery. ☎ 845-765-2199; www.foveaeditions .org; 143 Main St, Beacon; admission free; ☷ hours vary depending on exhibits

Storm King Art Center
Some 500 acres of untouched nature and all types of sculptures. ☎ 845-534-3115; www.stormking.org; Old Pleasant Hill Rd, Mountainville; adult $10, child & senior $9; ☷ 11am-5:30pm Wed-Sun Apr-Nov, 11am-8pm Sat May-Aug; ♿ ⛰

Van Brunt
Diverse artwork by modern and contemporary artists in print, multimedia and traditional mediums. ☎ 845-838-2995; www .vanbruntgallery.org; 460 Main St, Beacon; admission free; ☷ 11am-6pm Thu-Mon

LINK YOUR TRIP

West Point Academy
A bus tours the statue-filled grounds, or walk solo through the museum, 5 miles north of Bear State Park. ☎ 845-938-2638; www .usma.edu; Rte 9W, West Point; bus tour $7; ☷ 9am-4:45pm; ♿

EAT
Cup & Saucer Tea Room
Step into a world of high teas and flaky scones, quiches and biscuits at this Victorian-era-inspired café. ☎ 845-831-6287; 165 Main St, Beacon; mains $3-15; ☷ lunch; ♿

Piggy Bank
A cute name for a BBQ restaurant in an 1880s bank; this is food worth investing in. ☎ 845-838-0028; www.piggybankrestaurant.com; 448 Main St, Beacon; mains $8-18; ☷ lunch & dinner; ♿

SLEEP
Cromwell Manor Inn
Romantic fireplaces, wood floors and free wi-fi in the restored manor and detached cottage. ☎ 845-534-7136; www.cromwell manor.com; 174 Angola Rd, Cornwall-on-Hudson; r with shared bathroom $145, ste up to $380; ♿

Inn at Painter's
Eclectic and fun, this is an inn, a bar and an art gallery rolled into one. ☎ 845-534-2109; www.painters-restaurant.com; 266 Hudson St, Cornwall-on-Hudson; r $149-200; ☷ 11am-9pm; ♿

Storm King Lodge
Storm King's pool, gardens and back suites look right into the art center. ☎ 845-534-9421; www.stormkinglodge.com; 100 Pleasant Hill Rd, Mountainville; r $150-195; ♿

USEFUL WEBSITES
http://nysparks.state.ny.us/parks/

www.lonelyplanet.com/trip-planner

New York Wine Trail

WHY GO Follow the grapes from the sandy soil of Long Island, where vines are cooled by salty Atlantic breezes, to the grittier, mineral-filled land of upstate New York. You'll explore beautiful beaches and verdant mountains in your quest for the perfect vino.

No trip to the Hamptons is complete without a glimpse of at least one of its beach villages and a taste – or two – of its award-winning wines. You can enjoy both by starting your trip in the sandy enclave of ❶ **Southampton**, a village of sprawling old mansions and old money, where strolling down trendy Main St in beachwear is frowned upon, but partying late into the night at summer hot spots is an honored pastime.

Get your bearings at the ❷ **Golden Pear**, a favorite local café, followed by a walk around town. Before wine-making and catering to the celebrity crowd became Long Island's two most dominant industries, it was a whaling and seafaring community. Its colonial roots are evident at ❸ **Halsey House**, the oldest residence in the Hamptons, and the nearby ❹ **Southampton Historical Museum**, a perfect place to learn more about the region's former seafaring ways before diving into its wine country. It has a homey collection of local relics displayed in a restored 1843 sea-captain's house, plus ❺ **Rogers Mansion**, an old sea-captain's residence full of whaling lore.

Now that you've got a thirst going, drive along Montauk Hwy east from Southampton toward the first of three local wineries that you'll be visiting along the South Fork shore of the Hamptons. You'll know you've arrived at ❻ **Duck Walk Vineyards** when you spot a reddish-brick, Normandy-style chateau, fronted by spiky blue spruce trees and backed by row upon row of neatly clipped grape shoots clinging tightly to the sandy soil. Explore the 130 acres of the Damiano family estate,

TIME	**3 days**
DISTANCE	**170 miles**
BEST TIME TO GO	**Mar – Nov**
START	**Southampton**
END	**Keuka Lake**
ALSO GOOD FOR	

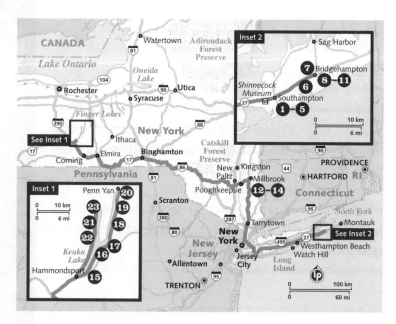

and you'll get an up close look at the startling variety of libations produced here: merlot, sauvignon, a late-harvest gewürztraminer, pinot grigio, blush wines, two kinds of port and even boysenberry wine.

Don't go overboard in the Duck Walk tasting room though – there's still the road to ❼ **Channing Daughters Vineyard** to navigate, following the ubiquitous "wine trail" signs. A 3.5-mile drive brings you to the vineyard's glass-paned French doors.

Step across the wide, stone patio, dotted with plush chaise lounges that look out on to 30 acres of vine trellises and grape plants, and taste your way through Channing's citrusy white wines and deep, oaky reds. Keep your eyes peeled for the Alice-in-Wonderland-like sculptures of owner Walter Channing – his works pop up everywhere, staring down at you from the end posts of vineyard rows and emerging in the shape of towering inverted trees against the horizon. Elsewhere, a 40ft pencil rockets skyward while draped nudes sleep on the patio floor, and a cluster of small footprints tempts you down an unknown path.

It's probably time for some solid food, so follow the road into nearby ❽ **Bridgehampton**, another quaint Hampton village packed with trendy boutiques and restaurants. Grab a gourmet slice on the outdoor patio at ❾ **World's Pie** – dishing up its deep-dish pizza to celebrities and locals with equal bonhomie – or sit down for a more substantial bite at ❿ **Pierre's**, a whimsical

French bistro. Slurp down some salty steamed mussels or power through an egg croque-monsieur while you gaze at the people wandering the main strip.

As you leave Bridgehampton, make a left at the first traffic light onto Sagg Rd. ⑪ **Wolffer Estates'** graceful, Tuscan-villastyle tasting room is 200yd down on your right. Inside the sun-faded ocher walls – with window shutters painted a bright Grecian blue – you can taste the crisp whites and earthy reds Wolffer is renowned for while lounging under massive, wooden beams. Experiment with some of the vineyard's more unusual brews, including an apple wine, verjus and rose wines, and sweet dessert drinks.

"...Alice-in-Wonderland-like sculptures pop up everywhere, staring down at you from the end posts of vineyard rows..."

It's time to say good-bye to the Hamptons and start moving north, into New York wine country. Head for the upstate enclave of Millbrook, where you can overnight at ⑫ **Old Drovers Inn**. The luxury B&B is a lot more welcoming now than when cattle herders used it as a stopover 150 years ago.

Refuel in the morning at ⑬ **Babette's Kitchen**, where you'll find fairtrade coffee in big country mugs, and fresh-from-the-oven organic muffins. Before you continue your wine journey northward, swing by one of New York's flagship upstate wineries: ⑭ **Millbrook Vineyards**. The rich smells of its loamy earth and flower-filled meadows are totally different to Long Island's salty, Atlantic tang – giving you a preview of how the flavors of their wines differ as well.

From here you can take a leisurely drive into the heart of the area's vineyards, keeping an eye out for shimmering ⑮ **Keuka Lake**, one of the many picturesque wine trails in the storied Finger Lakes region. Although small when compared to the Great Lakes of Erie and Ontario, Keuka is about 20 miles long and in some parts up to 2 miles wide, its lush vegetation uninterrupted except for the neat patches of grape plants in vineyards. Keuka is surrounded on both sides by two small state parks that keep it relatively pristine. One of its old canals has been converted into a rustic bike path, and it's a favorite lake for trout fishers. The biggest draw, however, has to be the nearly two dozen wineries that line its shores. The rich soil has been put to good use, and wineries are eager to have visitors sample their distinctive wares.

DETOUR

Before you leave Southampton, slip inside the Native American **Shinnecock Museum** at Stonybrook College, owned and run by members of the Shinnecock nation. Housed in a wood, cabinlike building are murals, carved totems, a wigwam, beadwork, old birchbark canoes and a large collection of bronze sculptures that tell the story of the ancient culture that once dominated Long Island. The college is on Montauk Hwy just outside Southampton.

As you pass through Hammondsport, follow Rte 54 to the east, and pull over for a Keuka Lake tradition – lunch at the **16** **Switz Inn**. This is a rowdy, outdoorsy burger joint that also serves up all-you-can-eat crab legs and a weekend fish fry. On hot days you can dive off the dock into the lake.

Follow the winding road as it curves around Keuka Lake and through the thick pine trees to your next destination: the **17** **Ravines Winery**, styled after the owner's family estate in Provence. The south of France vibe permeates the Ravines, from its sparkling whites and rose wines to the briny olives and Provençal-inspired snacks sometimes offered at its tastings.

The Keuka Lake Wine Trail has only just begun, however. Another short stretch of lakeside driving along Rte 54 brings you to **18** **Barrington Cellars**, 500ft off the lake and flush with Labrusca and Vinifera wines made from local grapes. Barrington's deck is a favorite place to stop for a drink – and for the abstemious, the cellars offer vitamin-packed organic grape juice.

WINDMILL FARM & CRAFT MARKET
On Saturdays in summer everyone flocks to this outdoor market to check out the Amish and Mennonite goods, ranging from hand-carved wooden rockers to homegrown veggies and flowers, and even old-fashioned hand-sewn quilts and duvets. There's plenty here to keep you busy. The market convenes just outside Penn Yan, the largest village on Keuka Lake's shores. Go to www.thewindmill.com for detailed directions.

Rte 54 continues north, curling around the top of Keuka Lake as you arrive at **19** **Rooster Hill** and **20** **Keuka Spring** vineyards – two more local favorites that offer tastings and tours in pastoral settings. Rooster Hill's fine whites – sparkling gewürztraminers and refined Rieslings – spark a buzz among wine aficionados, and Keuka Spring has won many awards for its oaky cabernet franc, a Lemberger grown from Austrian grapes and a cherry-infused pinot noir.

As you pass through the tiny village of Branchport, keep an eye out for **21** **Hunt Country Vineyards** and **22** **Stever Hill Vineyards**, the latter of which has its tasting room in a restored old barn. Both wineries are family run and edging into their sixth generation. On top of tastings there are tours of the grape-growing facilities, and snacks from the vineyard's own kitchens.

Backtrack into Branchport, and track down the **23** **Gone with the Wind B&B**. Every room in the old stone home is named after a character or theme from Scarlett O'Hara's fictional life – and the newly built adjacent mansion is referred to as "The Sequel." With the rippling lake at your feet, a huge, wrap-around deck to sit on, and the flicker of fireflies keeping complete darkness at bay, this is the perfect place to end a day of winery touring.

Ginger Adams Otis

TRIP INFORMATION

GETTING THERE
From Long Island, head north along the Taconic State Parkway to Millbrook, and I-86 toward Keuka Lake and Hammondsport.

DO

Barrington Cellars
An innovative family-run vineyard that experiments with grapes and fruit brews like peach and apple. ☎ 315-531-8923; www.barringtoncellars.com; 2794 Gray Rd, Penn Yan; admission free; 🕑 11am-5:30pm Mon-Sat, noon-5:30pm Sun; 🚻

Channing Daughters Vineyard
As much outdoor art park as winery, grab a fat cabernet to drink while you stroll. ☎ 631-537-7224; www.channingdaughters.com; 1927 Scuttlehole Rd, Bridgehampton; admission $5; 🕑 11am-5pm, with seasonal variations; 🚻

Duck Walk Vineyards
More than 100 acres of roots, vines and perfectly arranged trellises grace this family estate. ☎ 631-726-7555; www.duckwalk.com; 231 Montauk Hwy (Rte 27), Water Mill; admission free; 🕑 11am-5pm; 🚻

Halsey House
An original 1600s house (with a rare "Breeches Bible"), built by an English peer. ☎ 631-283-3527; www.southamptonhistoricalmuseum.org; 249 S Main St, Southampton; admission $4; 🕑 11am-4pm Fri-Sun, other times by appointment

Hunt Country Vineyards
Twenty-five years of wine-making and 30 gold medals translates into a good quality of grape grown here. ☎ 315-595-2812; www.huntwines.com; 4021 Italy Hill Rd, Branchport; admission free; 🕑 10am-5pm Mon-Sat, noon-5pm Sun; 🚻 🍷

Keuka Spring
Sit atop the lovely knoll overlooking the lake and sip some award-winning seyval blanc, chardonnay and pinot noir. ☎ 315-536-3147; www.keukaspringwinery.com; 243 Rte 54, Penn Yan; admission free; 🕑 11am-5pm Apr-Nov; 🚻

Millbrook Vineyards
A flagship upstate winery, Millbrook produces fantastic, fruity brews and offers tours of its sprawling vineyards. ☎ 845-677-8383; http://millbrookwine.com; 26 Wing Rd, Millbrook; admission free; 🕑 11am-6pm May-Sep, noon-5pm Oct-Apr; 🚻

Ravines Winery
Built on a high ravine, this winery has a Provençal flavor courtesy of its French-born owner. ☎ 607-292-7007; www.ravineswinecellars.com; 14630 Rte 54, Keuka Lake; admission free; 🕑 varied tasting hours; 🚻

Rogers Mansion
This old sea captain's perfectly preserved Greek Revival mansion is luxurious even by today's standards. ☎ 631-283-2494; www.southamptonhistoricalmuseum.org; 17 Meeting House Lane, Southampton; admission $4; 🕑 11am-4pm Fri-Sun, other times by appointment; 🚻

Rooster Hill
The mineral-rich soil has helped this winery win awards for its crispy, sweet Rieslings. ☎ 315-536-4773; www.roosterhill.com; 489 Rte 54, Penn Yan; admission free; 🕑 10am-5pm Mon-Sat, noon-5pm Sun, winter hours vary; 🚻

Southampton Historical Museum
Full of rare artifacts, colonial-era history and art exhibits from local artists. ☎ 631-283-4540; www.southamptonhistoricalmuseum.org; 17 Meeting House Lane, Southampton; admission $4; 🕑 11am-4pm Fri-Sun, other times by appointment

Stever Hill Vineyards
A well-tended family vineyard with a great old barn for tastings and other events. ☎ 315-595-2230; www.steverhillvineyard.com; 3962 Stever Hill Rd, Branchport; admission free; 🕑 11am-6pm Apr-Oct, winter hours vary; 🚻 🍷

Wolffer Estates
Tuscany isn't far away at this Italy-inspired winery. ☎ 631-537-5106; www.wolffer.com; 139 Sagg Rd, Sagaponack; admission free; 🕑 11am-6pm Sun-Wed, 11am-7:30pm Thu, 11am-7pm Fri & Sat, winter hours vary; 🚻

EAT

Babette's Kitchen
Organic croissants, muffins and sandwiches served up with ultra-fresh coffee in this cozy downtown café. ☎ 845-677-8602; www .babetteskitchen.com; 3278 Franklin Ave, Millbrook; mains $2-15; ☷ 7am-7pm Wed-Mon; ♿ 🐾

Golden Pear
Locals crowd this place for the fresh sandwiches, coffee, croissants, homemade fruit tarts and all sorts of baked goods. ☎ 631-283-8900; www.goldenpearcafe .com; 99 Main St, Southampton; mains $3-12; ☷ breakfast & lunch; ♿

Pierre's
It's always busy at this hipster and celebrity hangout with light, summery pasta and fish dishes, close to the beach. ☎ 637-537-5110; www.pierresbridgehampton.com; 2468 Main St, Bridgehampton; mains $3-26; ☷ 8am-10pm

Switz Inn
Hot summer fun at this pizza, burger and beer joint right on the lake. ☎ 607-292-6927; www .theswitz.com; 14109 Keuka Village Rd, Hammondsport; mains $8-16; ☷ 11am-10pm; ♿

World's Pie
Pizzas covered in fresh cheese, delectable sauce and any kind of topping you want – meatballs, basil, spinach and much, much more. ☎ 631-537-7999; 1402 Montauk Hwy, Bridgehampton; mains $8-22; ☷ 11am-midnight; 🐾

SLEEP

Gone with the Wind B&B
This lakeside B&B is every bit as beautiful as Tara, and it has a sweeping deck with great views. ☎ 607-868-4603; www.gonewith thewindonkeukalake.com; 14905 West Lake Rd, Branchport; r $148-190

Old Drovers Inn
A luxurious 150-year-old inn with plenty of opulent amenities and big, sexy four-poster beds. ☎ 845-832-9311; www.olddroversinn .com; Duncan Hill Rd & Old Rte 22, Millbrook; r $149-250

USEFUL WEBSITES
www.keukawinetrail.com
www.liwines.com

LINK YOUR TRIP   www.lonelyplanet.com/trip-planner

Niagara Falls & Buffalo

WHY GO Even the most jaded traveler will be impressed by the thundering spectacle of Niagara Falls, a gushing tribute to the power of nature that's inspired hundreds to take a leap of their own – either a daredevil jump over the falls in a barrel, or into a wedding chapel.

Jump right into the frothing power of ❶ **Niagara Falls** with a whirlwind tour on the ❷ **Maid of the Mist**. It's the closest you can get to the seething, soaking waters without going over in a barrel yourself. The half-hour boat cruise will give you a good perspective on the falls from the American vantage point – including the ❸ **Bridal Veil** that's the most famous – and a sense of the Canadian's panoramic view from ❹ **Horseshoe Falls**.

You'll need a little drying out after that, so walk or drive over the small bridge linking mainland Niagara to ❺ **Goat Island**. This small outpost in the middle of the Niagara River – the border between the US and Canada – is part of the ❻ **Niagara Reservation State Park**, the oldest state park in the country. From Goat Island there are sweeping views of both the Horseshoe Falls and the American cascades. From here it's an easy walk to ❼ **Three Sisters Island**, a series of small outcrops and rapid waters approaching Horseshoe Falls. There's also a walkway, a bit slippery in parts, down to Terrapin Point, the closest viewpoint to the Canadian falls.

For an intense look at the raging falls, take the elevator on Goat Island down to the ❽ **Cave of the Winds**. Its damp wooden walkways bring you to within 25ft of the cataracts.

❾ **Top of the Falls Restaurant** on Goat Island allows you to rest and nosh while still drinking in Niagara's ample, watery bounty. Cross the

TIME
2 days

DISTANCE
25 miles

BEST TIME TO GO
Apr – Nov

START
Niagara

END
Buffalo

ALSO GOOD FOR

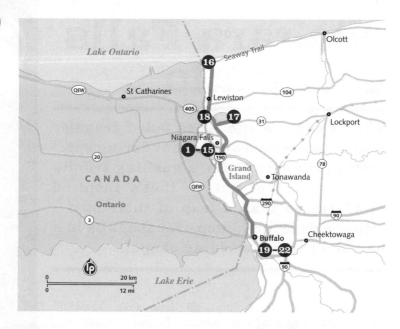

footbridge again to the mainland and enter the **10 Schoellkopf Geological Museum**, a nifty spot dedicated to explaining the area's unique geography. Its exhibits and displays overlook the Niagara Gorge, and there's information on additional nature trails you can hike around the museum. If you're a sure-footed type, consider one of the guided tours along the upper rim of Niagara Falls, or a trip down to the falls' base.

"There's even an old castle on the park grounds, haunted by a headless ghost in search of its missing bits."

Not far away, just north of the Rainbow Bridge that crosses into Canada, is the **11 Aquarium of Niagara Falls**, an often-overlooked family-friendly treat with more than 1500 types of fish, sharks and underwater creatures at hand. The Peruvian penguins, bottlenose dolphins and sea lions all clamor loudly to be fed by visitors – you can watch them romp from an observation deck that affords simultaneous views of the falls.

Even if you're not planning matrimony, consider staying at the **12 Rainbow Bridge B&B and Wedding Chapel**. It's a romantic, cozy Victorian house that's been renovated to perfection, with downy quilts and roaring fireplaces for those cold New York nights, and airy, flower-filled rooms in summer. It's also not far from **13 Seneca Niagara Casino & Hotel**, in case you're feeling lucky, or want to check into the high-end hotel there. **14 Buzzy's** is a local hangout that's been around since 1953, serving up cheesy pizza and buffalo wings, with sauces ranging from mild to atomic. Seafood lovers will want to try ⑮ **Goose's Roost**, with its massive fish platters and clam chowders, or save Goose's for tomorrow morning, when you'll be after fresh coffee and eggs before you head out of town.

Day two kicks off with a 15-mile drive north on the Robert Moses Parkway to the mouth of the Niagara River, not far from Lake Ontario, which you can see in the distance. This is the gateway to ⑯ **Fort Niagara State Park**, home to Old Fort Niagara, a French garrison built in 1726 and later used by the British and Americans in their Revolutionary battles. It has been stunningly restored and offers breathtaking views from its windblown ramparts. There's even an old French castle on the park grounds, supposedly haunted by a headless ghost in search of its missing bits. All around the old fort are well-maintained swimming pools and hiking trails.

NIAGARA SCENIC TROLLEY

It's wet and wild around Niagara Falls, but you don't have to trudge across the park's 3 miles in damp shoes. Take the local trolley that covers all six of the main attractions around the waterfalls. The trolley, an old-fashioned car like those in San Francisco, allows you to jump on and off at will, and one ticket is good for the whole day.

On your way back to Niagara, stop by the local university to check out the ⑰ **Castellani Art Museum**, a 4000-piece collection of works by Picasso, de Kooning, Dali, Modigliani and others. Take in one last look at Niagara's swirling waters at ⑱ **Whirlpool State Park**, about 2 miles outside of Niagara proper, sitting just above a sharp bend in the Niagara River – a bend that creates a giant whirlpool easily visible from your vantage point. Steps will take you 300ft to the gorge below, and mind you don't tumble into the vortex.

Continue your journey south, through Niagara and onto ⑲ **Buffalo**, via Grand Island, a low, scrubby stretch of land accessed by crossing two sky-high, arching bridges. Buffalo is known primarily for football and chicken wings. But it also has a surprising amount of early American architecture, courtesy of one Franklin Lloyd Wright. Spend your afternoon visiting the ⑳ **Albright Knox Art Gallery** and ㉑ **Erie County Botanical Gardens**, then wrap up the day by touring Wright's multilevel masterpiece, the ㉒ **Darwin D Martin Complex**. Wright produced this huge project at age 36, when he was at the height of his "prairie house" phase.

Ginger Adams Otis

TRIP INFORMATION

GETTING THERE
The New York State Thruway is a direct line into downtown Buffalo and north into the Niagara Falls area.

DO
Albright Knox Art Gallery
The heart of Buffalo's art scene is here, along with some major 20th-century works. ☎ 716-882-8700; www.albrightknox.org; 1285 Elmwood Ave, Buffalo; admission $10; ☺ 10am-5pm Wed-Sun

Aquarium of Niagara Falls
Come by at feeding time to hang with penguins, sea lions and other cold-water creatures. ☎ 716-285-3575; www.aquarium ofniagara.org; 701 Whirlpool St; adult/child $9/6; ☺ 9am-5:30pm; ♿

Darwin D Martin Complex
Frank Lloyd Wright's splendid "prairie house" offers a glimpse into the architect's mind. ☎ 716-856-3858, 877-377-3858; www .darwinmartinhouse.org; 125 Jewett Pkwy, Buffalo; admission $15; ☺ call for tours

Erie County Botanical Gardens
Make a reservation to tour these Victorian-era hothouses. ☎ 716-827-1584; www.buf falogardens.com; 2655 S Park Ave, Buffalo; admission $4; ☺ 8am-4pm Mon-Fri

Maid of the Mist
You'll get wet on this wild boat ride around the base of the falls. ☎ 716-284-8897; www.maidofthemist.com; Prospect Park, 151 Buffalo Ave; adult/child $12.50/7.30; ☺ 9:45am-5:45pm; ♿

Niagara Reservation State Park
Home to the Niagara Falls attractions that are accessible from the US side. ☎ 716-284-9449; www.niagarafallsstatepark.com; 151 Buffalo Ave, Niagara Falls; admission to visitors center free; ☺ 7:15am-8pm summer, 8am-6pm winter; ♿

Schoellkopf Geological Museum
The entire 12,000-year history of this natural wonder told through rocks. ☎ 716-278-1070; Niagara Reservation State Park, 151 Buffalo Ave, Niagara Falls; admission $1; ☺ 9am-7pm, winter hours vary; ♿

EAT
Buzzy's
New York–style pizza, spicy buffalo wings, calzones, subs and hoagies for hungry crowds who like to drink beer and watch sports. ☎ 716-283-5333; www.buzzyspizza.com; 7617 Niagara Falls Blvd, Niagara Falls; mains $6-15; ☺ 11am-9pm; ♿

Goose's Roost
Goose's is a hearty diner by day, seafood and Italian joint by night. ☎ 716-282-6255/297-7497; 343 4th St at 10158 Niagara Falls Blvd, Niagara Falls; mains $3-22; ☺ 7am-9pm; ♿

Top of the Falls Restaurant
Sandwiches, soups and salads served atop Goat Island for great views of the falls. ☎ 716-278-0340; www.niagarafalls statepark.com; Goat Island, Niagara Falls; mains $10-18; ☺ 10am-8pm; ♿

SLEEP
Rainbow Bridge B&B and Wedding Chapel
Stay in the honeymoon suite even if you're not getting married – this romantic Victorian oozes connubial bliss. ☎ 716-282-1135; www.rainbowhousebb.com; 423 Rainbow Blvd, Niagara Falls; seasonal rates

Seneca Niagara Casino & Hotel
High rollers love this mega-hotel above the teeming casino. Hit a big score and it'll comp you. ☎ 716-299-1100; www.senecaal-leganycasino.com; 310 4th St, Niagara Falls; r $160-250

USEFUL WEBSITES
www.infoniagara.com

www.lonelyplanet.com/trip-planner

LINK YOUR TRIP

Saratoga Springs: Spas & Races

WHY GO Slather yourself in mineral mud, bathe in Saratoga's sulfurous waters and try your luck with the ponies. This spa town was built around abundant natural springs and its high-energy horse-racing track only adds to the fun.

Start by exploring gracious and stately Saratoga Springs' rows and rows of well-tended ❶ **Victorian homes** in the heart of the city, focusing on Broadway at the north end of Congress Park, where crowds come to shop, eat and stroll up and down the pedestrian-friendly streets.

You'll find a beautifully restored example of 1840s Federalist architecture at 353 Broadway near Caroline St – the ❷ **Rip Van Dam**. The light gray facade is sparingly etched with ellipses, a common motif from the 1800s. Rip Van Dam is one of the few remaining mega-hotels that used to fill with long-term guests every summer. It's now a business center, but, just a few blocks south, at 365 Broadway, you'll find the gold-and-brown ❸ **Adelphi**, a spotlessly preserved Victorian-era hotel that's still in business. Its dark Italianate exterior rises four stories above the street, resting on slender white and cream columns topped with delicate Victorian molding. Step inside and admire the fancy hand stenciling along the lobby walls, or sip a fresh espresso at the turn-of-the-century café and courtyard in the back.

Across the street, not far from the ❹ **Saratoga Visitors Center**, is the formally landscaped ❺ **Congress Park** – make sure you have a cup with you so you can sample the various springs, each with its own flavor. Some taste clear and sweet, fresh as a mountain stream, others are tart and sulfurous, full of carbon from deep underground.

If you want to go all out on the spa experience, make reservations for the ❻ **Crystal Spa**, hidden behind the ❼ **Grand Union Motel**, a Georgian building with simple rooms with fireplaces, and wood and

TIME
2 days

DISTANCE
10 miles

BEST TIME TO GO
Apr – Sep

START
Saratoga Springs

END
Saratoga Springs

ALSO GOOD FOR

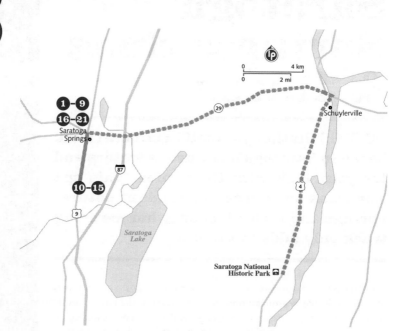

brick walls. Its guests have the run of the spa, which is a private-bath facility that pumps its water from Rosemary Spring. Step onto the smooth tile floors and take your pick from algae body wraps, aromatherapy, sterile mud baths, and other treatments that promise to take inches off your body.

Beyond the spa, about a mile away, is the country's only **❽ National Museum of Dance**, where everyone from Fred Astaire to Mr Bojangles is celebrated. Inside the spacious white marble building, formerly the Washington Bath House, are wall-size murals of tap-dancing greats and displays detailing the careers of masters like Balanchine. The museum is on the way to **❾ Lincoln Baths**, a Georgian-style building where men and women can take separate soaks in the healing waters in semiprivate tubs. The bubbly water at these democratic springs is said to contain 16 different minerals.

"Step onto the smooth tile floors and take your pick from algae body wraps, aromatherapy, sterile mud baths..."

Continue the pampering over lunch at **❿ Gideon Putnam Hotel**, a grand old colonial structure right in the middle of **⓫ Saratoga Spa State Park**, itself a sprawl of manicured lawns, shade-giving oak and maple trees, and gravelly hiking paths skirting mineral springs, picnic grounds and a deep blue pool. The Gideon's Georgian grandeur makes it a delightful place to spend the night, especially if you get one of the porch suites. Besides a big wooden bed, antique light fixtures and floor-to-ceiling windows that come with all the rooms, porch suites have

French doors that lead to your own private deck over the gardens. You can freely wander into the café outside, or step into the cool dark recesses of the hotel's woody pub. The on-site reservation-only spa, the ⑫ **Roosevelt Baths**, gives you a taste of what it was like back in the day, when wealthy New Yorkers came upstate and were scrubbed, wrapped and rubbed into glowing relaxation. The antique bathhouse shows its age, but it's easy to see why a soak here was considered the height of luxury 100 years ago.

Now that you can appreciate a good buffing, go ahead and check out the park's other attractions, starting with the glossy cars at the ⑬ **Saratoga Automobile Museum**, a reclaimed former bottling plant with three galleries full of classic autos and souped-up muscle cars.

In summer months there's almost always a concert or dance recital on at the beautiful outdoor amphitheater that houses ⑭ **Saratoga Performing Arts Center**, the seasonal home to both the New York City Ballet and the Philadelphia Orchestra. In downtown Saratoga Springs, the ⑮ **Saratoga County Arts Council** maintains a 2000-sq-ft art gallery and performance space that in summer presents local theater groups and avant-garde troupes from all around the country.

> **DETOUR** Anyone who paid even scant attention in high-school history remembers hearing about the Battle of Saratoga – a decisive rout of the British in October 1777. The 2800-acre **Saratoga National Historic Park** (www.nps.gov/sara), 14 miles southeast of Saratoga Springs along Rtes 29 and 4, commemorates the fight. Pick up a guide at the park entrance that will take you on a tour of key battle sites and attractions.

It's off to the races for the next morning. Get to the ⑯ **Saratoga Racecourse** early (around 7am) and you can slip in for free. A must-do experience is having breakfast while the horses and jockeys go through their fast-paced morning warm-up. There are also free tours of the backstretch and the stables to keep you occupied until post time – usually 1pm. Get a whiff of old leather at the ⑰ **Saratoga Harness Racing Museum and Hall of Fame**, on the racecourse grounds. Its high-wheeled sulkies, antique horseshoes and equine-loving artwork are worth looking over.

At night, you can blow your winnings at ⑱ **Siro's** jazz-filled steak house, the see-and-be-seen racetrack location, or go local at ⑲ **Hattie's**, a Saratoga institution since 1938, dishing up fried fish, Southern style. For a nightcap, swing by ⑳ **Parting Glass Pub**, usually full of beer drinkers whooping it up to the Irish bands that play here, or visit ㉑ **Caffé Lena**, where Bob Dylan once performed. Folk and acoustic artists, like Ani DiFranco, are regular performers in Saratoga Springs, bringing with them a new generation of travelers who enjoy the city's unique mix of history and pleasure.

Ginger Adams Otis

TRIP INFORMATION

GETTING THERE
Saratoga Springs is accessible along Rte 87 from Albany, and is within a few hours' drive from the Catskills along Rte 90 through Utica.

DO
Lincoln Baths
Saratoga's oldest public bathhouse offers inexpensive but effective super-steamy soaks and rub-downs in the local mineral waters. ☎ 518-583-2880; 65 South Broadway; admission free; ⏲ 10am-5pm Tue-Sun

National Museum of Dance
In an airy old bathhouse you'll find photographs, videos and costumes, and the best memorabilia of American dance. ☎ 518-584-2225; www.dancemuseum.org; 99 South Broadway; admission free; ⏲ 10am-5pm Tue-Sun

Saratoga Automobile Museum
A homage to the car, in all its various forms over the decades. ☎ 518-587-1935; www .saratogaautomuseum.org; 110 Ave of the Pines; adult/child $8/3.50; ⏲ 10am-5pm Tue-Sun; ♿

Saratoga Performing Arts Center
The city's premier performing arts center offers world-class music, dance and recital shows. ☎ 518-584-9330; www.spac.org; 108 Ave of the Pines; admission $20-65; ⏲ hours vary by show; ♿

Saratoga Racecourse
Watch New York–bred beauties race their hearts out on this historic, horseshoe-shaped racetrack. ☎ 518-584-6200; www.saratoga raceway.com; 267 Union Ave; admission $3; ⏲ May-Sep; ♿

EAT
Caffé Lena
Dylan played here, and you're still likely to find the next big acoustic act performing at this friendly, bohemian music venue. ☎ 518-583-0022; www.caffelena.org; 47 Phila St; mains $15-30; ⏲ 8pm-midnight

Hattie's
A tiny, blue-awning storefront restaurant with to-die-for Southern food, plus a full liquor license. ☎ 518-584-4790; www.hatties restaurant.com; 45 Phila St; mains $7-18; ⏲ 4-10pm; ♿

Parting Glass Pub
Traditional Irish pub fare and music, plus friendly, boozy crowds. ☎ 518-583-1916; www.partingglasspub.com; 40-42 Lake Ave; ⏲ 11am-1am

Siro's
A popular after-the-races steak house with a live jazz band that fills up super-fast. ☎ 518-584-4030; www.sirosrestaurant .com; 168 Lincoln Rd; mains $12-30; ⏲ 6-10pm Jun-Sep

SLEEP
Gideon Putnam Hotel
Saratoga's premier spa resort set amid sprawling acres of mineral springs, green lawns and leafy trees, with luxurious suites. ☎ 866-890-1171; www.gideonputnam.com; 24 Gideon Putnam Rd; r $119-300; ♿

Grand Union Motel
A comfortable though barebones motel with no-frills rooms and wood paneling, but a great downtown location. ☎ 518-584-9000; www.grandunionmotel.com; 120 South Broadway; r $84-120

USEFUL WEBSITES
www.saratoga.com
www.saratogaspastatepark.com

LINK YOUR TRIP
TRIP
www.lonelyplanet.com/trip-planner

Adirondack State Park

WHY GO New York's wide, northern territory is dominated by an untamed wilderness of craggy peaks with bushy tufts of spruce trees that loom over a series of idyllic, mirrorlike lakes. Strict land control has kept this park almost pristine; it's a treat to spend time in its rough-hewn, rustic confines.

Enter the Adirondack State Park through the attractive, tourist-friendly enclave of ❶ **Lake George**. This little village is centered on the southern end of the aptly named Lake George, a 32-mile mini-ocean that froths with white-caps on windy days and shines like the placid blue sky on sunny ones. Known as the "Queen of America's Lakes," Lake George has long been the haunt of city-weary artists, history buffs and summer fun seekers.

Not far from the water in downtown Lake George is the ❷ **Fort William Henry Museum**; the fort was built by the British during the French and Indian War (1754–63). It was used as a staging ground for attacks against the garrison that would later become Fort Ticonderoga, and its fall would become the focus of James Fenimore Cooper's epic novel, *The Last of the Mohicans*. Although it's a reconstruction of the 1755 original, the minimalist barracks and dank dungeons certainly seem authentic. Guides dressed in Revolutionary garb muster visitors along, with stops for battle reenactments that include firing period muskets and cannons.

If shivery dungeons aren't frightening enough for you, head along Canada St to the ❸ **House of Frankenstein Wax Museum**, a kitschy little delight that seems oddly out of place in serene Lake George. There are all sorts of monsters and madness in this haunted house (little kids might find it too intense) and if you didn't believe in the Wolfman before, you might after a stop here.

TIME
3 days

DISTANCE
180 miles

BEST TIME TO GO
Apr – Nov

START
Lake George

END
Lake Placid

ALSO GOOD FOR

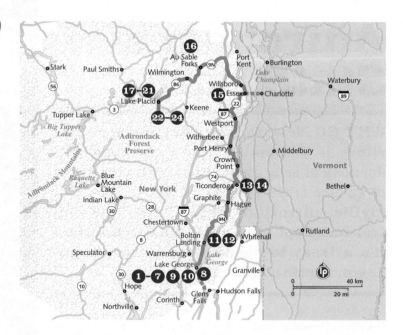

Clear your head with a quick trip around the lake to check out the teeming, wild shoreline and deep blue waters. ❹ **Lake George Steamboat Co's** boats departs from Steel Pier on downtown Beach Rd. Three boats – including the *Minnie Haha,* a paddle wheeler – go out in summer months on one-hour jaunts and half- or full-day trips. ❺ **Prospect Mountain Diner**, back on Canada St, can quench that fresh-air appetite with jumbo burgers, fries, hot dogs and fruity pies.

If you'd rather hit the beach, there's a perfect strip for lolling on the water- front drive appropriately called Beach Rd – but don't expect that crystal-clear ,spring-fed lake water to be as warm as the rough sand. Heat up with a vol- leyball game, or hang out in the picnic area in the sun. Directly behind the beach is the ❻ **Lake George Battlefield** area, a larger, grassier picnic spot. You'll spy the decaying remains of the original Fort William Henry on the green knolls, and a few monuments to long-gone soldiers.

Just south of the battlefield is the entrance to ❼ **Prospect Mountain**. Follow its 5-mile corkscrew drive upward and you'll find dramatic views of the lake and surrounding mountain ranges – the verdant tips of Vermont's Green Mountain range and even some of New Hampshire's granite peaks are visible.

❽ **Davidson Brothers Restaurant and Brewery** can serve you up an English pub dinner, but be prepared to eat buffalo burgers instead of shepherd's pie – that's the house specialty. You can spend the night at the ❾ **Georgian**, a luxury resort, or within the sprawling grounds and sumptuous suites of the ⑩ **Fort William Henry Hotel**.

An early start the next morning will see you at ⑪ **Bolton Landing**, north of Lake George, in time for breakfast. Bolton Landing is full of stately, stone megamansions that stretch along Lake George's western shore (Lake Shore Dr). These Tudor and Italianate summer houses were once owned by wealthy New Yorkers, who wryly referred to their piles as "cottages." Check out the Sagamore resort, Melody Manor, Sun Castle and Green Harbor Mansion for four of the best examples of what was once known as ⑫ **"Millionaires Row."**

Move from old money to old military as you leave Bolton Landing and follow the rough Adirondack road to ⑬ **Fort Ticonderoga**, 30 miles northeast. The small town of Ticonderoga is known essentially for two things: the No 2 pencil factory that's long since shut down, and its iconic fort. Since it was taken from the British in 1775 by the "Green Mountain Boys" (a group of independence-loving hotheads from

Take an afternoon visit to **Glens Falls**, about 10 miles south of Lake George along Rte 9. Its chief attraction is the Hyde Collection, a remarkable gathering of art amassed by local newspaper heiress Charlotte Pryun Hyde. In her rambling Florentine Renaissance mansion you'll stumble across Rembrandts, Rubens, Matisses and Eakins, as well as tapestries, sculptures and turn-of-the-century furnishings.

Vermont led by Ethan Allen and Benedict Arnold), Fort Ticonderoga has been synonymous with the American Revolution. Nowadays its buckling stone walls and rickety wooden outposts, affording stellar views of the surrounding lakes, can barely sustain their own weight, let alone that of a 300lb cannon. But every summer the carefully preserved fort opens its doors for tours and reenactments of famous war moments.

It's a good idea to fuel up on gas and food before leaving Ticonderoga. Grab a bite at the ⑭ **Hot Biscuit Diner**, and then hit the Lakes to Locks Passage – the famously curving, scenic Rte 22 that twists along Lake Champlain toward the historic village of Essex. Each turn brings a new view of Lake Champlain's sculpted shores, pushed up against the foothills of the Green Mountains. On the other side, it's all wavy gold meadows and carefully sculpted fields. A good place to stop for the night is ⑮ **Essex Inn**, built in 1810 when this village was a port stop for boats hauling goods north. The soft-yellow boarding house has all the creaky charm you'd expect from a 200-year-old landmark.

A drive north to Keesville kicks off your morning, as you head toward one of New York's most exciting natural wonders. For those who thrill to nature – or like their nature to be thrilling – there's no beating ⑯ **Au Sable Chasm**, formed by a gushing river that over thousands of years carved its way through deep layers of sandstone, creating 200ft cliffs, waterfalls and rapids.

Au Sable's hiking trails (aided in some places by swinging connecting bridges and a sleek cable car) wind up and down the canyon's nearly 2-mile length. Unique rock formations are marked on hiking maps – look for the Elephant's Head, Devil's Oven, Mystic Canyon, Rainbow Falls and more. When the call of the sun-dappled waters gets too hard to resist, lazily slide downriver in a rented kayak or inner-tube, gazing at the birds and butterflies that fill the light-filled gorge. If adrenaline is your drug, opt for the rafting tours – shooting between ancient rocks at white-water speeds really gets the heart pumping.

DETOUR Neighboring Vermont is within your reach at Essex – just jump on the stately ferry that crisscrosses Lake Champlain and in 20 minutes you'll be in **Charlotte**, VT, a quaint hamlet established in 1792 and dedicated to farming and rustic pursuits like making maple syrup and maple syrup candy. The ferry runs all day and can have you back on the New York side of the lake before nightfall.

By day's end, make tracks about 30 miles southwest to Lake Placid, where you can tuck into the **17 Mirror Lake Inn** or **18 Paradox Lodge** for the night, two quaint local-run retreats. Before you begin your Olympic odyssey next morning, stop in at **19 Blues Berry Bakery** or **20 Saranac Sourdough**, two of the best breakfast options.

Take a stroll around downtown Lake Placid and keep an eye out for the 30ft-tall Lake Placid Toboggan Chute (near the post office), one of many Olympic mementoes left in the area. The official **21 Olympic Center** is on Main St, a large white building where the inside temperatures are kept bone-chillingly cold, thanks to the four large skating rinks where athletes come to train. Hockey fans will recognize this complex as the location of the 1980 "Miracle on Ice," when the upstart US hockey team managed to defeat the seemingly unstoppable Soviets and win Olympic gold. You can relive that and other sports glory days with a visit to the Lake Placid Winter Olympics Museum, inside the center.

Not far from town on Rte 73 is the **22 Mackenzie-Intervale Ski Jumping Complex**, an all-weather training facility for ski jump teams. A 7-mile scenic drive south of the Kodak facility brings you to **23 Mt Van Hoevenberg**, home to Olympic bobsledding.

As you head back to Lake Placid on Rte 73, stop off at the **24 John Brown Farm State Historic Park**, former homestead and final resting place of the famous abolitionist who tried to spark a slave revolt at Harpers Ferry, West Virginia in 1859. Brown and his followers were executed and later interred on his 24-acre farm. You can take a quiet stroll around the fragrant grounds – full of buzzing bees and flowers in summer and icy cross-country ski trails in winter – and study the graves.

Ginger Adams Otis

TRIP INFORMATION

GETTING THERE
Follow Rte 87 north from Saratoga Springs into Adirondack State Park and to the village of Lake George.

DO
Au Sable Chasm
Hike, walk or inner-tube your way around this deep gorge, formed by gushing river waters. ☎ 518-834-7454; www.ausable chasm.com; 2144 Rte 9; adult/child/under 5 $16/9/free; ☾ year-round; ♿ 🐾

Fort Ticonderoga
An eerie, rickety and vivid reminder of Revolutionary soldiers' frigid hardships. ☎ 518-585-2821; www.fort-ticonderoga .org; Sandy Redoubt Rd, Ticonderoga; adult/senior/child $15/13.50/7; ☾ 9am-5pm May 10-Oct 20; ♿ 🐾

Fort William Henry Museum
Impeccably dressed guides lead informative tours and conduct battle reenactments at this old British fort. ☎ 518-668-5471; www .fwhmuseum.com; Canada St at Rte 9, Lake George; adult/senior/child $14.95/12.95/8; ☾ 9am-6pm May-Oct; ♿ 🐾

House of Frankenstein Wax Museum
An oddball attraction that's part haunted house, part museum; little kids might not like it. ☎ 518-668-3377; www.frankenstein waxmuseum.com; 213 Canada St, Lake George; adult/child $9/4.50; ☾ 9am-11pm Jun-Sep, noon-6pm Oct-May

John Brown Farm State Historic Park
Visit the famous abolitionist's former family farm, where he and his sons are buried. ☎ 518-523-3900; John Brown Rd, Lake Placid; admission $2; ☾ 10am-5pm Wed-Sat, 1-5pm Sun May-Oct; ♿ 🐾

Mackenzie-Intervale Ski Jumping Complex
Suit up and test your ability to withstand heights at this training/competition center. ☎ 518-523-2202, 800-462-6236; www.orda .org; 8 John Brown Rd, Rte 73, Lake Placid; adult/child $10/8; ☾ hours vary seasonally

Mt Van Hoevenberg
Trolley tour your way along the bobsled and luge training tracks. ☎ 518-523-4436; 8 John Brown Rd, Rte 73, Lake Placid; adult/child $10/8, bobsled rides $30; ☾ hours vary seasonally; ♿

Olympic Center
Details on 1980 Olympic sites, plus a glimpse at the training rigors undergone by world-class athletes. ☎ 518-523-1655; www.orda .org; 2634 Main St, Lake Placid; adult/child $5/3; ☾ 10am-5pm; ♿ 🐾

EAT
Blues Berry Bakery
A cheery bakery with fresh-from-the-oven cakes, croissants, brioches, cookies, tarts, éclairs and more. ☎ 518-523-4539; http: //bluesberrybakery.com; 26 Main St, Lake Placid; mains $2-22; ☾ 7am-6pm Mon-Sat, 8am-4pm Sun; ♿

Davidson Brothers Restaurant and Brewery
An old-fashioned pub, with stouts, ales and hearty lagers as well as heaping fish and meat platters. ☎ 518-743-9026; www.david sonbrothers.com; 184 Glen St, Glens Falls; mains $8-22; ☾ lunch & dinner; ♿

Hot Biscuit Diner
Heaping plates of fresh eggs, farm bacon, organic burgers, and biscuits from the wood stove oven. ☎ 518-585-3483; http://hot biscuitdiner.com; 14 Montcalm St, Ticonderoga; mains $5-15; ☾ 8am-7pm; ♿

Prospect Mountain Diner
Hoary fisherfolk, rustic locals and wealthy second-homers all rub elbows here over waffles, burgers and homemade pies. ☎ 518-668-9721; Canada St, Lake George; mains $3-12; ☾ 7am-9pm; ♿

Saranac Sourdough
A great deli with fantastic morning coffee and thick, meaty sandwiches that can be packed up to go. ☎ 518-523-4897; 2126 Saranac Ave, Lake Placid; mains $4-12; ☾ 7am-4pm; ♿

SLEEP

Essex Inn
A 200-year-old charmer, with seven rooms all decorated with period furnishings, and a wide veranda and back garden. ☎ 518-963-8821; www.theessexinn.com; 2297 Main St, Essex; r with shared bathroom $95, private bathroom $125-160

Fort William Henry Hotel
A gorgeous megaresort with sweeping mountain and lake views and modern, comfy rooms an arm's length from the water. ☎ 800-234-0267, 518-668-3081; www.fortwilliamhenry.com; 48 Canada St, Lake George; r $159-269

Georgian
A beautiful, sprawling lakeside resort with a marina and pools. The spacious rooms are marred slightly by outdated decor and furnishings. ☎ 518-668-5401; www.georgianresort.com; 384 Canada St, Lake George; r $189-289, ste $389

Mirror Lake Inn
Perched in the Adirondack Mountains, this high-end resort has large, plushly carpeted rooms with balconies overlooking the water. ☎ 518-523-2544; www.mirrorlakeinn.com; 77 Mirror Lake Dr, Lake Placid; r from $300

Paradox Lodge
A cedar-wood paradise, reminiscent of a well-appointed hunting lodge, with cozy fireplaces and Native American print rugs. ☎ 518-523-9078; www.paradoxlodge.com; 76 Saranac Ave, Lake Placid; r $135-245

USEFUL WEBSITES
www.adirondacks.com
www.visitadirondacks.com

LINK YOUR TRIP
www.lonelyplanet.com/trip-planner

St Lawrence Seaway

WHY GO Dive into the watery world of the St Lawrence Seaway, an island-studded stretch of small towns and fishing villages backed by the vivid blues of Lake Ontario and the St Lawrence River. Boldt Castle – a looming, Gothic wonder – is one of many turn-of-the-century dream homes dotting the Thousand Islands.

Head east out of Rochester and pick up the ❶ **Seaway Trail**, a National Scenic Byway, running alongside Lake Ontario on Rte 3. The twisting coastal road takes you through several little fishing hamlets, picturesque harbors, orchards and farmer stands stacked with brightly colored fruits and glass jars of plummy preserves.

Within a half-hour's drive is ❷ **Sodus Point**, home of a three-story, stone and clapboard lighthouse that's now a museum. You can take a break from driving and climb its 52 circular steps into the old lens room for a bird's-eye view of massive Lake Ontario, or just sit on its wide circular porch and enjoy the salty breezes.

Further northeast, still on the Seaway Trail, is the port town of ❸ **Oswego**. It's home to another old lighthouse just waiting to be explored – but this one involves a walk along a lengthy breakwater that juts well into the sea. An easier approach to ❹ **Oswego West Pierhead Lighthouse** is to take in its delicate silhouette in the distance as you stroll the historic waterfront that's backed by gorgeous resort homes, including the ❺ **Richardson-Bates House Museum**, an Italian villa built by a wealthy family in the late 1800s.

At the end of the town's main pier, you'll find the ❻ **H Lee White Marine Museum**, full of detailed information about the Pierhead Lighthouse. While you meander across the salt-flecked stones – courtesy of

TIME
2 – 3 days

DISTANCE
200 miles

BEST TIME TO GO
May – Sep

START
Rochester

END
Alexandria Bay

ALSO GOOD FOR

OUTDOORS

BEST TRIP

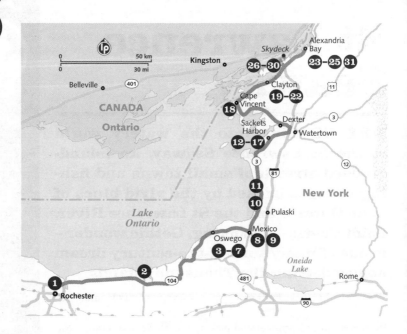

the brackish water in these parts – take note of the tugboat *Nash* moored at the pier; it served in the Normandy invasion in WWII.

Join the locals lining up for fresh fish and fries at **7** **Rudy's Lakeside Drive-Thru**, an Oswego institution that's straight out of the 1950s. Then continue north on the Seaway Trail. There's plenty of opportunity to get out and hike or bird-watch along the way.

You'll pass the **8** **Derby Hill Bird Observatory** in the woodsy and rural area north of Oswego, a state park that also contains the famous **9** **Salmon River** – the location fly-fishermen dream of when planning their perfect vacation. A walk around these challenging shores will bring you in close contact with northern New York's fiercely rampant nature – soaring trees, rough marsh grasses and big birds with sharp talons abound.

Next along the coast is **10** **Port Ontario**, which has its own protected light-house, the Selkirk, one of only four in the country with original hexagonal and iron lights intact. Beach lovers shouldn't miss a pit stop at **11** **Sandy Pond**, still on your northward route. This barrier beach has walkovers set up so pedestrians can enjoy the salty sand without disturbing fragile dunes and adjacent wetlands. There's plenty of wildlife to see, including frogs and turtles, especially if you arrive during the busy sunset hours, when the night crawlers start to stir.

A lovely place to spend the night is ⑫ **Sackets Harbor**, an old fishing village perched on a big lakeside bluff. Its history is worth exploring, but for tonight, content yourself with a few drinks and dinner at ⑬ **Tin Pan Galley**, an informal alfresco delight, or the more mainstream ⑭ **Sackets Harbor Brewing Company**, looking over the marina. Both are in easy walking distance of ⑮ **Ontario Place**, a classy, old waterfront hotel, and the more romantic ⑯ **Candlelight B&B**, a 19th-century Georgian with four-poster beds.

Swing by the ⑰ **Sackets Harbor Battlefield** before you leave town in the morning – two important battles were fought here in the War of 1812. When the battle reenactments are on – performed by history-loving locals who enjoy wearing uniforms – you can practically smell the cannon smoke as old shooters are wheeled around to take aim at the retreating Red Coats. You can also learn more about the coastal trail you're now driving with a stop at the Seaway Trail Discovery Center, nine rooms full of interactive displays and features about life on the St Lawrence River and the shores of Lakes Erie and Ontario.

As Rte 104 turns into Rte 12E, you'll pass numerous old lighthouses, including the white-stucco and red-roofed ⑱ **Tibbetts Point Lighthouse** at Cape Vincent, formerly a coast guard entity and now a lakeside youth hostel.

Next up is ⑲ **Clayton**, and the ⑳ **Antique Boat Museum**. If looking at old vessels doesn't sound like your kind of morning, consider that this museum lets you actually sail (or sometimes row) the boats while you learn. ㉑ **Thousand Islands Museum** has warehoused all kinds of photography and writing about island culture dating from the 1800s. The museum also has a rotating exhibit of local artists, plus examples of the fine carving for which the region is famous. Another big draw is the ㉒ **Handweaving Museum and Arts Center**. If you don't consider weaving is an art, you'll know better by the time you leave Clayton.

GO NATIVE

Paddle to the biggest and best of the Thousand Islands the old-fashioned way – in a canoe or a kayak. Clayton native Jan Brabant leads tours (www.tiadventures.com) along the historic coastline and into off-the-beaten-path wildlife reserves, but he saves his toughest trip – The Grinder – for those willing to muscle their way a mile and a half into the river to Grindstone Island.

The next leg of this easy drive will bring you to ㉓ **Alexandria Bay**, a great home base while you explore the Thousands Islands that dot the St Lawrence River. Get your bearings over burgers and fries at ㉔ **Dockside Pub**, a friendly hangout where visitors like to trade travel stories over beers at the dark-wood bar, or ㉕ **Chez Paris**, an unpretentious French café with fresh sandwiches, salads and homemade deep-dish peach and apple pies.

Take the afternoon to visit ㉖ **Wellesley Island State Park**, a 2600-acre floating village that's connected to the mainland by the Thousand Islands International Bridge. Its abundant wildlife, plus marina, ponds and ㉗ **Minna Anthony Common Nature Center** – which has exhibits on the islands' animal life – will further pull you into the mysterious allure of these sparsely inhabited islands.

DETOUR On the other side of Wellesley, at the end of the Thousand Islands International Bridge, is the fantastic **Skydeck** (☎613-659-2335), a 395ft observation tower that belongs to Canada – but you can enjoy it if you have valid ID on you (a passport is best). The elevator ride to the top gives excellent views of the sprawling Thousand Islands.

You can spend the night on the islands if you like, either camping or bedding down in huge, ski-lodge-sized ㉘ **Hart House Inn**. Pedal your way down shady lanes and along the sandy coastline on the inn's free bikes, or just wander among the flower- and gazebo-filled gardens of this romantic B&B. At night, step aboard for a dinner cruise around the inky darkness of the St Lawrence River. As you bob along the gentle waterway, surrounded by flickering candles, faint silhouettes of the nearby island castles come and go on the horizon.

The grandest and most romantic castle of them all will most likely be first on your list in the morning. Take a ferry to ㉙ **Boldt Castle**, built by George C Boldt, the former proprietor of Manhattan's famed Waldorf-Astoria Hotel. It's a replica of a 120-room Rhineland, Germany castle. Boldt began building it in 1900 for his dying wife Louise, who passed away well before it was finished. Boldt subsequently abandoned the project and it became the provenance of the island's woodland creatures. But since the late 1970s, millions have gone into its restoration, and now the structures are as magnificent as Boldt intended. Look for the big stag deer atop the welcoming Arch, the Hennery, his Alster Tower playhouse, and the grand buildings that would have been for family and guests.

"As you bob along the gentle waterway, silhouettes of the nearby island castles come and go on the horizon."

Another not-to-be-missed island experience means a trip to neighboring ㉚ **Singer Castle**, perched on Dark Island. Built by the president of the Singer sewing machine company, this 20th-century delight was modeled on a classic Scottish castle, giving it lots of long, spooky hallways and dimly lit passages.

Finish off the day with a fruity drink at ㉛ **Bonnie Castle**. Despite the name, this is actually a ritzy resort back on the mainland in Alexandria Bay. Its waterside bar, called Rum Runners, pulls in sunburned workers and tourists from the surrounding sites, all eager to unwind after a long day of island-hopping.

Ginger Adams Otis

TRIP INFORMATION

GETTING THERE
Pick up the Seaway Trail at Rochester, and follow it north, hugging the coast to Alexandria Bay.

DO

Antique Boat Museum
Explore *La Duchesse,* a 1900s luxury houseboat, build a powerboat and celebrate life on the St Lawrence River. ☎ 315-686-4104; www.abm.org; 750 Mary St, Clayton; admission $15; ⏱ 9am-5pm May-Oct; ♿

Boldt Castle
This fairy-tale-like castle was reclaimed from nature in the late 1970s, and is now showcasing its original splendor. ☎ 800-847-5263; www.boldtcastle.com; Heart Island; adult/child $6.50/4; ⏱ 10am-6:30pm May 10-Oct 5, to 7:30pm Jul & Aug; ♿

Derby Hill Bird Observatory
Hike this untouched stretch of land famous for its raptors and other wild birds of prey. www.derbyhill.org; 36 Grand View Ave, Mexico; admission free; ⏱ daily; ♿ 🐾

H Lee White Marine Museum
March through Oswego's maritime history in this old, white coast guard facility. ☎ 315-342-0480; www.hleewhitemarinemuseum.com; W 1st St Pier, Oswego; admission $5; ⏱ 10am-5pm Jul & Aug, 1-5pm Sep-Jun; ♿

Handweaving Museum and Arts Center
Catch a glimpse of amazing local weavers hard at work on old-fashioned looms. ☎ 315-686-4123; www.hm-ac.org; 314 John St, Clayton; admission free; ⏱ 9am-4:30pm Mon-Fri; ♿

Richardson-Bates House Museum
Explore this old Victorian haunt, full of amazingly opulent furnishings and curios. ☎ 315-343-1342; www.rbhousemuseum.org; 135 E Third St, Oswego; donations accepted; ⏱ 10am-5pm Tue-Fri, 1-5pm Sat & Sun; ♿

Sackets Harbor Battlefield
Relive the horrors and glories of battling the British Army at this Revolutionary site. ☎ 315-646-3634; www.sacketsharborbattlefield.org; W Main St, Sackets Harbor; admission free; ⏱ 10am-5pm Wed-Sat, 1-5pm Sun; ♿

Singer Castle
A craggy, Scottish-inspired, nook-filled castle on Dark Island. ☎ 315-324-3275; www.singercastle.com; adult/child $12/6; ⏱ 10am-5pm Sat & Sun May 17-Jun 22, 10am-5pm Jun 23-Sep 4, 10am-5pm Sat & Sun Sep 5-Oct 12; ♿

Thousand Islands Museum
Learn all about the history of these rocky islands and the pioneering people who settled them. ☎ 315-686-5794; www.timuseum.org; 312 James St, Clayton; admission $3; ⏱ 10am-4pm May-Oct; ♿

Tibbetts Point Lighthouse
A gorgeous stone structure with stellar views. ☎ 315-654-2700; www.lighthousefriends.com; Broadway St, Cape Vincent; admission free; ⏱ 10am-7pm Mon-Fri May 25-Jun 22 & Sep 4-Oct 8, 10am-7pm Jun 23-Sep 3; ♿

Wellesley Island State Park
Check out the old Victorian schoolhouse and village left intact on the island. ☎ 315-482-2722; http://nysparks.state.ny.us/parks; 44927 Cross Island Rd, Fineview; admission free; ⏱ daily; ♿ 🐾

EAT & DRINK

Chez Paris
Salads, wraps and renowned, fresh-fruit pies are Chez Paris' signature dishes, served in a cheery, waterfront minibistro. ☎ 315-482-9825; 24 Church St, Alexandria Bay; mains $4-15; ⏱ lunch & dinner; ♿

Dockside Pub
Unpretentious pub fare – burgers, fries, shepherd's pie – served dockside, overlooking the St Lawrence River. ☎ 315-482-9849; 17 Market St, Alexandria Bay; mains $7-18; ⏱ lunch & dinner; ♿

Rudy's Lakeside Drive-Thru
A 1950s-era diner with fresh, deep-fried clams, mussels and haddock. ☎ 315-343-2671; www.rudyshot.com; County Rte 89 & Fred Haynes Blvd, Oswego; mains $8-15; ⏱ 11am-11pm Mar-Sep; ♿

Sackets Harbor Brewing Company
Enjoy home-brewed beers with big burgers, tangy pizzas and spicy wings. ☎ 315-646-2739; www.1812ale.com; 212 W Main St,

Sackets Harbor; mains $8-20; ☺ lunch & dinner Jun-Sep; ⚄

Tin Pan Galley
Pretty, wrought-iron tables and chairs in a blooming garden give this outdoor café a New Orleans feel. ☎ 315-646-3812; www .tinpangalley.com; 110 W Main St, Sackets Harbor; mains $10-18; ☺ 7am-9pm; ⚄

SLEEP

Bonnie Castle
Bonnie Castle has a megaresort with a four-star restaurant, the popular Rum Runners bar that also doubles as a nightclub, and generous rooms. ☎ 315-482-4511; www.bonniecastle .com; Holland St, Alexandria Bay; ste $115-225; ⚄

Candlelight B&B
Big beds, love seats and armoires give this redbrick Georgian B&B a charming vibe. Views are of the battlefields. ☎ 315-646-1518; www.imcnet.net/candlelight; 501 Washington St, Sackets Harbor; r $85-125; ⚄

Hart House Inn
Expansive and lovely, Hart House is part homespun charm and part five-star resort, perfect for romantic getaways. ☎ 888-481-5683; www.harthouseinn.com; 21979 Club Rd, Wellesley Island; ste $200-500; ⚄ ✿

Ontario Place
Aside from the green carpets and chintzy bed covers, rooms are warm and welcoming, with great river views. ☎ 315-646-8000; www .ontarioplacehotel.com; 103 General Smith Dr, Sackets Harbor; r $150-350; ⚄

USEFUL WEBSITES
www.nysparks.com/regions/thousandis.asp
www.seawaytrail.com

LINK YOUR TRIP
www.lonelyplanet.com/trip-planner

Day Trips from New York City

DAY TRIPS

The big city is great, but sometimes you just have to break free. Luckily Manhattan is surrounded by off-the-beaten-track delights, like a European castle high in the hills, a flower-filled Bronx garden and the sandy dunes and lighthouses of Fire Island.

THE CLOISTERS

Gaze at medieval tapestries, frescoes, carvings and gold treasures including a St John the Evangelist plaque dating from the 9th century inside the Metropolitan Museum annex. Set in Fort Tyron Park overlooking the Hudson River, the Cloisters was built to look like an old castle. Works like a 1290 ivory sculpture of the Virgin Mary, ancient stained-glass windows, and oil on wood religious paintings are displayed in galleries connected by grand archways and topped by Moorish terra-cotta roofs, all facing an airy courtyard. The extensive grounds – blanketed in lush green grass and rolling hills – contain more than 250 varieties of medieval herbs and flowers. In summer concerts and performances happen almost nightly. **A 20-minute drive north on Henry Hudson Pkwy gets you to the Fort Tyron-Cloisters exit, right after the George Washington Bridge.**

WAVE HILL

Twenty-eight acres of scenic views, blooming gardens, art galleries, picnic spots and a conservatory will make you believe you've traveled far, far away from the boogie-down Bronx. Built in 1843 by a wealthy lawyer, Wave Hill is now a park, making its panoramic Hudson views available to anyone. Before it became public domain, it played host to the wealthy and well connected. Theodore Roosevelt's family often summered here, and Mark Twain called it home from 1901 to 1903. Its manicured gardens stretch on forever, offering up numerous shady paths, bucolic gazebos and strategically placed benches. The park's taken to setting up public art installations around the grounds – adding a sense of whimsy to the otherwise formal estate – and there are frequent summer dance and music recitals as well. **Go north on Henry Hudson Pkwy to exit 21, 246th-250th St. Continue northbound on the service road to 252nd St. Turn left onto the overpass and turn left again at the light. Turn right at 249th St and proceed to the Wave Hill gate.**

FIRE ISLAND

A skinny barrier island running parallel to Long Island, Fire Island contains much wonder, beauty and flaming adventure along its scant 32 miles, almost all of which are car free. Its federally protected white sand dunes, shrub-filled forests and beach hiking trails pull in thousands of sun-starved city folk every summer. Robert Moses State Park is home to the Fire Island Lighthouse – which holds a minimuseum – and also has a tiny corner dedicated to nude sunbathing. Popular residential hamlets are Davis Park, Fair Harbor, Kismet and Ocean Bay Park. The two most-visited villages are Cherry Grove and The Pines, home to thriving gay populations and Fire Island's best nightlife. **Take the I-495/Long Island Expressway out of Manhattan. For Sayville ferries (to The Pines and Cherry Grove), get off at exit 57 onto the Vets Memorial Hwy. Make a right on Lakeland Ave and take it to the end, following signs for the ferry.**

JAMAICA BAY

Salty, marshy Jamaica Bay Wildlife Refuge sits right on the perimeter of JFK airport. In spring and fall, more than 325 bird species stop in to rest and snack – snapping up all sorts of briny sea creatures, such as clams, turtles, shrimp and oysters. Each season brings different visitors: spring features warblers and songbirds, and American woodcocks in late March. Mid-August, shorebirds start to move south, landing here from Canada to fuel up for the trip to Mexico. Fall is when migrating hawks and raptors get mobile, along with ducks, geese, monarch butterflies and thousands and thousands of dragonflies. Birders and naturalists get the most action around the East and West Ponds, both about 1.5 miles in circumference and easily walkable. Wear shoes good for mud, bring bug repellent and sun screen, carry some water and watch out for poison ivy. **Follow the Belt Pkwy to exit 11S (Flatbush Ave), and follow it south to the third traffic light (before the Marine Pkwy Bridge toll plaza). Turn left at the traffic light and into the park.**
Ginger Adams Otis

NEW JERSEY & PENNSYLVANIA TRIPS

The Big Apple casts a large shadow, and Philadelphia and New Jersey can suffer identity crises because of it. Despite once being the more important American city, Philly now plays second fiddle while New York calls the tune. And Jersey remains, as Ben Franklin once noted, a "barrel tapped at both ends": in north Jersey, residents listen to WPLJ and root for the Yankees and the Giants; in south Jersey, they listen to WMMR and root for the Phillies and the Eagles.

Yet, these states have a lot to offer on their own terms, as these trips show. Jersey will always have its fabulous shore, as well as its quirky diners and famous musical sons and daughters. Jersey also has the overlooked Pine Barrens, a vast, vital wilderness in the midst of this huge urban corridor. Walkable, historic Philadelphia is one of the friendliest cities you'll ever meet, and it's coming into its own as a restaurant town. Relaxing getaways in Pennsylvania include artsy New Hope and Lambertville on the Delaware River and the radically antimodern charms of Dutch Country. What's the biggest surprise? Pittsburgh, that once-dirty steel-town, is now a beautiful, avant-garde delight. Really, go check it out for yourself.

 For classic rock, tune to WPLJ (95.5FM) and WMMR (93.3FM). The public radio station WXPN (88.5FM) broadcasts from UPenn. For more music, see the Jersey Rocks trip playlist.

- "Sherry," Frankie Valli
- "One O'clock Jump," Count Basie
- "Wee Willie," The Hooligans
- "All of Me," Sarah Vaughan
- "4th of July, Asbury Park (Sandy)," Bruce Springsteen
- "Jersey Girl," Tom Waits
- "Philadelphia Freedom," Elton John
- "That's Life," Frank Sinatra

NEW JERSEY & PENNSYLVANIA'S BEST TRIPS

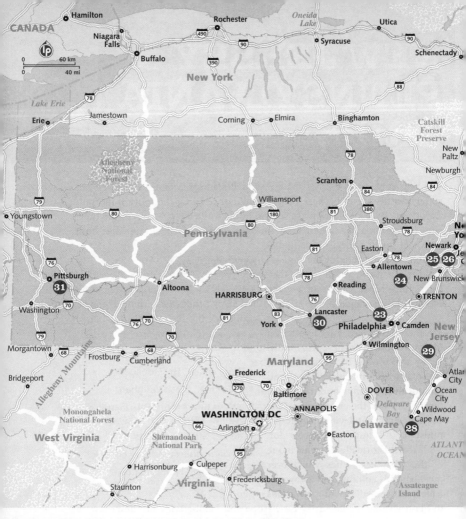

NEW JERSEY & PENNSYLVANIA TRIPS

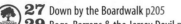

Slow Food & Sloe Gin in Philly

WHY GO Is Philly a foodie town? Kip and Sheri Waide, the husband-and-wife co-owners of Southwark, take us on a tour of their funky Queen Village neighborhood to make the case that, in fact, Philly is fast becoming a locavore's dream of creative cuisine and handcrafted cocktails.

At ❶ **Southwark**, Sheri is the chef and Kip is the bartender, and their hip restaurant/Prohibition-era bar – which opened in 2004 at the corner of Bainbridge and 4th Sts – reflects the marriage of their talents: Sheri is a passionate slow-food advocate, and Kip is a classic cocktail fanatic. They met in California, where they both trained in their respective arts, and in 1996 they moved to Philly, where Sheri grew up.

In 2004, Philadelphia had several top-end celebrity-chef destinations – Le Bec-Fin, Stephen Starr's Continental and Buddakan – but its larger dining scene was usually dismissed as a ho-hum collection of mom-and-pop BYOBs. It would be unfair to say Sheri and Kip started the trend, but they nevertheless opened their "labor of love" at the start of what has been a five-year renaissance of great dining and drinking in the City of Brotherly Love. Following Southwark has been the arrival of James, Ansill, Gayle, Xochitl, Horizons and more, as well as the demise of Le Bec-Fin. It's as if a slew of culinary Davids are conquering the dining Goliaths and transforming the way Philly eats.

It hasn't been easy. Today, Southwark's menu is "80% local," Sheri says, "and it's all sustainable." Achieving that meant building from scratch a network of a dozen or so small organic farms. Sheri says, "We had to grow into it. You need to get to know suppliers and trust the people you talk to. You develop a relationship. We're beyond a first-name basis with some of these people. We're supporting them and their families." Why go to the trouble? "We're antiglobal, to be honest. It's about carbon miles."

TIME
2 – 4 days

DISTANCE
2 miles

BEST TIME TO GO
Dinnertime

START
Philadelphia

END
Philadelphia

ALSO GOOD FOR

CITY

BEST TRIP

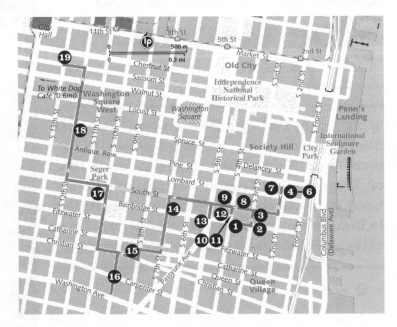

Sheri admits she gets as much satisfaction from *how* she gets her ingredients as what she does with them, but what she does has drawn raves, earning "three bells" from tough-to-please Philly food critic Craig LaBan (who awarded three bells to all the restaurants here except Xochitl). "We try to be playful, fun, rustic – not fine dining or stuffy," Sheri says. She makes her own terrine and smokes her own fish, and "we serve pork belly with the rib to give it that Flintstones look."

"...a slew of culinary Davids are conquering the dining Goliaths and transforming the way Philly eats."

Just as much praise has been heaped on Southwark's bar, which is a gorgeous, handcarved masterpiece with a speakeasy vibe. While Prohibition-era bars are old news in New York, Philly had none till Southwark opened. Kip wasn't riding a trend, though: "I'm following my own taste buds. I've always been into the supper club feel, and we love the classic cocktails. I like dirty gin." His Manhattan is made "the way it's supposed to be made. We're the only place that makes a real old-fashioned, a real Sazerac. We're the old-school guys." Like Sheri, Kip is passionate about his ingredients: "We have up to 22 different rye whiskeys. Almost a national record." Vodka, he says with a grin, "is on the bottom shelf." And as for flavored vodka: "I can't stand that."

Kip explains, "You have to build a place you'd like to go to because you'll be there a lot."

Indeed, passion and individuality now define Philly's restaurant scene. Even better, much of that scene can be reached on foot – unlike, say, in Manhattan. Sheri says, "Philly is very much a small town. It has everything a big city has but it's very neighborhoody. It's much more walkable."

And so we walk, and our first destination is just down the street, ❷ **Ansill**. Chef and owner David Ansill earned his stripes as a Philly bartender and later a chef for 14 years before opening his own place in 2006. He achieved instant notoriety for his culinary skills *and* his featured ingredients: offal, sweetbreads, marrow, pig's trotters etc. Ansill's approach – straightforward and direct – is reflected in his menu: baked duck egg truffles cream and crispy lamb's tongue chickpeas mint. It takes courage to challenge diners like this, without handholding, but Ansill quickly inspires trust and loyalty.

BUY LOCAL, EAT SLOW

Where exactly can aspiring Philadelphia locavores turn to buy locally and eat slowly? First, check out **Local Food Philly** (www.localfood philly.org), which links to a number of national organizations (such as the Buy Fresh Buy Local initiative) and lists city farmers markets, restaurants and retailers devoted to a sustainable food economy. Then, attend an event by (or join) the **Philadelphia Slow Food Convivium** (www.slowfoodphilly.org).

Not 20 yards away is ❸ **Gayle**, where Daniel Stern, formerly of Le Bec-Fin, is giving free reign to his personal gastronomic visions, on the plate and in a cocktail glass. Gayle has a comfy, neighborhood feel – photos of Stern's family line the walls and the eclectic music shifts from Dylan to Smokey Robinson to U2 – and the short, constantly evolving menu reflects an unpretentious perfectionism (such as seared ahi with curry ice cream).

A few blocks north, we reach ❹ **Headhouse Square**, aka Irish Alley. Irish pubs dominate the brick-and-cobblestone rectangle. For a pint, try the multi-level ❺ **Dark Horse Pub**, and on weekends don't miss the ❻ **Headhouse Farmers Market** in the Shambles (a colonial-era covered market). However, definitely nip into fun-loving ❼ **Xochitl**, where the Pueblan chef rose from immigrant dishwasher to become a culinary star. The unusual ceviches are dreamy concoctions only matched by the selection of tequilas (over 50) and the uses to which they are put: infused with ancho chili, muddled with pineapple and mixed with tropical fruits.

As we continue on, Kip and Sheri become ambivalent about ❽ **South St**, which Kip describes as "always fun and funky, but it's in transition. Too many chains." South St recalls San Francisco's Lower Haight district before the 1990s internet boom: a mix of partying suburbanites, die-hard punks, and transients. Still, they point out notable stops, like the authentic punk havens ❾ **Crash Bang Boom** and ❿ **Jinxed**. Of ⓫ **Eddie's Tattoo**, Sheri says, "All our staff seem to get tattoos here." Another must is the ⓬ **Eyes Gallery**, run by the wife of famed folk artist Isaiah Zagar, whose striking mosaic murals pop up throughout the neighborhood. Then there is the sexy **13 Passional**, "an institution for handmade corsets," Sheri says.

We next come to **14 Horizons**, a gourmet vegan restaurant as equally devoted to slow food as Southwark. At Horizons, the humble medley of tofu, seitan and tempeh are transformed by a globe-spanning variety of spices and preparations and fresher-than-fresh vegetables.

Then we reach another slow-food stalwart: **15 James**, which is the first stop exuding a fine-dining ambience, with service and atmosphere turned up a notch. Chef/owner Jim Burke was named one of 2008's best new chefs by *Food & Wine* because, similar to all the restaurants we visited, James displays the zestful daring that makes eating fun. Definitely order Burke's *risi e bisi*, a risotto topped with bacon gelato that regulars won't let him rotate off the menu.

DETOUR

The doyenne and den mother of slow food in Philly is Judy Wicks, whose **White Dog Cafe** (www.whitedog.com) has mixed politics with pancakes for over two decades. Wicks advocates not just for organic, sustainable farming but argues that "food sovereignty" is a global civil rights issue. The White Dog hosts events, live music and food celebrations, and dishes up such delicious cuisine that just might make you a believer. It's near UPenn, on Sansom and 34th St.

But Sheri and Kip aren't quite done: no food trip to South Philly is complete without visiting the **16 Italian Market**. Of this ranging, outdoor collection of butchers, produce, cheese shops and delis, Sheri quips, "Nothing here is really slow food unless the trucks got stuck in traffic, but we do use Di Brunos." Back on South St, muralist Isaiah Zagar's greatest epiphany is his **17 Philadelphia's Magic Gardens**, an indescribable, artful, cheeky maze of tile, mirrors, bicycle rims and bric-a-brac.

As for a night's stay, the affable, queer-friendly **18 Alexander Inn** in the heart of the midcity gayborhood is Kip and Sheri's hands-down favorite. And for that final nightcap before bed, Kip suggests nearby **19 Apothecary**, even though this ultracontemporary "cocktail lab" is his polar opposite. "It's just a different style of bartending," Kip allows, while no doubt fantasizing about that record-breaking 23rd rye.

Jeff Campbell

TRIP INFORMATION

GETTING THERE
Via I-95, Philadelphia is two hours from Manhattan and 2½ hours from Washington DC.

DO

Crash Bang Boom
It's the renowned Zipperhead with a new name and new location, but still punk, punk, punk. ☎ 215-928-1123; www.crashbang boomonline.com; 528 S 4th St; ☽ noon-9pm Mon-Thu, to 10pm Fri & Sat, to 8pm Sun

Eddie's Tattoo
Co-owner Troy Timpel also runs the Philly Tattoo Arts Convention. ☎ 215-922-7384; http://philadelphiaeddiestattoo.com; 621 S 4th St; ☽ noon-midnight

Eyes Gallery
In 1968, Zagar's first mosaic was for his wife's store, which contains three floors of Mexican art, pottery, carvings and tchotchkes. ☎ 215-925-0193; www.eyesgallery.com; 402 South St; ☽ 11am-7pm Mon-Thu, to 8pm Fri & Sat, noon-7pm Sun; ♿

Headhouse Farmers Market
This new farmers market is better Sunday than Saturday, and contains a full range of produce, cheese and meat. ☎ 215-575-0444; www.thefoodtrust.org/php/headhouse; The Shambles, 2nd & Lombard Sts; ☽ 10am-2pm Sat & Sun; ♿

Italian Market
The main action is along 9th St between Christian and Washington Aves; of the Italian delis, Di Bruno is the godfather. www.phillyitalian market.com; 9th St btwn Fitzwater & Wharton Sts; ☽ 9am-5pm Tue-Sat, to 2pm Sun; ♿

Jinxed
An anarchist's delight for books, art, T-shirts and strange, cuddly punk toys. ☎ 215-978-5469; www.jinxedphiladelphia.com; 620 S 4th St; ☽ noon-9pm

Passional
Silk and leather corsets so hot your palms will sweat; they run $200 to $500, and you can custom order any fabric with any design. ☎ 215-829-4986; www.passionalboutique .com; 704 S 5th St; ☽ noon-10pm

Philadelphia's Magic Gardens
For 35 years Isaiah Zagar has crafted over 100 murals in Philly, but he'd be famous forever if he'd only done this. ☎ 215-733-0390; www.philadelphiamagicgardens.org; 1020 South St; admission $3; ☽ 11am-6pm Tue-Sun; ♿

EAT & DRINK

Ansill
Take heart: Ansill also serves spicy shrimp, house-cured salmon and a perfect hanger steak. ☎ 215-627-2485; www.ansillfoodand wine.com; 637 S 3rd St; mains $8-15; ☽ 5:30-10pm Mon-Thu, to midnight Fri & Sat, bar menu 10pm-1am Mon-Sat

Apothecary
The irreverent cocktail menu (hmmm, a Booty Collins or a Dermis Fantasticus?) includes bottled libations. ☎ 215-735-7500; http://apothecarylounge.com; 102 S 13th St; mains $9-12, cocktails $11-14; ☽ 5pm-2am Tue-Sun

Dark Horse Pub
The pub has six barrooms over two floors, and serves classic Irish grub with its Guinness. ☎ 215-928-9307; www.dark horsepub.com; 421 S 2nd St; mains $9-12; ☽ 11:30am-11pm Mon-Thu, to midnight Fri & Sat, 11:30am-10pm Sun, bar to 2am daily

Gayle
When the weather's right, the back patio is divine, and the tasting menus are satisfying adventures. ☎ 215-922-3850; www .gaylephiladelphia.com; 617 S 3rd St; mains $28-34; ☽ 5:30-10pm Tue-Sat

Horizons
Owners Rich Landau and Kate Jacoby have literally written the book on vegan cuisine. Yes, you *can* do this at home. ☎ 215-923-6117; www.horizonsphiladelphia.com; 611 S 7th St; mains $18-21; ☽ 6-10pm Tue-Thu, to 11pm Fri & Sat

James
They infuse their own vodkas and gins, and summer finds fish paired with fresh fruit. ☎ 215-629-4980; www.jameson8th.com; 824 S 8th St; mains $25-35; ☽ 5-10pm Mon-Thu, to 11pm Fri & Sat

Southwark

Eat in the bar; everybody does. And Sunday is one mean, all-day brunch. ☎ 215-238-1888; www.southwarkrestaurant.com; 701 S 4th St; mains $20-29; ⏱ 5:30-10:30pm Tue-Thu, to 11:30pm Fri & Sat, bar to 2am, Sun 11am-5pm

Xochitl

Serves a late-night menu till 1am. Any excuse for another Vuelve a la Vida ceviche. ☎ 215-238-7280; www.xochitlphilly.com;

408 S 2nd St; mains $16-40; ⏱ 5-10pm Tue-Thu, to 11pm Fri & Sat, bar 5pm-2am Tue-Sat

SLEEP
Alexander Inn

Philadelphia's best value sleep just got better, as all the rooms here recently received pretty facials. ☎ 215-923-3535, 877-253-9466; www.alexanderinn.com; 301 S 12th St; r $120-170

LINK YOUR TRIP   www.lonelyplanet.com/trip-planner

Impressions of the Delaware River

WHY GO As with the weather, East Coast hearts soften in spring and fall, which paint the landscape ever-so-briefly in scarlet and gold, buttercup yellow and amethyst. When this happens, seize the moment and enjoy a romantic getaway along the Delaware River in New Hope and Lambertville.

TIME
2 – 3 days

DISTANCE
15 miles

BEST TIME TO GO
Apr – Jun,
Sep – Nov

START
New Hope

END
Bull's Island Recreation Area

ALSO GOOD FOR

You won't, of course, be the first to be taken by the soothing beauty of the riverbanks and lazy canals. Since the turn of the 20th century, painters have found inspiration in the region's bucolic scenery, which became the focus and epicenter of American impressionism. Not that that matters to your plans, but it's always nice when fancy-pants artists confirm what's right before your eyes.

New Hope and Lambertville nestle across from each other, with a pretty, walkable bridge connecting them over the wide, powerful Delaware. Like siblings, these towns have grown up together and resemble each other, but they'd stalk off in a pouty huff if you called them the same. Presuming you're arriving from Philly along Hwy 202, we'll start with ❶ **New Hope**, the jewel of Bucks County.

In this two-town relationship, New Hope has always played the pink-haired troublemaker: more emotional, artsy and rebellious. New Hope has long had a comfortably open gay community, and, until recently, it was equally welcoming to the leather-and-tat biker crowd. However, killjoy town fathers have been enforcing parking regulations more strictly, more chains have moved in, and New Hope has settled into a middle-aged post-punk boomerhood.

Entering town along W Bridge St, turn left onto Union Square Dr for the ❷ **James A Michener Art Museum**. A satellite of the Doylestown

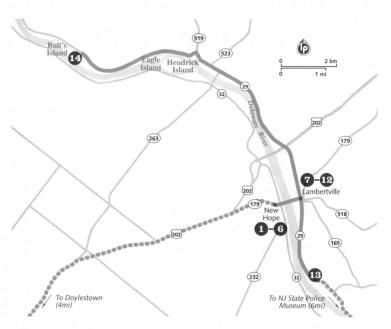

museum, it provides a succinct overview of the many painters and writers (like SJ Perelman, Dorothy Parker and Moss Hart) who called Bucks County home.

The intersection of Bridge and Main Sts is the center of the action. Long hours can be spent strolling the trinkety, crafty, boutiquey, vintagey shoppes (Love Saves the Day is a retro fave). For a secluded stay just off the main drag, nip down Fisher's Alley to **3 Porches on the Towpath**. Romance is a little cozy, quirky Victoriana with canal views that (like the inn's affable owner) doesn't take itself too seriously.

DETOUR In 1898–99, painters Edward Redfield and William Langson Lathrop moved to New Hope and cofounded an artists' colony that changed American painting. Redfield, in particular, became famous for painting outside *(en plein air)* in winter storms so bad he had to tie his easel to a tree. He worked fast, not even sketching first, creating moody, muted landscapes in a day. For the whole story on the New Hope School, visit Doylestown's **Michener Art Museum** (www.michenermuseum.org).

Wandering south on Main St, you'll find **4 Coryell's Ferry**, which offers pleasant paddlewheel cruises with colonial history narrated by Bob Gerenser, New Hope's star George Washington reenactor. Down the street, another recommended lodging is the venerable 1722 **5 Logan Inn**, which has a modern, friendly tavern downstairs and a clutch of ghosts wandering the halls. At intimate, handsome **6 zoubi**, you'll find what one local told us was "the only authentic Frenchman left in town." We think he meant the Gallic chef;

drop by and show him some love, and he'll return the favor, deliciously. (The same folks run the popular bohemian bar/restaurant, Karla's, next door.)

Now amble over the bridge, home to nesting cliff swallows (awww), and meet **❼ Lambertville**, the well-mannered, well-dressed, well-off sophisticate of the pair. Walking Bridge and Union Sts, you'll find Lambertville to be a quaint, inviting, historical town where, as one Princeton mother commented, "it looks like an antique store threw up all over the place." She means, in a *good* way.

Yes, Lambertville has antiques, and top-notch art galleries too, all shoulder-to-shoulder with independent coffeehouses and snuggly restaurants. Anchoring Lambertville's end of the bridge is **❽ Lambertville Station**. This gorgeously restored 19th-century train station was single-handedly saved from decay 25 years ago by Daniel Whitaker and his business partner. Today the Station's swell, gleaming dining rooms and pub are nearly the town's signature.

One notable art gallery across from the station is **❾ Jim's of Lambertville**, which specializes in Pennsylvania impressionists (the suitably well-heeled can purchase a Redfield to take home). Further up Bridge St is **❿ Sneddon's**, a homey diner and gathering spot that's one of the last remaining bits of "old" Lambertville (pre-antique-explosion).

For another, find the Porkyard (an alley off Coryell St) and grab a leisurely afternoon cocktail at the century-old **⓫ Boathouse**, crammed with so much atmospheric nautical hoo-haw the building seems to bob in the canal (or is that the cosmos?). Don't worry about dinner. When cocktail hour ends, stumble next door to **⓬ Hamilton's Grill**, a favorite for straight-up, perfectly done seafood and local shad.

Finally, if you love old stuff, don't miss the outdoor **⓭ Golden Nugget Antique Market** (about a mile south of Lambertville on Rte 29). Serious treasure hunters arrive, elbows flying, first thing Sunday morning.

> **DETOUR**
>
> Enough art. We're going to police headquarters to visit the **NJ State Police Museum.** Where else can you gawk at confiscated sawed-off shotguns, Colt .45s, or the electric chair that killed Bruno Hauptmann? Yes, the guy who kidnapped Lindbergh's baby – or did he? A fantastic exhibit guides you through the trial. Then test your detective skills on a fictional crime-scene. Need romance? Hold hands while you solve a murder! HQ is at I-95 exit 1; get directions online.

However, the reason all this is here is the river itself, and the most romantic thing you can do is walk or bike the lovely canal paths on either side. Spend an afternoon at **⓮ Bull's Island Recreation Area**, seven miles north of Lambertville, and you too may become overwhelmed with the urge to capture the scene with paint and canvas.

Jeff Campbell

TRIP INFORMATION

GETTING THERE
From Philadelphia, take Hwy 611 north to Hwy 202 east to New Hope.

DO

Bull's Island Recreation Area
For those inclined, camping is available. ☎ 609-397-2949; www.state.nj.us/dep/parksandforests/parks/bull.html; 2185 Daniel Bray Hwy (Rte 29); ⏱ dawn-dusk; 👶 🐾

Coryell's Ferry
Get tickets at Gerenser's Ice Cream on Main St; 35-minute trips leave every hour. ☎ 215-862-2050; 22 S Main St, New Hope; adult/child $10/5; ⏱ 10am-5:30pm May-Oct; 👶

Golden Nugget Antique Market
Over 250 dealers, outside and in, plus produce, restaurants and free parking. ☎ 609-397-0811; www.gnmarket.com; 1850 River Rd (Rte 29), Lambertville; ⏱ 6am-4pm Wed, Sat & Sun; 👶

James A Michener Art Museum
Has the wall-size "Artist Among Us" mural and multimedia exhibit focusing on 12 famous Bucks County artists. ☎ 215-862-7633; www.michenermuseum.org; Union Square Dr, New Hope; adult/child $5/2; ⏱ 11am-5pm Tue-Sun; 👶

Jim's of Lambertville
Mecca of impressionism, including paintings by Daniel Garber, Charles Rosen, Edward Redfield and William Langson Lathrop. Jim's also hosts exhibitions. ☎ 609-397-7700, 215-280-8650; www.artnet.com/gallery/574/jims-of-lambertville.html; 6 Bridge St, Lambertville; ⏱ 10:30am-5pm Wed-Sun

EAT & DRINK

Boathouse
Locals fill this bar on weekdays, tourists on weekends. ☎ 609-397-2244; 8½ Coryell St,

Lambertville; ⏱ 4pm-midnight or so Mon-Sat, from 2pm Sun

Hamilton's Grill
This trusty Mediterranean-style surf and turf is also BYOB. ☎ 609-397-4343; www.hamiltonsgrillroom.com; 8 Coryell St, Lambertville; mains $18-32; ⏱ 6-10pm Mon-Sat, 5-9pm Sun

Lambertville Station
Don't just eat and drink, stay: the adjacent modern Inn offers dependable upscale lodgings. ☎ dining 609-397-8300, inn 609-398-8461; www.lambertvillestation.com; 11 Bridge St, Lambertville; mains $11-30, r $125-300; ⏱ 11:30am-9:30pm Mon-Thu, to 11pm Fri & Sat, 10am-9:30pm Sun; 👶

Sneddon's
Posters of the owner's smiling grandkids set the tone. Serves diner-style breakfasts and voluminous hot sandwiches. ☎ 609-397-3053; 47 Bridge St, Lambertville; mains $4-8; ⏱ 6am-2pm daily, plus 5-8pm Fri; 👶

zoubi
Stylish, gourmet French cuisine with Latin and Asian influences; reserve on weekends. ☎ 215-862-5851; www.zoubinewhope.com; 5-7 Mechanics St, New Hope; mains $28-38; ⏱ 5:30-9:30pm, to 10pm Fri & Sat

SLEEP

Logan Inn
Rooms are very nice, just more standard than the evocative building itself. ☎ 215-862-2300; www.loganinn.com; 10 W Ferry St at Main St, New Hope; r $100-200; 👶

Porches on the Towpath
Ten unique rooms with skylight showers and private fountains. A delight! ☎ 215-862-3277; www.porchesnewhope.com; 20 Fisher's Alley, New Hope; r $95-250

USEFUL WEBSITES
www.buckscountycvb.org
www.dandrcanal.com
www.lonelyplanet.com/trip-planner

LINK YOUR TRIP

TRIP 23 Slow Food & Sloe Gin in Philly p183

OPEN 24 HRS

WHY GO What makes a diner? Is it the hours, the neon, the counter, the menu? Is it the jukebox, the clientele? New Jersey and its diners are inextricably linked; to know one is to know the other. On this trip, then, we seek the existential truth of this 3am-coffee-and-cheesecake conundrum.

New Jersey has over 600 diners, more than any other state, so we'll start by restricting ourselves to the boomerang of urbanized northeast Jersey. Locals, save your howls of indignation: we know this leaves out all the great diners elsewhere, but whatta ya gonna do? You really want them all?

Let's begin with a burger. Specifically, a White Mana. Diner scholarship generally acknowledges that the oldest diner in New Jersey is Max's Grill, a 1927 shingle-roofed, maroon O'Mahoney on Harrison Ave (at Manor St) in Harrison. Sadly, Max's Grill is closed, perhaps forever; though the cream-colored lettering announces "Ladies Invited," the grill is quiet.

The Jersey City ❶ **White Mana** likes to claim it pioneered the fast-food hamburger, which some still call a "slider." First or not, it's a classic of the genre. The tiny chrome-and-white building with the red roof was featured at the 1939 New York World's Fair, and sitting at the circular linoleum counter is a true time warp – as well as a rite-of-passage for diner aficionados and Jersey City kids.

To get there: from Manhattan's Holland Tunnel, take Hwy 1-9 and follow it north onto frenetic, truck-packed Tonnele Ave. White Mana comes up fast, at Manhattan Ave, but everyone risks the turnoff: from gray-haired matrons to truckers to businessmen to the quintessential lost souls who frequent Edward Hopper paintings.

TIME
2 – 3 days

DISTANCE
150 miles

BEST TIME TO GO
Year-round

START
Jersey City

END
Wall

ALSO GOOD FOR

FOOD &
DRINK

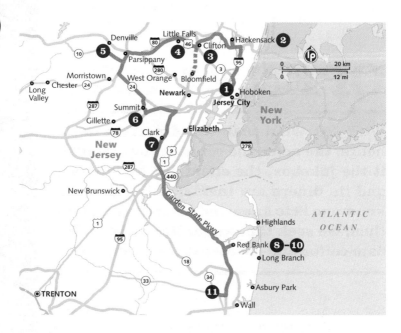

The menu is simplicity itself: burgers, hot dogs, eggs, fries. The equipment? Two small grills, a deep fryer, a toaster oven, and a blender for shakes. The burgers are fresh; no frozen, preformed patties, oh no. The chef grabs a hunk of raw meat with his hand, flattens it with a spatula, tops it with grilled onions and pickle, lays it on a soft bun, and there you go. For $1.12. Cheese is another 10 cents. A "Big Web" – the equivalent of a quarter pounder – is $3.36. Atmosphere is on the house.

For purity, for history, for architecture, this chrome wonder is the quintessential truck-stop diner, and they are a vanishing breed. Another prime example, which in fact argues that *it* was first, is the Hackensack ② **White Manna** (two ns, no explanation, also c 1939); it's got a glass-brick front, more red trim, and smaller potato buns. Are the burgers better? Some make that case, but it's the same experience – order three at a time, and skip lettuce and tomato. They just get in the way.

To get from White Mana to White Manna, continue north on Hwy 1-9 to Rte 46 west, and exit onto River St north (Rte 503/Bergen Turnpike). Then, from White Manna, take Rte 503 back south to I-80 west, take the Garden State Parkway south to exit 153, and take Rte 3 to the ③ **Tick Tock Diner**. "The Tick" is a legend, and it epitomizes another aspect of diner-osity: the restaurant-diner with the mile-long menu. How is it that places offering only a handful of things and others offering everything are both equally and essentially diners? Discuss.

The original Tick was a 1949 Silk City, but the current building was made by Kullman in 1994: the original clock and the neon motto "Eat Heavy" were kept. Though it applies to much, the Tick's motto certainly covers the ever-popular "Disco Fries," which arrive smothered in cheese and gravy. The Tick has the retro chrome and neon, the wry waitstaff, the overwhelming dessert case, the 24-hour breakfasts. It's a home-away-from-home for high schoolers and families and a cure-all for postclub, predawn hangovers. All it lacks are tabletop jukeboxes.

In the same vein is the **4** **Park West Diner**; to get here, go west on Rte 3, which becomes Rte 46. The Park West has an even classier retro vibe, with a fun planet-and-stars Googie carpet, two-tone booths, a dramatic two-story glass-brick entry, and the scalloped ceiling and inset lights of a Pullman railcar. It's a spruced-up vision of the doo-wop, streamline moderne, art deco '40s and '50s. But the Park West really shines with its food, highlighting, of all things, salads: they arrive like crafted events, towering with mango, straw-berries, perfectly grilled tuna, black-ened shrimp, and feta. Each meal starts with fresh bread and a tasty chickpea salad, and the waitstaff are *nice*.

DETOUR It's not a diner, but it's des-tination dining, Jersey-style: **Holsten's** (www.holstens.com) was the setting for the final scene in the final episode of *The Sopranos*, but it's long been a gourmand's delight. Cheap, fresh hamburgers, homemade ice cream (the shakes are out of this world), and a glass-front confectionery. You'll find Holsten's at 1065 Broad St in Bloomfield; from Rte 3, take exit 153/Broad St.

Yet, with its cutesy mural of Elvis and a pink Cadillac, the Park West tips danger-ously close to pandering nostalgia. Which begs the question: at what point does refurbishing and re-creating an authentic building and time-period fall into irredeemable kitsch, becoming yet another *American Graffiti*–style Mel's Diner rip-off? The Park West is not, making the case that authenticity is less about the right look than fresh food, which creates regulars like the actor who played Furio in *The Sopranos*, a native of Paterson, who would no doubt club our kneecaps if we broke bad about the Park West. Which we wouldn't, ever. Sir.

Furthering this particular looks-don't-matter argument is the **5** **Alexis Diner** in Denville (take Rte 46 west to I-80 and then west to I-287 south to Rte 10 west). There are lots of ugly New Jersey diners; many are flagstone-sided monstrosities with mediocre food served by indifferent staff. As your stomach will tell you, that Jersey boasts 600 diners is not always a good thing.

From the outside, the nondescript Alexis could be mistaken for one of these, though, inside, its pink neon and plum-and-gray decor have a tacky appeal. The Alexis isn't even 24 hours. But it doesn't matter. What matters – the reason the Alexis is voted Morris County's best diner year after year – is the food. Like at the Park West, dishes are fresh and display evidence of thought. The Italian BLT just might be the best sandwich ever made: fresh mozzarella, smoky bacon, green-leaf lettuce and deep-fried tomato on a seasoned focaccia.

GARDENS OF THE GARDEN STATE

New Jersey is called the Garden State, not the Diner State, for a reason: it's packed with farms. Imagine that? And Jersey corn, tomatoes, peaches, apples, and blueberries inspire their own pilgrimages. Here are four farms convenient to north Jersey. All are open daily year-round, but pick-your-own fun only happens in fall. Ya' know, harvest season.

- Alstede Farm, Chester (www.alstedefarms.com)
- Hillview Farms, Gillette (www.hillviewfarmsnj.com)
- Ort Farms, Long Valley (www.ortsfarm.com)
- Wightman's Farm, Morristown (www.wightmansfarms.com)

The Alexis is the ideal place to go Greek: its gyros and Greek salads are delicious and its "taverna specials" are hearty meals that exemplify the best of this particular strain of restaurant-style Jersey diner cuisine. Like '50s nostalgia, what you get at many diners is bland fakery, but not here.

Now we come to another major category of diner: the gleaming, silver roadside railcar, the diner of fantasy – the one photorealist painter John Baeder has made a living capturing and the kind architectural buffs drool over. Like the White Mana, these are prefabricated buildings (though the first were real train cars), and New Jersey has had at least nine manufacturers: such as Silk City, Jerry O'Mahoney, DeRaffele, Kullman and Paramount. Only the last two remain in business.

But are any of them places you'd actually want to eat?

From the Alexis, take Rte 10 east to I-287 south to Rte 24 east; at exit 8, follow Summit Ave to downtown Summit and the **❻ Summit Diner**, a 1938 chrome-sided O'Mahoney facing the train station. It's a little worn, inside and out; waitresses display a level of impatience some might call surly. The menu is long, but limited to the grill and the fryer; no shakes. When a despairing customer asked, "How about spinach? You got any green vegetables?" the waitress casually shrugged him off, "Nah, we got green peppers. That's it." The cook uses so much butter, cheese and bacon, the doorway should be posted with instructions: sit, eat, wait for irregular heart rhythm.

"...so much butter, the doorway should be posted with instructions: sit, eat, wait for irregular heart rhythm."

And yet, this is the real deal: the Summit is often packed with contractors, pensioners and high school kids. It's an inexpensive working-class place in a town (and a state) that is less working class by the day. It's not *too* worn, and jokes aside, the food is good. So, here we are: diners are not just about the menu and pert greens. They are clientele, history, some attitude.

From Summit, take I-78 east to the Garden State Parkway south; take exit 135 to Central Ave and stop at the ❼ **Clark White Diamond**. This is another, teeny-tiny chrome haven for top-quality burgers, though here the burgers are bigger and the bun has substance (and poppy seeds).

Keep going south on the Parkway to exit 109 and Red Bank. Here, the ❽ **Broadway Diner** is another classic railcar that glows in bubble-gum pink, from the tables to the booths to the ceiling. It's got the rotating dessert case, fluffy pancakes, and, at last, tabletop jukeboxes. Yet they don't work. They almost never do. Clearly, the once-essential connection between diners and popular music is gone, so let's mourn and move on: diners are no longer about music.

❾ **Red Bank** is a great town to explore (and window-shop those burgers off), but if you just can't continue, roll yourself into the ❿ **Molly Pitcher Inn** for a well-earned rest.

Finally, there's one more stop, perhaps the most famous of all: the ⓫ **Road-side Diner**. The Roadside is a movie star: it was in 1983's *Baby It's You*, it made a Bon Jovi album cover *(Cross Road)*, and in 2008, the Boss himself featured it in the music video "Girls in Their Summer Clothes." Tour buses stop at the Roadside, a burden it somehow overcomes.

This 1950 Silk City railcar has a cool sliding-door entry, 18 counter stools and six booths. It's clean and neat, with original red-and-white tile and wood-work, and exudes a low-key nostalgia (tin advertising signs, a photo of Babe Ruth, golden oldies music). Like Park West, it evokes its era without overdoing it. Best of all, the standard, everything-under-the-sun menu is made to order. Burgers are great, and of the chef's egg and tuna salads, a customer nodded reassuringly: "He mixes everything fresh. It doesn't sit."

The Roadside pulls it all together at a nowhere location near the intersection of Rtes 33 and 34. It doesn't epitomize *all* a diner can be – nothing could. In the end, the best diner is always the one where we feel comfortable, the one we call home, the one where we're known and where we'll forgive the occasional bad meal because, like our home, that diner is us.

Jeff Campbell

TRIP
25

OFFBEAT

TRIP INFORMATION

GETTING THERE
From New York City, take the Holland Tunnel to Hwy 1-9 north/Tonnele Ave to White Mana.

EAT
Alexis Diner
The friendly Alexis gives you fresh baked cookies; if the Italian BLT isn't on the menu, ask for it. ☎ 973-361-8000; http://alexis dinernj.com; 3130 Rte 10, Denville; mains $5-20; ☽ 7am-midnight Sun-Thu, to 1am Fri & Sat; ⚹

Broadway Diner
Gotta love the undersea mural and the bad pop music: get down, boogie oogie oogie! ☎ 732-224-1234; 45 Monmouth St, Red Bank; mains $6-18; ☽ 24hr; ⚹

Clark White Diamond
The burger is bigger than the paper plate; the staff are very friendly and they have an Elvis gold record! Cash only. ☎ 732-574-8053; 1207 Raritan Rd at Central Ave, Clark; mains $2-5; ☽ 24hr; ⚹

Park West Diner
Park West gets props for challah bread French toast and buffalo burgers. ☎ 973-256-2767; www.parkwestdiner.com; Rte 46 W, Little Falls; mains $7-23; ☽ 24hr; ⚹

Roadside Diner
Big, fresh burgers, and don't overlook the dinner specials here. Cash only. ☎ 908-449-1060; Rtes 34-33, Wall; mains $4-13; ☽ 5:30am-8pm Tue-Sat, to 4pm Sun & Mon; ⚹

Summit Diner
Great for breakfast and cheesesteaks, but the grilled cheese is a killer. Cash only. ☎ 908-277-3256; Summit Ave & Union Pl, Summit; mains $4-11; ☽ 5:30am-8:30pm Mon-Sat, 6:30am-1pm Sun; ⚹

Tick Tock Diner
If it's not on the menu, it hasn't been invented yet. Ask for sweet-potato fries instead of regular. ☎ 973-777-0511; www.tictock diner.com; 281 Allwood Rd, Clifton; mains $7-19; ☽ 24hr; ⚹

White Mana
Celebrity clients here include Mike Tyson and Sty Stallone. Cash only. ☎ 201-963-1441; 470 Tonnele Ave, Jersey City; mains $1-4; ☽ 24hr; ⚹

White Manna
You could get milk in a Styrofoam cup and a hot dog, but why? Just decide: cheese or no cheese. Cash only. ☎ 201-342-0914; 358 River St, Hackensack; mains $1.05-3; ☽ 24hr; ⚹

SLEEP
Molly Pitcher Inn
It's fancy for this trip, but you'll appreciate going upmarket to sleep. Plus, you know where to go for breakfast. ☎ 732-747-2500; www.mollypitcher-oysterpoint.com/molly pitcher; 88 Riverside Ave, Red Bank; r $160-200; ⚹

USEFUL WEBSITES
www.dinercity.com
www.njdiners.com

LINK YOUR TRIP
www.lonelyplanet.com/trip-planner

TRIP
26 Jersey Rocks opposite
27 Down by the Boardwalk p205

Jersey Rocks

WHY GO Jersey rocks, it raps, it croons, it swings. So much good music and so many great musicians have come from Jersey – some so famous they're known by titles alone: the Boss, the Voice, the Divine One, the Empress, the Queen. Truth be told, this trip could last a lifetime.

Let's get right to it by paying respects to the Chairman of the Board, Frank Sinatra, who was born and raised in ❶ **Hoboken**. Pick up a walking tour of Sinatra sights at the ❷ **Hoboken Historical Museum**, and definitely visit ❸ **415 Monroe St**. Though the house is gone, a bronze sidewalk star commemorates the 1915 birthplace of "the Voice."

Then make sure to visit ❹ **Frank Sinatra Drive**, which runs along the waterfront and takes in the magnificent view of Manhattan that surely tantalized the young singer, who nevertheless always defended his rough-and-tumble Jersey roots. The Sinatra shrine of shrines remains ❺ **Leo's Grandevous**, at the corner of Grand and 2nd Sts. Leo's lovingly preserves an amazing collection of photos and memorabilia, and the long curved bar is an ideal place to order a martini and remember as Sinatra wafts from the jukebox.

Hoboken has also been fertile ground for indie rock, so much so that in the 1980s it developed the "Hoboken Sound" – epitomized by local groups The Bongos and Yo La Tengo. The scene revolved almost entirely around the famed, East Village–like ❻ **Maxwell's**. The club remains a significant venue for punk and indie bands; the dining room is hung with skateboard art, and double swinging doors lead to the dark, intimate backroom. Another place to catch live music is at the ❼ **Goldhawk Bar & Lounge**, which is part-owned by Sinatra's granddaughter, AJ Azzarto, who at one time sang here with the New Hoboken Four.

TIME
2 days – 20 years

DISTANCE
100 miles

BEST TIME TO GO
Weekends

START
Hoboken

END
Asbury Park

ALSO GOOD FOR

HISTORY & CULTURE

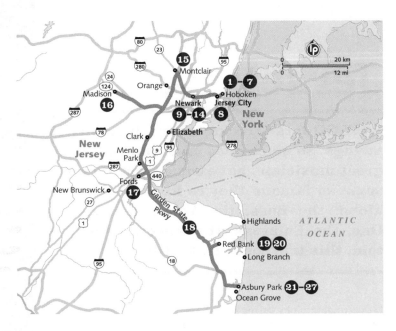

About a mile south of Hoboken off I-78, Jersey City's Liberty State Park was the site of the August 2008 inaugural **8** **All Points West Festival** (headlined by Radiohead), which aims to finally give New Jersey a rock festival to rival Coachella and Bonnaroo.

Next up is **9** **Newark**, the birthplace and childhood home of the Divine Sarah Vaughan, Whitney Houston, Frankie Valli, Queen Latifah, Paul Simon, Dionne Warwick, Connie Francis (the "Empress of New Jersey") and others. In a story celebrated in the Tony-winning musical *Jersey Boys*, and which is repeated a thousand times over across the state, Frankie Valli was a hard-luck kid from the wrong side of the tracks who sung his way out of a nowhere, impoverished life.

Newark has two major venues. The gorgeous theaters at the **10** **New Jersey Performing Arts Center** (NJPAC) host a diverse slate of jazz, classical and world music year-round. During summer, its entrance (along Sarah Vaughan Way) is the scene of Sounds of the City, a free outdoor series, which features music ranging from hip-hop to reggae to jazz. The latest arrival is the **11** **Prudential Center** (aka "the Rock"), a huge arena for pro hockey and concerts. Appropriately enough, in 2007, Jersey rocker Jon Bon Jovi inaugurated the venue by declaring, "I'm a Jersey devil, and this is my house!"

Perhaps the nicest, and certainly the most convenient, place to stay in Newark is the historic ⑫ **Robert Treat Hotel**, across the street from NJPAC. Rooms are small but stylishly done in sophisticated browns and tans; it's a great after-concert crash pad. For a meal, head for Newark's ⑬ **Ironbound District**, an old Portuguese neighborhood centered along Ferry St. The Ironbound is known for Iberian cuisine, and the stalwarts are Sagres, Fornos of Spain and Iberia Tavern (look for the Christmas lights and brick castle gate). However, a younger crowd and live Latin music – bossa nova, flamenco, Spanish guitar – can be found at ⑭ **Mompou**, a newer tapas restaurant and wine bar.

PLAYLIST 🎵

How does Jersey rock? Here's a little old, a little new, a little silly, a little serious.

- "Rosalita (Come Out Tonight)," Bruce Springsteen
- "Exit 140A," Maybe Pete
- "Beanbag Chair," Yo La Tengo
- "Dead!" My Chemical Romance
- "Bomb. Repeat. Bomb," Ted Leo & the Pharmacists
- "U.N.I.T.Y." Queen Latifah
- "Bad Medicine," Bon Jovi
- "I Don't Want to Go Home," Southside Johnny & the Asbury Jukes

North Jersey's musical heritage, the progeny it's unleashed, goes well beyond these highlights. Consider, for instance, hip-hop: the Sugarhill Gang, who helped launch rap music with "Rapper's Delight," were from Englewood. Admittedly, rap fermented to life in the South Bronx, but Jersey remained at the forefront. In addition to Queen Latifah – who won a 1994 Grammy for her single "U.N.I.T.Y." and who once worked at a Newark record store – Ice-T, Lauryn Hill, Redman, Sister Souljah and Naughty by Nature are all from Jersey. The master of funk George Clinton grew up in Plainfield.

What of heavy metal and punk? The Misfits, Overkill, and Karen O of the Yeah Yeah Yeahs – all from Jersey. Plus, Megaforce Records, the label that launched Metallica, Anthrax and countless others, was based in Old Bridge. Members of My Chemical Romance are from Newark and Belleville. And the "stoner rock" movement would be bereft without Jersey's Monster Magnet, the Atomic Bitchwax, guitarist John McBain and Ted Leo & the Pharmacists.

Jersey has had a major influence on jazz. The legendary Van Gelder Studio in Hackensack (later Englewood Cliffs) was one of *the* bebop recording hotspots in the 1950s. Thelonious Monk, John Coltrane, Bill Evans (born in Plainfield), Sonny Rollins and Milt Jackson recorded landmark albums there. As a teenager, Sarah Vaughan sang in a Newark church choir before she got her big break.

Two jazz venues that continue to put together excellent bills are ⓯ **Trumpets** in Montclair (next to the train station), which also serves meals, and ⓰ **Shanghai Jazz** in Madison, which combines an evocative supper-club atmosphere, good Chinese cuisine and serious music.

As we head south, make a pilgrimage to ⓱ **Vintage Vinyl** in Fords (near the intersection of I-287 and Rte 1). One of Jersey's last remaining old-school record shops, it has both new and used vinyl, tons of CDs and hosts live music and signings.

DETOUR In 1877, Thomas Alva Edison invented the phonograph in Menlo Park, New Jersey, and could we have rock without records? Hell no! Pay tribute at the tiny **Menlo Park Museum** (www.menloparkmuseum.com; open Thursday to Saturday), where several original phonographs are demonstrated by eager guides. The museum is on Rte 27 (take Garden State Parkway exit 131B).

Now, continue south on the Garden State Parkway. Consider catching a show at the ⓲ **PNC Bank Arts Center**, an outdoor venue, at exit 116, that nearly every Jersey youth has at least one blurry memory of. Then, pull into ⓳ **Red Bank**, where jazz pioneer Bill "Count" Basie was born. Here, the beautiful ⓴ **Count Basie Theatre**, painstakingly renovated in 2008, presents an extremely eclectic range of concerts, from Blondie to doo-wop to the New Jersey Symphony Orchestra.

Let's see, have we missed anything? Oh right. Silly us. Greetings from ㉑ **Asbury Park**. Bruce Springsteen did not actually grow up in Asbury Park, and he is only the most famous of a group of musicians who developed the Asbury Sound in the 1970s. Several of these musicians – like Steve Van Zandt, Garry Tallent, Danny Federici (who died in 2008) and Clarence Clemons – formed Springsteen's supporting E Street Band, maybe the tightest, most celebrated backing band in rock history. Others included Southside Johnny & the Asbury Jukes.

"Let's see, have we missed anything? Oh right. Silly us. Greetings from Asbury Park."

The main venue is the ㉒ **Stone Pony**, a low-ceilinged club with the stage in your lap and the seen-it-all black walls crammed with signed guitars. Another small club that nurtures emerging bands is the ㉓ **Saint**, while bigger acts hold forth at the boardwalk's evocative ㉔ **Paramount Theatre** (which boasts Asbury's neon greeting). June's ㉕ **Wave Gathering** is Asbury Park's main music festival.

You will need a place to sleep, so book a room at the ㉖ **Empress**, a large, clean, gay-friendly hotel on the boardwalk. The Empress is noisy because its gay club ㉗ **Paradise**, snug next to the mirror-ball-festooned pool, shakes till all hours. But that's fine. You won't be coming home early.

Jeff Campbell

TRIP INFORMATION

GETTING THERE
From Manhattan, take the Holland Tunnel and turn right on Luis Munoz Marin to reach Hoboken.

DO

All Points West Festival
For three days in August, over 40 top acts like Ben Harper, Cat Power and Jack Johnson rock three stages at Liberty State Park. www .apwfestival.com; Liberty State Park, Jersey City; tickets $90-260

Count Basie Theatre
In addition to music, see movies, dance and theater at this restored jewel. ☎ 732-842-9000; www.countbasietheatre.org; 99 Monmouth St, Red Bank; tickets $20-150; ♿

Goldhawk Bar & Lounge
This laid-back neighborhood lounge has live music Tuesday to Thursday, and DJs on Friday and Saturday. ☎ 201-420-7989; www .thegoldhawk.com; 936 Park Ave, Hoboken; ⌚ 5pm-2am Sun-Thu, to 3am Fri & Sat

Hoboken Historical Museum
Ask for the Sinatra walking tour; exhibits are small and change often. ☎ 201-656-2240; www.hobokenmuseum.org; 1301 Hudson St, Hoboken; admission donation $2; ⌚ 2-9pm Tue-Thu, 1-5pm Fri, noon-5pm Sat & Sun; ♿

Maxwell's
The club side has multiple bills almost every night. The restaurant side serves fancy diner food. ☎ 201-653-1703; www.maxwellsnj .com; 1039 Washington St, Hoboken; tickets $8-25, mains $8-17; ⌚ from 5pm

New Jersey Performing Arts Center
Three theaters, plus Sounds of the City Thursday nights (5:45pm to 9:45pm) in July and August. ☎ 888-466-5722; www.njpac.org; One Center St, Newark; tickets $20-150; ♿

Paradise
DJs work the dancefloor weekends only, but the poolside tiki bar is open daily. ☎ 732-774-0100; www.paradisenj.com; Asbury & Ocean Aves, Asbury Park; ⌚ bar 11am-10pm, to 2am Fri & Sat, club 10pm-2am Fri & Sat, sometimes Thu & Sun

Paramount Theatre
The Paramount and attached Convention Hall host the big shows, roller derby, dance parties etc; see website for schedule. ☎ 732-897-8810; www.asburyparkconventionhall .com; Ocean Ave, between Fifth and Sunset, Asbury Park; tickets $35-75

PNC Bank Arts Center
All the top groups go through the Arts Center; lawn seats are a cheap way to go. ☎ 732-203-2500; www.artscenter.com; Garden State Pkwy, exit 116, Holmdel; tickets $40-200 and over; ♿

Prudential Center
The Rock is walkable from Newark Penn Station. ☎ 973-757-6000, tickets 201-507-8900; www.prucenter.com; 165 Mulberry St, Newark; tickets $45-200; ♿

Saint
Only 175 people can fit in this tiny space; check the schedule for exact times and dates. ☎ 732-775-9144; www.thesaintnj.com; 601 Main St, Asbury Park; tickets $7-15; ⌚ from 7pm or 8pm to late most nights

Shanghai Jazz
No cover for music, but table minimums. There are two seatings Friday and Saturday; call for the exact schedule. The diverse Chinese menu includes dim sum. ☎ 973-822-2899; www.shanghaijazz.com; 24 Main St, Madison; mains $16-27; ⌚ from 6pm or 7pm to late Tue-Sun

Stone Pony
It's elemental: white stucco and brick exterior, black-and-white sign, lines down the block. ☎ 732-502-0600; www.stoneponyon line.com; 913 Ocean Ave, Asbury Park; tickets $10-25; ⌚ from 6pm or 7pm to late most nights

Trumpets
Live jazz Tuesday to Sunday nights, with two seatings Friday and Saturday; the short dinner menu features pasta and steaks. ☎ 973-744-2600; www.trumpetsjazz.com; 6 Depot Sq, Montclair; tickets $5-15, mains $10-20; ⌚ from 6pm Tue-Sat, from 7pm Sun, plus brunch 11:30am-3pm Sun

Vintage Vinyl

Hard to find, in the small Fords Shopping Plaza on Rte 1; download directions. ☎ 732-225-6948; www.vvinyl.com; Rte 1 & Ford Ave, Fords; ⊙ 10am-10pm Mon-Sat, noon-8pm Sun

Wave Gathering

Since 2006, hundreds of emerging musicians and bands have made noise in Asbury Park for three days in late June. www.wavegathering.com; various locations, Asbury Park; tickets $25-40

EAT & DRINK

Leo's Grandevous

Serves an Italian menu, in addition to a full bar of Sinatra nostalgia; cash only. ☎ 201-659-9467; www.leosgrandevous.com; 200 Grand St, Hoboken; mains $8-15; ⊙ 4-11pm Mon-Sat, to 10pm Sun; ♿

Mompou

Fresh updates of classic tapas (salt cod, *camarones*, *patatas bravas*); live music

Wednesday and Thursday and DJs Friday and Saturday. ☎ 973-578-8114, 866-998-2727; www.mompoutapas.com; 77 Ferry St, Newark; mains $7-14; ⊙ noon-2am Mon-Fri, 5pm-3am Sat, 5pm-1am Sun

SLEEP

Empress

An older but nicely renovated hotel; ample sunning decks and two poolside bars. ☎ 732-774-0100; www.asburyempress.com; Asbury & Ocean Aves, Asbury Park; r midweek/weekend from $160/230

Robert Treat Hotel

Renovated in 2007, with flat-screen TVs and fridges in 160 rooms; floor-to-ceiling mirrors increase the sense of space. ☎ 973-622-1000, 800-780-7234; www.rthotel.com; 50 Park Pl, Newark; r $165-300; ♿

USEFUL WEBSITES

www.asburymusic.com
www.northjerseymusic.com

LINK YOUR TRIP

www.lonelyplanet.com/trip-planner

TRIP
25 OPEN 24 HRS p193
27 Down by the Boardwalk opposite

OUTDOORS

Down by the Boardwalk

WHY GO Jersey girls in bikinis, too-hot-to-eat funnel cakes, mile-long boardwalks, clanging arcades, neon-lit Ferris wheels, steamed crabs, sweaty beers, and 127 miles of Jersey coast washed by the Atlantic Ocean: when temperatures soar in July and August, pack the car. It's time to go down the shore.

But let's be honest: in summertime, the Jersey shore can be hell. Traffic's a nightmare, parking's impossible, the beaches are packed, the cover bands are terrible, and a day of boardwalk amusements can drain your wallet faster than a flock of seagulls on a dropped slice of pizza. The perfect boardwalk exists only in Springsteen songs, which echo like a siren's call in the heat-addled brains of tri-state-area residents, who in a fevered dementia descend en masse, all trying to get to the water at once.

Don't let this happen to you. We love the shore, but Parkway backups and sand rash have taught us a few lessons. Simply put, as Edna Mode would say, "Luck favors the prepared." Pack the car – *the night before*. Leave at dawn, or soon thereafter. If at all possible, come midweek. If you want to stay, make reservations. And if you want something besides a run-down, sun-bleached, musty, three-blocks-from-the-water, sand-crusted flea box, make reservations six months to a year in advance.

While Jersey is flush with all types of beaches (see also other trips in this book), this trip highlights classic Jersey boardwalks, which are not all made the same (well, technically, they are all raised wooden piers running parallel to the shore, but you know what we mean).

Let's start with the boardwalk Bruce made famous: **❶ Asbury Park**. Like a song, the Asbury Park boardwalk lives as much in memory as in reality – its beachfront, and the town, exist in a perpetual cycle of

TIME
1 – 7 days

DISTANCE
120 miles

BEST TIME TO GO
Jun – Sep

START
Asbury Park

END
Wildwood

ALSO GOOD FOR

ROUTE

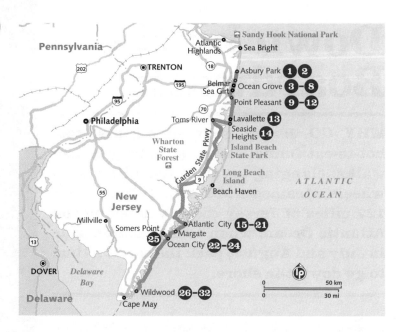

renewal and decay. Construction crews have been as busy as ever recently, so perhaps that's about to change, but that's been said before.

The boardwalk itself is short, by Jersey standards: at one end is the gorgeous but empty carousel building, and near the other is the majestic, red-brick Grand Arcade, which houses the quite-active Paramount Theatre, the Convention Hall, and a clutch of restaurants and bars. The boardwalk is pretty much just a boardwalk – without frantic amusements and arcades – fronting an attractive, well-cared-for stretch of sand. Asbury Park's amusements tend to be more for adults than children: its clubs and bars rock late into the night, it has decent surf, and it has the shore's best gay scene.

It also has one of the shore's best breakfast spots: **2 Sunset Landing** is like a Hawaiian surf shack transported to a suburban Asbury lakeside. Vintage longboards crowd the wooden rafters (including one of Greg Knoll's), cheesy omelettes are super-fresh, and delicious specialty pancakes come with cranberries, cinnamon, coconut, macadamia nuts and other island flavors. As Rob, the owner, told us: "I'm from Maui, so this was as close as we could get."

Next to Asbury Park is **3 Ocean Grove**, and there couldn't be two more different towns. Ocean Grove ("God's Square Mile at the Jersey Shore") is as perfectly coifed, sober, conservative and quaint as Asbury Park is scuffed, scraggly, gay and hungover. Originally a Methodist Camp Meeting summer colony, Ocean Grove's "tent city" – a crowded mass of wood shacks with tented fronts and bright striped awnings – became permanent, and around it grew one of the cutest Victorian seaside towns anywhere, with a boardwalk boasting not a single business to disturb the peace and quiet.

Towering over the tents, the 1894 mustard yellow ❹ **Great Auditorium** shouldn't be missed: its vaulted interior, meticulous acoustics and historic organ recall Utah's Mormon Tabernacle. Make sure to catch a recital or concert. Main Ave and the streets off it are silly with adorable eateries like the ❺ **Starving Artist**, with a big outdoor patio, tasty ice cream, and even live theater. For a more serious meal, the coolly modern ❻ **Seagrass** specializes in the tasty critters swimming off the coast.

> **ASK A LOCAL**
>
> "I like Sea Bright. There's no boardwalk. It's very quiet and has pretty sand dunes. To me, just to be close to the ocean, to have the breeze and the warm water, is heaven on earth. Because of the way it's situated, Sea Bright doesn't have as rough a sea as other places, like Point Pleasant. I go to the Point Pleasant boardwalk later, for ice cream, pizza, cotton candy. It's nice. The food is nice and the kids are nice."
>
> *Lynn Quinones, Nutley*

For a comfortable, unfussy night's sleep in a historic Victorian, try the ❼ **Quaker Inn** (with small, well-priced, attractive rooms) and the ❽ **Manchester Inn**, a homey, rambling building with endearing personal touches (like hand-painted murals), not corporate-slick luxury.

Now, follow Rte 71 south through a string of sleepy towns (Bradley Beach, Belmar, Sea Girt) to reach ❾ **Point Pleasant**, the first of five quintessential bumper-car-and-Skee-Ball boardwalks. On a July weekend, Point Pleasant's long beach is jam-packed: squint, cover up all that nearly naked flesh with striped unitards, and it could be the 1920s – umbrellas shading every inch of sand and the surf clogged with bodies and bobbing heads.

Families with young kids love Point Pleasant, as the boardwalk is big but not overwhelming, and the squeaky-clean amusement rides, fun house and small aquarium – all run by ❿ **Jenkinson's** – are geared to the height and delight of the 10-and-under set. That's not to say Point Pleasant is only for little ones. ⓫ **Martell's Tiki Bar**, a place margarita pitchers go to die, makes sure of that: look for the neon-orange palm trees and listen for the live bands. Point Pleasant's motel selections are uninspiring, but a dependably clean place right on the beach is the ⓬ **Windswept Motel**.

"…squint, cover up all that nearly naked flesh with striped unitards, and it could be the 1920s…"

As you head south on Rte 35, stop in Lavallette for an ice cream at the ⓭ **Music Man**, a true crowd-pleaser where every evening is "dessert theater," with servers belting out Broadway show tunes tableside. Go on, order a sundae; you'll smile all the way home.

Just south is **14 Seaside Heights**, a truly overwhelming boardwalk so long it has a sky ride and two rollicking amusement piers with double corridors of arcade games and adult-size, adrenaline-pumping rides, roller coasters, and various iterations of the vomit-inducing 10-story drop. During the day, it's as family friendly as Point Pleasant, but once darkness falls Seaside Heights becomes a scene of such hedonistic mating rituals that an evangelical church has felt the need for a permanent booth on the pier. Packs of young men – caps askew, tats gleaming – check out packs of young women in shimmering spaghetti-strap micro-dresses as everyone rotates among the string of loud bars with live bands growling out Eagles tunes. It's pure Jersey.

Jumping down to **15 Atlantic City**, we find the same conundrum that bedevils Asbury Park: the city and its boardwalk couldn't be more famous and enjoy more goodwill – after all, its real estate has been bought and sold in "Monopoly" for over 70 years. And AC's casinos have spent Monopoly-like amounts of money (just ask Donald Trump) to bring to life the ultimate boardwalk fantasy, in which the pier's kiddie games and their plush-doll prizes morph into real-stakes gambling for hard cash. Yet, this somehow dampens the charm of those harmless seaside arcades, and Atlantic City, for all its efforts at rejuvenation, has never quite rid itself of the poverty that sits side by side with the glitz.

As for the long boardwalk itself, its beach sometimes feels too narrow and cramped. The Steel Pier is the destination for games and rides, though the amusements are tame compared to Seaside Heights. The **16 Trump Taj Mahal** towers over Steel Pier, making it ideally situated to combine sunning and slots. Further down, **17 Caesars** is next door to the concert hall, across from its namesake pier (an upscale mall with a clever dancing fountain), and in walking distance to the corporate-sanitized outlet shopping along Michigan Ave.

About six miles west of Seaside Heights in Toms River, the sarcastically named **Shut Up and Eat!** (☎ 732-349-4544) could be the silliest breakfast joint ever: waitresses in pajamas (wear yours for a 13% discount), snappy repartee, mismatched furniture and a cornucopia of kitsch (Shaun Cassidy records, dial phones, cartoon lunch boxes). Even better: the stuffed French toast with real maple syrup, plus top-quality omelets, pancakes and more. It's tucked away in the Kmart shopping plaza at 213 Rte 37 east.

AC isn't bereft of authentic charms, of course. Make sure to see the frankly somber **18 Korean War Memorial** near the Central Pier; and at the Garden Pier, the **19 Atlantic City Historical Museum** preserves an appealingly self-amused nostalgia for the AC of yesteryear. Take the bridge to Brigantine to visit the **20** **Marine Mammal Stranding Center**, which rehabilitates lost and injured seals in winter and sea turtles in summer. Finally, absolutely don't leave before visiting **21** **White House Subs**, an icon of old AC whose wall of fame includes Tiny Tim, Roddy McDowall, Ellen DeGeneres, CCH Pounder and the Beatles. Plus, its gigantic oily subs (say "yes" to hot peppers) and cheesesteaks really are the best. Some stop in AC simply to grab a number here.

Take your sub and head to **22** **Ocean City**, an almost heavenly amalgam of Ocean Grove and Point Pleasant: it's a dry town with a roomy boardwalk packed with genuine family fun and facing an exceedingly pretty beach. There's a small water park, and Gillian's Wonderland has a heart-thumpingly tall Ferris wheel, a beautifully restored merry-go-round, kiddie rides galore – and no microphoned teens hawking carnie games. The mood is light and friendly (a lack of alcohol will do that).

Minigolf aficionados: dingdingdingding! You hit the jackpot. Pint-size duffers can play through on a three-masted schooner, around great white

> **DETOUR**
>
> She's the most famous icon of the Jersey shore, and you can look out her eyeballs: she's **Lucy the Margate Elephant** (www.lucytheelephant .org). A six-story novelty built in 1881, Lucy was saved by a truly remarkable restoration effort. Tours take you inside her roomy belly, where you get the whole story, and then up to the "howdah" for the sweeping view. Pat her red toenails for us. From Atlantic City, take Atlantic Ave south to Decatur Ave in Margate.

sharks and giant octopus, under reggae monkeys piloting a helicopter and even in black light. If you haven't yet, beat the heat with a delicious Kohr's soft-serve frozen custard, plain or dipped. While saltwater taffy is offered many places, **23** **Shriver's Taffy** is, in our humble opinion, the best: watch machines stretch and wrap it through plate-glass windows, and then fill a bag with two dozen or more flavors.

Shake off those sandy motel blues at Ocean City's **24** **Flanders Hotel**: every room is a modern, immaculate, 650-sq-ft (or larger) suite with full kitchen, and the blue-and-yellow decor evokes a pleasantly low-key seaside feel. At dinnertime, make like a local and head five minutes out of town to Somers Point, where the popular **25** **Crab Trap** does classic seafood just right – not too fancy, not too plain.

Whether by design or serendipity, Jersey saves what many consider its best boardwalk for last. **26** **Wildwood** very nearly has it all. Not that we can't quibble. For instance, the beach is really *too* wide: from the boardwalk, you can barely see the waves break. But once you eventually trek to where sea meets sand, all is forgiven. With its sweetly lapping waves, Wildwood's beach is ideal for crafting those intricate, all-day sand castles.

Wildwood tops Seaside Heights for amusements, with a brilliantly lit Ferris wheel, two fantastic water parks and *three* piers shaking with rides – all run by **27** **Morey's Piers**. All ages can play happily for a week and not get bored (though, perhaps, annoyed by the incessant recording: "Watch the tram car, please"). If you're here for waterslides and roller coasters, book a room at **28** **Heart of Wildwood**, facing the amusement piers. It's not fancy, but gets high marks for cleanliness (the tile floors help), and from the heated rooftop pool you can watch the big wheel go round and round.

WE'RE HAVIN' A PARTY

Yes, in summer, every day is a party at the Jersey shore. But here are some events not to miss:

- Gay Pride Parade, Asbury Park, early June (www.gayasburypark.com)
- Polka Spree by the Sea, Wildwood, late June (www.polkaspree.com)
- New Jersey Sandcastle Contest, Belmar, July (www.njsandcastle.com)
- New Jersey State Barbecue Championship, Wildwood, mid-July (www.njbbq.com)
- Ocean City Baby Parade, Ocean City, early August (www.ocnj.us)
- Clownfest, Seaside Heights, mid-September (www.clownfest.com)

Wildwood is also famous for its 1950s-era doo-wop motels, a 100% kitschy nostalgia that infects businesses of all stripes. A drive along Ocean Ave provides an orgy of retro signage, neon starbursts and art deco curves, but many of the motels themselves are tired. Of the standouts, the sea-green-and-white **29** **Starlux** has the soaring profile, the lava lamps, the boomerang-decorated bedspreads and the sloopy-shaped mirrors, plus it's clean as a whistle. Even more authentically retro are its two chrome-sided Airstream trailers.

North of the noise and lights, in an unassuming white house, is the coolest vintage experience of all: **30** **Summer Nites B&B**. It's unalloyed fun, top to bottom. Real jukeboxes play 45s; the breakfast room is a perfectly re-created diner, with vinyl booths and tabletop jukes. The eight themed rooms are dominated by wall-size murals and framed, signed memorabilia: over the Jacuzzi in the pinkalicious Marilyn room, the sexy starlet poses wearing only bubbles, while the standout Elvis suite has gold couches, a black Jacuzzi and pouty, smoldering portraits designed to make your knees go weak.

Finally, no Jersey shore town worth its sea salt lacks a perfect, diner-style breakfast joint and a dependable seafood shack: in Wildwood, these roles are filled admirably (and respectively) by **31** **Uncle Bill's Pancake House** and **32** **Schellenger's**.

Now, go join the sunburned masses creeping home along the Parkway, or take one last dip and let the traffic leave without you.

Jeff Campbell

TRIP INFORMATION

GETTING THERE
All Jersey shore-towns are signed and accessible from the Garden State Parkway.

DO
Atlantic City Historical Museum
AC built the first seaside amusement pier in 1882 and launched the golden age of boardwalks; it's all here. ☎ 609-347-5839; www.acmuseum.org; Garden Pier, Atlantic City; admission free; ⊙ 10am-4pm; ⚅

Great Auditorium
Of course it sounds great, that organ's got 10,000 pipes! ☎ 732-775-0035, tickets 800-965-9324; www.oceangrove.org; Pilgrim Pathway, Ocean Grove; recitals free, concerts $13; ⊙ recitals 7:30pm Wed, 10am or noon Sat; ⚅

Jenkinson's
The amusement park is free, but rides are $2 to $5 a pop. Discount wristband promotion hours are listed online. ☎ 732-295-4334, aquarium 732-899-1659; www.jenkinsons.com; 300 Ocean Ave, Point Pleasant; aquarium adult/child $10/6; ⊙ rides noon-11pm, aquarium 10am-10pm, hours vary off-season; ⚅

Marine Mammal Stranding Center
Call to confirm hours and what animals you'll see; winter is busiest. Has a nice sea-life exhibit. ☎ 609-226-0538; www.marinemammalstrandingcenter.org; 3625 Brigantine Blvd, Brigantine; admission by donation; ⊙ 10am-4pm; ⚅

Morey's Piers
Hours and prices vary by day/season/type of ride/package. The website lays it all out. ☎ 609-522-3900; www.moreyspiers.com; at 25th, Schellenger & Spencer Aves, Wildwood; day passes $33-55; ⊙ piers noon-midnight, water parks 9am-7pm; ⚅

Shriver's Taffy
Not just taffy, but handmade chocolates and classic candies, too. ☎ 609-399-0100, 877-668-2339; www.shrivers.com; 9th & Boardwalk, Ocean City; ⊙ 9am-midnight, shorter hours off-season; ⚅

EAT & DRINK
Crab Trap
The quintessential surf and turf, with great crab cakes, fresh oysters, the works. ☎ 609-927-7377; www.thecrabtrap.com; Somers Point Circle, Somers Point; mains $17-35; ⊙ 11am-10pm, to 11pm Fri & Sat; ⚅

Martell's Tiki Bar
Martell's is actually several bars, inside and out (one even serves sushi), plus a sit-down restaurant and multiple food counters. ☎ 732-892-0131; www.tikibar.com; Boardwalk, Point Pleasant; mains $5-30; ⊙ 11am-11pm, to 12:30am Fri & Sat; ⚅

Music Man
Get takeout ice cream all day. Ticket-only kiddie events at 4pm, and music shows (free with sundae) start at 6pm. ☎ 732-854-2779; www.njmusicman.com; 2305 Grand Central Ave (Rte 35), Lavallette; mains $3-8; ⊙ takeout 6am-midnight, shows 6pm-midnight; ⚅

Schellenger's
The menu ranges widely, but the simpler the preparation, the more successful the dish. ☎ 609-522-0433; 3516 Atlantic Ave, Wildwood; mains $15-30; ⊙ 2:30-10pm; ⚅

Seagrass
Above-average, creative seafood, with a dash of Cajun spices, a sprinkling of panko crumbs, a splash of teriyaki sauce. ☎ 732-869-0770; 68 Main Ave, Ocean Grove; mains $16-29; ⊙ 11am-3pm & 5-9pm Wed-Sun; ⚅

Starving Artist
Menu highlights breakfast, the grill, and fried seafood; ice cream is at the adjacent shop. ☎ 732-988-1007; 47 Olin St, Ocean Grove; mains $3-9; ⊙ 8am-3pm Mon-Sat, to 2pm Sun, closed Wed; ⚅

Sunset Landing
"Surf Dawgs Rule"! It's on Deal Lake, about 10 blocks from the beach. Cash only. ☎ 732-776-9732; 1215 Sunset Ave, Asbury Park; mains $5-8; ⊙ 7am-2pm Tue-Sun; ⚅

Uncle Bill's Pancake House
As the name says, the specialty is pancakes, but all the breakfasts are good. No reservations; cash only. ☎ 609-729-7557; 4601 Pacific Ave, Wildwood; mains $5-9.50; ⊙ 7am-2pm; ⚅

White House Subs
A half is bigger than most subs elsewhere; a whole could feed a family of four. ☎ 609-345-8599; 2301 Arctic Ave at Mississippi, Atlantic City; mains $6-15; ⏰ 10am-9:30pm; ♿

SLEEP

Caesars
Weekend rates are insane, but at least you get a flat-screen TV and no sandy carpets. ☎ 800-443-0104; www.caesarsac.com; 2100 Pacific Ave, Atlantic City; r $220-520

Flanders Hotel
You'll wish every shore hotel were this nice. Parking and beach tags included. Great deals off-season. ☎ 609-399-1000; www.flandershotel.com; 719 E 11th St, Ocean City; r $260-440; ♿

Heart of Wildwood
Thirteen room types fit all needs; it's well-run and easy-clean functional, right on the boardwalk. ☎ 609-522-4090; www.heartofwildwood.com; Ocean & Spencer Aves, Wildwood; r $125-245; ♿

Manchester Inn
The cheapest rooms share a bath; breakfast is included. Open year-round. ☎ 732-775-0616; www.themanchesterinn.com; 25 Ocean Pathway, Ocean Grove; r $115-190; ♿

Quaker Inn
The 135-year-old inn has 29 rooms, all with air-con and TV, and some with balconies.

Open year-round; no breakfast. ☎ 732-775-7525; www.quakerinn.com; 39 Main St, Ocean Grove; r $90-150; ♿

Starlux
Parking included; open year-round. Heart-shaped pool, Airstream trailers and a cottage. ☎ 609-522-7412; www.thestarlux.com; Rio Grande & Atlantic Aves, Wildwood; r $130-310; ♿

Summer Nites B&B
Full hot breakfast, working Zenith TV, pool table, pinball machines, loaner bicycles; small bathrooms are the only knock. ☎ 609-846-1955; www.summernites.com; 2110 Atlantic Ave, Wildwood; r $145-275

Trump Taj Mahal
Rooms are nicely appointed and, outside summer, very competitively priced. ☎ 800-825-8786; www.trumptaj.com; 1000 Boardwalk at Virginia Ave, Atlantic City; r $250-350

Windswept Motel
Includes a parking space and beach pass; no fridge in queen rooms. Open year-round. ☎ 732-899-1282; www.windsweptmotel.net; 1008 Ocean Ave, Point Pleasant; r $170-295; ♿

USEFUL WEBSITES
www.jersey-shore-region.com
www.nj.com/shore

LINK YOUR TRIP
www.lonelyplanet.com/trip-planner

Cape May: Seaside Idyll

WHY GO Nowhere does the Jersey shore reach a more perfect summation than at its southern tip – in Cape May. What's so idyllic? Try a walkable historic downtown chockablock with fine cuisine and elegant Victorian inns, dolphins frolicking offshore, and pristine beaches littered with "diamonds." And that's just for starters.

TIME
2 – 4 days

BEST TIME TO GO
May – Sep

START
Cape May

END
Cape May

ALSO GOOD FOR

Cape May satisfies everyone – from history buffs to families to nature lovers to hyper-social teens – but it's particularly appealing to couples seeking seaside romance. Despite the crush of summer crowds and the ensuing traffic jams on the tiny one-way streets, it's easy to nestle in the plush secluded splendor of gorgeous B&Bs, get moon-faced over candlelit gourmet meals, and walk silken strands of sand till the splashing, boogie-boarding tweens are a distant echo. Outside summer, Cape May calms down but remains open, making it an ideal choice for a lovely beach getaway year-round.

The heart of the Cape May scene is the pedestrian ❶ **Washington St Mall**, a stretch containing every seashell trinket, jokey T-shirt and dripping hamburger a beach vacation requires – and ice cream (so much ice cream). At Ocean St, ❷ **Washington Commons** is the horse-carriage turnaround, and the streets leading to the beach are lined with richly painted, gingerbread-laced Victorian homes (and look at that – many are inns!). Between Grant and Jefferson Sts, ❸ **Beach Ave** is lined with bars, cheap eats and mini-golf.

Anchoring the Washington St Mall, and Cape May itself, is the grand, lemon-yellow ❹ **Congress Hall**. A favorite for weddings, Congress Hall overlooks the ocean and evokes a breezy seaside mood, with uneven floors, understated but generous contemporary rooms, and playful wood-shuttered interior screen doors (covering actual room doors).

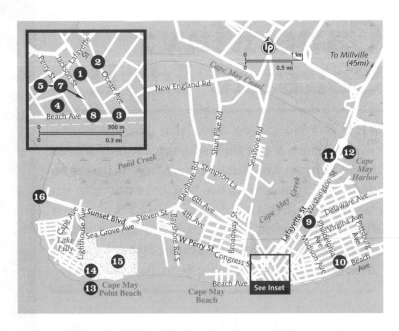

Nearby on Jackson St, the **5** **Virginia Hotel** is a sophisticated interpretation of the Victorian good life, with flat-screen TVs, modern furnishings and a cocoa and powder-blue palette. The Virginia's **6** **Ebbitt Room** whips up gourmet dining that stands out in a crowded field.

ASK A LOCAL

"Why does Cape May have so many ghosts? I don't know – it just does. People say a washing machine will turn on for no reason. The nuns at St Mary's say a ghost likes to mop – they find the mop moves around. There's lots of children downtown. They're waiting for their parents to come home. People take pictures in front of the lighthouse and find blurs in them."

Ed Levine, Cape May

Next door, the **7** **Mad Batter** is another institution: a friendly, unfussy destination serving fluffy pancakes and crazy-good lump-crab eggs Benedict. It's the sort of popular breakfast-place-cum-bar every good beach town needs. Down the street, **8** **Hot Dog Tommy's** is the perfect hole-in-the-wall: definitely order two dogs, one with homemade cranberry slaw, one with chili. Tommy is the guy cracking wise in the hot-dog hat.

Cape May's preeminent Victorian mansion is the 1879 **9** **Emlen Physick Estate**. Forty-five-minute tours immerse you in tea-drinking turn-of-the-century life, and here you can also book popular trolley tours of other Victorian homes, plus ghost tours, moonlight tours and scores more.

To escape Victoriana entirely, get thee to the ❿ **Mission Inn**, a historic Spanish home thoroughly reimagined as a fantastical paean to California's Spanish missions. Each sumptuous room is cleverly painted in indescribable floor-to-ceiling trompe l'oeil murals of actual missions. It's so egregiously comfy you'll never want to leave.

North of downtown, Cape May's wharf is the place for ⓫ **Cape May Whale Watcher** tours; year-round you'll see juvenile finback and humpback whales as well as oodles of dolphins. Also here, ⓬ **Lobster House** provides the classic waterfront experience: buy fresh fish to cook yourself, wait forever for a restaurant seat or, best of all, order from the raw bar or takeout window, grab a wharfside table and make a full-blown mess with a wooden mallet, drawn butter and steamed lobster.

West of town, take Sunset Blvd to ⓭ **Cape May Point**, which is the best place to bike, as traffic downtown is a drag. Here, the ⓮ **Cape May Lighthouse** is one of Jersey's most attractive, with 199 steps to the top affording opulent views. The adjacent ⓯ **Cape May Point State Park** has a bounty of wildlife. A small wildlife museum has exhibits on the point's dramatic erosion, and trails lead through wetlands favored by over 300 species of migratory birds, monarch butterflies and even dragonflies. In fall, tens of thousands of hawks, eagles, falcons and raptors fill the skies. Meanwhile, the beach is quieter because you can't swim, but dolphins feed and play seemingly at arm's length all day, more than making up for it.

Head to ⓰ **Sunset Beach** an hour or so before the appointed moment for Cape May's best show. Since 1973, from Memorial Day to October, Sunset Beach has held a genuinely moving flag-lowering ceremony. The beach flies casket flags of American war veterans, and just before sunset, the national anthem and taps are played, and the sacrifice of each individual is remembered. Then, everyone turns around to watch the blazing sun lower into the goblet of the sea, and to sift the pebbly beach for Cape May "diamonds" – bits of crystal quartz that, over eons, have washed down the Delaware River to land here. When polished and faceted, the opaque gray rocks become clear or milky semiprecious stones worthy of a gold setting. And that's how perfect Cape May is – it gives diamonds to anyone who troubles to look.

DETOUR An hour northwest of Cape May, off Hwy 55 in Millville, **WheatonArts and Cultural Center** (www.wheatonarts.org) presents one of the world's finest historic and artistic glass collections. Resident artists give glass-blowing and pottery demonstrations daily, and the Down Jersey Folklife Center highlights Jerseyan cultural expression. If the names Chihuly and Tiffany make you drool, WheatonArts will blow your mind.

Jeff Campbell

TRIP INFORMATION

GETTING THERE
From Philadelphia, take the Atlantic City Expressway to the Garden State Parkway, and head south till the road runs out.

DO
Cape May Lighthouse
Run by the Mid-Atlantic Center for the Arts. ☎ 609-884-5404; www.capemaymac.org; Cape May Point State Park; adult/child $7/3; ⊙ 9am-9pm, shorter hours off-season; ♿

Cape May Point State Park
Accessible short hikes, bird-watching, wildlife museum; no swimming on the beach. ☎ 609-884-2159; www.njparksandforests .org/parks/capemay.html; Lighthouse Ave, Cape May Point; admission free; ⊙ 9am-7pm, shorter hours off-season; ♿

Cape May Whale Watcher
Two- and three-hour tours nearly always see dolphins and usually whales. ☎ 800-786-5445; www.capemaywhalewatcher.com; 2nd Ave & Wilson Dr; adult $30-40, child $20-25; ⊙ daily tours, times vary; ♿

Emlen Physick Estate
Ask about combination tickets; reserve ahead on rainy days, when tours book up lickety-split. ☎ 609-884-5404, 800-275-4278; www.capemaymac.org; 1048 Washington St; estate adult/child $10/5, trolley tours $10-15; ⊙ multiple tours daily, hours vary by day/season; ♿

EAT
Hot Dog Tommy's
Frozen sodas are a great accompaniment to an all-beef BAD (black angus dog). ☎ 609-884-8388; www.hotdogtommys.com; Jackson St

at Beach Ave; hot dogs $1.30-4; ⊙ 10:31am-5:17pm, with seasonal variations; ♿

Lobster House
No reservations, but between the fish market, takeout counter, raw bar and restaurant, options abound. ☎ 609-884-8296, takeout 609-884-3064; www.thelobsterhouse.com; Lafayette St, Fisherman's Wharf; mains $7-50; ⊙ 11:30am-10pm, with seasonal variations; ♿

Mad Batter
No reservations for breakfast, so arrive by 9am or expect to wait. ☎ 609-884-5970; www.madbatter.com; 19 Jackson St; breakfast $7.50-12, dinner $24-31; ⊙ 8am-3pm, dinner from 5pm; ♿

SLEEP
Congress Hall
Rates vary widely year-round and with ocean or town view; on-site spa, restaurant, concierge and lovely pool. ☎ 609-884-8421, 888-944-1816; www.congresshall.com; 251 Beach Ave; r $125-540; ♿

Mission Inn
To the eight uniquely designed rooms, add fireplaces, flat-screen TVs, central air-con, jacuzzi tubs and a three-course breakfast. ☎ 609-884-8380, 800-800-8380; www .missioninn.net; 1117 New Jersey Ave; r $205-310

Virginia Hotel & Ebbitt Room
Room rates vary by day and season; live jazz enlivens the restaurant on weekends. ☎ 609-884-5700, 800-732-4236; www.vir giniahotel.com; 25 Jackson St; r $270-500, mains $26-36; ⊙ restaurant 5:30-9:30pm

USEFUL WEBSITES
www.capemaychamber.com
www.capemaytimes.com

LINK YOUR TRIP
www.lonelyplanet.com/trip-planner

Bogs, Barrens & the Jersey Devil

OUTDOORS

WHY GO To explore New Jersey's Pine Barrens is to leave much of the urbanized Eastern seaboard far behind. Sandy trails and meandering rivers lead through a habitat of bogs, wetlands and stunted forests – home to carnivorous plants, pygmy pines, cranberry bogs and chilling ghost stories of one legendary devil.

Officially named the Pinelands National Reserve, the Pine Barrens is a 1.1-million-acre biosphere reserve that is the coast's largest protected habitat between Boston and Richmond. The forests were originally considered barren because the acidic, sandy soil wouldn't grow normal crops. So, by the mid-1800s, most folks had washed their hands of the place; those who remained were dubbed "Pineys." Like the trees, they were rough-barked and tough but surprisingly friendly when you got to know them. It's no different today.

The best place to begin is at the well-preserved historic village of ❶ **Batsto**. Founded in 1766, Batsto forged "bog iron" for the Revolutionary War and remained an important ironworks until the 1850s. Batsto is also the main Wharton State Forest visitors center, with slickly updated exhibits on the Pinelands' entire cultural and natural history. From here, several 1- to 4-mile loop trails provide a great taste of the scrub oak and scrub pine, swamp maple and Atlantic white cedar that make up these scruffy woods.

The most famous trail is the epic 50-mile ❷ **Batona Trail** (long but moderate). Highlights are the magnificent views from the Apple Pie Hill fire tower and the Carranza Memorial, honoring a Mexican pilot who crashed in 1928. Look for endangered pitcher plants, which get nutrients from insects that they can't get from the soil.

TIME
2 – 3 days

DISTANCE
130 miles

BEST TIME TO GO
Apr – Oct

START
Batsto

END
Harbor City

ALSO GOOD FOR

OFFBEAT

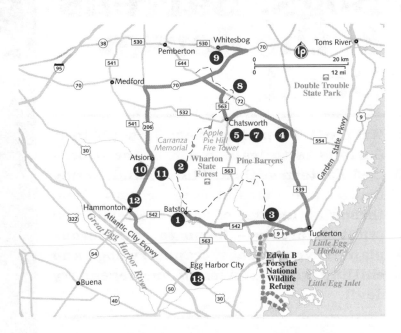

Next, from Batsto, take Rte 542 east and follow the signs for ❸ **Bass River State Forest**, which gets packed in summer because of its swimming lake and large campground. Facilities are kept relatively spiffy, but know that all camping is "buggy." Hey, it's the Pine Barrens! In summer, prepare to fend off mosquitoes, strawberry flies, greenheads and other quaintly named biting pests, all of which diminish in spring and fall.

The **Edwin B Forsythe National Wildlife Refuge** (www.fws.gov/northeast/forsythe) protects 50 miles of coastal wetlands and provides habitat for over 300 species of migratory birds. To glimpse egrets, herons, ibis and osprey yourself (spring and fall are best, but flocks migrate through year-round), visit refuge headquarters south of Smithville. An 8-mile drive and hiking trails get you into the middle of the wetness. It's about 20 miles from Batsto, off Hwy 9 at Great Creek Rd.

From Bass River, take Stage Rd to Tuckerton and then Rte 539 north to Hwy 72 west. Around this intersection, you pass sections of ❹ **pygmy forest**, where crabbed pines gnarl their way to 6ft, tops. Several dirt roads lead into them (there are no official trails), but assess carefully: Pine Barrens backroads can have sand traps and hip-deep puddles that swallow your average sedan.

From Hwy 72, take Rte 532 to ❺ **Chatsworth**, a small "Piney" town made famous in John McPhee's 1967 book *The Pine Barrens*. The ❻ **Chatsworth General Store & Buzby's Cafe** is the perfect stop for breakfast or lunch, to buy a Pine Barrens nature guide, and to get acquainted with the cranberry bog workers and hardy folk who call this land home. In October, the **7** **Chatsworth Cranberry Festival** is a don't-miss event.

Refreshed and enlightened, take Rte 563 north to Hwy 72, then Hwy 70 north to **8** **Brendan T Byrne State Forest**. With a paved, 10-mile loop road, and 14 more miles of sand-slippery trails, this is the best place to bike, on- or off-road (plus, the roads to/from Chatsworth have generous bike lanes). Brendan T Byrne also contains enormous cranberry bogs, which, when flooded, become surreal, undulating lakes of shimmering garnet jewels. The cranberry harvest occurs over six weeks around October.

"…enormous cranberry bogs, which, when flooded, become surreal, undulating lakes of shimmering garnet jewels."

For a real education in berry-ology, head for **9** **Whitesbog** (take Hwy 70 north and Rte 530 west). Here, in the early 20th century, Elizabeth White developed the first cultivated blueberry. The last Saturday in June, the blueberry harvest festival inspires rapture, while more working cranberry bogs paint fields red in October. Whitesbog's General Store is an atmospheric relic, and loving tours take in White's gardens, the bogs and the historic village, which is still occupied by workers' families.

The last major destination is **10** **Atsion**, part of Wharton State Forest. More camping and cabins and a large, sandy swimming lake make this extremely popular with families. And Atsion provides another quintessential Pinelands experience: leisurely **11** **Mullica River canoe trips**. The nearby Batsto River is an equally scenic choice; do a day trip or overnight at backcountry campgrounds along the rivers.

THE JERSEY DEVIL IS BORN

Pull over at roadside stands and pickup trucks selling fresh berries and produce, but don't leave without tasting the fruits of the Barrens the way they're meant to be experienced – in a pie. Far and away the best – heaving tin vessels of crumble-topped, oozing sugary goodness – are made at **12** **Penza's Red Barn Cafe**, along Hwy 206 south of Atsion. End your trip with a sip of blueberry champagne at the 140-year-old **13** **Renault Winery** in Egg Harbor City, and you'll have enjoyed all that is sweet and salty, sandy and enduring, about New Jersey's legendary Pine Barrens.

In 1735, a certain Mrs Leeds, not wanting more children, let fly that if she had another child, she wished it would be "a devil." Sure enough, she became pregnant and gave birth to a creature with a horse head, bat wings, cloven hooves and a forked tail. Ever since, the "Leeds Devil" has stalked the Pine Barrens, filling night-shrouded forests with blood-curdling shrieks, haunting the dreams of children and frightening campers.

Don't believe us? Ask locals. Just *don't camp alone…*

Jeff Campbell

TRIP INFORMATION

GETTING THERE
From Philadelphia, take I-76 to Atlantic City Expressway. At exit 28, take Hwy 206 north and Rte 542 east to Batsto.

DO
Adams Canoe Rental
Next to Atsion; pick-up/drop-off service. Minimum age 6; no credit cards. ☎ 609-268-0189; www.adamscanoerental.com; 1005 Atsion Rd, Atsion; kayak/canoe $45/75; 🚻 ♿

Batsto Village
A restored mansion, 33 historic buildings and state forest backcountry camping reservations. ☎ 609-561-0024; www.njparksandforests.org/parks/wharton.html; Rte 542, Batsto; mansion tour $2; 🕐 visitors center 9am-4:30pm; 🚻 ♿

Chatsworth Cranberry Festival
The October festival's main draw, besides the bogs, is its huge craft fair; south of Chatsworth on Rte 563 are some huge cranberry farms. ☎ 609-726-9237; www.cranfest.org; Chatsworth, NJ; 🕐 2 days in mid-Oct

Renault Winery
Winery tours and tastings occur daily, plus two restaurants, gourmet and Italian. ☎ 609-965-2111; www.renaultwinery.com; 72 N Bremen Ave, Egg Harbor City; tours $3, mains $15-30; 🕐 shop & tours 10am-5pm, later Fri & Sat, restaurant from 11:30am

Whitesbog
General Store sells berry jam and gifts; tours by reservation. ☎ 609-893-4646; www.whitesbog.org; Rte 530, Whitesbog; admission free, tours $5; 🕐 store 10am-4pm Sat & Sun Feb-Dec; 🚻

LINK YOUR TRIP

EAT
Chatsworth General Store & Buzby's Cafe
Lazy ceiling fans, eggs, pancakes and sandwiches; cash only. ☎ 609-894-4415, 609-726-9000; Rte 563 & First St, Chatsworth; mains $5-7; 🕐 7am-2pm Thu-Sun; 🚻

Penza's Red Barn Cafe
The simple café closes after lunch, but the pie shop does brisk business all day. ☎ 609-567-3412; www.penzaspies.com; Hwy 206 & Myrtle St, Hammonton; pies $16-23, mains $4-8; 🕐 store 8am-6pm, café 8am-1:30pm; 🚻

SLEEP
Atsion
Roomy, wooded, full-service campground and big cabins, with grills and picnic tables. ☎ 609-268-0444; www.njparksandforests.org/parks/wharton.html; Hwy 206, Atsion; lake parking midweek/weekends $5/10, campsites $20, cabins $45-85; 🕐 dawn-dusk; 🚻

Bass River State Forest
Just like Atsion, but add enclosed lean-tos. ☎ 609-296-1114; www.njparksandforests.org/parks/bass.html; 762 Stage Rd, Tuckerton; lake parking midweek/weekends $5/10, campsites $20, lean-tos $30, cabins $45-85; 🕐 dawn-dusk; 🚻

Brendan T Byrne State Forest
Just like Atsion, but add yurts. ☎ 609-726-1191; www.njparksandforests.org/parks/byrne.html; junction Rtes 70 & 72; parking free, campsites $20, yurts $30, cabins $45; 🕐 dawn-dusk; 🚻

USEFUL WEBSITES
www.nps.gov/pine
www.pineypower.com

SUGGESTED READS
• *The Pine Barrens*, John McPhee
• *A Pine Barrens Odyssey*, Howard Boyd

www.lonelyplanet.com/trip-planner

Dutch Country Timewarp

WHY GO The Amish really do drive buggies and plow their fields by hand. In Dutch Country, the pace is slower, and it's no costumed reenactment. This is modern life in a world where autos feel somehow indecent. Happily park yours and travel by train, horse, bike and foot instead.

TIME
2 – 3 days

DISTANCE
35 miles

BEST TIME TO GO
Mar – Sep

START
Lancaster

END
Lancaster

ALSO GOOD FOR

FOOD & DRINK

It's tempting to say the Amish have turned their backs on the modern world, but they see it every day. They are surrounded by powerlines, asphalt and tourists. And while they're good marketers and have packaged their lives into visitor-friendly morsels, they're not kidding either. They'd rather walk a mile than drive a hundred. It makes for some interesting questions and anachronisms (Why is a gasoline-powered refrigerator OK but an electric one not? Why is a push scooter preferred over a bicycle? Why don't they like to be photographed?) Yet, after a few relatively unplugged days, you'll start to think the Amish might be onto something.

A good place to start is ❶ **Lancaster**, a bustling, diverse city with all the 21st-century conveniences. In the walkable, red-brick historic district, just off Penn Sq, is the ❷ **Central Market**, which is like a smaller version of Philadelphia's Reading Terminal Market. Sample all the regional gastronomic delicacies – fresh horseradish, whoopie pies, soft pretzels, sub sandwiches stuffed with cured meats and dripping with oil. You'll find surprises, too, like Spanish and Middle Eastern food. Plus, of course, the market is crowded with handicraft booths staffed by bonneted, plain-dressed Amish women.

Next door is the ❸ **Lancaster Quilt & Textile Museum**, which has a beautifully displayed collection of 82 historic Amish quilts. Exhibits do an eloquent yet succinct job of describing the bold, bright geometric-patterned artworks as well as the culture of the people who make them; a hands-on kid's area lets you "make" your own.

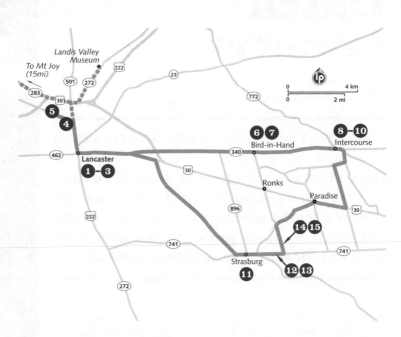

Those wishing to visit Dutch Country by day but luxuriate by night should bunk down at the **4** **Lancaster Arts Hotel**, which has artfully transformed a tobacco warehouse into a sophisticated boutique property. Down the street, **5** **Iron Hill Brewery** handcrafts beer, which some consider no less an art.

From Lancaster, take Rte 340 to **6** **Bird-in-Hand**, one of several delightfully named Amish towns. Shops and gift stores abound along the highway, but make sure to visit the **7** **Bird-in-Hand Farmers Market**, which is pretty much a one-stop shop of Dutch Country highlights. There's fudge, quilts and crafts, and you can buy scrapple, homemade jam and shoofly pie.

A more satisfying town is **8** **Intercourse** (named for the crossroads, silly), since it's more amenable to walking. **9** **Horse-drawn buggy rides** are offered seemingly every few yards, and they can be great fun. How much fun depends largely on your driver: some Amish are strict, some liberal, and Mennonites are different again. All drivers strive to present Amish culture to the "English" (the Amish term for non-Amish, whether English or not), but some are more openly personal than others.

You may be tempted by the many advertisements for all-you-can-eat, family-style Dutch restaurants, and a good place to give in is **10** **Stoltzfus Farm**. It's just country cooking, plain and plentiful, but served by waitresses so preternaturally friendly you wonder for your own hardened soul.

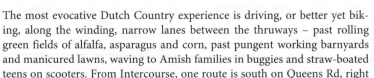
The most evocative Dutch Country experience is driving, or better yet biking, along the winding, narrow lanes between the thruways – past rolling green fields of alfalfa, asparagus and corn, past pungent working barnyards and manicured lawns, waving to Amish families in buggies and straw-boated teens on scooters. From Intercourse, one route is south on Queens Rd, right on Harvest Dr and left on Belmont Rd to Hwy 30. Go west on Hwy 30 and exit on Paradise Lane, following that into Strasburg.

The main attraction in ⓫ **Strasburg** is trains, the old-fashioned, steam-driven kind, which somehow seem of-a-piece. Since 1832, the ⓬ **Strasburg Railroad** has run the same route (and speed) it does today, and wooden train cars are gorgeously restored: with stained glass, shiny brass lamps and plush burgundy seats. Several rides are offered; plan ahead and you can get off halfway along the route for a picnic.

 **DETOUR** In the 18th century, German immigrants flooded southeastern Pennsylvania, and only some were Amish. Most lived like the costumed docents at the **Landis Valley Museum** (www.landisvalley museum.org), a re-creation of Pennsylvania German village life that includes a working smithy, weavers, stables and more. The museum is a few miles north of Lancaster, off Rte 272/Oregon Pike.

The ⓭ **Railroad Museum of Pennsylvania** has 100 gigantic mechanical marvels to climb around and admire, but even more delightful is the HO-scale ⓮ **National Toy Train Museum**. The push-button, interactive dioramas are so up-to-date and clever (ie a "drive-in movie" that's a live video of kids working the trains), and the walls are packed with so many gleaming railcars, that you can't help but feel a bit of that childlike Christmas-morning wonder.

Dutch Country's most unusual place to stay is, in fact, in a train, at the ⓯ **Red Caboose Motel**. Historic railcars have been spruced up with tempura-bright cobalt blue and burnt umber, brick red and canary yellow, and the insides converted into hotel rooms. Accommodations are small, but memorable – the Strasburg Railroad toots by all day.

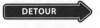 **DETOUR** Dutch Country's least-serious historical visit awaits at **Bube's Brewery** (www.bubesbrewery .com) in Mt Joy, 15 miles northwest of Lancaster off Rte 283 on N Market St. This well-preserved 19th-century German brewery now contains several atmospheric bars and dining rooms (one underground), hosts costumed "feasts" and, naturally, brews its own beer.

From Strasburg, a relaxing route back to Lancaster is via Lancaster Ave/Strasburg Pike. There's nothing here but countryside, and that's just fine.
Jeff Campbell

TRIP INFORMATION

GETTING THERE
From Philadelphia, take I-76 to Hwy 222 south into Lancaster.

DO
Horse-Drawn Buggy Rides
From Kitchen Kettle Village, a 35-minute ride takes you along backroads. ☎ 717-391-9500; www.aaabuggyrides.com; 3529 Old Philadelphia Pike, Intercourse; adult/child $12/6; ⏰ 9am-7pm Mon-Sat, hours vary; ♿

Lancaster Quilt & Textile Museum
In addition to quilts, rotating exhibits display needlework and other textiles. ☎ 717-299-6440; www.lancasterheritage.com; 37 N Market St, Lancaster; adult/child $6/free; ⏰ 9am-5pm Mon-Sat; ♿

National Toy Train Museum
All trains, all gauges, plus the actual Lionel factory keystone. ☎ 717-687-8623; www.nttmuseum.org; 300 Paradise Lane, Strasburg; adult/child $5/2.50; ⏰ 10am-5pm May-Oct, call for hours off-season; ♿

Railroad Museum of Pennsylvania
Over 100 locomotives and cars, inside and out. ☎ 717-687-8628; www.rrmuseumpa.org; Rte 741, Strasburg; adult/child $8/6; ⏰ 9am-5pm Mon-Sat, noon-5pm Sun; ♿

Strasburg Railroad
Regular 45-minute trips daily, cheese-and-wine trips on weekends, and "Thomas" arrives thrice yearly. ☎ 717-687-7522; www.strasburgrailroad.com; Rte 741, Strasburg; adult $12-19, child $6-13; ⏰ multiple trips daily, times vary by season; ♿

EAT & DRINK
Bird-in-Hand Farmers Market
Bring a cooler and hit the meat counters here on your way home. ☎ 717-393-9674; Rte 340 at Maple Ave, Bird-in-Hand; items $2-8; ⏰ 8:30am-5:30pm Wed-Sat Jul-Oct, weekends only off-season; ♿

Central Market
The nation's oldest farmers market lives in an 1889 brick marvel. It's only open three days a week. ☎ 717-735-6890; 23 N Market St, Lancaster; items $2-8; ⏰ 6am-4pm Tue & Fri, 6am-2pm Sat; ♿

Iron Hill Brewery
Huge, contemporary brewpub with fancy grub like salmon BLTs and crab cakes. ☎ 717-291-9800; www.ironhillbrewery.com; 781 Harrisburg Pike, Lancaster; mains $8-11; ⏰ 11am-close daily; ♿

Stoltzfus Farm
All you can eat of chow chow, pepper cabbage, fried chicken, homemade sausage, shoofly pie and more. ☎ 717-768-8156; www.stoltzfusmeats.com; Rte 772, near Rte 340, Intercourse; mains $16.50; ⏰ 11:30am-8pm Mon-Sat Apr-Nov; ♿

SLEEP
Lancaster Arts Hotel
Artist-designed suites set the tone for the hip decor throughout; loaner bikes are free. ☎ 717-299-3000, 866-720-2787; www.lancasterartshotel.com; 300 Harrisburg Pike, Lancaster; r $180-370

Red Caboose Motel
Bring extra blankets outside summer; shower at night for best hot water; all have private bath. ☎ 717-687-5000, 888-687-5005; www.redcaboosemotel.com; 312 Paradise Lane, Strasburg; r $70-130; ♿

USEFUL WEBSITES
www.800padutch.com
www.padutchcountry.com

www.lonelyplanet.com/trip-planner

LINK YOUR TRIP

Warhola
Without the A

WHY GO In 1949, Andy Warhola dropped the last "a" in his name, fled Pittsburgh for New York, and changed pop culture forever. Yet the "a" Andy left behind has grown up, so much so that his working-class hometown now produces avant-garde art the way it once produced steel.

TIME
2 – 5 days

BEST TIME TO GO
Year-round

START
Pittsburgh

END
Pittsburgh

ALSO GOOD FOR

CITY

As you drive across western Pennsylvania's undulating farmland, arriving via I-376, Pittsburgh seems to magically materialize: all of sudden, you're hugged by steep-sided green valleys cradling an epiphany of skyscrapers and riveted steel bridges, like a fantasy model-train set come to life. Pittsburgh is beautiful, like an old-world European city: at its heart are three rivers nestled among forested hills, and its convoluted streets and walkable neighborhoods snuggle inside them.

Over a dozen bridges span this meeting of the Ohio, Monongahela and Allegheny Rivers, but the three you'll become most familiar with are the bright-yellow, pedestrian-friendly 6th, 7th and 9th St Bridges, which arch over the Allegheny to connect downtown with ❶ **Northside**. Here, along the riverbank, are ❷ **Heinz Field** (home to football's Steelers), ❸ **PNC Park** (home to baseball's Pirates) and ❹ **Allegheny Riverfront Park**, a green swathe perfect for taking in Pittsburgh's majestic confluence.

The ❺ **7th St Bridge**, renamed Andy Warhol Bridge, leads directly to the ❻ **Andy Warhol Museum**, which is the magnetic pole orienting the metallic shavings of Pittsburgh's art community and where our tour officially begins. This mecca of modernism crams seven floors of galleries with the full breadth of Warhol's prodigious talent: including his first Campbell soup can (tomato rice), his "Death and Disaster" series, his award-winning 1950s commercial art, Brillo boxes, *Interview* covers, candy-colored celebrities, children's wallpaper, the giddy

BEST TRIP

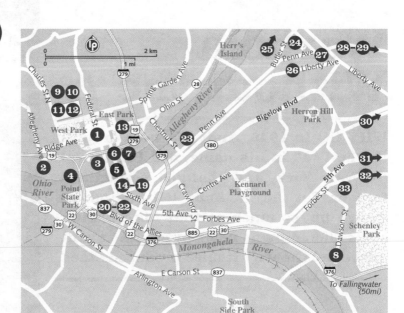

Silver Clouds and more. There's a café underground (get it?), a photo booth for instant self-portraits, a theater showing Warhol's TV shows and movies, and regular "happenings."

Without question, though, the place to get properly acquainted with the be-wigged, bizarre, pouty Warhol is in the 1st-floor **7 Introduction Gallery**. In a few swift, succinct strokes, it drives home the realization that understanding Warhol is a necessity not just for art students but for students of the 21st century. Warhol's radical 1960s pop innovations – emphasizing manufactured repetition, celebrity, banal irony and the idea that "anybody could do anything" – have become the consumer culture we live and breathe, leading one to wonder: did Andy create our world, or did he just see it first? As he said, "Once you 'get' Pop, you could never see a sign the same way again. And once you thought Pop, you could never see America the same way again."

For the record, Andy Warhol was 5ft 11in tall, weighed about 140lb and had dark brown hair. He was born on August 6, 1928, at 73 Orr St to Carpatho-Russian immigrants, the youngest of three brothers. The Orr St house is gone, but the home he grew up in, at **8 3252 Dawson St**, still stands – a nondescript tan-brick working-class duplex (not open to the public), identical to those on either side. Ask at the museum for directions to Warhol's grave, which is next to his parents in a Catholic cemetery on Pittsburgh's outskirts. Relatives still run Paul Warhola Scrap Metals on Pennsylvania Ave at Brighton Rd.

If Warhol graduated from the Carnegie Art School today (as he did in 1949), he might not have been so quick to leave. But then, would Pittsburgh be what it is now? From the Warhol museum, walk north through the quaint, red-brick Mexican War Streets (Pittsburgh's gayborhood) and head for the ⑨ **Mattress Factory**, which hums with the anything-goes, installation spirit of *the* Factory, the one Warhol founded in Manhattan in 1964. The Mattress Factory gives artists entire rooms to play with, and they do: messing with light, time, perspective and expectation. James Turrell's *Pleiades* and Yayoi Kusama's *Infinity Dots Mirrored Room* are goose-bump-inducing permanent exhibits. Nor do artists confine themselves to the building; walk along ⑩ **Sampsonia Way** for more.

ASK A LOCAL "How did Pittsburgh become an art town? We have lots of disgruntled kids from disgruntled families. And it's on the cheap. Pittsburgh's a place where you can still rent a big warehouse space like the Factory. I don't think we're losing artists as quickly as we once did. It used to be art students graduated and got on I-80 as fast they could get outta here."
Greg Knox, Pittsburgh

The gayborhood is a great place to stay: the ⑪ **Inn on the Mexican War Streets** is a whimsical riff on Victorian elegance (favoring marble mantels holding stuffed squirrels, gilt mirrors and tiger-print chairs) in a bona fide mansion; it's run by a charming gay couple eager to share their city. Around the corner, the ⑫ **Monterey Pub** is *Cheers* come to life – if Cliff were gay, Norm were black, and Carla was Carla. Nearby, in an old German neighborhood, the family-run ⑬ **Priory Hotel** is an appealing, refurbished monastery exuding a European-style B&B ambience.

From Northside walk the 7th St Bridge into downtown's ⑭ **Cultural District**, which holds Pittsburgh's major performance venues and a dozen or so lively art galleries along Penn and Liberty Aves between 6th and 11th Sts. Several are small, funky, free spaces devoted to multimedia and installation art by emerging artists; stroll by ⑮ **Space**, ⑯ **Future Tenant**, ⑰ **707-709 Penn Galleries** and ⑱ **Wood Street Galleries** and check out what's going on. Every self-respecting art town needs an arthouse cinema, and that would be Pittsburgh's

DETOUR Andy Warhol considered himself a quintessentially American artist, as did architect Franklin Lloyd Wright – and one of Wright's most revolutionary homes, **Fallingwater** (www.fallingwater.org), is 1½ hours from Pittsburgh. Don't miss the chance to experience Wright's visionary creation, a glass-and-stone symphony of human-scaled spaces cantilevered over a waterfall. One-hour tours leave continually (daily March to November), but reserve ahead or expect a long wait.

Take I-76 to exit 91, then Rte 31 to Rte 381 south and follow signs.

⑲ **Harris Theater**, showcasing all manner of ironically obscure, foreign-language pictures.

Pittsburgh's most iconic downtown structure is ⑳ **PPG Place**, a towering black-glass castle. The building presides over downtown's sunny-day lunch spot: ㉑ **Market Square**, a cobblestoned city block filled with outdoor tables and rimmed with restaurants. Try ㉒ **Primanti Bros**, who pioneered the only-in-Pittsburgh innovation of throwing french fries on sandwiches.

Now, we pick up the pace in Pittsburgh's outer neighborhoods. Closest to downtown is the ㉓ **Strip District**: Penn Ave is lined with food markets, while Smallman St is a warehouse zone of nightclubs. This leads into grittier ㉔ **Lawrenceville**, where funky galleries and designer shops are interspersed with boarded-up storefronts and empty lots. Butler St, running between 41st and 47th Sts is best; check out ㉕ **Everyone an Artist Gallery**, showcasing disabled artists.

ART HAPPENS

Art "happenings" are regular Pittsburgh fare.

- Good Fridays: the Warhol stays open late Fridays, with a cash bar and special events.

- Unblurred (www.pennavenuearts.org/unblurred): the first Friday every month, art explodes on Penn Ave.

- Cultural District Gallery Crawl (www.pgharts.org): a free quarterly art party.

- Three Rivers Arts Festival (www.artsfestival.net): a June festival of art and performance.

- Hothouse (www.sproutfund.org/hothouse): a major art party benefit in August.

On Liberty Ave, ㉖ **Church Brew Works** is destination dining, only because you don't often see a church altar replaced with stainless-steel beer vats and eat Kobe beef on pews beneath cathedral ceilings. Further out on Penn Ave, ㉗ **Brillobox** is a quintessential East Village restaurant/bar/gallery – all black T-shirts and red vinyl. ㉘ **Pittsburgh Glass Center** showcases intriguing glass artistry, and offers classes, while, almost next door, ㉙ **Quiet Storm** is a hip vegetarian café.

For trendier gallery browsing, head for Ellsworth St (between Spahr and Summerlea Sts) in ㉚ **Shadyside**. This leads to another major art destination: the ㉛ **Pittsburgh Center for the Arts**, where nine city artist guilds present eclectic, experimental works in the gardens and rooms. Then, as a reminder of all that art in Pittsburgh isn't, visit the ㉜ **Frick Art & Historical Center**, which focuses on 14th- to 18th-century European and religious art.

A good way to end our art tour is at the ㉝ **Carnegie Museum of Art**. It's worth visiting for the building itself (don't miss the *Crowning of Labor* fresco in the Grand Staircase), and the Scaife Galleries walk you through the entire evolution of modern and postmodern art. If you're lucky enough to attend the Carnegie's International, held every four years, you'll be witness to one of the art world's most prestigious events.

Yes, Andy, there really is art in Pittsburgh.
Jeff Campbell

TRIP INFORMATION

GETTING THERE
From Philadelphia, take I-76 west to I-376 west; it's about 310 miles (five hours).

DO
707-709 Penn Galleries
These side-by-side galleries emphasize Pittsburgh artists and Carnegie Art School graduates. ☎ 412-325-7017, 412-224-4651; www .pgharts.org; 707 & 709 Penn Ave; admission free; ⊙ 11am-6pm Tue-Thu, to 8pm Fri & Sat

Andy Warhol Museum
The Weekend Factory (noon to 4pm Saturday and Sunday) lets patrons make art like Andy! ☎ 412-237-8300; www.warhol.org; 117 Sandusky St; adult/child $15/8; ⊙ 10am-5pm Tue-Sun, to 10pm Fri; 👤

Carnegie Museum of Art
Art Museum admission includes the huge Natural History Museum, and the café is quite good. ☎ 412-622-3131; www.cmoa .org; 4400 Forbes Ave; adult/child $15/11; ⊙ 10am-5pm Tue-Sat, to 8pm Thu, noon-5pm Sun; 👤

Everyone an Artist Gallery
Warhol believed anyone could make art, and that's the credo at this gallery devoted to artists with disabilities. ☎ 412-681-2404; www.aemhmr.org; 4128 Butler St; admission free; ⊙ 10am-noon Tue & Fri, 10am-2pm Mon, Wed & Thu; 👤

Frick Art & Historical Center
In addition to art, a Guilded Age carriage museum and huge greenhouse; Clayton home tours $12. ☎ 412-371-0600; http://thefrick pittsburgh.org; 7227 Reynolds St; admission free; ⊙ 10am-5pm Tue-Sun; 👤

Future Tenant
You could find anything at this art lab run by Carnegie Mellon University students. Only open during installations; call to check. ☎ 412-325-7037; www.futuretenant.org; 819 Penn Ave; admission free; ⊙ 12:30-6pm Tue-Sat

Harris Theater
Also a venue for November's Three Rivers Film Festival (www.3rff.com). ☎ 412-682-4111; www.pghfilmmakers.org; 809 Liberty Ave; admission $7; ⊙ 1-2 screenings nightly

Mattress Factory
Four floors of wonder-inducing installations, plus a sculpture garden and café. ☎ 412-231-3169; www.mattress.org; 500 Sampsonia Way; adult/child $10/7; ⊙ 10am-5pm Tue-Sat, 1-5pm Sun

Pittsburgh Center for the Arts
Both playful and provocative, a mix of hung art, installations and outdoor sculpture. ☎ 412-361-0873; www.pittsburgharts.org; 6300 Fifth Ave; admission free; ⊙ 10am-5pm Tue-Sat, noon-5pm Sun; 👤

Pittsburgh Glass Center
This major glass studio runs classes and gives demos, and provides glass artists a dedicated venue. ☎ 412-365-2145; www.pittsburgh glasscenter.org; 5472 Penn Ave; admission by donation; ⊙ 10am-7pm Tue-Thu, to 4pm Fri-Sun; 👤

Space
Huge plate-glass windows along the sidewalk announce strange things inside. ☎ 412-325-7723; www.spacepittsburgh .org; 812 Liberty Ave; admission free; ⊙ 11am-6pm Tue-Thu, to 8pm Fri & Sat

Wood Street Galleries
In the building above the Wood St T-station, top-notch exhibits rotate frequently. ☎ 412-471-5605; www.woodstreetgalleries.org; 601 Wood St; admission free; ⊙ 11am-6pm Tue-Thu, to 8pm Fri & Sat

EAT & DRINK
Brillobox
Live music, movies and spoken-word performances while you nosh, hiply. ☎ 412-621-4900; www.brillobox.net; 4104 Penn Ave; mains $9-20; ⊙ kitchen 5pm-midnight Tue-Sat, 8pm-midnight Sun, bar to 2am

Church Brew Works
Get happy beneath the glare of stained-glass saints. Generous steaks and homemade beer make a holy pair. ☎ 412-688-8200; www .churchbrew.com; 3525 Liberty Ave; mains $16-32; ⊙ 11:30am-11pm Mon-Sat, noon-9pm Sun; 👤

Monterey Pub

Belly up to this Irish bar and make friends while enjoying above-average pub grub. ☎ 412-322-6535; www.montereypub.com; 1227 Monterey St; mains $8-12; ⏲ kitchen 5-10pm, bar 3pm-midnight Mon-Sat

Primanti Bros

Every sandwich comes with fries, coleslaw and tomatoes – *inside* the sandwich! Bring an appetite. ☎ 412-261-1599; www .primantibros.com; 2 S Market Sq; mains $5-7; ⏲ 11am-11pm; ♿

Quiet Storm

Bargain-priced gourmet vegetarian diner food: try the faux-loaf, curries, lasagne, refreshing mockamole and tasty shakes. ☎ 412-661-9355; www.quietstormcoffee .com; 5430 Penn Ave; mains $6-9; ⏲ 8am-9pm Mon-Fri, 10am-9pm Sat, 10am-4pm Sun; ♿

SLEEP

Inn on the Mexican War Streets

The gorgeously restored, ornate Boggs Mansion is romantic, quirky, relaxed and memorable. ☎ 412-231-6544; www.inn onthemexicanwarstreets.com; 604 W North Ave; r $140-190

Priory Hotel

The Benedictine monks never lived this well, with satiny bed covers, iron bed frames, wi-fi and downtown shuttle service. ☎ 412-231-3338; www.thepriory.com; 614 Pressley St; r $140-220; ♿

USEFUL WEBSITES

www.pittsburghgalleryguide.com
www.visitpittsburgh.com

SUGGESTED VIEWING

- *Basquiat* (1996), Julian Schnabel
- *Chelsea Girls* (1966), Andy Warhol
- *I Shot Andy Warhol* (1996), Mary Harron

LINK YOUR TRIP

www.lonelyplanet.com/trip-planner

TRIP
1 Ultimate Urban Adventure p35
5 The Boys of Summer p75

Day Trips from Philly

From Philly much of the mid-Atlantic, and many trips in this chapter, can be done as day trips. Here are four more jaunts worth checking out.

HAWK MOUNTAIN

When the East Coast gratefully turns the page on August's heat and humidity, it's time to head for the mountains. Not only do cooler temperatures make hiking more pleasant, but as the leaves turn, nature paints her masterpiece in the mid-Atlantic's deciduous forests. With so many mountains to choose from, why Hawk Mountain? Because raptors start their annual migration south, and over the three months of September, October and November, some 18,000 hawks, eagles, osprey, kestrels and vultures pass this particular windy updraft along the Kittatinny Ridge. From Hawk Mountain's North Lookout, over 17 species fly by, some at eye level. On a good day, observers count a thousand birds, though broad-winged hawks, the rare raptor that flies in a group, have been known to arrive 7000 at a time. At other times of the year, the soft carpeted hills of the Appalachians are just as beautiful, and those for whom Hawk Mountain's relatively short trails are not enough can pick up the Appalachian Trail from here. The visitors center (www.hawkmountain .org) has loaner optics and trail guides. **Take I-476 north to I-78 west, then take exit 35 to Rte 143 north; after 4 miles, turn left on Hawk Mountain Rd, which continues 7 miles to the mountain.**

PRINCETON

It's still preppie personified – a bastion of Ivy League smarts and privilege – but despite that or perhaps because of it, Princeton makes an ideal day trip. The university (www.princeton.edu) is such a relaxing and stately place you feel more intelligent just walking through it; if you like books – and we notice, you're holding one – definitely visit the campus' stunning Firestone Library. Running along the campus' edge is Nassau St, which is the town's principal retail street, a place where Albert Einstein once window-shopped. For breakfast, hit PJ's Pancake House, and for drinks later, stop off at Triumph, a fun brewpub. Off ritzy Palmer Sq, you'll rub elbows with both students and professors at the underground Tap Room, which sports a mural by Norman Rockwell over the bar. You can also admire the portraits of famous alumni (Ralph Nader, Donald Rumsfeld, Brooke Shields, James Stewart) and wonder who getting drunk in the booths behind you will some day join them. **From I-95 north, exit at Rte 206/Lawrenceville Rd, which leads directly to Nassau St and downtown Princeton.**

HERSHEY PARK

The name represents either hell or a necessary rung of parental purgatory. But in the right spirit, it's not so bad. Just know this: Hershey's real chocolate factory, the tantalizing brick building with the double smokestacks in town, is closed to the public, as it has been since 1973. Where's Willy Wonka when you need him!? Hershey's Chocolate World (www.hersheypa.com) is a completely separate place, essentially a mall with a handful of clever, silly diversions (a 3D movie, a "factory tour" ride, custom-labeled chocolate bars with your photo) and stacks and stacks and stacks of Hershey-brand chocolates. Next door is the amusement park, which is great as amusement parks go, including a super-fantastic water park for younger kids. There's other stuff, like a history museum and trolley tours, but it's all secondary to chocolate-ing up and going nuts in the water park. **From I-76 west, take exit 266 onto Rte 72 north. Then take Rte 322 west to Hershey Park.**

ATLANTIC CITY

Atlantic City (www.atlanticcitynj.com) is Philly's playground, one that is constantly getting new equipment. The Sands is gone, to be replaced by a $2-billion pleasure palace (ironically, further blocking the view from the Absecon Lighthouse, the tallest in NJ). The Trump Marina is being renovated and rebranded by Jimmy Buffet into a Margaritaville casino. And so it goes. Yet AC is no Vegas, no matter how hard it tries. It's "supermarket gambling," as one local dubbed it, but then Vegas doesn't have the Atlantic Ocean lapping its feet. It's a fair trade-off: play the slots and blackjack till you're broke, then swim and sleep it off on a real beach. At night, the casinos have nice restaurants and loud nightclubs to keep you in town: try the Pool at Harrah's and mur.mur at the Borgata. For a casino on the boardwalk, aim for Trump Taj Mahal and Caesars. **The Atlantic City Expressway cuts straight across Jersey and right to the casinos.**

Jeff Campbell

WASHINGTON DC, MARYLAND & DELAWARE TRIPS

There are few better places in which to see America condensed than the capital and the state that immediately surrounds it. Maryland's unofficial motto for years has been "America in Miniature," and since Delaware is basically an extension of Maryland (sorry Delaware, we mean this in the best possible way), you could say the 42nd- and 49th-largest states in the union also happen to encapsulate said Republic.

Culturally, Delaware balances the gritty northeast edge of Philly and south Jersey with the redneck lassitude of a tidewater good old boy. Maryland's even tougher to pin down. Green mountains in the panhandle to aristocratic horse country in the center, the disfiguring appendage of the Chesapeake Bay running throughout, a north–south intermarriage of cultures and the cross-pollination of enormous immigrant groups, creates a state that mixes up some of the nation's poorest ghettos and wealthiest estates with sharp cliffs and soft, tide-kissed wetlands.

PLAYLIST 🎵 From jazz to hip-hop, go-go to country and plenty of rock on the side, the area's musical heritage is as diverse as everything else that characterizes this corner of the country.

- "Overnight Scenario," Rare Essence
- "Down in Mary's Land," Mary Chapin Carpenter
- "Bad to the Bone," George Thorogood and the (Delaware) Destroyers
- "Mood Indigo," Duke Ellington
- "Jiggle It," Young Leek
- "We'll Be Together Again," Billie Holiday
- "Projects," Tyree Colion
- "That was a Crazy Game of Poker," O.A.R.

Then there's Washington DC, whose hard outer shell is being pushed past the city's periphery by waves of new restaurants, cafés and art galleries, additions that are making the capital more livable – though not to its working-class African American community.

WASHINGTON DC, MARYLAND & DELAWARE'S BEST TRIPS

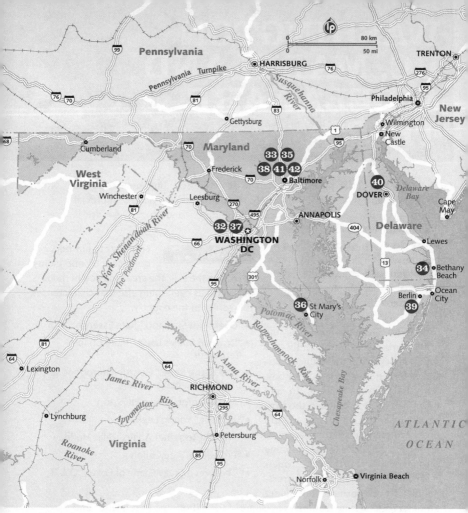

WASHINGTON DC, MARYLAND & DELAWARE TRIPS

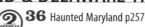

48 Hours in DC

WHY GO The nation's capital is more than monuments, museums and government buildings. It's an international entrepôt, a simmering kettle of jazz and go-go, an exercise in double-edged gentrification and home for thousands of immigrants, idealists and political pragmatists. Experience this, plus the accompanying tension that defines this unique city.

TIME
2 days

BEST TIME TO GO
May, Sep – Oct

START
Washington DC

END
Washington DC

ALSO GOOD FOR

HISTORY & CULTURE

In April 2008, the Washington DC *City Paper,* the local alternative newsweekly, ran a front-page story on the great DC novel, or lack thereof. No one author, the paper argued, could bridge in one narrative the multiple identities of this town.

No one neighborhood does, either, although it can be fun trying to find one. Take the U Street corridor, which sits on the rapidly expanding frontier of DC gentrification, a multicolored, multicultural, multilingual neighborhood where students, professionals and Ethiopians have supplanted the heart of one of DC's oldest African American communities.

Trenchant political ambition, creative class renovation and the lingering traces of this 'hood's black identity are all realized at the unabashedly intellectual meat-market that is ❶ **Busboys and Poets**. This is the spot for a civilized coffee and rant about Third World debt relief/climate change/ Tibet. Unlike similar protest-chic coffeehouses across the country, Busboys isn't lily white; this is U Street, and the 'hood's history of black nationalism sits easily at the crowded table of opposition ideologies.

The displacement of the poor by the middle class makes U Street a controversial choice for the quintessential DC neighborhood. But ultimately, it is tension – between rich and poor, politicos and proles, white and black and, increasingly, brown – that defines DC.

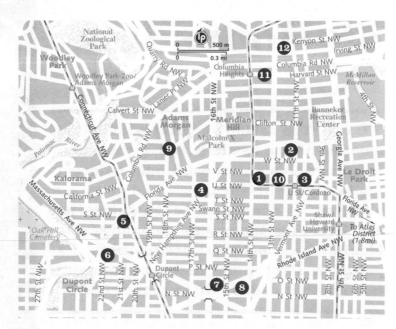

The balance between organic and administrative Washington is the soul of this city, and is manifested in beautiful, alive edges: a go-go drummer pounding paint buckets on V St, a café packed with diplomats and college students in Dupont Circle, or the sun setting over the Capitol dome glimpsed from a brick row house.

"The balance between organic and administrative Washington is the soul of this city..."

Plenty of places exemplify this relationship. The ❷ **Florida Avenue Grill**, for example, is perhaps the most quintessential of DC's old-school diners. It's a black institution that does reliable soul favorites and fields a clientele of local regulars in a town where the regulars can be Kwanice from around the way or the Ambassador of Kazakhstan. Where else do you find signed pictures of cabinet officials *and* Lionel Richie sharing a wall? ❸ **Oohs and Aahs**, near the African American Civil War Memorial, is another soul food contender and a complete (in its way) contrast to Florida Avenue Grill. It does the fried whiting and greens, and mac-and-cheese (give us a minute, while we reverentially remember the mac-and-cheese), but where the Grill is a greased-out corner fixture, Oohs and Aahs was opened by a Stanford-educated homegirl.

If you want a sense of DC's social mobility (or lack thereof), start your trip in College Park, MD and head south on Rte 1, past basketball courts and takeaways, until it becomes Rhode Island Ave, which plunges into the capital's center. You'll pass through Hyattsville and Mt Rainier, where local black joints run up against community halls, often church-organized, for migrants from Latin America.

What's this got to do with Washington DC? Well, nothing, if you think DC is just the National Mall, America's front lawn. And everything, if you recognize that the folks who mow that lawn and sweep the corridors of power romanticized by shows like *The West Wing* commute out here each day.

This is the hard end of the DC metro's Red Line, which also spits into Bethesda, a bedroom suburb for the other kind of DC workforce: journalists, policy wonks, think-tank staff, lobbyists and consultants all competing to get their opinions heard by someone who matters. When these guys, particularly the younger crowd, need a break from the grind of getting noticed in a city where everyone wants some attention (and deserves it; DC has one of the biggest concentrations of post-graduate degrees in the world), they hit the rails hard. Their behavior is pretty fun to watch, and when we're on a DC-nightlife safari we rarely pass up ❹ **Stetson's**. With its excellent backdoor beer garden, this is the sort of place where congressional interns flirt on the sly with Defense Department employees, who throw back shots with kids from the Maryland 'burbs looking to party.

UNDERRATED INSTITUTIONS

These museums are all gems of their genre. The **Corcoran Gallery** (www.corcoran.org) is the nation's oldest art museum, but has never rested on its laurels, despite free Smithsonian competition around the block. The **National Museum of African Art** (http://africa.si.edu) is beautiful, in terms of both exhibitions and layout. And out in Anacostia, the **Frederick Douglass National Historic Site** (www.nps.gov/frdo) and **Anacostia Museum & Center for African American History & Culture** (http://anacostia.si.edu) are excellent glimpses into black American history and current affairs.

Stetson's is just north and over from Logan Circle. Arriving here from Maryland, it's hard not to notice that while the row houses remain brick, their residents are no longer black; here, around 14th St NW, you're straddling DC's color line. But, in exploring the capital's transition zone, you're not relegated to the U Street corridor; from here you can walk to Adams Morgan and Dupont Circle, which have always been benchmarks for urban lifestyle in this town.

Architecturally, the Circle is a Victorian playground of gay hotspots, ethnic restaurants and Embassy Row, which runs along Massachusetts Ave (you'd be surprised at the kind of real estate that small countries can afford here). Have a coffee at a local chic café, but save some room for a glass of wine (and, if you can fit them in, the excellent steak *frites*) at ❺ **Bistro du Coin**, a roll-up-your-sleeves French diner that, in true Gallic style, heroically fought off the DC smoking ban for as long as it could before surrendering.

After comparing Camels to Gauloises with the French ambassador, break the rules and add some grain to that grape with a beer, any beer, at **6** **Brickskellers**, a perennially popular watering hole that claims to have the largest selection of brews in the world (we believe it). The specially tailored food-for-beer menu is brilliant to boot.

Dupont is a good place to rest your head in sleek, sexy environs that are nothing like the conventioneer hotels and chandeliered grand dames most people associate with capital-area lodging. The **7** **Hotel Rouge**, decked out in dark leather and neon red, is still one of the hottest girls in this classroom, and one of the first contemporary design boutiques to challenge DC's usual button-down conservatism. For a bit of punky playfulness and sassy staff, we love **8** **Hotel Helix**, which, with its "Andy Warhol rockets into the future" sensibility, feels like it could house both the staff of nearby embassies and an all-star lineup plucked from VH1's "I Love the '80s."

But before you go to sleep, you need to head up 18th St NW into the thumping heart of DC nightlife: Adams Morgan. There's no shortage of bars (or folks behaving badly in them) along this strip of sin and watchful cops. The best way to go about the night generally involves enjoying a drink and getting a good booty-shake on at a West African, Latin-fusion or all-American bar. You're spoiled for choice, but we love a coke and a small bottle of whiskey in the sweatbox that is **9** **Dan's Cafe**, which eschews *Sex and the City* flash for a more criminal-needs-to-get-wasted-before-robbing-a-bank ambience.

DETOUR

What U Street was before the yuppies arrived, the **Atlas district**, over a three-block stretch of H St centered on the 1200 block, is where old DC (pool halls and soul food) mashes up on indie gigs, punk bars, freak shows and a Belgian beer-and-*frites* hall. Some standouts on this still lovingly seedy strip include **Granville Moore's** (www.granvillemoores.com) for its pub fare, the **Red and Black** (www.redandblackbar.com) for its knife-edged smile, and **Palace of Wonders** (www.palaceofwonders.com) for its sheer madness.

Need a soaking agent? Head back to U Street for the ultimate DC late-night nosh: a chili-soaked half-smoke (the local, meatier version of the hot dog) from **10** **Ben's Chili Bowl**, where the hungry lines curve around the block.

The next morning (assuming you've slept last night off), head back down Rhode Island Ave and swing right onto M St, which takes you into the patrician heart of Georgetown. This has long been the seat of DC aristocracy, from Kennedy Northeast liberals to modern Young Republicans, where Bill Clinton went to college, the Bush twins partied, and diplomats and academics make their home in a neighborhood unserved by any Metro lines (a situation that pleases some local residents who prefer to not have "undesirables" accessing the area). This is a nice area to linger in until early evening, when it becomes a mad cruising strip for rich kids; wander up Wisconsin Ave past the big-brand-label parade. From Hyattsville we've physically come about 25 miles; economically, we might as well be in Dubai.

We don't want to end these 48 hours in Georgetown; it's too removed from the everyday DC experience. But we don't have to end in the ghetto either.

Instead, we'll go to ⓫ **Columbia Heights**, an emerging neighborhood – plenty of new immigrants, young families and professionals looking for starter homes, are concentrated here – along with a hip, chill vibe. As night falls, we're heading to a place that mixes a dive's edge with a club's sense of careless hedonism. ⓬ **Wonderland** is a sweaty shack, where the wooden walls creak to bass and folks get a low, full of punk vibe and upstairs is hip-hop dancing all smooshed into one ball of fun.

MONUMENTAL ANTICIPATION

We've listed our favorite museums and monuments in the Ultimate Urban Adventure trip; two more spots may be open when you read this. The **National Museum of American History** (http://americanhistory.si.edu) is an exhaustive peek into the nation's memory. The civil rights side of that memory will be jogged by the **Martin Luther King Jr National Memorial** in West Potomac Park. And try the newly opened **Newseum** (www.newseum.org), dedicated to journalism and lots of kid-friendly bells and whistles.

And there you have it. In 48 hours, you've crossed the borders between poverty, gentrification, aristocracy, immigrant hopes and artsy intelligentsia. About the only thing studiously avoided is politics, because those airs always overlay whatever you do here. You may not have captured Washington's soul, but you've seen more of its facets than most dignitaries (and tourists) generally experience. If you can't write the great DC novel, you've at least cribbed the footnotes.

Adam Karlin

TRIP INFORMATION

GETTING THERE
College Park is at the end of Rhode Island Ave, where it becomes Rte 1 and intersects with MD 410.

EAT
Ben's Chili Bowl
Chili dogs and cheese fries and the night-lit storefront are the quintessential DC beer-soaker. ☎ 202-667-0909; 1213 U St NW; items $3.70-7; ◔ to 2am Mon-Thu, 4am Fri & Sat, 8pm Sun

Bistro du Coin
It's big, it's unabashedly French, the food is fantastic and the staff and clientele are as Euro as. ☎ 202-234-6969; 1738 Connecticut Ave NW; meals $8-24; ◔ 11:30am-11pm Sun-Wed, to 1am Thu-Sat

Florida Avenue Grill
This quintessential DC diner does Southern soul food takes on classic countertop favorites. Grab some hot sauce to go. ☎ 202-265-1586; 1100 Florida Ave; meals $7-15; ◔ 8am-9pm Tue-Sat, to 4:30pm Sun

Oohs and Aahs
Thank you, God, for gracing the hand of whoever makes the mac-and-cheese, collard greens and fried catfish here. ☎ 202-667-7142; 1005 U St NW; meals $12-20; ◔ noon-10pm Tue-Sat

DRINK
Brickskellers
Pick one brew among thousands and complement it with some of the capital's best pub grub. ☎ 202-293-1885; 1523 22nd St NW; ◔ lunch to 2am Mon-Thu, 3am Fri & Sat, midnight Sun

Busboys and Poets
There's excellent food here, but BB&P is best known for the coffee, from-the-hip philoso-phizin' and rainbow clientele vibe. ☎ 202-387-7368; 2021 14th St NW; ◔ to midnight Mon-Fri, 2am Sat & Sun

Dan's Cafe
Somehow, Dan's has maintained its ultimate dive status here at the frat-boy cruisey end of Adams Morgan. Long may it reign. ☎ 202-265-9241; 2315 18th St NW; ◔ to late

Stetson's
Stetson's has a rough exterior, but this stale-beer-and-dark-wood bar (and its beer garden) is extremely popular with DC politico types. ☎ 202-667-6295; 1610 U St NW; ◔ to 2am Mon-Fri, 3am Sat & Sun

Wonderland
Tattooed rockers, pretty blondes in floaty sundresses, old-school DC derelicts and thug lifers all mingle at this fun place in Columbia Heights. ☎ 202-232-5263; 1101 Kenyon St; ◔ to late

SLEEP
Hotel Helix
Step into a VH1 teaser crossed with a Warhol painting in this wild, wonderful hotel perched near Dupont Circle. ☎ 202-462-7777; www.hotelhelix.com; 1430 Rhode Island Ave NW; r $140-270

Hotel Rouge
With sleek rooms divided into contemporary chic categories, expect a stylish, somewhat attitude-heavy sleep at the edge of Embassy Row. ☎ 202-232-8000; www.rougehotel.com; 1315 16th St NW; r $190-370

USEFUL WEBSITES
www.dcnites.com
www.washingtoncitypaper.com/neighborhoods

www.lonelyplanet.com/trip-planner

LINK YOUR TRIP
TRIP
1 Ultimate Urban Adventure p35
37 The Ethnic Epicurean p261

The Tolerance Tour

WHY GO From integrated swathes of urban America to the secret tunnels of the Underground Railroad, Maryland's history is wrapped up in extending rights to all of its citizens. On this trip, you can travel the lines of struggle and acceptance for which state residents have spent hundreds of years fighting.

There are certain qualities – religious freedom, emancipation, suffrage and other great American abstractions like diversity, tolerance and equality – that define this country. Marylanders are lucky, in that their state and its history embodies the fight for all of the above. And the physical traces of these struggles for fundamental rights are deeply etched into the state's contours.

❶ Baltimore, a city that has weathered segregation, slavery and the dreams of millions of new immigrants, is a good place to start. The logical jump-off is the **❷ Maryland Historical Society**. The state's well-put-together archive of historical bric-a-brac is worth a linger, and from here you can move on to see how patterns of past discrimination and diversity manifest themselves in Maryland today.

The row houses, for example, that spread across the city in graceful sine waves and ordered grids, are not just Baltimore's signature structure; they're a concrete example of uneasy equality as well. If this town was a nature video, David Attenborough would comment on how working-class whites, newly arrived immigrants and upwardly mobile blacks all share the same habitat: terraced formstone 'hoods.

While North Ave has long marked the dividing line between Baltimore's right and wrong side of the tracks, this rough edge has also

TIME
2 – 3 days

DISTANCE
310 miles

BEST TIME TO GO
May – Jun, Oct

START
Baltimore

END
St Mary's City

ALSO GOOD FOR

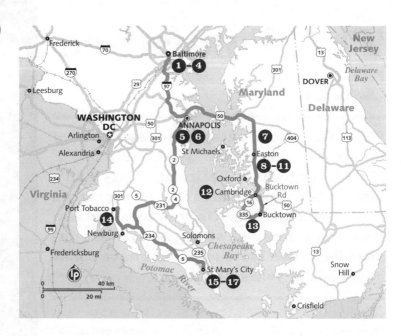

been softened by paint. The children's storybook–bright ❸ **murals** by local son Tom Miller are Maryland art of the best sort – playful subversions of racist memes (African American subjects are purposely drawn with big lips, to demonstrate how attractive their smiles are) and little artistic dollops of hope plopped onto some of Baltimore's grittiest corners. Miller himself was an African American homosexual, and although he struggled with this identity throughout his life, his prolific work, which can be spotted at 1339 E North Ave and North Ave and Harford Rd, speaks to the degree of acceptance he won before his death from AIDS complications at the age of 54.

"…playful subversions of racist memes and little artistic dollops of hope plopped onto Baltimore's grittiest corners."

If you're exploring the state's past, lodge in some local historical digs; one of the nicest is the ❹ **Baltimore Hostel**, in a beautiful 1857-era apartment building. In the 1990s this lovely grand dame had become a crackhouse and derelict shelter, but has since been restored by grassroots community activists into one of the finest hostels on the Eastern seaboard.

Maryland's state capital of ❺ **Annapolis** is barely an hour from B'more, and feels like an open-air history museum in itself. The ❻ **History Quest** museum is an informative, flashy (well, as flashy as a restored 18th-century house can be) interpretive center, but far more attractive is the cobblestoned area surrounding the capital building; under winter snow it feels like it should be the center set for a Dickens adaptation.

A memorial to Thurgood Marshall, the Maryland-born first black justice on the US Supreme Court, is uncommonly well put together, combining a sense of open space with dignified solemnity. Marshall himself stands framed in the middle of the exhibit, while the clients he fought for as a civil rights lawyer occupy the remainder of the memorial complex.

When you've finished in Annapolis, cross Rte 50 into the flat clumps of marshes, pine islands and weblike waterways of the Eastern Shore. These narrow channels and brackish skeins devour the individual; it's a land to get lost in, and was used primarily as such by slaves slipping north to freedom in the 19th century.

BALTIMORE'S BUILDING BLOCKS

Note as you drive in Baltimore the grayish, tannish stone that fronts so many local buildings. This is "formstone," or more accurately, "form-plaster-compound." It's not stone at all, and is jokingly called "styrofoamstone" because of its cheapness, but it's one of Baltimore's defining features, a comforting material that practically screams to locals, "Welcome home."

These slaves were led along the Underground Railroad, a series of secret passageways and escape routes, by local abolitionists and free blacks. Riding the railroad was a dangerous journey; escaped slaves and anyone caught helping them faced harsh justice in the then-slaveholding Shore. Maryland was a border state between North and South, whose black population was split between slave and free, and a large local population of the latter well understood the cost of slavery and the opportunities of freedom.

Driving along Rte 328, through an overgrown stream valley of flat fields and low bogs, leads you to ❼ **Tuckahoe Creek**. This was where Frederick Douglass was born into slavery. He eventually freed himself and wrote a memoir, *The Narrative of the Life of Frederick Douglass*, which became the seminal text of the abolitionist movement.

Follow Rte 328 back south to ❽ **Easton**, MD, into a well-integrated community whose compact town center includes yuppie coffee shops like ❾ **Coffee East** and international lodgings like the ❿ **Inn at Easton**, where American, Maryland and Australian flags flutter over a quintessentially small-town, filigree-fenced grid of lanes and antique shops. The food scene reflects the town's mixed identity of boho day-trippers from DC, who can dine at Pacific-rim-Chesapeake-tide fusion joints, and more down-home, Formica-and-fried-chicken-and-oysters soul-food shacks, such as ⓫ **Darnell's Grill**.

Easton may be an artsy getaway for DC types, but further down Rte 50 is ⓬ **Cambridge**, a more typical rural Shore community tied to the water –

and history. As in many towns in this region, local blacks were employed in seafood processing plants and kept segregated from whites. As a result, Cambridge is divided evenly between white and black residents, a bit of a rarity in rural America, where small towns tend to consist of either all blacks or all whites. Today, numerous migrant Latinos are adding their voices to local community relations.

From here, drive south along Rte 16, pausing to admire salt-swept, clapboard houses that seem frozen in a permanent state of Southern gothic rot. Follow Rte 16 to Rte 335 through a series of nowhere fields and scattered lot developments; if you detour west and head up small streets like Laurie Lane and White Haven Dr, you're following the Underground Railroad "line" that delivered slaves to the Choptank River, where they could be ferried northeast into Delaware and free Pennsylvania.

Often enough the railroad "conductor" was Harriet Tubman, who was born a slave on the Shore. Despite marrying a free black (most black families in Maryland at that time had free and slave members), she only found freedom after running away from captivity. But Tubman frequently returned to Maryland, at the risk of being resold into slavery, to guide slaves along the Choptank and through the swamps to abolitionist Quaker and free black communities in nearby Caroline County.

As you drive east on Rte 335 into the ⓭ **Blackwater National Wildlife Refuge**, a Jurassic-like marsh of snakes, wild grass and interlacing marsh flats gives a nice impression of the physical and historical landscape that the fugitive slaves slipped across. The road also loops past Tubman's likely birthplace and settlements, such as Bucktown, that are associated with her childhood. Follow the Bucktown road north to Rte 16 to the now privately owned Leverton House, the central Underground Railroad "station" for those about to cross into the free North.

The next day drive back to Annapolis and south along Rte 2/4 into southern Maryland, the triangle of three counties from which modern Maryland originates. If you head west and south on Rtes 231 to 234, and north on Rte 301 (note the classic 1950s roadside marquee of the Thunderbird Apartments) you can pop into Port Tobacco's ⓮ **St Ignatius Church**, founded in 1641, and the oldest operating Catholic parish in the country. This pretty church commands a majestic, sylvan lookout over the Potomac River; the grassy areas near the cemetery are perfect for a picnic.

Colonial Maryland was built on the two pillars of tobacco and Catholicism. Follow Rte 234 south, past another lovely view over Allen's Fresh Creek, and go south on Rte 5 to the very tip of the state. Along the way you'll pass through the pasture of the southern Maryland Amish, who reject post-19th-century technology (by and large; most Amish villages keep a payphone on hand for convenience). Their businesses are often recognizable by Germanic surnames like Zimmerman.

The end of the line (and the state) is ⓯ **Historic St Mary's City**, one of the prettiest corners of Maryland. This preserved former capital spreads over a green mesh of fields and forest that feels a bit like tidewater Chesapeake Bay marshland mixed with rolling English countryside, all overlaid with a hint of fairy-tale geography. Crash out at the nearby ⓰ **Woodlawn** estate and winery, which captures much of the English-estate-and-tidewater ambience described above. Or opt for a (far) less civilized beer at the ⓱ **Green Door**, the peanut-shell-strewn local where someone's dog is as likely to greet you at the door as a bouncer.

TOBACCY SHACKS

One of the defining landmarks of southern Maryland is its tobacco barns, recognizable by their lean-to, jaunty wooden frames. They're as integral to this landscape as trees and water, and the smell of air-cured tobacco leaves is a sensory milestone for people who've grown up in the area. The barns are the leftovers of a once-thriving tobacco farming industry that was the economic backbone of this region, but today they are in danger of being lost to fast-scaling development.

St Mary's City was where Leonard Calvert first landed a crew of Catholics escaping the religious tensions of the English Civil War, and it was an uncommonly progressive town for its day. A black-Portuguese sailor, Mathias de Sousa, went on to become the first elected black politician in America, while Margaret Brent was the first woman in the North American colonies to act as an attorney and demand her own representative voice. In the meantime, the early Maryland assembly passed some of the earliest freedom of religion ordinances in North America, laying the base values of the Bill of Rights (which came 100 years later).

Today the site is dominated by a living history museum, some scattered archaeological digs and a replication of the 17th-century trading ship *Dove*, which ferried supplies from Europe to the New World. It's all quite captivating, but the most enjoyable activity is a gentle stroll through the trails that crisscross the historic city and next-door St Mary's College. Wander by the perfect riverbanks of Godiah Spray Plantation, or bushwhack trails cut by the long gone Piscataway and Yaocomaco Indians, vanished tribes that speak to Maryland's imperfect – if still respectable – track record for tolerance.

Adam Karlin

TRIP INFORMATION

GETTING THERE
Begin this delve into Maryland's history at the Maryland Historical Society at 201 W Monument St in Baltimore.

DO
Blackwater National Wildlife Refuge
You can be forgiven for thinking you had left Maryland for the Everglades once you enter this mammoth tidal wetland refuge. ☎ 410-228-2677; www.fws.gov/blackwater; 2145 Key Wallace Dr

Historic St Mary's City
Costumed interpreters keep the historical atmosphere fun yet educational amid rolling fields, thick forests and gorgeous river ridges. ☎ 800-762-1634; www.stmaryscity.org; off Rte 5; ⊙ 10am-5pm

History Quest
This well-executed museum offers the definitive glimpse into the background of Annapolis, and Maryland in general. ☎ 410-990-4538; www.annapolis.org; 99 Main St, Annapolis; ⊙ 9:30am-5pm, to 7pm Sat

Maryland Historical Society
The original copy of the "Star Spangled Banner" tops the excellent collection of historical detritus assembled here. ☎ 410-685-3750; www.mdhs.org; 201 W Monument St, Baltimore; admission $4; ⊙ 10am-5pm Wed-Sun

St Ignatius Church
This beautiful church, the oldest Catholic one in North America, overlooks an even more beautiful, picnic-perfect bend of the Potomac River. ☎ 301-934-8245; www.chapelpoint.org; 8855 Chapel Point Rd, Port Tobacco

EAT
Coffee East
There's no better spot for a cup o' Joe, some artsy events, community activities and plenty

of succulent sandwiches in Easton. ☎ 410-819-6711; 3 Goldsborough St, Easton; meals $4-10; ⊙ from 6am

Darnell's Grill
Get the friendly man behind the counter to fry up something delicious and drenched in hot sauce, you lucky thing. ☎ 410-770-5534; 22 North Harrison St, Easton; meals $8-18; ⊙ 7am-2pm Mon-Fri

DRINK
Green Door
Surly rednecks and hippies from St Mary's College compete for beer-pong champion of the world in this sawdust-strewn, dog-friendly dive. ☎ 301-863-7000; Rte 5, St Mary's City; ⊙ to late; 🐾

SLEEP
Baltimore Hostel
This converted mansion is a fine example of historical renovation gone completely right. Staff are friendly and knowledgeable. ☎ 410-576-8880; www.baltimorehostel.org; 17 W Mulberry St, Baltimore; dm/r $25/$60

Inn at Easton
Dreamtime artwork pushes the Australian edge of the Pacific Rim into the Chesapeake tidewater in this Federal home. ☎ 410-822-4910; www.theinnateaston.com; 28 S Harrison St, Easton; r from $200

Woodlawn
This beautiful mansion is at the quietest end of one of the quietest spots in Maryland – and comes with a winery. ☎ 301-872-0555; www.woodlawn-farm.com; 16040 Woodlawn Lane, off Rte 5; r $140-210

USEFUL WEBSITES
www.msa.md.gov/msa/mdslavery
www.sha.state.md.us

LINK YOUR TRIP

www.lonelyplanet.com/trip-planner

ROUTE

Delaware's Beaches

WHY GO Don't dismiss Delaware: the beach resorts of her southern coast are some of the best on the Eastern seaboard, especially if you crave a traditional boardwalk-and-pizza-saturated summer escape. The addition of an older artsy gay colony in Rehoboth Beach is the diverse icing on this excellent salt-and-sea cake.

The signs of a good mid-Atlantic beach resort can be summed up thus: a boardwalk. A surplus of eating establishments selling multiple variations on New York pizza, Philly cheesesteaks and fried…well, everything. A long, dusty beach that's a good stretch of sand. And some Confederate flag paraphernalia sitting storefronts from retiree-run art studios and a glut of gay bars.

Welcome to Delaware and its 30 or so miles of summery beach goodness, which combine the country-fried outlook of the rural Eastern Shore, Northeastern blue-collar roughneck 'tude and the intellectual yuppieness of trippers escaping DC, Philly and New York.

There's only one real road here: State Rd (SR) 1, also known as Coastal Hwy, a flat horizon of scrub, dune grass and blue skies. Starting from the south is ❶ **Bethany Beach**, the family-friendly grandma of local beach towns that greets you with a surrealist totem poll: Chief Little Owl, a Nanticoke Indian topped by a north-facing eagle carved from an Alaskan red cedar log.

The beach here (and elsewhere on the Delaware shore) is a pretty swathe of gold sand, and the town of Bethany is probably the coziest local oceanside community. A small grid of gift shops, bookstores and cafés is walkable and generally packed with family-on-holiday pedestrians.

TIME
2 days

DISTANCE
15 miles

BEST TIME TO GO
Jun – Aug

START
Bethany Beach

END
Rehoboth Beach

ALSO GOOD FOR

OFFBEAT

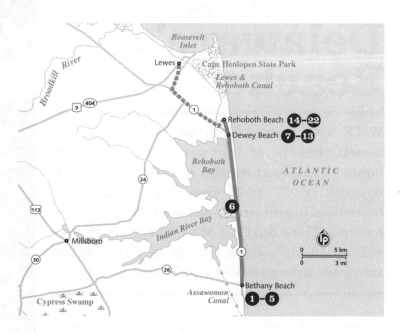

There are three good eating options for the three meals of the day. **2** **Frog House** looks deceptively like a diner gone stale, but don't judge this frog by its warts – try a dozen fluffy "sand-dollar" flapjacks instead. When lunch calls, have a pit-smoked sandwich at a patriotic country song given restaurant form: **3** **Bethany Blues BBQ Pit**. Assuming you're not saluting the giant American flag hanging over the bar, gorge out on the Pit's "Delmarva BBQ" (pretty much imported Texas mesquite style, but for the East Coast this is some fine, woodsy, pleasantly acrid, slow-smoked meat).

Bethany's most inconspicuous restaurant happens to be its best. Huddled like a vale of humility between flashy mountains of culinary gaudiness, the storefront **4** **Kingston Grille** is the embodiment of, "Honey, let's find a nice, romantic French place." The cuisine is organic, well-crafted and rural – filling and rich – and the ambience is nice enough for a good night out, yet still aware that this is the beach and no one wants to get too dressed up.

There's a glut of same-same mediocre motels and much better (and pricier) B&Bs in Bethany. Our favorite specimen of the latter genre is **5** **Addy Sea**, which strikes up a good posh-linens-to-lacy-curtains ratio without feeling stuffy, although it is a bit ornate for the beach.

If Bethany's beach (or any beach) gets too crowded you can always head to **6** **Delaware Seashore State Park**, about 6 miles north of Bethany. There's an end-of-the-world quality to this barrier island, with its long, lonely stretches of windswept dunes and surprisingly fierce gray-capped waves surging in the distance. It all feels slightly out of place given that, y'know, you're in Delaware, but it's a nice surprise, especially for surfers.

North of the park (watch out for sudden shifts in speed limit) is **7** **Dewey Beach**. Now if Bethany is a sweet grandma, what's Dewey? How about a bride-to-be on her bachelorette party shrieking around in a rhinestone-studded tiara? No, that's just someone we spotted at the **8** **Starboard**, Dewey's most raucous bar, on "Suicide Sunday," over a powerful (and well-mixed) Bloody Mary.

If you want to add dancing of the thumpa-thumpa variety, head west to **9** **Northbeach** resto-club, which overlooks a pretty bend of Rehoboth Bay (not that anyone's checking out the water). During the day the large back porch is a lovely spot from which to squint and moan off your hangover.

The **10** **Bottle and Cork** self-promotes as the best rock venue in the world; we're willing to concede it tops the competition in Sussex County and certainly attracts the biggest names on the Delaware shore. If you need to wind down with coffee, wi-fi and general tranquility, **11** **Booksandcoffee** awaits you with civilized respite.

Dewey has the leanest eating options of Delaware's beach towns, but it makes up for this lack of choice with one of the best arguments for death-by-caloric overload we've ever seen: **12** **Ed's Chicken and Crabs**. This converted chicken coop-cum-crab shack specializes in fried things, steamed things, things covered with melted cheese and all those other elements that make life worth living. Ask for the "shrimp jammers" – when we did, someone in the kitchen yelled, "Them shrimps is the shit, yo!", to which we can only reply: indeed.

While Dewey is good for a drink, the best beach town around is only a 1.3-mile drive away (or ride on the **13** **Jolley Trolley**, a hop-on and hop-off bus that runs constantly through the season) away.

DETOUR

Once named Zwaanen-dael (Valley of the Swans) by newly arrived Dutch settlers (who were eventually massacred by the local Nanticoke), **Lewes**, nine miles northwest of Rehoboth, is a hybrid between Delaware's dollhouses and the coast. This is the place to catch the **Cape May Ferry** (www.capemaylewesferry.com) to New Jersey, dine in impeccably cute grandeur at the **Buttery Restaurant** (www.butteryrestaurant.com) or just wander amid the quaint blocks of this quiet burg, which still carries a whiff of well-organized, provincial Northern Europe.

14 **Rehoboth Beach** calls itself "The Nation's Summer Capital"; its name has a biblical root ("Place for all") and both titles are fitting. Everyone from first ladies to rednecks to young professionals to an older gay community calls this town (summer) home; it's the sort of place where men hold hands, lesbians belt out karaoke, dudes slam shots and families munch on saltwater taffy, peanut oil–soaked french fries and pizza.

There are some lovely hotels here, but a more economical option, especially for large groups, is renting one of the many short-lease properties; we've had good experiences with **15** **Ocean Atlantic** real estate agency. Otherwise, the new, bright, beautiful place for sleeping is **16** **Hotel Rehoboth**, where the soft shades of blue, white and cream and the thoughtful turn-down service make for a respectably luxurious doss. Two top gay sleeps include the **17** **Shore Inn**, which looks a bit like a rainbow flag–bedecked Motel 6 run through a flower garden (with a clothing-optional sundeck), and the very sweet and civilized **18** **Royal Rose**, a great spot for older couples or those just seeking a quiet escape.

GREASE = GOOD

Not mentioned in our eating reviews are three quintessential beachfront dining options you pretty much have to partake of when on the Delaware shore. To wit: saltwater taffy from Dollie's, pizza from Grotto's (which, as one put it, "has the beach on lock") and fries doused in vinegar and Old Bay at Thrasher's. All available on the boardwalk in Rehoboth, and all definitely delicious.

Across the street on gay-nexus Baltimore Ave is **19** **Café Sole**, a typically Rehoboth joint where a macho man with a Village Person mustache dips his pita in spicy garlic hummus next to weekend-tripping urbanites drooling over the sweet-and-savory Turkey Stuffer, which drips stuffing, cranberry sauce and deliciousness. If you need a nice dinner date locale, the dim red and black interior, Hindu-accented art and lovely fusion cuisine of **20** **Planet X** are well worth your time; an *escabeche* (pickled fish) with chickpea puree mixes up the peppery, the fresh and the pleasantly starchy in one wonderful package.

More straight–gay mishmash occurs at the **21** **Purple Parrot** when night falls. It's the sort of place where working-class Pennsylvanians sing karaoke with canoodling lesbians and white-collar DC types. But our favorite Rehoboth bar is the **22** **Dogfish Head Brewery**. A must for beer lovers, Dogfish is one of the best brewers in the country, well known for its innovative deployment of hops and barley (and, in the past, mashed raspberries, pumpkin, brown sugar, cocoa and chilies – this, friends, is the beer frontier). Kick back, sip a five-beer sampler, listen to a North Carolina alt-country band with friends or family, feel the summer creep up your spine and your worries slip, if ever-so-briefly, away.

Adam Karlin

TRIP INFORMATION

GETTING THERE
The easiest way to get from DC to SR 1 is by following Rte 50 through Maryland to MD/DE 404.

DO

Booksandcoffee
This perfectly cute spot is a wonderful place to pick up seaside reading, nice strong coffee (the mochas are divine) and some wi-fi besides. ☎ 302-226-9959; 113 Dickinson Rd, Dewey Beach; ☽ 7:30am-7pm

Delaware Seashore State Park
One of the prettiest parks in the state mixes some soft, fluffy dunes with a wild stretch of Atlantic coastline near Bethany. ☎ 302-227-2800; www.destateparks.com; 39415 Inlet Rd; ☽ 8am-sunset

Jolley Trolley
This tourist and drinkers' bus runs between Rehoboth and Dewey. ☎ 302-227-1197; www.jolleytrolley.com; along Rehoboth Ave, Rehoboth Beach; one-way $2, after midnight $3; ☽ 8am-2am

EAT

Bethany Blues BBQ Pit
It's hokey, it's all-American and everyone basically loves the theme, to say nothing of the pit BBQ. ☎ 302-537-1500; 6 Pennsylvania Ave, Bethany Beach; meals $8-21; ☽ lunch & dinner

Café Sole
The sandwiches here are so outstanding that they may well have figured out the recipe for sex between bread. ☎ 302-227-1707; 44 Baltimore Ave, Rehoboth Beach; meals $8-26; ☽ lunch & dinner

Ed's Chicken and Crabs
By all that is holy: damn this place can fry. Fry what? Fry *every-freaking-thing*. ☎ 302-227-9484; Rte 1 & Swede St, Dewey Beach; meals $5-20; ☽ lunch & dinner Apr-Nov

Frog House
The quintessential family diner on the quintessential family beach is a great place for the kids. ☎ 302-539-4500; 116 Garfield Pkwy, Bethany Beach; meals under $15; ☽ breakfast, lunch & dinner

Kingston Grille
You couldn't get better food if you washed Montmartre straight onto Bethany Beach, which is basically the vibe here. ☎ 302-539-1588; Pennsylvania Ave & Campbell Pl, Bethany Beach; meals $22-40; ☽ dinner

Planet X
Crimson lighting, Asian bric-a-brac and an excellent fusion menu make X the natural choice for those tripping the culinary light fantastic. ☎ 302-226-1928; 35 Wilmington Ave, Rehoboth Beach; meals $20-30; ☽ dinner

DRINK

Bottle and Cork
If you're on the Delaware coast and in the market for some live music and decent headliners, look no further. ☎ 302-227-7272; 1807 Hwy 1, Dewey Beach; ☽ to late

Dogfish Head Brewery
One of our favorite microbreweries operates one of Rehoboth's best bars, with live tunes and great (natch) artisan-crafted brews. ☎ 302-226-2739; www.dogfish.com; 320 Rehoboth Ave, Rehoboth Beach; ☽ from 4pm Mon-Fri, from noon Sat & Sun

Northbeach
On the bay side of Dewey Beach, Northbeach has a giant porch and buzzing ambience that's perfect for soaking up sun, sexiness and Smirnoff. ☎ 302-226-8673; www.deweybeachlife.com/dning_nb.html; 125 McKinley St & the Bay, Dewey Beach; ☽ to late

Purple Parrot
This epitome of Rehoboth nightlife manages to mix up rednecks, gay party boys and a raucous lesbian scene – often with karaoke! ☎ 302-226-1139; 247 Rehoboth Ave, Rehoboth Beach; ☽ to 2am

Starboard
You wanna be bad? You better be here. Dewey's parties don't get crazier, or more in your face, than in this madhouse. ☎ 302-227-4600; 2009 Hwy 1, Dewey Beach; ☽ to late

SLEEP
The following are high-season rates; expect half-price or lower in the off-season.

Addy Sea
Addy just edges the line of over-the-top, but it's certainly one of the plushest, most attractive sleeps in Bethany Beach. ☎ 302-539-3707; www.addysea.com; 99 Ocean View Parkway, Bethany Beach; r $250-400

Hotel Rehoboth
The Rehoboth provides all the filigreed luxury of an elegant B&B with all the corporate amenities of a big box chain. ☎ 302-227-4300; http://hotelrehoboth.com; 247 Rehoboth Ave, Rehoboth Beach; r $269-379

Ocean Atlantic
It's not a hotel per se, but this friendly rental agency does rent out some outstanding properties if you need a longer stay. ☎ 302-227-6767; www.oceanatlantic.net; 330 Rehoboth Ave, Rehoboth Beach

Royal Rose
Probably the most sedate gay B&B we've ever seen, the Rose is quietly romantic, perfectly charming, tastefully decorated and centrally located. ☎ 302-226-2535; www.royalroseinn.com; 41 Baltimore Ave, Rehoboth Beach; r $130-190

Shore Inn
The Shore is a good spot for older gay travelers looking for a bit of fun to complement their sun. ☎ 302-227-8487; www.shoreinn.com; 703 Rehoboth Ave, Rehoboth Beach; r $130-235

USEFUL WEBSITES
www.beach-net.com
www.delawarebeaches.com

LINK YOUR TRIP
www.lonelyplanet.com/trip-planner

Cinematic Baltimore

WHY GO Baltimore is eminently cinematic, and the true star of productions that showcase her kooky eccentrics, American dreamers and what most critics call the best show to grace American TV: The Wire. This trip highlights sites from all of these tributes to Charm City.

A great controversy rocked Baltimore and its surrounds in 2007, and it had nothing to do with the usual crime, corruption and scandal. No. At issue: the latest version of *Hairspray* (the John Waters homage to 1960s Baltimore) was being filmed in…Toronto.

Waters forms one angle of a triumvirate of filmmakers whose work seizes three distinct angles of the Baltimore experience: Waters with the weirdos, Barry Levinson and his socially mobile immigrants, and David Simon, who captures the Baltimore of drug corners, flawed cops, failing labor unions and indifferent bureaucracy. Waters' kitsch is part of Baltimore's brand, to the chagrin of locals who want to be known for more than backyards inhabited by mad transvestites. The temple to this image is recognized as W 36th St in Hampden, better known as "the Avenue."

Still one of Balty's old-school, working-class white 'hoods, Hampden is the home of Waters HQ, ❶ **Atomic Books**, the sort of bookstore where edgy Japanese soft-core gets stacked near the greeting cards. Hampden's a-flux today; two blocks away, tatted-up skinhead-look-alikes in denim shorts kick back on porchfronts, while on the Avenue, yuppies grab coffee at artsy coffeehouses like ❷ **Common Ground Café** and go vintage-and-art shopping in boutiques such as ❸ **Passion Fish**. Here the tatted dudes rub shoulders with hipsters, most notably in ❹ **Frazier's on the Avenue**, where the clientele fits the mold of either cute musician (skinny jeans and thick glasses) or meth-ed out rock warrior–god.

TIME
1 day

DISTANCE
25 miles

BEST TIME TO GO
Year-round

START
Baltimore

END
Baltimore

ALSO GOOD FOR

OFFBEAT

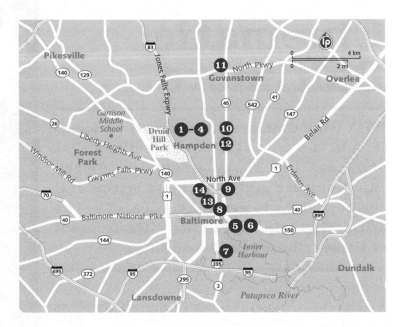

From the city's north to its northwest: head to Forest Park, along the road that serves as the title for the Levinson film *Liberty Heights*. Another take on integration-era Baltimore through the lens of interracial dating, Garrison Middle, on Barrington Rd, stands in for the movie's high school. Unfortunately, Levinson's parable on community come-togetherness seems off the mark today, as this once-white suburb has become, due to white flight, part of Baltimore's black periphery.

 **PLAYLIST** This playlist showcases some of the best tunes from Baltimore-based movies and TV like *Diner, Hairspray* and *The Wire*.

- "It's All in the Game," Tommy Edwards
- "Come Go with Me," The Del Vikings
- "Baltimore, You're Home to Me," Dave Hardin
- "Good Morning Baltimore," *Hairspray*
- "Way Down in the Hole," The Blind Boys of Alabama
- "Jail Flick," Diablo
- "I Walk on Gilded Splinters," Paul Weller
- "What You Know about Baltimore?," Ogun, featuring Phathead

You remain in that world rolling down Druid Hill Ave toward North Ave, which feels like driving into a filming day from Simon's TV "novel," *The Wire*. Low-rises like the ones used by the show's drug crews huddle near West Preston, along with the shuttered doors of Edward Tilghman Middle, the focal point of season four. The motel where gay gangster Omar ambushes a rival hit man stands at the end of North Ave, where, in the summer, kids dance in the jet stream of a knocked-out fire hydrant.

Drive southeast to Eutaw past the art deco–tabulous ❺ **Hippodrome Theater**, which Levinson used as a stand-in for the James Brown–showcasing Royal Theater in *Liberty Heights*. Nearby is the ❻ **Hollywood Diner**, a stainless steel wonder where young chefs train in the sacred art of short-order frying. It also served as the centerpiece of *Diner*, Levinson's coming-of-age chick flick for dudes.

Waters fans (and anyone who likes art) should detour to the nearby ❼ **American Visionary Art Museum**; wander through its collection of unpretentious, inspiring outsider art and pay homage to the 20ft statue of Divine, mad transvestite star of *Pink Flamingos*. Then make your way back to Fell's Point and drive up N Calvert St, past the

HONFEST...HONEST?

Honfest (www.honfest.net) is Baltimore's most famous festival, a studied celebration in the local kitsch scene (often embraced by members of the cult of John Waters) that occurs every June in Hampden. But to be honest, the Baltimore of beehive hairdos has vanished, and Bawlmerese, the local, lovely slurred accent, is dying the death of regional accents everywhere. Enjoy the gaudiness, but recognize that "Hon" hairdos are more rooted in Chamber of Commerce boosterism than living, breathing Baltimore.

❽ **Baltimore Sun building** (all three directors mentioned here have used the newspaper in their films) and up Greenmount Ave past ❾ **Green Mount Cemetery**, used as a negotiating spot between criminals and cops in *The Wire*.

Greenmount becomes a long, quintessentially Baltimore street: bail bonds offices, convenience stores, T-shirt stands (doing a ripping trade in Barack Obama shirts in 2008) and soul-food and lake-trout takeaways like ❿ **Waverly Grill**, where the whiting is fried right and the greens are pleasantly salty.

After Greenmount becomes York Ave, Baltimore moves into a white area again. The transition is marked by the gorgeous Senator Theatre, a major art deco set piece in Levinson's *Avalon*. Have a burrito at the rockabilly restobar ⓫ **Zen West** and then head back down Greenmount, pausing to wander through the musty, dusty shelves of ⓬ **Normals Books and Records**, one of Baltimore's best indie bookstores.

If you're tired by the time you reach Mount Vernon, check into ⓭ **Phoenix Risin'**, which balances B&B fluffy comfort with three eclectic, ethnic-themed bedrooms. It's a good place to crash after a tipple in the ⓮ **Drinkery**: an attitude-free, friendly neighborhood gay bar. Your trip ends here, where, appropriately enough, *Pink Flamingos* wrapped – with Divine's infamous consumption of...well, watch the movie. We recommend having a beer.

Adam Karlin

"...rolling down Druid Hill Ave toward North Ave feels like driving into a filming day from The Wire."

TRIP INFORMATION

GETTING THERE
To get to Hampden, take Exit 8A (Falls Rd) from I-83. Turn onto W 36th St to reach "the Ave."

DO
American Visionary Art Museum
Our favorite Baltimore art museum show-cases self-taught "outsider" art by vagrants, mental patients, wanderers, convicts and other geniuses. ☎ 410-244-1900; www.avam.org; 800 Key Hwy; adult/child $12/8; ⏲ 10am-6pm Tue-Sun; ♿

Atomic Books
What, you've got a thing against graphic novels about dominatrix robots? Then never, ever enter this shop. ☎ 410-662-4444; www.atomicbooks.com; 1100 W 36th St; ⏲ 11am-7pm, to 6pm Sun

Normals Books and Records
This is a fantastic indie bookstore, full of quirky and edgy titles that reflect the char-acter of the city it serves. ☎ 410-243-6888; www.normals.com; 425 E 31st St; ⏲ 11am-6pm

Passion Fish
This is one of Hampden's better indie galleries-cum-vintage-clothing shops. The son of the owner was a location photogra-pher for *The Wire*. ☎ 410-925-4133; 1129 W 36th St; ⏲ Wed-Sun

EAT
Hollywood Diner
Top-quality diner fare is cooked and served by at-risk kids training in the Chesapeake Center for Youth Development. ☎ 410-962-5379; 400 E Saratoga St; meals $4-10; ⏲ 7am-2pm Mon-Fri; ♿

Waverly Grill
This is a clean, tasty spot for Baltimore soul food favorites like lake trout served with thick mac-and-cheese. ☎ 410-962-5379; 3011 Greenmount Ave; meals $6-12; ⏲ 7am-2pm Mon-Fri

Zen West
Cross a Baltimore hipster with a Tex Mex menu and some healthy rockabilly vibe and you get this swinging joint. ☎ 410-323-3368; 5916 York Rd; meals $8-21; ⏲ lunch & dinner

DRINK
Common Ground Café
Coffee, Bawlmer style: loads of local artwork, playful hipster vibe and back alleyway graffiti. ☎ 410-235-5533; 819 W 36th St; ⏲ 7am-5pm

Drinkery
This queer (in every sense) dive is one of the friendliest gay bars around, anywhere, with a neighborly vibe. ☎ 410-225-3100; 207 W Read St; ⏲ 11am-2am

Frazier's on the Avenue
A good grime-and-grot dive for enjoying Natty Boh and watching dem 'Os (Orioles) on the TV, hon. ☎ 410-662-4914; www.fraziersontheavenue.com; 919 W 36th St; ⏲ 9am-2am

SLEEP
Phoenix Risin'
Chintzy B&B vibe gets mixed with con-temporary Baltimore attitude and Haitian, African and Native American–themed rooms. ☎ 410-462-2692; www.phoenixrisin.com; 1429 Bolton St; r $95-140; ♿

USEFUL WEBSITES
www.dreamlandnews.com
www.hbo.com/thewire

LINK YOUR TRIP

www.lonelyplanet.com/trip-planner

Haunted Maryland

WHY GO Tour some of the most haunted places in this spooky state: Point Lookout, crawling with the spirits of hundreds of Civil War POWs; Leonardtown, home of the original Blair Witch; and other dead zones, including some suitably dreary nooks and crannies associated with Edgar Allen Poe.

TIME
2 – 3 days

DISTANCE
200 miles

BEST TIME TO GO
Oct – Dec

START
Baltimore

END
Baltimore

ALSO GOOD FOR

Let it be said: the ❶ **Brome Howard Inn** is perfectly lovely. It's one of southern Maryland's nicest digs, combining the grace of an historical home and the stunning surrounds of 30 acres of prime Chesapeake riverfront. The on-site restaurant is excellent, too. Just be aware that if you bunk here, you may be doing so with the spirits of two girls.

That, at least, is the story of a Mexican dishwasher who was working at the Brome in 2002. The tale didn't surprise us. Maryland is an old state blanketed in gothic scenery that could have been sketched out of Alvin Schwartz's *Scary Stories to Tell in the Dark*.

❷ **Point Lookout State Park**, at the tip of Maryland's western shore, has an entire prison camp full of restless dead. Located at the marshy confluence of the Chesapeake Bay and Potomac River is a watery, dark peninsula, long-shadowed under thin copses of loblolly pine. During the Civil War, the Union Army placed a Confederate prisoner of war camp here as a warning to pro-secessionist elements in southern Maryland. Many of the camp guards were in fact black soldiers.

Some 4000 out of 50,000 POWs died in the camp. Their ghosts are often spotted in woods, among creeks and crossing fields next to an obelisk dedicated to the prison dead. A nearby lighthouse, closed to the public, has been called "the most haunted lighthouse in America"; a Navy friend who worked on the building's electronics says he was once hounded out of the basement by a disembodied voice.

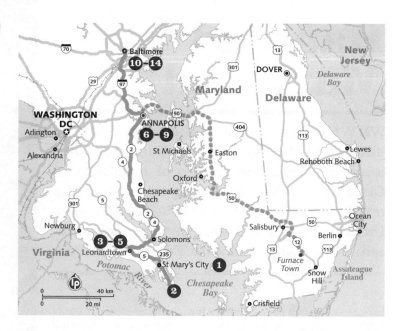

North on Rte 5 is **3 Leonardtown**, the charming seat of St Mary's County. A cozy main street ensconces the corny-named yet lovingly elegant (and delicious) **4 Café Des Artistes**, which gives the best ingredients of the tidewater an appropriate French twist.

Up the street is the county historical society building, and a boulder marked by the knee (or hand) prints of one of colonial America's oldest ghosts, **5 Moll Dyer**, who lived in late-17th-century Leonardtown. During a winter's serious epidemic she was accused of being a witch, cast out of town and froze to death, kneeling (some say with her hands splayed) on the rock that now sits near Leonardtown courthouse. As she died, Dyer cursed the town.

HAUNTED HALLOWEEN

Every Halloween park, rangers in Point Lookout lay out tape recorders and lead volunteers on ghost walks into the lonely southern Maryland marshes. It's not uncommon for visitors to spot ragged Confederate prisoners in the woods, or for the recorders to pick up agonized pleas for help drawled out in thick, Southern accents...

Does this sound familiar? That legend helped inspire the 1999 movie *The Blair Witch Project*. There's a Moll Dyer Rd south of Leonardtown, and some say an angry ghost haunts the area on the coldest day of winter. Traces of her knee prints are supposedly visible in the rock as well, although we failed this spiritual Rorschach test on our visit.

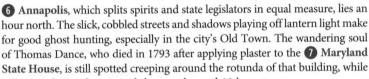

6 **Annapolis**, which splits spirits and state legislators in equal measure, lies an hour north. The slick, cobbled streets and shadows playing off lantern light make for good ghost hunting, especially in the city's Old Town. The wandering soul of Thomas Dance, who died in 1793 after applying plaster to the **7** **Maryland State House**, is still spotted creeping around the rotunda of that building, while in St Anne's Parish, it is said that an obsessed 19th-century gravedigger named Joe Simmons still haunts his old workplace cemetery.

"...slick, cobbled streets and shadows playing off lantern light make for good ghost hunting..."

If all of the above frightens you, best ward off supernatural discomfort at the **8** **Ram's Head**, the capital's own brewpub, restaurant and live music venue. Just beware of the rumors of the ghost of a "working girl" who apparently crashed through the ceiling of the joint in the 1800s. **9** **Annapolis Ghost Tours** is an excellent way of accessing the city's spooky sites amid suitably scary company (spirit spotting becomes a lot easier after a haunted-pub crawl).

10 **Baltimore**, city of whores, drunks and authors, is another prime Maryland "haunt." The town is, after all, Edgar Allen Poe's old stomping ground; the grave of the father of the modern horror story is still visited by a cloaked stranger who leaves roses and a bottle of brandy for the author on his birthday. Poe's tiny **11** **house** instills a telltale fear of a different sort (ie that of the rough neighborhood that surrounds it), but it's also a nice museum, although you'll want to call ahead for opening hours.

The **12** **Annabel Lee Tavern**, named for one of Poe's poems, is a chintzy, gloomy, yet cozy pub/dungeon in Highlandtown; envision one of those dark houses Poe must have lived in enlivened by friendly bartenders, laughing clientele and fine food, and you have this spot imagined.

13 **Baltimore Ghost Tours** follows the Annapolis example (or vice versa), taking tourists around the salt-spray-and-death-stained historic Baltimore waterfront. When you're ready to retire (with the lights on), head for the **14** **Inn at Henderson's Wharf**. Housed in an evocative old tobacco warehouse, this hotel consistently excels, provid-

DETOUR Deep in the Lower Eastern Shore, about 110 miles from Annapolis, are the eerie ruins of an iron-smelting foundry. **Furnace Town** (www .furnacetown.com) was abandoned in the 19th century, tended amid thick marshes and red-barked pines by its last inhabitant, an ex-slave named Sampson Hart who lived to the ripe age of 106. Hart is still supposed to wander this muddy relic, now a living-history museum still under the shadow, like so much of Maryland, of the restless dead.

ing the right old-school atmosphere to send a few more shivers up your spine before the lights go off and the spirits of Maryland come out to play.

Adam Karlin

TRIP
36

TRIP INFORMATION

GETTING THERE
St Mary's County is at the far end of Rte 5, about 60 miles south of Washington DC.

DO
Annapolis Ghost Tours
Discover Annapolis' rain-slicked, spirit-touched alleyways, plus (if you opt for the haunted-pub crawl) raging party people. ☎ 800-979-3370; www.ghostsofannapolis.com; Main St & Church Circle, Annapolis; adult/child $16/10

Baltimore Ghost Tours
Baltimore is a haven for thieves, smugglers, murderers, even politicians, whose spirits are subjects of this tour. ☎ 410-522-7400; 731 S Broadway St, Baltimore; adult/child in advance $13/8, from departure $15/10

Edgar Allen Poe House
The father of American noir lived here, in this pretty noir-ish – OK, bad – Baltimore neighborhood. ☎ 410-396-7932; 203 N Amity St, Baltimore; adult/child under 13 $3/1; 🕑 noon-3:45pm Wed-Sat

Maryland State House
The oldest state house in continuous use is also one of the prettiest. Look for the upside-down, wisdom-representing acorn atop the dome. ☎ 410-974-3400; 25 State Circle, Annapolis; 🕑 9am-5pm Mon-Fri, 10am-4pm Sat & Sun

Point Lookout State Park
A strip of sand, thin trees and wide marshes mark where Maryland gets pinched out by the Potomac and Patuxent Rivers. ☎ 410-925-4133; St Mary's County; 🕑 Wed-Sun

EAT
Café Des Artistes
If you ignore the corny name, you'll appreciate the excellent menu of rich, rural French favorites often served here. ☎ 301-997-0500; 41655 Fenwick St, Leonardtown; meals $15-30; 🕑 lunch & dinner

Ram's Head
A good spot for burgers that is made even better by home-brewed beers, talk of a local ghost and decent live music acts. ☎ 410-268-4545; 33 West St, Annapolis; meals $11-20; 🕑 from 11am

DRINK
Annabel Lee Tavern
Although named for Poe's gloomiest poem, the tavern is as elegiac, if a hell of a lot more fun, than its namesake. ☎ 410-522-2929; 601 S Clinton St, Baltimore; 🕑 4pm-1am

SLEEP
Brome Howard Inn
As evocative and charming as B&Bs get, the food here is as lovely as the digs and surrounding tidewater countryside. ☎ 301-866-0656; www.bromehowardinn.com; 18281 Rosecroft Rd, St Mary's City; r $80-160

Inn at Henderson's Wharf
Have a sleep in a former warehouse, which happens to have been converted into one of Baltimore's best hotels. ☎ 410-522-7777; www.hendersonswharf.com; 1000 Fell St, Baltimore; r $179-259

USEFUL WEBSITES
www.angelfire.com/scary/marylandhauntings
www.marylandghosts.com

LINK YOUR TRIP
www.lonelyplanet.com/trip-planner

TRIP

The Ethnic Epicurean

WHY GO The suburbs of Washington DC are home to some of the mid-Atlantic's best culinary diamonds in the rough. Hidden among long lines of stale strip malls are well-established ethnic enclaves and the favorite chow halls and watering holes of those communities, waiting to be discovered by intrepid travelers.

Let's just be totally honest: Langley Park, MD, is not going to be the international tourism hot spot of the 21st century. Like most of the 'burbs within the Beltway, it's a congested, ill-defined mess of gas stations, service centers and residential blocks; a sponge for the working-class, mainly immigrant population priced out of the nation's capital.

Still, if it isn't a tourism hot spot, it is a center for international travel: according to the *Washington Post,* Langley Park is now essentially the site of a relocated Guatemalan village whose residents have all picked up sticks to chase the American dream. The Park also hides one of the region's best culinary gems: all across DC's outskirts are excellent restaurants, patronized by either immigrants who crave mom's meatloaf (or cow tongue taco), or foodies seeking the perfect wave of their obsession: the utterly authentic and delicious ethnic eatery.

Ironically, though, Langley Park's contribution to the ethnic eatery trail isn't Central American; it's pure-veg Indian. ❶ **Woodlands** is a true Indian restaurant, in that there is no soft sitar music, nor are there paintings of the Taj Mahal. Rather, you are confronted with a Krishna-speckled bare cafeteria packed with Indian families and several delicious troughs of veg curry, from paneer to okra to lentils.

We kinda feel bad taking you to this most Latin of neighborhoods and feeding you curry (good as it is), so we scouted out some excellent

TIME
3 days

BEST TIME TO GO
Year-round

START
Langley Park, MD

END
Adams Morgan, Washington DC

ALSO GOOD FOR

CITY

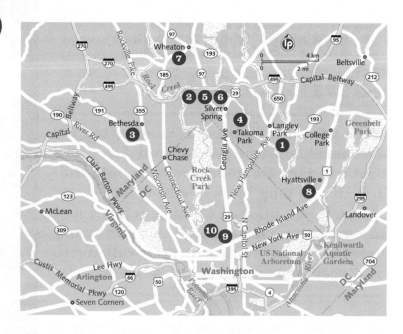

Central American cuisine, too. ❷ **Dona Azucena Pupuseria**, on an entirely nondescript stretch of Piney Branch Rd, happens to be a beating heart for DC's Salvadoran community. *Pupusas,* small meat-and-cheese-filled turnovers (similar to empanadas), fly in and out of the kitchens by the thousands and on to the tables for hundreds of hungry Salvadorans.

If you head toward Bethesda, MD, you'll find a restaurant that pulls in appreciative chicken lovers as much as local Latino families: ❸ **Chicken On the Run**.

"…in the DC 'burbs they take their seared, juicy, savory chicken with sides of yucca and dipping sauce seriously."

The question, "Who does the best *pollo brasa* (roast chicken; a Peruvian specialty) around here?" is a contentious one in the DC 'burbs; they take their seared, juicy, savory chicken with sides of yucca and dipping sauce seriously. But you'll always get an appreciative nod of approval if you vote for COTR.

There are plenty of Latin American churches here, where the *iglesia* is still the heart of social life. In church basements, men scream *"Dios en mi corazón"* (God in my heart) to the accompaniment of an ancient Casio keyboard played by an even more ancient Salvadoran (or Guatemalan, Nicaraguan or Honduran) grandmother. But, eventually, Latinos give way for Caribbeans in Takoma Park, where the chicken is jerked, not roasted. ❹ **Caribbean Palace** is a favorite with local Jamaicans and Trinidadians, where the reply to "How's it goin'?" is an enthusiastic "Rough and tough."

We'll shift ethnic gears back to Asia and a restaurant widely considered one of the best deals in the DC area. ❺ **Mandalay**, in Silver Spring, is one of the friendliest neighborhood restaurants this side of anywhere, and it also happens to be Burmese. The green-tea salad gets rave reviews from well-taste-budded travelers, who also enjoy the spacious, well-appointed interior. Also in Silver Spring is an example of ethnic Americana: ❻ **Tastee**, a 24-hour, clean-countertop and comfort-food exemplar of the American contribution to global cuisine: the diner. Go for the Reuben, and thank us later.

There's all kinds of lousy Chinese food available in DC, but it's our good fortune to eat at ❼ **Good Fortune** in Wheaton. One of those enormous Chinese restaurants that seems to employ half of Shanghai and is decorated like a color clash given wings, the Fortune is renowned for its excellent dim sum lunches, which attract those who're craving shrimp balls from hours away.

"Washington is a vibrant and cosmopolitan city. Unfortunately, this does not always extend to the world of authentic ethnic cuisine. The city's need to cater to tourists and those on an expense account are sometimes a challenge to the development of urban, ethnic fare. Getting to a strip mall in Maryland or Virginia can sometimes prove this point. So many kinds of cuisine from around the world seem underrepresented in Washington, but are really barely beyond the Beltway."

Vijay Rajendran, Cleveland Park

Heading into DC via Hyattsville you'll see culinary evidence of an ethnic enclave that's not generally considered as such: African Americans. In this case, Southern blacks, who love the seafood, fried chicken and ribs buffet at ❽ **Bubba's Muscogee**, a veritable (and delicious) heart attack served on Formica.

We've tried to maintain this ethnic foodie tour outside of Washington DC, as the DC eating scene is nowhere near as unnoticed, but in a tip to some of the best overseas cuisine in the capital, we have to mention ❾ **Dukem**, which shines above a huge array of Ethiopian competition with its fluffy *injera* (bread), spicy lamb stew and excellent honey wine. With prices topping out in the $20s for entrées, this is easily as expensive as the ethnic epicurean tour gets. If you've saved some money, have a snooze in ❿ **Adam's Inn**, a luxurious if chintzy B&B. This Victorian row house is truly fuzzy and comfortable, but it's best noted for its location – in Adams Morgan, near another strip of ethnic eating exploration.

While we've mostly kept to Maryland in this trip, we can't wrap without mentioning the **Eden Center**, at the corner of Wilson Blvd in Seven Corners, VA. You might as well change that "VA" to "VN," though; the Eden Center is the central nervous system of area Vietnamese. The vibe here is more South Vietnam than Northern Virginia, and if you need some *pho*, pop into any restaurant here and emerge smiling.

Adam Karlin

TRIP INFORMATION

GETTING THERE
Drive out here by heading north from DC on Wisconsin Blvd or Rhode Island Ave.

EAT
Bubba's Muscogee
This is real soul food served in a real Southern setting. ☎ 202-269-1871; 1544 Rhode Island Ave NE; meals $8-22; ☽ lunch & dinner Tue-Sun, breakfast Sun

Caribbean Palace
Bright, tropical attitude gives way to bright, tropical dishes that are all the rage with local Caribbeans and Takoma Park yuppies. ☎ 301-431-1563; 7680 New Hampshire Ave; meals $5-15; ☽ lunch & dinner

Chicken On the Run
The amount of food you get for the price you pay makes COTR one of the best takeaways in suburban Maryland. ☎ 301-652-9004; 4933 St Elmo Ave; meals $5.50-13.50; ☽ 11am-9pm, slightly reduced Sun

Dona Azucena Pupuseria
Surprisingly large for a *pupuseria*, Dona's needs to be kinda roomy to accommodate its loyal mobs of Salvadoran regulars. ☎ 301-434-4230; 8728 Piney Branch Rd; meals under $10; ☽ 10am-6pm Tue-Sun

Dukem
Having a communal Ethiopian meal with loved ones at a place like this is a defining DC-area experience. ☎ 202-667-8735; 1118 U St NW; meals $11-30; ☽ 11am-2am, to 3am Fri & Sat

Good Fortune
It comes off as the Wal-Mart of Chinese restaurants, but the dim sum truly is the stuff of local legend. ☎ 301-929-8818; 2646 University Blvd W; meals $11-20; ☽ 11am-midnight

Mandalay
The friendly Burmese staff and the excellent food at this extremely popular place have carved the Mandalay into its surrounding community's heart. ☎ 301-925-4133; 930 Bonifant St; meals $9-13; ☽ lunch & dinner

Tastee Diner
This is as good as diners get this far south of the Mason–Dixon Line, and a Silver Spring landmark to boot. ☎ 301-589-8171; 8601 Cameron St; meals $6-15; ☽ 24hr

Woodlands
Some of the best pure-veg Indian in the DC area isn't in DC, but at this Guatemalan strip mall. ☎ 301-434-4202; 8046 New Hampshire Ave; meals under $20; ☽ lunch & dinner

SLEEP
Adam's Inn
It may look like the sort of B&B grandma would stay at, but it's in the neighborhood your wild cousins party in. ☎ 202-745-3600; www.adamsinn.com; 1746 Lanier Pl NW; r $99-159

USEFUL WEBSITES
http://amandamc.blogspot.com
www.dcfoodies.com

LINK YOUR TRIP
www.lonelyplanet.com/trip-planner

HISTORY &
CULTURE

Maritime Maryland

WHY GO Maryland's culture is drenched in the Chesapeake's brackish tides. In the past, water shaped Marylanders' working lives; today it's their recreational backyard. Even the state's mixed population seems physically well-matched by its defining geographic feature: the estuary – the body of water that mixes fresh and salt into a fertile whole.

We all have smells that remind us of home, that root us in a space where we know we belong. For anyone born on the Eastern Shore, southern Maryland and Delmarva (Delaware/Maryland/Virginia – get it?) peninsula, it's the mix of salt and fresh water around the legs, the bloom of chlorophyll in acres of deciduous forest and the musky dark odor of marsh.

If there was a structure to define Maryland it would be the ❶ **USS Constitution**, a boat, of course, and a beautiful one at that, with her clean lines, dark siding and fresh sails. She's docked near the ❷ **Baltimore Maritime Museum**, a good place to learn about the Baltimore clippers, greatest ships of the Age of Sail, which carried the name of the city far and wide, along with goods from around the world back to a port that once contained the bustle of industry and travel and languages.

Head down Rte 97 to where it intersects Rte 50 and drive over the ❸ **Bay Bridge**, which crosses the Chesapeake Bay at a narrow neck. The Bay isn't so much mighty as heart-breakingly lovely, a quiet, salty womb where the sun dances on the mirror tides.

Rte 50 is the main road here, but to experience Shore small towns, with their chicken-and-crab-and-dumpling church dinners, Royal Farms gas stations, rotting houses, elevated graves (the shallow soil has a habit of

TIME
2 days

DISTANCE
200 miles

BEST TIME TO GO
May – Jun

START
Fell's Point, Baltimore

END
Crisfield

ALSO GOOD FOR

OUTDOORS

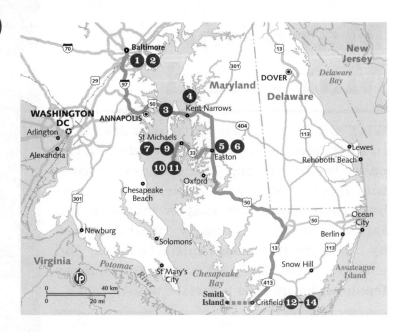

ejecting bodies after hard rainfalls) and low-slung chicken coops (this is America's fifth-largest poultry producing area), you have to get off the highway.

Take exit 42 off Rte 50 into Kent Narrows to see the oddly proportioned local ④ Waterman's Monument – the two subjects look like Goya's idea of crabbers. Further down Rte 50, Easton is a nice spot to eat and rest before tackling the rest of the deceptively large Shore. The restored art-deco ⑤ Avalon Theater on Dover St serves as a gorgeous anchor for the town's well-restored historic district, which never met a colonial renovation it didn't like. Take, for example, the lace-curtained loveliness of the ⑥ Tidewater Inn, which manages to combine B&B coziness and an historic building with the professionalism of a well-managed corporate sleep.

MISS MUSKRAT

Shore girls have many qualities, including the ability to skin a muskrat. That's what goes down at Maryland's Miss Outdoors pageant, when beauty queens in full makeup "clean rats" for an appreciative audience. It might seem odd, but some think it's a nice way of combining a pageant with respect for local traditions. Check Dorchester County's tourism bureau for more info: www.tourdorchester.org.

Further west on Rte 33, the village of St Michaels is squeezed between two watery "necks" (rivers) of the Bay. The local ⑦ Chesapeake Bay Maritime Museum is well-run and friendly, overflowing with Bay memorabilia and, often enough, real-life water workers volunteering their time to explain the exhibits.

There's another B&B with friendly owners and doily-overkill at the **8** **Parsonage Inn**, which keeps a well-appointed lounge room dotted with chintzy furniture. Across the street, **9** **208 Talbot** feels like a dark and intimate hunting lodge (and, indeed, it will cook game and fish if you bring some); it specializes in that sort of haute, elegant take on American Southern food that makes you cry into your cornmeal-fried oysters.

"...back in 1900 a quarter of registered boats in America worked the Chesapeake Bay..."

You don't have to eat fancy. There's a certain workingman way Marylanders have with seafood that eschews the delicate preparation techniques of the rest of the world. It's hearty and filling without sacrificing the pure, salt-and-spray clean flavors of whatever's on the table, and **10** **Harrison's Chesapeake House**, on Tilghman Island (at the tip of this peninsula) exemplifies the best of this sort of cuisine.

On a nearby working waterfront (which means the docks are used for commercial fishing rather than recreational boating) the lovely **11** **Rebecca T Ruark** remains the oldest skipjack (sail-powered oyster dredger) in the country and is available for tours. She's the last of a breed; back in 1900 a quarter of registered boats in America worked the Bay, harvesting 15,000,000 bushels of oysters a year. Today, due to diseases, overharvesting and overdevelopment, only 53,000 bushels of oysters emerge from the Bay annually, and the 30,000 Maryland oystermen of the early 20th century are down to less than 300.

Way at the end of the road and the tip of the Shore are the crustacean-signed streets of **12** **Crisfield**, Maryland, the "crab capital of the world." The most evocative spot in town is **13** **Gordon's Confectionary**, where watermen come in for 2am morning coffee (supposedly brewed with rainwater collected from the tin roof) before they set out at dawn to set crab pots and fish traps. The trials of their work are lovingly examined in the small but enthusiastic **14** **J Millard Tawes Historical Museum**; the name "Tawes," for the record, is present in many Lower Shore family trees. When you're done here, head out for a salt marsh. Watching the herons glide over the creeks, and the saw grass bend under the Bay wind, you might understand why the Shore always brings its children back to the water's edge.

DETOUR The state's only inhabited offshore island, **Smith Island** actually consists of three islands inhabited by three interrelated families who live off the water. The appeal isn't immediate (the big activity is driving around local marshes in a rented golf cart) but this is, as the cliché goes, stepping back into time. Except this time travel demonstrates how hardscrabble, insular, but also close-knit the character of a true fishing village is. It's not romantic. But for many Marylanders, it's roots.

Adam Karlin

TRIP INFORMATION

GETTING THERE
Take exit 4, Rte 97 south to Rte 50 east from Baltimore Beltway (I-695) for the Shore.

DO
Baltimore Maritime Museum
B'more's identity is rooted in her docks towns. That legacy – and plenty of boats, including the *USS Constitution* – is examined here. ☎ 410-396-3453; www.baltomari timemuseum.org; adult/child from $10/5, under 5 free; 802 1 E Pratt St, Baltimore; ⊙ 10am-5:30pm; 🚻

Chesapeake Bay Maritime Museum
Delves into one of the most fascinating ecosystems of North America, and its associated human communities. ☎ 410-244-1900; www.cbmm.org; 800 Key Hwy, St Michaels; admission $13; ⊙ 10am-6pm Tue-Sun

J Millard Tawes Historical Museum
Explains the backbreaking work of watermen, Bay ecology and leads good walking tours of Crisfield. ☎ 410-968-2501; www.crisfield heritagefoundation.org/museums.htm; 3 Ninth St, Crisfield; adult/child $3/1; ⊙ 10am-4pm Mon-Sat

Rebecca T Ruark
One of America's last working sailboats, this beautiful wooden skipjack still dredges oysters under wind power. ☎ 410-829-3976; www.skipjack.org; 21308 Phillips Rd, Tilghman Island; charters adult/child $30/15

Waterman's Monument
This small memorial honors both Maryland's signature profession and the period when most of the state's population lived off the water. **Kent Narrows Rd, off Rte 50**

EAT
208 Talbot
A cozy, intimate lodge that serves up excellent rustic yet refined takes on the local land's field-and-stream bounty. ☎ 410-745-3838; 208 N Talbot St, St Michaels; mains $26-33; ⊙ dinner, closed Mon

Gordon's Confectionary
OK, the food may not win any awards (although the scrapple's decent); the reason to come is to chat with men still working the water. ☎ 410-968-0566; 831 W Main St, Crisfield; meals under $10; ⊙ from 4am

Harrison's Chesapeake House
A Shore legend, Harrison's does Maryland seafood with all the grease and flair the genre demands. ☎ 410-886-2121; 21551 Chesapeake House Dr, Tilghman Island; mains $8-25; ⊙ 6am-9pm Mon-Fri, to 11pm Sat & Sun

SLEEP
Parsonage Inn
It may be too quaint for some travelers, but if you need lovely service and doilies, your train has arrived. ☎ 410-745-5519; www.parson age-inn.com; 210 N Talbot St, St Michaels; r $110-215

Tidewater Inn
The Tidewater manages to provide all the flower-accented edges you'd expect out here, but amenities are refreshingly modern. ☎ 410-822-1300; www.tidewaterinn.com; 101 E Dover St, Easton; r $144-280

USEFUL WEBSITES
www.bayweekly.com
www.cbf.org

LINK YOUR TRIP
www.lonelyplanet.com/trip-planner

A Summer Frozen in Time

WHY GO Maryland in the summer is like a grab bag of all-American, mid-Atlantic vacation nostalgia, from small-town cute-boxes like Snow Hill and Berlin to the boardwalk-strapped, salt-and-sea-scented itinerary of an old-school beach holiday in Ocean City, the East Coast's "OC."

TIME
2 – 3 days

DISTANCE
30 miles

BEST TIME TO GO
Jun – Aug

START
Berlin

END
Ocean City

ALSO GOOD FOR

Summer's a special time in the mid-Atlantic. Florida and Hawaii might have better beaches, but we have *seasons*. They appreciate the sun here, because it's gone for six months of the year.

We like tradition, too. Three of Maryland's best summer towns encapsulate timeless, sometimes corny, sometimes welcoming Americana. The towns of Berlin and Snow Hill overwhelm the cute-o-meter with their tree-lined streets, neighborliness and miniature sense of perfection, and, judging by their brick-faced old town squares, wrought-iron accents and, well, *niceness*, exist about 100 years in the past. Ocean City brings to mind weekend seaside holidays: boardwalks, carny rides and saltwater taffy, which speak to an older America that hasn't learned how to roll with the five-star glitz of Vegas and South Beach sexy.

1 Berlin is so ingratiatingly cute it formed the small-town setting for one of Julia Roberts' chickest of flicks, *Runaway Bride*. In the **2 Pink Box Bakery**, on Main St, the friendly owner greets guests with a "Hey hon" and a smile before making custom Smith Island cakes. Named for the offshore isle they hail from, the thin, stacked (usually 10 layers) cakes are traditionally chocolate flavored, but come in peanut butter and Oreo cookie variations here.

Around the corner (well, everything's around the corner), the immaculate **3 Atlantic Hotel**, built in 1895, rises over the surrounding handsome Federal architecture in both size and quality, forming a lovely navigation

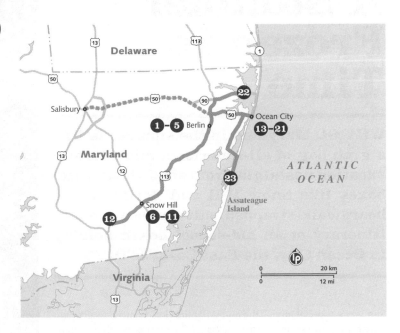

hub. The hotel's attached restaurant, **④ Solstice**, boasts an interior that's a study in Zen rusticity; it's understated and all the more elegant for being so, although the tidewater-fusion menu provides an (appropriately) offsetting exuberance.

Berlin's centerpiece, as it were, is the **⑤ Globe Theater** restaurant, which has warm-copper autumnal highlights, afternoon matinees in a screened theater, an on-site art gallery and an American-deli-meets-Asian-noodle-bar menu. Take in a matinee or live-music show, browse the surrounding antique shops and art galleries, see where Julia Roberts got her cut in *Runaway Bride* (it's the salon at 17 N Main St), then settle in for an evening at one of the local restaurants. Every week in Berlin there's also some kind of arts walk, auction, church recital or crafts festival; check www.berlinmdcc.org.

Fifteen miles south on Rte 113 is **⑥ Snow Hill**, even cuter and quieter than Berlin. If it suits you (and it suits many folks fine) there's nothing to do here but nothing. Or you can go on a wander through "downtown," the area between N Washington St and N Church St. There are several nice art galleries here, including the **⑦ Fine Needle**, which showcases the town's long tradition of expert knitting and quilting, and **⑧ Artiques**, stuffed with locals' art and (imagine that) antiques.

At the **⑨ River House Inn** the friendly, enormous poodles and equally friendly owners are a plus, but the standout is its postcard-perfect backyard view over the Pocomoke River that deserves a spot in a landscape painting from the height of the Romantic era. An ideal meal out in Snow Hill is best enjoyed over wine, conversation and safely eccentric creative touches (imagine if your mom opened an art studio) at the **⑩ Palette**. The menu draws off local ingredients and international recipes; comforting and unpretentious, as contemporary as Snow Hill gets.

Flashes of cosmopolitan, tourist-friendly fare sometimes clash with the flag-draped, front-porch character of these and neighboring towns but, ironically, the latter aesthetic probably couldn't survive without tourism. These small towns may have been saved, at least partially, by city folk.

"...the boardwalk is the epitome of its genre: a souvenir- and fried-food-packed permanent carnival..."

Still, these communities comprise more than just decamped city slickers. The **⑪ Julia Purnell Museum** in Snow Hill is tiny and, in the grand scheme of things, easily passable. But the little touches in this annex – an embroidery by the museum's namesake or a wanted poster for runaway slaves probably culled from someone's attic – serve to flesh out the details of this blink-and-miss-it village.

Heading southwest, Snow Hill vanishes into long fields and the acidic smell of freshly tilled and sprayed soil, hemmed in by clotted masses of broadleaf and pine forest where the branches grow into kissing canopies; you can camp amidst all of the above in **⑫ Pocomoke River State Park**, accessible from Rte 12 or Rte 113. There's also canoeing, kayaking and a series of lovely trails, none of which, as per the gentle prettiness of this region, are particularly taxing.

That's enough small town life. Who likes drunk Pennsylvanians, seaside kitsch and T-shirts that run the gamut from tacky to obscene? Good, because we're taking either Rte 90 or Rte 50 to **⑬ Ocean City** and its excellent **⑭ boardwalk**, which encapsulates all of the above. "The OC" is another exemplar of traditional mid-Atlantic summer, but this isn't the model of carefully manicured preservation one gets in Berlin and Snow Hill. It's all about fun: this is where locals who didn't have the time or money to go to Florida (let alone overseas) let their hair down, and by hair, we mean near every physical inhibition in the book.

The OC is the first seaside memory for many residents of this region. The water is actually pretty good for bodysurfing, the sand is soft and tan and the boardwalk is the epitome of its genre: a souvenir- and fried-food-packed permanent carnival whose scents constantly unearth an inner child who never got too old for cotton candy and Skee-Ball. On the downside, same-same boxy hotels weigh down an otherwise perfectly attractive beachfront. All of these serve up essentially identical rooms, but there are some accommodations standouts amidst the sameness.

⑮ Inn on the Ocean is just that: a seashore-shaded collection of jewel-box rooms that make you feel like Lord Sandypants on a Victorian seaside holiday. The **⑯ King Charles Hotel** turns it down a few notches, making the beachfront-home theme a little more accessible and casual. The gabled grounds are still far more elegant than the uninspiring options elsewhere.

In Salisbury, about 30 miles from Ocean City, and 22 miles from Berlin, is one of America's unique art museums: **The Ward Museum of Wildfowl Art** (www.wardmuseum.org). Which is to say, yes, the museum of wooden ducks. The Ward is dedicated to showcasing the North American art of carved hunting decoys. This may provoke raised eyebrows, until you see the feather-to-feather detail, scientists' precision and artists' flair evident in the excellent collection.

In the midst of all this we're missing some modern, well-designed digs, and that's when the **⑰ Edge** hotel comes to the rescue. Boasting 12 enormous suites with sweeping views of Assawoman (you read it right) Bay, the Edge is a study in individualized cool.

You can walk from here to **⑱ Fager's Island**, one of the OC's legendary shots-in-the-sun bars, where crowds swell over the deck after a long day of walking the boardwalk. The quintessential eating options in town are all-you-can-eat buffets. **⑲ Phillip's**, the king of the Maryland crab-packing industry, runs an excellent example of this; it's a bit of a state tradition to get rolled out of here in a wheelbarrow. A little less excessive, the **⑳ Crab Bag** is an intimate but enjoyably rowdy crab house on the OC's northern end.

If you've ever wanted life to be one of those 3am commercials for "Girls Gone Wild," the place to go is **㉑ Seacrets**. It's basically a slice of Cancun dropped in the middle of Delmarva, which you'll find either awesome or an expansion of hell's fifth circle. Take it for what it is: a chance to drink in an inner tube and witness the over-the-top fun Ocean City is (for better or worse) famous for.

Two local state parks balance out the above bacchanal. The **㉒ Isle of Wight Wildlife Management Area**, on a narrow strip of land off Rte 90, is a marsh island of saw grass encircling a copse of loblolly pine. It's a major migration point for waterfowl, and a quiet respite from the OC madness. But nature's most beautiful local curves are best glimpsed on **㉓ Assateague Island National Seashore**. This long stretch of sand dune and salt marsh is inhabited by a herd of wild horses. Come to watch the horses dance over the tide line and spot large, lovely flocks of shorebirds. All the cheesy goodness of beachside summer pales next to the sight of a palomino kicking up sand and surf at full gallop on a blue day. It's the sort of vision that reminds us summer could be, or should be, endless.

Adam Karlin

TRIP INFORMATION

GETTING THERE
From DC, take Rte 113 to reach Berlin and Snow Hill, and Rte 50 to Ocean City.

DO

Artiques
Showcases the work of dozens of Eastern Shore artists and the antiques of everyone in Worcester Count. ☎ 410-632-3885; 310 N Washington St, Snow Hill; ☼ 10am-4pm Tue-Sat, from noon Sun, to 8pm first Fri of month

Assateague Island National Seashore
This beautiful stretch of windswept dunes conceals a herd of wild horses. ☎ 757-336-5956; www.assateagueisland.com; 7206 National Seashore Lane (off Rte 611); individual/vehicle $3/10; ☼ 5am-10pm summer

Fine Needle
Get your knit on, or a quilt made, at this fabulously fabric-focused gallery. Call ahead to inquire about classes. ☎ 410-632-0772; 121 South Dr, Snow Hill; ☼ 10am-5pm Thu & Fri, to 3pm Sat

Isle of Wight Wildlife Management Area
This park's 200 acres of wetland and abundant waterfowl make for a good marshy escape from OC's sandy debauchery. ☎ 410-543-8223; www.dnr.state.md.us/public lands/eastern/isleofwright.html; Rte 90 & St Martins Neck Road; ☼ to dark

Julia Purnell Museum
A peek into the Lower Eastern Shore's psyche and attic. ☎ 410-632-0515; 208 W Market St, Snow Hill; adult/child aged 5-12 $2/0.50; ☼ 10am-4pm Tue-Sat & 1-4pm Sun Apr-Oct; ♿

Pocomoke River State Park
In one of the Shore's prettiest corners is this beautiful state park, with miles of excellent trails. ☎ 410-632-2566; www.dnr.state .md.us/publiclands/eastern/pocomokeriver .html; 3461 Worcester Hwy; admission $5; ☼ to dark; ♿

EAT

Crab Bag
Of OC's many Maryland crab shacks, this one smacks of authenticity and dedication to its crustaceans (and customers). ☎ 410-250-3337, 410-430-8332; 130th St & Coastal Hwy, Ocean City; mains $12-30; ☼ 11am-8pm

Globe Theater
At the heart of Berlin's preservation district and town center is this mind-bogglingly cute restaurant-cum-afternoon-matinee house. ☎ 410-641-0784; 12 Broad St, Berlin; mains incl show $10-34; ☼ lunch daily, dinner Mon-Sat

Palette
An enclave of fine dining and boho-oriented service in the middle of "downtown" Snow Hill. ☎ 410-632-0055; 194 W Green St, Snow Hill; mains $12-22; ☼ lunch & dinner Tue-Sat, brunch Sun

Phillip's
This enormous, neon-lit temple to saying "yes" is the essence of Ocean City dining: big, brash, all-you-can-eat, unapologetic excess. ☎ 800-799-2722; 14101 Coastal Hwy, Ocean City; mains $7-15; ☼ from 4pm Mon-Fri, 3:30pm Sat & Sun

Pink Box Bakery
This friendly (and tiny) bakery does up some excellent baked goods, perfect for a picnic on a perfect summer weekend. ☎ 410-641-2300; 120 Main St, Berlin; ☼ 10am-3pm, to 1pm Sun

Solstice
As fine as tidewater-fusion gets in small-town Eastern Shore: upscale, elegant and refreshingly innovative. ☎ 410-641-3589; 2 N Main St, Berlin; dinner $21-28; ☼ lunch & dinner Tue-Sat, brunch Sun

DRINK

Fager's Island
Fager's is fun by daylight, when it's a beer-on-the-deck spot, and at night, when it's utter madness. ☎ 410-524-5500; 60th St & the Bay, Ocean City; ☼ to late

Seacrets
Come here once to see Ocean City party with abandon, and glimpse the first cracks in the

collapse of American civilization. ☎ 410-524-4900; 49th St & the Bay, Ocean City; 🕐 to late

SLEEP
Atlantic Hotel
Located above Solstice, this red-brick centerpiece of Berlin's historic district is a nicely outfitted hotel and a gorgeous spot for sleeping. ☎ 410-641-3589; www.solsticegrill.com; 2 N Main St, Berlin; r $150-250

Edge
Behind (and owned by) Fager's, this is as modern as Maryland's Eastern Shore gets; it's pretty sleek and swish. ☎ 888-371-5400; www.fagers.com/edge; 60th St & the Bay, Ocean City; ste $329-425

Inn on the Ocean
All in a name: the Inn, a cute conglomeration of blue-and-white, is on the ocean and is simply lovely. ☎ 410-289-8894; www.innontheocean.com; 1001 Atlantic Ave, Ocean City; r $165-360

King Charles Hotel
A nice break from the OC's big box blah is the King Charles, a sort of mega-sized, well-located, very friendly beach cottage. ☎ 410-289-6141; www.kingcharleshotel.com; 1209 N Baltimore Ave, Ocean City; r $105-148

River House Inn
One of our favorite B&Bs in the state, the River House combines excellent service with an immaculate, riverfront setting. ☎ 410-632-2722; www.riverhouseinn.com; 201 E Market St, Snow Hill; r $250-300

USEFUL WEBSITES
www.ococean.com
www.visitworcester.org

LINK YOUR TRIP

www.lonelyplanet.com/trip-planner

Dollhouse Delaware

WHY GO Besides being one of the most obscure states in the union, Delaware weathers a schizophrenic split between rampant overdevelopment on her highways and some of the prettiest small towns and well-tended green spaces on the East Coast. On this trip we focus, firmly, on showing off the latter.

You can go on a quest, a journey, if you will, anywhere – even in Delaware. The goal: to find St Andrew's School, where *Dead Poets Society* was filmed. Many American public high schools are architectural monstrosities, but St Andrew's clearly represents something else: nicely manicured greenness, boarding school sensibility and an almost English sense of place.

A love of this particular aesthetic is lost and found in Delaware, a state that blends lush woodland and romantic small roads with long stretches of dreary highway development.

Drive east from Washington DC through Maryland onto Rte 8, which cuts across an overpowering sense of green kept in check by frequent villages, poultry farms and antique shacks, and eventually row after monotonous row of gas stations and vinyl townhouse blocks – the outskirts of **①** **Dover**.

Past this peripheral ring, Dover unfolds into an attractive grid of redbrick and walkable serenity. This character is exemplified in quaint hotels like the **②** **State Street Inn**, which splices a refined sense of Old South charm with typically exuberant Northeast hospitality (kind of like Delaware itself).

Around the way are two of Delaware's better free museums: the inordinately packed **③** **Biggs Museum of American Art**, stuffed with

TIME
1 – 2 days

DISTANCE
60 miles

BEST TIME TO GO
May – Jul

START
Dover

END
Wilmington

ALSO GOOD FOR
ROUTE

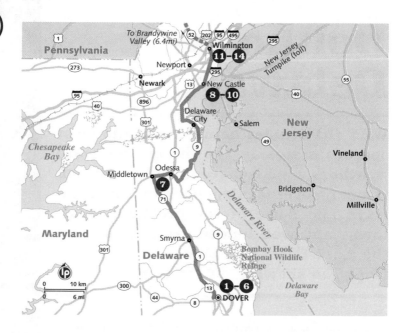

darling examples of Delaware silverware and a nice smattering of American landscapes, and the ❹ **Delaware Public Archives**, where an original signed copy of the Bill of Rights can be viewed for the first six months of the year. The rest of the time it's on display in the National Archives in Washington DC, according to a security guard who clearly resented this state of affairs.

There's a hint of rowdiness afoot in Dover; the town meshes military personnel from nearby Dover Air Force Base (first stop for all returning American war-dead) and the work-hard, play-hard staff of the Delaware state legislature. Seriously – Delaware can party! On a typical Dover Friday night, a legislative aides on the town drink tequila and order buffalo wings in ❺ **WT Smithers**, while Annapolis rockers Jimmy's Chicken Shack tear the roof off at the nearby ❻ **Loockerman Exchange (LEX)**, a surprisingly kick-ass gig venue.

Hwy 13 north of Dover is a stretch of commercial ugliness dominated by the casino horse-racing complex of Dover Downs – a preservationist's most lurid nightmare. Leave this behind and veer onto Rte 71 and Noxontown Rd, the turnoff for ❼ **St Andrew's School**. Technically, unless you're a prospective student you can't visit these grounds; call ahead and try to arrange a tour. Friends tell us the school is far more liberal than the strict academy portrayed in *Dead Poets* (it's a co-ed boarding school – do we need to spell it out for you?).

St Andrew's, with its red-brick pavilions, dark wood corridors and lush, rolling lawns, embodies the balance of historic and organic charm that is still Delaware's most attractive feature. But it's not the only example of the style.

Heading up Rte 9 takes you to lovely **8** **New Castle**. Unlike many other communities of its size, which tend to give in to quick development cash in the form of fast-food outlets and gas stations, New Castle has realized it can trade in on something better: its aesthetic appeal. The cobblestoned town square, a fringe of lovely park that fronts the Delaware River and well-plotted, dignified middle-class row houses make one weep to think of the McMansions that mar so much of the American suburban landscape.

The right way to sleep and eat in New Castle is old-school style, with colonial banquets heavy on the butter, cream and ye olde hearte attackes, all available at **9** **Jessop's Tavern**. Round out the whole powder-wigged theme with a sleep in the alluringly stone-shod coziness of the **10** **Terry House B&B**, and ask the owner to accompany your breakfast with his excellent ivory-mashing skills on the piano.

ROUTE 9 ON OUR MINDS

It's not rife with dollhouses, but Rte 9 between Odessa and New Castle is one of the prettiest roads in the state, cutting through a picture-perfect wetland-scape of countless swamps draining into the mirror-flat Delaware River. Well, practically perfect; the looming smokestacks of Salem Nuclear Power Plant in New Jersey, visible from across the river, aren't the most flattering touch.

It's a scant few miles north of here to **11** **Wilmington**, which epitomizes Delaware class in different angles: from her art deco Design and Art College to blocks of handsome townhouses that conceal a surpassingly delicious local dining scene. **12** **Moro** surprises with a decadently excellent Pacific-rim-cum-steakhouse fusion menu (you don't expect Kobe Pork Milanese in this somewhat bypassed corner of the mid-Atlantic corridor). For more blue-collar countertop fare, **13** **Leo and Jimmy's** has been doing up excellent eats of a meat-between-bread nature for years.

DETOUR One of the reasons Delaware has so many dollhouses is because it was basically built by the uberwealthy Dupont family, who turned the Brandywine Valley (6 miles northwest of Wilmington on Rte 52) into their personal Camelot. Today the valley is stuffed with dozens of estates, but the grandest of them all is the old Dupont mansion, **Winterhur** (www.winterhur .org), which stands today as a 175-room country mansion and museum of decorative arts.

As for sleeps, it is universally acknowledged that the grandiose **14** **Hotel du Pont** is the best in the state. The palatial grounds and elegantly over-the-top rooms provide a nice offsetting touch to the accumulated cuteness of Delaware's dollhouses.

Adam Karlin

TRIP INFORMATION

GETTING THERE
Drive east from Washington DC onto Rte 50 and then Rte 8 in Maryland to get to Dover.

DO
Biggs Museum of American Art
Come here if you're into Delaware's contributions to fine arts and expert silverware – and who isn't? ☎ 302-674-2111; www.biggsmuseum.org; 406 Federal St, Dover; ☻ 9am-4:30pm, from 1:30pm Sun

Delaware Public Archives
The archives' museum gives good insight into the quirks of America's first state. ☎ 302-744-5000; www.archives.delaware.gov; 121 Duke of York St, Dover; ☻ 8am-4:30pm Mon-Fri, to 8pm Wed, 9am-5pm Sat

St Andrew's School
The campus used as the filming location of *Dead Poets Society* is one of the prettiest boarding-school grounds in the country. ☎ 302-285-4231; www.standrews-de.org; 350 Noxontown Rd, Middletown

EAT
Jessop's Tavern
Colonial decadence is the name of the culinary game here, as is a general sense of firelit hospitality. ☎ 302-322-6111; 114 Delaware St, New Castle; mains $13-22; ☻ lunch & dinner Mon-Sat

Leo and Jimmy's
One of Wilmington's oldest and greatest delis is an urban institution, well-deserving of both your gnosh and patronage. ☎ 302-656-7151; 728 N Market St, Wilmington; mains $4-12; ☻ 5:30am-4pm; ♿

Moro
Wilmington shocks with prosciutto and melon, "baked fog" and truffles and other fusion wonders. Call ahead and the chef will prepare a personalized menu. ☎ 302-777-1800; 1307 N Scott St, Wilmington; mains $24-42; ☻ dinner Tue-Sat

DRINK
Loockerman Exchange (LEX)
LEX attracts some consistently excellent talent throughout the year. Don't miss a show while you're here. ☎ 302-741-2223; 1 W Loockerman St, Dover; ☻ to 1am

WT Smithers
This excellent bar is usually packed, and is a great spot for wings, beers and general bad behavior of the all-American kind. ☎ 302-674-8875; 140 South State St, Dover; ☻ 11am-1am

SLEEP
Hotel du Pont
The storied du Pont is the grandest of grande-dame hotels, and the service is nicely laid-back for such a beautiful beast. ☎ 302-594-3100; www.hoteldupont.com; cnr Market & 11th Sts, Wilmington; r $260-430

State Street Inn
The Victorian rooms and vibe at this B&B are well complemented by an exuberantly friendly management team and central location. ☎ 302-734-2294; www.statestreetinn.com; 228 N State St, Dover; r $110-135

Terry House B&B
It's corny and comforting, but that's what you're looking for in New Castle, and Terry House doesn't disappoint. ☎ 302-322-2505; www.terryhouse.com; 130 Delaware St, New Castle; r $90-110

USEFUL WEBSITES
www.preservationde.org
www.visitdelaware.com

www.lonelyplanet.com/trip-planner

LINK YOUR TRIP

Maryland Crab Quest

WHY GO Come, ye foodies, for the food that best defines Maryland: Callinectes sapidus. The "beautiful swimmer" is better known as the blue crab, served steamed in large shell-flecked social gatherings. Attending a crab feast in a true crab house is the gastronomic distillation of all things Maryland.

TIME
4 days

DISTANCE
320 miles

BEST TIME TO GO
Jun – Sep

START
Baltimore

END
Whitehaven

ALSO GOOD FOR

OFFBEAT

In some states, when you want to get your smooth on with a girl, you take her out for a nice French meal, or to a cozy Italian joint, or book a table at some cutting-edge fusion culinary chicness.

In Maryland, nothing says "I love you" like spreading newspapers on a table, sticking your thumb up the ass of a bottom-feeding spider, ripping the body of said arthropod cleanly in two and then dismantling the rest of the creature with a mallet and knife. A few beers only add to the romance.

Yes, they know affection in the Old Line State. Although to be honest, a crab feast, Maryland's state meal (thanks to an abundance of the crustaceans in the Chesapeake Bay) is usually not a pairs event. While any self-respecting Maryland girl would go gaga over a good plate of blue crabs, the event tends to be a group affair, an occasion for friends and family to come together and celebrate good food and casualness in that most hallowed of state social halls: the crab house.

These institutions are quintessentially Maryland, and a distinct identifier for a state that lies in an amorphous cultural penumbra between the North, the South and the shadow of the nation's capital. Let's be honest, Maryland is often insecure of its identity. Crabs are the one thing they do best, even better than New Orleans. (Boiled crabs? Pah! Steaming releases the juices.) How much does Maryland care about

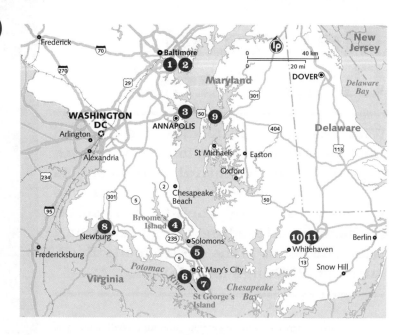

its crabs? Well, they put them on their driver's licenses (no, really). And the physical act of eating together in messy camaraderie, working hard for a little meat that is oh-so-sweet, complemented by sweet white corn, Budweiser and hush puppies, is a ballet most Marylanders are trained in from early childhood, a dance they all know the steps to.

Herein we have described a quest for the best of Maryland's crab houses, yet we've got to admit: the statewide appeal of the venue is partially attributable to its essential sameness across the board. Crabs are comforting, and so are the restaurants they're served in. Inevitably, the crab house decor is uniform: maritime memorabilia, wooden tables, jars of Old Bay, apple vinegar and melted butter, and the smell of fish, frying grease, beer and sawdust.

"Done right, the result is sweet, juicy white crabmeat cut by the sharp edge of cayenne, onion and salt."

Crabs are cooked the same way across the state: steamed in water and beer and Old Bay seasoning; if Old Bay is added afterwards, beware. Done right, the result is sweet, juicy white crabmeat cut by the sharp edge of cayenne, onion and salt.

We'll start in Baltimore, which calls itself the "Crab Cake" to New York's Big Apple. In urban Maryland, this is as good as crabs get, although we are firmly of the opinion that you need to go to the marshy boonies for the best crabs in the state.

❶ **Waverly Crabs & Seafood**, on Greenmount Ave, is a slightly tatty joint in a slightly tatty neighborhood, but the prices tend to be cheaper than the competition and the jumbos (the largest class of crab) are really jumbo. The clientele is local, which is another positive sign, as is the mixed Salvadoran, Filipino, black and white staff of pickers, steamers and spicers cooking the crabs behind the counter.

This is a takeout, so you'll be eating your crustaceans at home. For the record, these crab take-aways are more common than actual crab houses, and, often-times, crabs sold out of the back of a waterman's pickup are of the best quality (and guaranteed to be local; sadly, due to depletion of the Chesapeake Bay and run-off pollution, many "local" crabs are shipped in from southern states. Pre-picked crabmeat sold in grocery stores is often from Southeast Asia).

The best sit-down crab joint in Baltimore is ❷ **LP Steamers**, which is a quick drive from Fort McHenry. The "LP" stands for Locust Point, one of Charm City's classic blue-collar southside 'hoods; lots of residents here have been employed on the Baltimore docks or are a family member removed from working the waterfront. Steamers stands in the middle of a thin block of Baltimore row houses, and bustles with business from dedicated tour-ists and working-class neighbors. Everything on the menu is good, and everyone working the line is local.

MALES ONLY

Crabs are priced seasonally, so you can expect to pay anywhere from $30 to $80 for a dozen. When buying crabs, be sure to always ask for large or jumbo males. Females shouldn't be har-vested, since they're the mothers of the next generation of dining goodness.

Munching on a fried oyster sandwich doused in hot sauce, we couldn't help smiling when our server asked her friend, in a true Bawlmer accent, about the weather "deeyown the ayshun" (down the Ocean – ie in Ocean City).

It may be the state's capital, but Annapolis isn't the best city in Maryland for crabs – better options are closer in Southern Maryland and the Eastern Shore (by close we mean an hour or so away; Marylanders will drive long distances, even making day trips, for specific crab houses). Still, state politicos do have an excellent option for the vaunted government practice of committee-ing a bill over blue crabs at ❸ **Cantler's**, just outside of the city.

Like many crab houses, Cantler's can be approached by road (Forest Beach Rd by Rte 50 east) or boat (a waterfront location is crab-eating industry stand-ard). The soft crabs here are particularly well-respected, probably due to the large on-site peeling sheds, where crabs are allowed to molt.

Some of the tastiest crabs in Maryland are served in the rural trifecta of coun-ties that makes up Southern Maryland. In thin Calvert County, about 45 miles south of Annapolis, the crab cakes at ❹ **Stoney's** on Broome's Island are regarded as the best in the state: large, pleasantly lumpy and served amid excellent waterfront ambience. Calvert is good for post-crab drinks, too; on Rte 4, at the tip of Solomons Island is one of the most inexplicably popular bars in the state: the ❺ **Tiki Bar**. It's not much more than an outdoor bar with a sand-and-Polynesian-idol-strewn courtyard, but hundreds of party people and boaters from across the Chesapeake create a mini–Bourbon Street vibe here on weekends.

BEST. SEASONING. EVER.

You see it everywhere down here: Old Bay seasoning, the deep red, pleasantly hot but unmistakably estuarine spice of Maryland. Made from celery salt, mustard, black and red pepper and other secrets, we put it on our corn, our french fries, our potato chips and, of course, our crabs. A large container of the stuff is the perfect Maryland souvenir, but beware of wiping your face after partaking of the spice: Old Bay in the eyes is incredibly painful.

The crab houses seem to stack thicker the closer you come to the tip of the state's Western Shore, in St Mary's County. Only 60 miles long, yet surrounded by hundreds of miles of water due to its heavily indented coastline, the pineclad beaches of Maryland's oldest county conceal excellent crab shacks, particularly along the Patuxent River. The seafood joints we recommend are known for their steamed crabs and just a bit more. ❻ **Evans**, down Piney Point Rd off Rte 5, does good crabs, but is also worth a stop for its quintessentially tidewater location: St George's Island, a speckle of perfectly packaged nature hemmed in by tall, whispering trees, softly lapping tides and loblolly-needle trails.

The further south, the more spread out houses become, as if they are trailing into the Chesapeake Bay and its surrounding forests. Another pretty view and more excellent seafood awaits at the river-encircled end of Wynne Rd, also located off Rte 5. ❼ **Courtney's** is run by perennially gruff waterman Tom Courtney and his perennially chatty Filipino wife, Julie. This isn't technically a crab house, but it's one of the most authentic seafood restaurants in Maryland, where anything you're served (well, any seafood) was caught by Tom earlier that day.

Heading north on Rte 5, with a side trip on Rte 234 and a turn onto Hwy 301, leads you to Pope's Creek Rd. The road twists and turns through copses of trees overgrown with ivy and gold-flecked fields, which once hid John Wilkes Booth; Abraham Lincoln's assassin fled into this hinterland after his infamous performance in Ford's Theater.

Today, Pope's Creek (about 4 miles from Newburg) conceals one of the top seafood restaurants in Maryland, a crab-shack-cum-sit-down spot that overlooks the marsh-accented, slow meandering creek itself. ❽ **Captain Billy's** is as famous (if not more so) for its oysters as its crabs. Billy's combines the essential elements of Maryland seafood dining: talented frying, casual ambience and beautiful location.

The Eastern Shore is the part of Maryland most connected to water, but it's not as packed with crab houses as one might think; many locals buy their crustaceans directly from watermen or catch them themselves. **9** **Harris Crab House** off Rte 50 in the Kent Narrows, just after crossing the Bay Bridge, is highly regarded for its food and enormous wooden waterfront deck, even if it's a bit of a tourist trap.

CRUSTACEAN VARIATION

Steamed crabs are never the only item available at crab houses; Maryland menus mix up their shellfish. Try these favorites: crab cakes (crabmeat mixed with bread crumbs and secret spice combinations, fried); crab balls (as above, but smaller); soft crabs (crabs that have molted their shells and are fried, looking like giant breaded spiders – they're delicious); red crab and cream of crab soup; and fish stuffed with crab imperial (crab sautéed in butter, mayonnaise and mustard, occasionally topped with cheese).

Finding the best food on the Shore requires a bit of effort and driving. Well, we're loathe to call it Maryland's "best" crab house, as such proclamations have been known to start bar brawls, but it's as sure a contender as any. To reach the grail of this Crab Quest, you need to take Rte 50 all the way to tiny MD 347, turn right onto tinier MD 349, and left at even tinier MD 352, before hanging a right onto the thin track that is Clara Rd. There's a gorgeous, friendly B&B down this way, the **10** **Whitehaven Hotel** (in Whitehaven, pop: roughly 30) that overlooks one of the oldest, still-operating ferry crossings in the state.

Also here, nestled in a heart-melting river-and-stream-scape, is the low-slung, laughter-packed **11** **Red Roost**. It's a former chicken coop where the lamp shades are crafted from watermen's crab buckets and the waitresses are local teenagers. A bow-tied piano player pounds the keys and croons corny ballads (causing a family sitting next to us to mutter, "we best get out of here"), but that's the only potential drawback. Otherwise, the all-you-can-eat corn (served unshucked!), hush puppies, clam strips, fried chicken and steamed crab feasts are…well, it's a meal fit for a Roman emperor, were Roman emperors from Wicomico county.

Adam Karlin

TRIP INFORMATION

GETTING THERE
Start in Baltimore, on the north side of Greenmount Ave, before moving through the rest of the state.

EAT
Cantler's
The by-consensus best crab house in Annapolis is a little ways outside of the city, and well worth the drive. ☎ 410-962-5379; 400 E Saratoga St, Annapolis; mains from $20; ☺ 7am-2pm Mon-Fri

Captain Billy's
Getting here, driving through perfect Charles County countryside, is half the fun. The other half: the delicious food. ☎ 301-932-4323; 11495 Pope's Creek Rd, Pope's Creek; mains $10-30; ☺ 11am-9pm Tue-Sun

Courtney's
This is a small, barebones and thoroughly excellent seafood shack perched over a quiet bend of a picture-perfect river. ☎ 301-872-4403; 48290 Wynne Rd; mains $7-25; ☺ lunch & dinner

Evans
The only thing that could make the woodsy Potomac island of St George's more approachable is this lovely seafood house. ☎ 410-994-9944; 16800 Piney Point Rd; mains $10-32; ☺ lunch & dinner

Harris Crab House
Although it gets a bit flooded with tourists, Harris' reputation is well deserved and its crabs are frankly better. ☎ 410-827-9500; 425 Kent Narrow Way; mains $11-30; ☺ lunch & dinner

LP Steamers
LP's the best in Baltimore's seafood stakes: working class, teasing smiles and the freshest crabs on the southside. ☎ 410-576-9294; 1100 E Fort Ave, Baltimore; mains $8-28; ☺ lunch & dinner

Red Roost
The original legend: tell someone from the Eastern Shore you cracked crabs here and your street (well, Bay) cred rises immediately. ☎ 410-546-5443; 2670 Clara Rd, Whitehaven; mains $15-40; ☺ dinner

Stoney's
Another Maryland epic: that of the perfect crab cake, just lumpy, crispy, melty and fat enough for a Chesapeake king. ☎ 410-586-1888; 3956 Oyster House Rd, Broome's Island; mains $12-34; ☺ lunch & dinner

Waverly Crabs & Seafood
If you're picking up take-away crabs in Baltimore, there's no better spot in no more authentic environs. ☎ 410-243-1181; 3400 Greenmount Ave, Baltimore; crabs priced seasonally; ☺ to 10pm

DRINK
Tiki Bar
Imagine Bourbon Street in New Orleans with all the trashiness and none of the history, plus sand and tidewater breezes. ☎ 410-326-4075; 85 Charles St, Solomons Island; ☺ sunset to late, spring & summer

SLEEP
Whitehaven Hotel
Run by some lovely Baltimore ladies, the Whitehaven has excellent rooms and views and is nestled on a postcard-corner of the Eastern Shore. ☎ 410-873-2000; http://whitehaven.tripod.com; 2685 Whitehaven Rd, Whitehaven; r $110-150

USEFUL WEBSITES
www.bluecrab.info
http://skipjack.net/le_shore/crab/picking_index.htm

LINK YOUR TRIP

www.lonelyplanet.com/trip-planner

BaltiNoir

WHY GO Baltimore Sun reporter Julie Scharper knows her city at night is more than itself. It's more beautiful, more dangerous and more alive. It's everything that makes this city great, but fattened by moonlight, hidden by shadows and stumbling from too many drinks in a row-house bar.

While waiting for Julie Scharper on the corner of Eager St, "Maryland's biggest drag show" was going down at ❶ **Club Hippo**, "Baltimore's Best Gay Club." (Clearly a matter of intense debate. Does "best" equal big lights, big sounds and big cross-dressers? If so, rest on thy laurels, Hippo.)

A drag show, one of humanity's best expressions of surrealism, would have been a good way to open up a night of exploring Baltimore, surrealist of towns, at night, that surrealist of times. The demons come out to play when darkness falls on B'more, creating a city of poetic, maddening edges and imagery: John Hopkins undergrads buying cans of Natty Boh from an Ethiopian liquor store clerk; moonlight on firefighters stumbling out of a formstone pub; the gothic accents of spidery cathedrals and smokestacks blowing their hellish glow over the Patapsco River.

Yeah, Baltimore's like that.

Scharper takes us for dinner on Mulberry St, a quiet stretch of nothingness at night. It's the sort of street that, in the 1920s, would have housed a speakeasy. And, in fact, it did – a hidden bar that today is one of the city's strangest restaurants. Scharper gets us into ❷ **Martick's** by addressing the owner (Mo) through a slit-peephole, before we're led into a snakeskin-wallpapered, armless-Greek-goddess-festooned bistro. Mo, who picked up his culinary skills in 1970s Paris, cooks the excellent dishes (try the pâté) and handwrites the photocopied menu. Closing time is when Mo says.

TIME
1 – 2 days

BEST TIME TO GO
Year-round

START
Baltimore

END
Baltimore

ALSO GOOD FOR

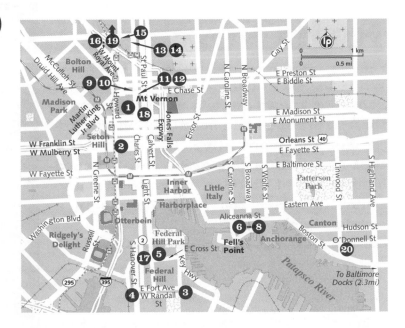

A good French meal only kicks off Baltimore by dark. A city built as a smuggler's cove and port lends itself to drinking, particularly in bars with a whiff of wharf about them, and not in a yo-ho-ho and a bottle of rum way, either.

③ Captain Larry's is Scharper's pick as exemplar of the genre. It's a stone-slicked corner pub, divey in a welcoming way, where our expert unites with a buddy from high school and South Baltimore toughs with shaved heads and long shorts slam whiskey under a bullet-pock-marked ceiling. The Bay seafood goes well with beer; get the fried clams and crab dip, then man up, and dip your strips in the dip.

> *"A city built as a smuggler's cove and port lends itself to drinking..."*

Scharper tells us about **④ Schaefer's**, located near the train tracks, as workingman as Baltimore pubs get: spread out over two formstone row houses, stuffed with longshoremen and Ravens memorabilia, and bearing a name shared with one of the state's most memorable good old boy politicians.

For more civilized (on the surface) drinking, try the horse-tranquilizer-strength margaritas at **⑤ Blue Agave**, which has provided South Baltimore with a facelift in the form of an upscale Mexican restaurant that actually serves Mexican regional cuisine, as opposed to refried glop on a tortilla.

Scharper feels that ❻ **Fell's Point**, on the waterfront east of the Inner Harbor, has gotten a little dilapidated in the nightlife stakes, but she and her friends still come here for a tipple now and then. The loyal patrons of ❼ **One-Eyed Mike's** buy bottles of Grand Marnier, which are stored in glass cases at the bar to be sipped upon each return – a sort of cognac quota for pirates. Nearby, the mussels at ❽ **Bertha's** (progenitor of famed Maryland bumper sticker, "Eat Bertha's Mussels") are a bit overrated, but the dark interior and frat-boy-meets-off-duty-cop crowd make for exciting evenings.

Grab a cab and head back to Scharper's home 'hood of ❾ **Mount Vernon**, where the booze flows fast in a well-scattered series of pubs, all of them classy (even if some are beautiful in their dilapidation). ❿ **Brewer's Art** (hey, it has its own brewery!) occupies a well-appointed townhouse and attracts a good mix of appreciative boozehounds; it's a place, Scharper says, for beer aficionados, not snobs (who have no place in Baltimore).

YO, MR BOH

National Bohemian beer (Natty Boh) is cheap, gets the job done, and is the earliest drinking memory for many Marylanders. Winking, one-eyed "Mr Boh" is Baltimore's unofficial mascot (look for Smyth Jewelers' ad of him proposing to Pennsylvania's Utz Girl by Penn Station – it's a ridiculously mid-Atlantic moment). Once brewed here in "The Land of Pleasant Living," today Natty Boh is owned by Miller and distributed by Pabst. For local beer, try any of Clipper City Brewery's excellent concoctions.

The ⓫ **Owl Bar**, like Martick's, echoes the 1920s: the long, wooden bar and stained-glass windows put you in mind of a place where gangsters would indulge in a Roman feast after shooting through the gins at the speakeasy. The food matches the decadent decor; the Monte Chessco is a happy diet-breaker – crabmeat slathered on egg-dipped bread, topped with Virginia ham.

Scharper sips an absinthe (one of which should carelessly murder your sobriety) with us. Upstairs is the ⓬ **13th Floor** (guess which floor it's on). It's a pretty plush club, but Baltimore has never taken itself seriously enough to attract pill-popping, house music elitists. People get into fake dance-offs, while outside the city shimmers under a gorgeous view and the smog-laced night.

There are two Charles that Scharper says are worth your attention on Charles St, Mount Vernon: firstly, the ⓭ **Charles Theater**, which regularly shows excellent indie flicks in its lovely showrooms, and also ⓮ **Club Charles**. The latter is a red-lit, hellish gin joint that doesn't shout, but always whispers, "badass" – it's the sort of bar that, were it human, would be tattooed, pierced, reek of vodka and cigarettes, but would be able to hold its own in a discussion of Descartes.

Further north of Penn Station the neighborhoods become Korean, then black (sometimes both). At the west end of North Ave, which is evolving into a left bank-ish artists' colony of cheap studios and warehouse space, Scharper takes us to **⑮ Joe Squared**, which serves both pizza and the city's best selection of rums (we don't get the connection either).

The town doesn't just drink, or, at least, it does other stuff while drinking, like listen to live music, which dominates a lot of the scene here. **⑯ Ottobar** tends to crank a well-mixed lineup, from local hip-hop to hardcore punk. While **⑰ 8x10**, down in Federal Hill, is a small, sweaty box that's arguably the best small venue in town.

Baltimorean cooks know their town comes alive at night, and there are all kinds of restaurants serving the by-the-moon foodie crowd. Nothing ends a good night out like a 3am run to **⑱ Never on Sunday**, where the menu calls for gravy fries doused in Old Bay and a Greek pita.

DETOUR On I-95, take exit 56 after the Fort McHenry tunnel onto Keith Ave and drive around the Baltimore docks, one of America's most evocative urban landscapes: rows of giant, rusting container ships, boarded-up diners, the gasping smoke of industrial mills and oil-slicked water running shiny and sinister under the moon. Run this little caper in the dead of night, but don't sneak into any security-restricted docks unless you want to get arrested, or seriously injured by smuggler-types.

For her own late-night eats, Scharper prefers **⑲ Papermoon Diner**, where the folks seem to understand their customers often arrive drunk or having recently inhaled something liable to make them unaccountably hungry. The decor – spaceship chandeliers, fractured fantasy color-scheme and rows of toys – reflects this mental state. And the food – the sweet-potato fries are killer, while the deep-fried ravioli might just kill you – is the king of late-night chow.

When you're ready to crash out after all this madness, the **⑳ Inn at 2920** is, wonder of wonders, a hip B&B. Contemporary funk and green sensibility put this smart boutique as close as Baltimore gets to gracing *Wallpaper* magazine, although locals like Scharper are probably glad they've avoided falling under the eyes of design pretensionistas. They'd never be able to survive, or appreciate, this town's wild nights.

Adam Karlin

TRIP INFORMATION

GETTING THERE
Take I-95 from DC to Baltimore. Get off on the MLK Ave exit to Charles St.

DO
Charles Theater
Baltimore's best movie house showcases plenty of arthouse, indie talent and anything else you'll probably never see in the cineplex. ☎ 410-727-3456; www.thecharles.com; 1711 N Charles St; ☼ Wed-Sun

EAT
Bertha's Restaurant & Bar
She's still famed for her mussels, but, to be honest, Bertha's is probably best appreciated for her piratical atmosphere. ☎ 410-327-5795; 734 S Broadway St; mains $12-20; ☼ from lunch to 2am, kitchen closes 10pm

Blue Agave
Our favorite Mexican place in Baltimore is a high-end, brilliant take on the genre; the *carnitas* (pork chunks) are heavenly. ☎ 410-576-3938; 1038 Light St; mains $12-25; ☼ dinner Mon-Sat

Joe Squared
Baltimore hipsters sip Haitian rum, chow homemade pizza and listen to local hip-hop at this awesome institution. ☎ 410-545-0444; 133 W North Ave; mains $9-25; ☼ from lunch to 2am

Martick's
The coolest restaurant in town is a secret speakeasy, staffed by salty locals, that serves luxurious French cuisine. ☎ 410-752-5155; 214 W Mulberry St; mains $15-24; ☼ lunch Tue-Fri, dinner Tue-Sat

Never on Sunday
If you're hungry, on Charles St, and it's 3am (and not Sunday), why aren't you here? ☎ 410-727-7191; 829 N Charles St; mains under $10; ☼ 24hr Mon-Sat

Papermoon Diner
If you fed a late-night diner through a really good regimen of hallucinogens, your reward:

Papermoon! ☎ 410-889-4444; 227 W 29 St; mains $6.50-15.50; ☼ 7am-midnight Sun-Wed, 24hr Thu-Sat

DRINK
8x10
As live-music venues go, the 8x10 is compact, crowded and loud enough for the rocker in all of us. ☎ 410-625-2000; 10 E Cross St; ☼ to late

13th Floor
One of Baltimore's most chic clubs is still comfortably down to earth, even as it commands some posh, sky-high nightline views. ☎ 410-347-0888; 1 E Chase St; ☼ to late Tue-Sat

Brewer's Art
This brewpub gets artesian with its beers, hip with the atmosphere and young, sexy and professional with its clientele. ☎ 410-547-9310; 1106 N Charles St; ☼ dinner & late night

Captain Larry's
Run by some local Latvian-Baltimoreans, this is the sort of corner spot, whiskey-soaked nautical pub that defines local drinking holes. ☎ 410-727-4799; 601 E Fort Ave; ☼ 4pm-2am

Club Charles
This dark red bar is popular with John Waters and Baltimore's associated cast of villains, criminals, artists, hipsters, musicians, writers and nighthawks. ☎ 410-727-8815; 1724 N Charles St; ☼ to late

Club Hippo
There are gay clubs and there are gay clubs. And then there's the Hippo and its drag shows, like a personification of the wildest edge of the queer psyche. ☎ 410-547-0069; 1 W Eager St; ☼ to late

One-Eyed Mike's
Get drunk as a sailor in this piratical pub overlooking the slick cobblestones of Fell's Point. ☎ 410-327-9823; 708 S Bond St; ☼ 11am-1am Mon-Sat

Ottobar
This live-music joint can get raucous and pulls in performers and crowds that regularly

cross this city's color lines. ☎ 410-662-0069; 2549 N Howard St; ☽ to late

Owl Bar
Comfortably old-school, the Owl Bar still attracts a young, hip-to-trip crowd. ☎ 410-347-0888; 1 E Chase St; ☽ to 11pm Mon-Thu, to midnight Fri & Sat, to 10pm Sun

Schaefer's Sports Bar & Restaurant
This bar exemplifies the gritty friendliness that is Baltimore's soul. 121 W Randall St; ☽ to 2am

SLEEP

Inn at 2920
The Inn is as hip as Baltimore gets, although it's still very warm and welcoming. ☎ 410-342-4450; www.theinnat2920.com; 2920 Elliot St; r $190-225

USEFUL WEBSITES
www.baltimoresun.com
www.citypaper.com

LINK YOUR TRIP
www.lonelyplanet.com/trip-planner

Day Trips from DC

Lying at the crossroads of the Northeast, Upper South and the immigrant melting-pot that is the Capital Region, Washington DC is surrounded by excellent day-tripping possibilities that cross some of the most diverse ground and communities in America.

FORT MCHENRY

Maryland was the epicenter of the oft-ignored War of 1812. You know, the one where the British re-invaded America and burned down Washington DC? Well, the US got a few licks in, especially in Maryland. Take Fort McHenry, which guards the entrance to Baltimore harbor. An invading fleet included local lawyer Francis Scott Key, who was negotiating on a British warship at the time. Key watched the fort withstand enemy fire throughout an all-night assault, and the next morning, "by the dawn's early light," saw the American flag still waving over the battlements. Inspired, he penned a flowery poem with impossible lyrics, which was then set to a popular drinking song and has since become our national anthem. The event is immortalized in film at Fort McHenry National Park, one of those '80s flicks where a costumed guy writing with a quill turns around and says, "Oh! I didn't see you there!"; at the end of the movie everyone has to stand, hand on heart, for the entirety of the Star Spangled Banner. Take *that*, England. **Fort McHenry is accessible from I-95; exits to the park are clearly marked from the highway. To reach the site, follow Fort Ave to its eastern end.**

ANNAPOLIS

If Baltimore is the quintessential Maryland town for her diversity and toughness, Annapolis deserves laurels too. The state's capital represents Maryland at her most leisurely, aristocratic, and history-obsessed. Luckily enough for the visitor, it rarely takes itself too seriously despite all of the above. The town's historic center is a great place for getting lost amidst winding cobblestone alleyways, small studios and pubs, and coffee shops that are distinctly of the "charming" school. Or have an all-you-can-eat seafood buffet. Or enjoy a day watching the boats slip into the harbor; this is pretty much the yachting capital of the Chesapeake Bay. Or enjoy some chopped liver at Chick and Ruth's deli, which is basically the cafeteria of the Maryland state legislature. Broadly, anything between city docks and State House is worth some time and aimless sightseeing. **To get to Annapolis, take Rte 50 (New York Ave) west of Washington DC. Rte 50 also leads past Annapolis onto the Bay Bridge and into the heart of Maryland's Eastern Shore.**

ST JOHN'S & THE NAVAL ACADEMY

Head to Annapolis and its most interesting schools: St John's and the US Naval Academy. They present an interesting contrast in learning styles. St John's is built on a "great books" curriculum; rather than having set-in-stone majors, each student reads dozens of great works of literature and discusses them in free-flowing, intellectually rigorous circles with their professors and peers. It's an innovative but old concept (St John's was established in 1784) that's produced a lot of great minds. During spring it's fun to stroll and listen to students debate the logic of Aquinas vis-à-vis the moral lessons of St Augustine's confessions. The nearby Naval Academy, on the other hand, is all about discipline; when students aren't studying they're supposed to be jogging across campus (where the classroom buildings have nuclear-fallout proof shelters). Yet good academy cadets must be, in their own way, just as intellectually creative and flexible as the students at St John's. Our favorite building here is the memorial hall, where a large banner, set in what looks like a Hapsburg grand ballroom reads, "Don't Lose the Ship," and there are long lists of names dedicated to those academy cadets who died while serving their country. **St John's and the Naval Academy are very close to each other. St John's is at 60 College Ave, and the Academy is three blocks to the east; the Blake Rd entrance is off Maryland Ave.**

DEEP CREEK LAKE

Maryland is a surprisingly large state, and one of the best ways of making this truth hit home is by driving out to the panhandle of Garret County and Deep Creek Lake. This is the largest (albeit artificial) lake in the state, and while it may not be too impressive when ranked against the "Greats" out in the Midwest, it's still a beautiful place, and visits here are ingrained in the childhood memories of most Marylanders. The best time of year to come is mid-fall, when the stifling humidity of summer is blown away by dry, clean winds and the surrounding Allegheny Mountains explode in a full-on sensory assault of reds, yellows and oranges. The vista frankly rivals the best Vermont has to offer during the height of its leaf-turning season, although there's no maple syrup. With all that said, Deep Creek is lovely anytime of year, although winters can get cold and snowy, and the area snowed-in during the height of the season. Then again, the snow is gorgeous out here. **Come here by taking Rte 219 (exit 14) off Rte 68. Rte 68 can be accessed from Rte 270, which can be reached from the DC Beltway.**

UNIVERSITY OF MARYLAND

If you're only in the capital for a few days and want to take a public transport–accessible trip to a traditional American university campus, hop on the Green Line of the DC metro to College Park. This is where you'll find the University of Maryland's main campus. UM (or UMCP, for University of Maryland, College Park) may not possess the prettiest college grounds in the country, but they are a study in fairly traditional bucolic American academia. There's a long, frisbee-cluttered grass lawn, splashing fountains, red-brick buildings of the stately sort scattered about, and several large stadiums where students can cheer on the Terrapins (yes, the turtles), the university's sports team. The town of College Park itself has some decent restaurants and bars; Plato's Diner on Baltimore Ave is a standout for good, greasy Greek and American fare. Greek life is big on campus and the social scene leans towards frat row. **Take the Green Line to College Park station to get here, or take Rhode Island Ave in DC northeast until it becomes Rte 1, which eventually leads into the heart of campus.**

NORTHERN VIRGINIA

There are many nice benefits to being a NoVA resident. For example: Wolf Trap, one of the country's prettiest outdoor concert venues, where you can enjoy music set against a lush backdrop of spilling Virginia farmland and, if you're lucky, an evening of spangled stars; and the Birchmere, a psyche-delic warehouse that happens to house America's premier folk-music venue. There is also Alexandria, as quaint and cute as American cities get (which is interesting, since it started life as a slave port that seceded from DC's refusal to facilitate the slave trade). The big attraction here is Torpedo Factory Art Center, a former munitions factory that now houses publicly supported arts spaces and studios (admission is free). Another 33 miles from DC, the Steven F Uvar-Hazy Center houses the spillover from the National Air and Space Museum; it's an amazing (and apparently alliterative) annex of all things avionic. **To get out here take Rte 66 west of Washington DC, and then take VA 267 west and get off at exit 15 toward Wolf Trap National Park. Take Rte 1 to VA 120 to Birchmere and Alexandria.**

ACCOKEEK

When the capital gets too crazy and we need a leisurely escape infused with fresh air and green space, it's great to head south of town to Accokeek, Maryland. This really is a local escape; most of DC's residents couldn't place Accokeek on a map. It's just a little intersection in southern Prince George's County, MD, but it's beautiful. Turn down Bryan Point Rd, crank up some classical music and enjoy the lovely countryside. If the folks at the Hard Bargain Farm are game, maybe you can enjoy a picnic on their picturesque grounds overlooking the Potomac River. Or drive to the end of the road, past a large, cypress tree–strewn black-water marsh thick with herons and other

waterfowl. Or take a side street and wander among the country lanes, tobacco barns and cornfields, or find a Thai Buddhist temple that appreciates all this serenity down on Farmington Rd. If you're feeling nerdy, head to the great comic-book store near Bryan Point. **Get here by taking Rte 210 south from the Beltway – it's the first exit in Maryland past the Woodrow Wilson Bridge coming from Virginia. Follow MD 210/Indian Head Hwy until it passes through Accokeek.**
Adam Karlin

VIRGINIA TRIPS

Virginia, named in honor of the "Virgin Queen," is America in a nutshell. Purple mountain majesties and amber waves of grain? Check. Vineyards? Beaches? NASCAR? Got it. Often overlooked, this vacation paradise is conveniently located right in the middle of the East Coast.

This region has something for everyone. Admire Jeffersonian architecture. Stew over politics at the watering holes in Alexandria. Ride horses with the gentry in "hunt country." See headlights winding slowly along Skyline Drive from one of the best restaurants in the world, tucked away at the foot of the Blue Ridge Mountains.

You can have the time of your life at the real-life resort from *Dirty Dancing*. Or kick up some dust at the Carter Family Fold, home to the founding family of country music.

PLAYLIST 🎵 There are many scenic highways and byways crisscrossing Virginia, so here are few tunes to accompany your drive across the "Old Dominion State."

- "Take Me Home Country Roads," John Denver
- "My Blue Ridge Mountain Boy," Dolly Parton
- "The Lees of Old Virginia," cast of *1776*
- "Virginia Is for Lovers," Jordin Sparks
- "Sweet Virginia," The Rolling Stones
- "Carry Me Back to Old Virginy," Louis Armstrong
- "Walkin' After Midnight," Patsy Cline
- "Crash Into Me," Dave Matthews Band

More interested in sitting than dancing? Try beating the front porch at the Martha Washington Inn or the boardwalk on Virginia Beach.

There is not one, but *two,* opportunities to solve a garden hedge-maze, as well as a full-scale replica of Stonehenge made of foam. Whatever you desire, from highbrow to low-brow, Virginia grows it locally.

 VIRGINIA'S BEST TRIPS

VIRGINIA TRIPS

Another Roadside Attraction

WHY GO Skyline Drive is one of America's classic road trips. Befittingly, it comes studded like a leather belt with natural wonders and artificial oddities one has to see to believe. Cruising through Virginia's Blue Ridge Mountains and Shenandoah Valley is the only way to do it.

The centerpiece of the ribbon-thin Shenandoah National Park is the jaw-dropping beauty of Skyline Drive, which runs for just over 100 miles high-atop the Blue Ridge Mountains. Unlike the massive acreage of western parks like Yellowstone or Yosemite, Shenandoah is at times only a mile wide. This lack of territorial expanse has allowed plenty of enterprising businesspeople to dream up their own amusements to lure the tourist dollar. We all know what a tree looks like, so let's find the hidden gems and one-of-a-kind attractions that sing their siren songs to road-weary travelers passing by.

Straddling the northern entrance to the park is the tiny city of ❶ **Front Royal**. Although it's not among Virginia's fanciest ports-of-call, this lush riverside town offers all the urban amenities one might need before a camping or hiking trip up in the mountains.

Those looking for a place to rest in Front Royal, and those with an Irish fetish, should be quite pleased with the ❷ **Killahevlin B&B**. Located in an Edwardian mansion on the National Register of Historic Places, Killahevlin offers all the usual amenities of a B&B, but also boasts its own in-house Irish pub. Guests can help themselves to the Irish beer on tap before singing a lively rendition of "Danny Boy." Stay in the tower rooms for that oh-so-Euro feel. Nearby, in the center of town, ❸ **Main Street Mill & Tavern** offers a tasty, if basic, lunch selection, including taco salads and hamburgers. This friendly place is

TIME
3 days

DISTANCE
150 miles

BEST TIME TO GO
May – Nov

START
Front Royal

END
Lexington

ALSO GOOD FOR

ROUTE

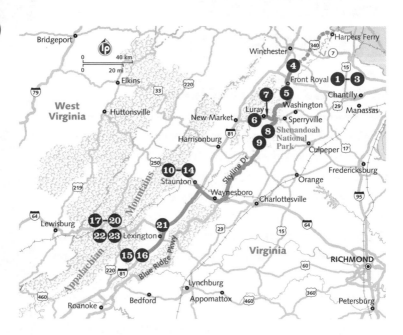

popular with the locals, and the Front Royal Visitors Center is conveniently located right across the parking lot.

Before you head into the national park, drive a few miles north of Front Royal (towards Winchester) to ❹ **Dinosaur Land**. This spectacularly low-brow shrine to concrete sculpture is not to be missed. Although it's an "educational prehistoric forest," with over 50 life-size dinosaurs (and a King Kong for good measure), you'd probably learn more about the tenants by fast-forwarding through *Jurassic Park 2*. But that's not why you've stopped here, so grab your camera and sidle up to the triceratops for memories that will last a millennium. The gift shop offers postcards and T-shirts that are almost as old as the lizards themselves (along with plenty of tacky, non-dino-related objets d'art).

❺ **Skyline Drive** is the scenic drive to end all scenic drives. The 75 overlooks, with views into the Shenandoah Valley and the Piedmont, are all breathtaking, even after you've seen the first 70. In spring and summer, endless variations on the color green are sure to enchant, just as the vibrant reds and yellows will amaze in autumn. A stop at the Dickey Ridge Visitors Center at Mile 5 will provide you with information on the numerous trails you can stop to hike along the route. This might be your chance to finally hike a section of the Appalachian Trail, which crosses Skyline Drive at 32 places.

When you get to Thornton Gap (about Mile 32) take a break from the twists and turns of Skyline Drive and head west to Luray, where you'll find the wonderful ❻ **Luray Caverns.** Here you can take a one-hour, roughly one-mile guided tour of these caves, opened to the public over a hundred years ago. Among the largest and most famous caverns in the East, Luray boasts what is surely a one-of-a-kind – the Stalacpipe Organ – in the pit of its belly. This crazy contraption has been banging out melodies on the rock forma-tions for decades. As the guide says, the caves are 400 million years old "*if* you believe in geological dating." No matter what you believe in, you'll be impressed by the fantastic under-ground expanses.

DETOUR If you're still not ready to go sightseeing in Shenan-doah, drive 30 miles further north on Rte 340 to Harpers Ferry, West Virginia, for the **John Brown Wax Museum** (www.johnbrownwax museum.com). Located on the town's main drag, it tells the dramatic story of this famed (if not quite successful) abolitionist in several waxy dioramas. Yes, it's a wax museum about slav-ery, riots, treason, and, ultimately, the gallows. Bizarre and generally unsettling, this place is a must-see for aficionados of the wax arts.

If you're traveling with kids, or are a big Hanna-Barbera fan, you may want to consider staying at ❼ **Yogi Bear's Jellystone Park Camp & Resort**, just outside Luray. Mini-ature-golf courses, water slides and paddleboats await inside its fanciful campus. The bargain-basement campsite and cabin prices don't even reflect the possibility that you might strike it rich while panning for gold at their Old Faceful Mining Company. For those just interested in passing by and taking a peek, there are a few oversized figures of Yogi and Boo Boo that are ready-made photo-ops. The park's convenience shop has the usual road food and a satisfying if not electrifying assortment of Jellystone character-related junk to buy.

Horse-fanciers will want to book a trail ride through Shenandoah at ❽ **Skyland Stables**. Rides last up to two-and-a-half hours and are a great way to see the wildlife and epic vistas. Pony rides are also available for the wee members of your party.

Ten miles south of the stables, another overnight possibility is the ❾ **Big Meadows Lodge** at Mile 51.2 on Skyline Drive, rather redundantly named for the adjacent, deer-filled "big meadow." The atmosphere here is very peace-ful, as chipmunks and birds go flitting about the branches. You can stay in either the 1939 stone lodge or one of the rustic cabins that are the picture of 1950s vacation paradise. This is a perfect place from which to stage hiking or biking excursions into the beautiful Shenandoah National Park. The helpful staff is more than happy to point you in the right direction, and rangers at the nearby visitors center can give you more specifics about what awaits you on the various trails.

The main dining room at Big Meadows is crowned by a huge A-frame chestnut roof and serves surprisingly good meals. Dinner entrées, like the Thanksgiving-esque turkey platter with stuffing and mashed potatoes, evoke a yesteryear Americana. Cap it off with the scrumptious blackberry ice cream. Afterwards, relax in the convivial Tap Room with a cocktail or beer and while away the evening hours listening to the local talent who perform music here nightly.

After a welcome rest, it's time to start working your way further south on Skyline Drive towards Staunton. Make sure to stop every now and again if for no other reason than to marvel at the grand panoramas and take the obligatory photo that will never fully communicate the serenity of the moment.

GARDEN MAZE ALERT

Next to the Luray Caverns is an excellent opportunity to let your inner Shelley Duvall or Scatman Crothers run wild. Go screaming *Shining*-style through the **Garden Maze**, but beware! This maze is harder than it looks and some could spend longer inside it than they anticipated. Paranormal and psychic abilities are permitted, but frowned upon, when solving the hedge maze. Redrum! Redrum!

By this point you're probably dreaming of ditching your 9-to-5 job and moving to the country to buy one of those gorgeous little farms you keep seeing from the scenic overlooks. A good way to snap yourself out of this fantasy is by taking a trip to the ❿ **Frontier Culture Museum** in Staunton. The hard work of farming comes to life via the familiar Virginia trope of employing historically costumed interpreters. The museum has Irish, German and English farms for exploring, and period farmhouses, which have been brought over from their respective Old Countries and rebuilt, brick by brick, here in Shenandoah Valley.

For something a little less historically edifying, try the model-train stores in precious downtown ⓫ **Staunton**. Nestled amidst these well-restored old buildings are several good eateries. For lunch, try the exceedingly quaint ⓬ **Pampered Palate Café**, which serves sandwiches and quiches, of both the carnivorous and vegetarian variety. Come here for $1 espressos during "Cappy Hour," 2:30pm to 4:30pm daily. The café also has takeout and boxed lunches for anyone who wants to go Goth and dine in the cemetery of Trinity Church down the street, or head back up the mountain to Shenandoah National Park. If you're looking for something a little more sophisticated, seek out the black chairs and banquettes of the supper-clubby ⓭ **Dining Room**. The seafood salad with grilled salmon, shrimp and crab cakes is a delicious starter before the double-crusted chicken potpie. The enticing contemporary dinner menu goes well with the modern art covering the walls – it could fit perfectly in Midtown Manhattan.

History buffs should check out the ⓮ **Woodrow Wilson Presidential Library** across town. Despite the fact that Virginia is the proud birthplace of eight presidents, this is the only presidential library in the state. Stop by and

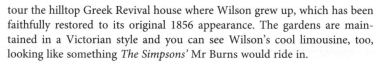
tour the hilltop Greek Revival house where Wilson grew up, which has been faithfully restored to its original 1856 appearance. The gardens are maintained in a Victorian style and you can see Wilson's cool limousine, too, looking like something *The Simpsons'* Mr Burns would ride in.

Head south on Hwy 81 and past Lexington to the gorgeous ⑮ **Natural Bridge** and its fantabulous potpourri of amusements. Natural Bridge is a legitimate natural wonder – even claimed to be one of the "Seven Natural Wonders of the World," though just who put together that list remains unclear. That said, this centuries-old rock formation is wondrous in its beauty and provides true respite from the trials and tribulations of the road. Soaring 200ft in the air, Natural Bridge was surveyed by the young George Washington and, legend has it, he also carved his initials in the rock face. What's certain is that Thomas Jefferson was so enamored of Natural Bridge that he built a cabin here. Those who aren't afraid of a little religion should hang around for the "Drama of Creation" light show that plays nightly underneath and around the bridge.

"…this crown jewel is one of the most ridiculous and incredible sights in Virginia."

Around Natural Bridge are several other attractions of varying kitsch value. The historical wax museum offers a tour of its factory but somehow it doesn't have that certain sense of theater one looks for in a waxen encounter. There are also nature trails, but they pale in comparison to those of the Shenandoah National Park.

Best to keep moving to the most truly unnatural part of the Natural Bridge complex: the outrageously out-of-place and therefore ingenious ⑯ **Foamhenge**. What's that you say? Foamhenge? You mean a life-size replica of England's most famous mystery site built entirely out of foam? Yes, and this crown jewel of the Blue Ridge foothills in the Shenandoah Valley is one of the most ridiculous and incredible sights in the entire state of Virginia. A pure distillation of the American Dream, this magical temple to creativity is worth every dollar you spend on gas to get to it. The utter ludicrousness of Foamhenge is its sole reward, and will change your life like a trip to Fatima. Bring your druid/pagan claptrap and see if anything happens at sundown on the solstice.

After all the wackiness of the Shenandoah National Park and Valley, it might be time for a little taste of civilized society. You can wander the streets of sexy ⑰ **Lexington**, a very well-heeled, immaculate town, like a Virginian version of Greenwich, Connecticut. Admire the classical architecture of ⑱ **Washington & Lee University,** or the imposing fortresses of the ⑲ **Virginia Military Institute**. Out-of-towners won't be able to help glancing sideways at all the military hard-bodies milling about, and there are several streets lined with shops and curiosities, such as Stonewall Jackson's house.

Bed down at the comfortable, pretty ⑳ **Sheridan Livery Inn**. Nine guest rooms and three suites make up this li'l charmer in a turn-of-the-century building positioned right on Main St. The location can't be beat and the Sheridan also has a fine restaurant serving lunch and dinner. You can dine on the shady patio while enjoying crab stuffed shrimp or pork with steamed clams. Naturally, delicious libations are also on the menu.

But don't go to bed because its date night at the drive-in! Just a few miles north of Lexington on Rte 11 is ㉑ **Hull's Drive-In Movie Theater**. Saved from demolition after the owner's death by a consortium of friends, this totally hardcore artifact of the golden age of automobiles is a living museum to the road trips your parents remember. It plays only new releases (sadly no *American Graffiti* or *Pee-Wee's Big Adventure*) on weekends, so you are left at the mercy of Hollywood's latest trifle. But even the latest installment of *Traveling Pants* should look good on a warm, starry Virginia night, especially when nuzzled next to your special someone.

LATE NIGHT BRIDGE PARTY

Too much to see and too little time? Those looking to spend the night at Natural Bridge can check into the **Natural Bridge Hotel** (☎ 540-291-2121; www.naturalbridgeva.com). A well-maintained roadside hotel, it offers specialty and holiday Southern buffets in the Colonial Dining Room. Now you might have time to check out their **Haunted Monster Museum** or "Virginia's Largest Gift Shop," which is perhaps equally frightening.

You can pick up some fresh movie snacks from the best joint in Lexington, the ㉒ **Patisserie Café**. Situated in what looks like a French farmhouse at the head of the loop through town, this superb bakery has dozens of homemade choices that come prepackaged for easy takeout. If you want to eat onsite, the staff will reheat the delicious lasagna or other daily offering for you.

On Fridays and Saturdays, they set up a grill and serve made-to-order burgers, bratwurst, and portobello mushrooms for the crowd that bops along to the live music acts, and there's brunch on Sundays.

If you're looking to get your drink on with the college kids (and who isn't, really?) you'll want to grab a beer at the ㉓ **Palms**. This very cozy, purple bar and grill has an upscale tavern vibe and an extensive menu if you want some onion rings with your Sam Adams. It has a great dark interior with big windows overlooking a grassy expanse across the street. Sidle up to the bar and buy a drink for, or offer a cigarette to, some of the young'uns and maybe they'll tell you where that night's party is.

When you've had your fill of officers and gentlemen, peel yourself away from the gracious Southern charms of Lexington. Fortunately, you'll have all the trinkets and receipts of roads well traveled to remind you of the myriad wonders of Shenandoah and its many, many outlandish attractions.

David Ozanich

TRIP INFORMATION

GETTING THERE
From Richmond you can take the I-64 west to the I-81 north. Or go via I-66 west from Washington DC.

DO
Dinosaur Land
Virginia's own Jurassic Park with 40 or so "life-size" dino "sculptures." ☎ 540-869-2222; www.dinosaurland.com; 3848 Stonewall Jackson Hwy, White Post; adult/child $5/4; 🕑 9:30am-5:30pm, to 6:30pm in summer; 👤

Foamhenge
A replica of Stonehenge made entirely of foam. Part of the Natural Bridge complex. Believe! ☎ 540-291-2121; www.natural bridgeva.com; Rte 11 just north of Rte 130, Natural Bridge; admission incl in Natural Bridge fee; 🕑 8am-dark; 👤

Frontier Culture Museum
A living farm-museum "that brings the past to life." ☎ 540-332-7850; www.frontier .virginia.gov; 1290 Richmond Rd, Staunton; adult/child $10/6; 🕑 9am-5pm; 👤

Hull's Drive-In Movie Theater
Step back in time to the 1950s. Utterly fab. ☎ 540-463-2621; www.hullsdrivein.com; 2361 N Lee Hwy, Lexington; admission $5; 🕑 double feature starts 9:15pm; 👤

Luray Caverns
The coolest caverns in Virginia – with the unique Stalacpipe Organ and a garden maze. ☎ 540-743-6551; www.luraycaverns.com; 970 US Hwy 211 West, Luray; adult/child $19/9; 🕑 9am-7pm summer, to 4pm or 5pm winter; 👤

Natural Bridge
A truly marvelous natural formation at the base of the Blue Ridge Mountains. ☎ 540-291-2121; www.naturalbridgeva.com; Rte 11 just north of Rte 130, Natural Bridge; adult/child $13/8; 🕑 8am-dark; 👤

Skyland Stables
Guided trail rides through Shenandoah National Park. ☎ 540-999-2210; www.visit shenandoah.com; Mile 41 on Skyline Dr; rides $30-50; 🕑 8:45am-5pm, closed winter; 👤

Skyline Drive
The main feature of Shenandoah National Park with several entrances. ☎ 540-999-3500; www.nps.gov/shen; north entrance at Front Royal; per car $10; 👤

Woodrow Wilson Presidential Library
Tour the birthplace and museum of one of our most important presidents. ☎ 540-885-0897; www.woodrowwilson.org; 18 N Coalter St, Staunton; adult/child $12/3; 🕑 9am-5pm Mon-Sat, 12-5pm Sun

EAT & DRINK
Dining Room
Supper-clubby, dark and refined restaurant in Staunton. ☎ 540-213-0606; www.the diningroomstaunton.com; 29 N Augusta St, Staunton; mains $11-25; 🕑 11am-10pm Mon-Sat, to 9pm Sun

Main Street Mill & Tavern
Folksy restaurant in a spacious renovated 1880s feed mill. ☎ 540-636-3123; 500 E Main St, Front Royal; mains $6-15; 🕑 10:30am-9pm Sun-Thu, to 10pm Fri & Sat; 👤

Palms
Popular restaurant and bar in downtown Lexington. ☎ 540-463-7911; www.the palmslexington.com; 101 W Nelson St, Lexington; mains $6-15; 🕑 11:30am-1am Mon-Sat, noon-11pm Sun

Pampered Palate Café
A quaint café in downtown Staunton. Also has boxed lunches. ☎ 540-886-9463; 26 & 28 W Beverley St, Staunton; mains $5-15; 🕑 9:30am-5:30pm Mon-Sat

Patisserie Café
Fantastic, yummy bakery in a French farm-house, with food to go or stay. Grilling on weekends. ☎ 540-462-6000; www.patis seriecafe.net; 107 N Main St, Lexington; mains $5-10; 🕑 11am-3pm Mon-Wed, 8:30am-6:30pm Thu, 8:30am-10pm Fri & Sat, brunch Sun

SLEEP
Big Meadows Lodge
Wonder Years–style lodge and campsite right in the heart of Skyline Drive. A worthwhile

stay. ☎ 800-999-4714; www.visitshenan doah.com; Mile 51.2 on Skyline Dr; r $74-166; 🅰

Killahevlin B&B
Irish-ish B&B in an old building on the National Register of Historic Places. Free beer on tap for guests. ☎ 540-636-7335; www .vairish.com; 1401 N Royal Ave, Front Royal; r $155-255

Sheridan Livery Inn
A gracious little inn in sexy Lexington. There's an in-house restaurant, too. ☎ 540-464-1887; 35 N Main St, Lexington; r $89-170

Yogi Bear's Jellystone Park Campsite
Family-friendly campsite with a Yogi Bear and Boo Boo theme and tons of activities. ☎ 800-420-6679; www.campluray.com; 2250 Hwy 211 East, Luray; campsites & cabins $125-200; 🅰

USEFUL WEBSITES
www.nps.gov/shen
www.visitshenandoah.com

SUGGESTED READS
• *Another Roadside Attraction*, Tom Robbins
• *The Height of Our Mountains: Nature Writing from Virginia's Blue Ridge Mountains and Shenandoah Valley*, Michael P Branch & Daniel J Philippon

LINK YOUR TRIP
www.lonelyplanet.com/trip-planner

TRIP
9 Upscale Appalachian Trail p107
44 Virginia Is for Lovers opposite
50 The Crooked Road: Heritage Music Trail p339

Virginia Is for Lovers

WHY GO Steal away from the endless trials of the day-to-day to the mythic land of romance: no, not Fantasy Island, but fabulous Virginia. It's not just for lovers anymore, as there are myriad options for admirers of food and luxury in both urban and rural scenes.

One of the most famous (and romantic) tourist slogans around, "Virginia Is for Lovers" is also one of the most true. Virginia has oodles of magical little hideaways where you can leave the world behind to focus on the most important person (or people) in your life. And, even better, these places are never more than two hours away from Washington DC or Richmond.

Start your trip with a Friday night out in ❶ **Alexandria**, one of Virginia's most historic, yet still contemporary, cities. Despite the focus on its attention-grabbing neighbor, Washington DC (just across the Potomac River), this bedroom community still maintains its unique identity thanks to the plethora of immaculately maintained historic buildings in (you guessed it) Old Town Alexandria. The shop-lined cobblestone streets and townhouse-flanked avenues are perfect for strolling on a weekend evening. Alexandria offers all the charms of a quaint town without leaving the amenities of a major city behind.

Check into the one of the 45 rooms or three suites at the ❷ **Morrison House** hotel. This impressive and luxurious, yet still intimate, hotel is the best in Alexandria. The recently updated rooms have fireplaces, honor bars stocked with top-shelf liquor and snacks, as well as four-poster beds. The Morrison's design evokes a refined elegance of centuries past that belies its comparatively brief history. If you don't want to leave the hotel for food, eat at the in-house restaurant, or drink an old-fashioned in the tony bar on the red-leather, high-back chairs.

TIME
3 days

DISTANCE
85 miles

BEST TIME TO GO
Year-round

START
Alexandria

END
Washington, VA

ALSO GOOD FOR

HISTORY &
CULTURE

BEST TRIP

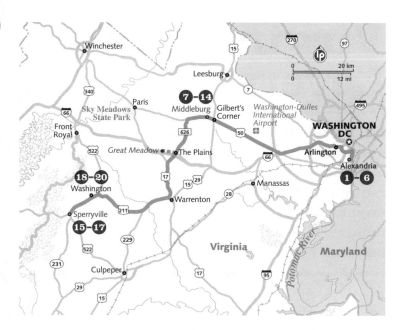

Less pricey (but only slightly) is the ❸ **Hotel Monaco**. A boutique hotel with a funkier, more youthful vibe, it's situated right at the epicenter of bustling downtown Alexandria. The staff's bright, groovy Cynthia Rowley–designed uniforms are an indication of this hotel's commitment to the fashionable edge, yet their attitude is never imperious or dismissive. The Monaco is pet-friendly and they offer goldfish for company if you left Spot at home. Once ensconced in one of the 242 rooms, you can order some low-country Southern cuisine 24 hours a day from their restaurant.

Politicos and their admirers will want to stop by the understandably trendy ❹ **Restaurant Eve**. Catering to beltway boys and government gals on dates, Eve is hidden down a cloistered entryway, giving the restaurant a secluded, private ambience. Its menu packs a sophisticated French-American punch that's delicious but never overly precious. Chef Cathal Armstrong has quite a following and was named one of *Food & Wine* magazine's best chefs of 2006. There's also a relaxed bar, with mixologists that really know how to stir a drink – try their perfect mojito made with mint-infused syrup. You get the expected deep, cool taste without the pesky mottled green leaves stuck in your teeth.

❺ **Vermilion** is another top-tier food palace (and lounge), located in the quieter section of downtown Alexandria west of Washington St. The high ceilings and red velvety decor create a smoldering setting for a rendezvous with a foreign diplomat lover. Share state secrets over charcuterie while sipping a glass of the rich, buttery Alexander Valley Claret. The braised short rib proves tender and tasty, while the Swiss chard and sweet-potato ravioli with pork tenderloin is a smidge more adventurous and just as well prepared.

If it's too early to return to the hotel, you might consider catching a movie at the nearby **6** **Old Town Theater**. This former dance hall and vaudeville theater shows first-run films. Plus, they serve drinks, so there's no need to lose the buzz from dinner.

The next morning, wake up with a room-service breakfast, and get ready to head out to horse country. Less than an hour away from Alexandria is **7** **Middleburg**, a splendid town in "hunt country," whose residents are just as likely to be wearing jodhpurs and riding boots as they are Cartier and Chanel. The much-married Liz Taylor lived near Middleburg in the 1970s during her stint as a senator's wife. Another siren, Jackie Kennedy, came here often to escape the flashbulbs of Washington. It's just far enough from the city to give the illusion of being of a more relaxed and gracious world. The surrounding countryside is dotted with large estates where gentleman farmers keep immaculate lawns and, of course, horses. Lots and lots of horses.

KIDS OF ALL AGES

Parents feeling guilty about leaving the tykes at home, and looking to buy back their affection, might want to browse the puppets, models, toys, and fairy costumes that fill **Why Not** (☎ 703-548-4420), a shop on King St in the heart of Old Town. Stop in to be delighted by the marvelous and curious items for sale – everyone will find something they "just have to have."

The town's main drag, Washington St, is brimming with upscale shops for the preppy gentry. **8** **Crème de la Crème** offers table linens, pottery, obscure cooking utensils and other fantastic little French-y doodads that you simply shouldn't live without. Special props go to their stationery annex, which has scores of cards for every conceivable occasion. The **9** **Home Farm Shop – Traditional Butchers & Graziers** is a good stop if you need some new gourmet items to pair with your bounty from Crème de la Crème. Housed in an old building, it has a regal feel that gives even the most oddball chutneys an air of tantalizing superiority.

A nifty local place for lunch is the **10** **Coach Stop**, which boasts "fine dining since 1958." They're probably still serving the same menu, and the interior design most definitely hasn't changed in that time either. That's why it's awesome. Feel like a background extra on an episode of *Alice* and snarl "Kiss my grits!" in this friendly, family-owned restaurant. Watch the locals pass through and you'll notice that everyone seems to know each other: Washington businessmen and their step-kids mix it up with aging blue bloods and horse-lovers taking a break from the stables. The food and service could best be described as "upscale diner" – minestrone soup represents, as do burgers and sandwiches. Some of the more complicated offerings, like pork porterhouse with fried apples and whipped potatoes, are really worth a try. For dessert, get the bread pudding. They have a full bar, too.

Want some fresh pepper with that? Delve into the edge of fashion at **❶ Highcliffe Clothiers**, Wendy Pepper's design and clothing store hidden away in an historic 1800s building. Who's Wendy Pepper, you ask? If you must be updated – she was a finalist on *Project Runway* and, more interestingly, she was the show's "villain," so you know her stuff is fierce. Worship at her feet, just watch her make dresses, or, even better, buy one of her originals for yourself.

ASK A LOCAL

"Places I particularly like in Middleburg are **Nobel Neilson Shoes**, run by my friend Troye Plaskitt. It's right across the street from my store (Highcliffe Clothiers). Also, around the corner is a place called **Mello Out**, specializing in homemade marshmallows. It is owned and operated by my friend Lisa."

Wendy Pepper, Highcliffe Clothiers, Middleburg

If you're just looking for a brew and little derby pie, head to the other side of town (about a quarter mile down Washington St) to the **❷ Red Horse Tavern**. Hunker down at one of the outdoor tables and watch the passersby on the street, which is surprisingly active for such a small town. They also serve a basic tavern menu with hot dogs, chicken sandwiches and onion rings.

Just north of town on Rte 626 is **❸ Glenwood Park**, a picturesque steeplechase whose highlights are the spring and fall races. They also host fox hunts open to both pros and amateurs. Even when there are no races, it's still a beautiful complex to visit, with large grassy expanses surrounded by gorgeous countryside.

For dinner you'll want to get a table at the **❹ Red Fox Inn**, which is convenient, because this is also where you'll want to spend the night. First built in 1728, it was home to Chinn's Ordinary, a pit stop at the halfway point between Alexandria and the frontier post of Winchester (hence the town's name, Middleburg). This flagstone building, remodeled in 1812 and naturally modernized since, is home to one of the best country inns in Virginia. The Red Fox Inn has six rooms in the main building and a handful of others in the Stray Fox out back. The rooms have four-poster beds and are decorated in a lovely, not cloying, 18th-century style. Couples planning to get drunk on romance and song may want to reserve the Belmont suite, which has a baby grand piano among its amenities.

The restaurant at the Red Fox features Virginia staples like peanut soup (among the finest and creamiest in the state), along with plenty of seafood and chops. The plating is quite modern and helps bring the restaurant out of the past and into the present. Firelight from the enormous hearths bounces off the low-slung ceilings in the five intimate dining rooms. Like many a previous visitor, plan for a coming revolution while working through a bottle from the Red Fox's fine selection of international and local vintages. After dinner, go stargazing in the garden behind the main building.

A continental breakfast is served in the main dining room. You can also have the Washington papers delivered, so you can enjoy the *Post* with your cup of coffee. Once you've caught up with the Sunday columnists, step into the Middleburg Information Center just up the street and grab a map of the surrounding countryside. The weblike crisscrosses of scenic byways and highways will take you through the rolling, grassy hills of the Virginia countryside into the numerous small towns, like Leesburg and Waterford. Ultimately, drive west towards the Blue Ridge Mountains into Rappahannock County.

 Less than 10 miles south of Middleburg off Rte 626 is **Great Meadow** (www.greatmeadow.org), another steeplechase course that also hosts twilight polo matches every Saturday in summer. It is home to the prestigious Virginia Gold Cup, a 4-mile course considered one of the premier steeplechase events in the US. If all the equine activity is making you thirsty, sample the local wine on sale here under the early-evening sun and stars.

⓯ **Sperryville** is a pleasant town right at the base of the Blue Ridge Mountains with a couple of eateries and sleeperies, but it's most highly recommended stop is ⓰ **Central Coffee Roasters**. A tiny family-run outfit, they sell self-roasted beans that hail from Africa, the East Indies and South America. They also offer coffee tasting and biscotti on weekends, and rightfully claim to have the best java in the area. Another interesting place for browsing is the huge ⓱ **Glassworks Gallery**. You'll cross a petite suspension bridge over a rushing creek to get to the building. Inside is just about everything that can be made out of glass, from hummingbird feeders to oil lamps. Even if you aren't a glass nut, it's worth taking a look.

Or you could stop at one of the local churches that spring like wildflowers from the landscape, and pray to the culinary gods, thanking them for the existence of your next destination: the ⓲ **Inn at Little Washington**. Even if you swear allegiance to French Laundry or Gramercy Tavern as your favorite restaurant ever, you'll be bowled over by the sheer fabulosity of this sacred destination on the epicurean trail.

Head back north on Lee Hwy to Washington. "Little" barely describes the pinprick proportions of this town, which, like Sperryville, is at the foot of the Blue Ridge Mountains. A few stores and a couple of dozen homes and B&Bs constitute the hamlet, but it's no matter because you're here to go to one place. Though the Inn was founded 30 years ago, back before "destination dining" existed, it didn't stop Patrick O'Connell and his partner from creating one of the most famous restaurants on the East Coast. Among the billions of accolades, stars, and diamonds it has racked up, the Inn was named one of the "10 best restaurants in the world" by the *International Herald Tribune*.

But the Inn's pleasures come at a price so beware – the dinner prix fixe starts at $148 on weekdays and goes higher on weekends. It is worth every penny. First of all, the service is, unsurprisingly, impeccable, and the food hits all the grace notes. For the first course you might try the beet fantasia or the eggs in an egg (once prepared for the queen of England on her visit to the US). Next, you could try the pecan-crusted soft-shell crab tempura with Italian mustard fruit. The "pepper crusted tuna pretending to be a filet mignon capped with seared duck fois gras on charred onions with a burgundy butter sauce" is a popular main course. Others prefer the "medallions of rabbit loin wrapped in house cured pancetta surrounding a Lilliputian rabbit rib roast resting on a pillow of English pea puree." So, yeah, any questions? Naturally the desserts are just as elaborate. Maybe the passion fruit dreamsicle or the seven deadly sins? Go. Toss your credit score to the winds and just go.

"Al and Tipper Gore have rested their weary heads here, as have Warren Beatty and Annette Bening."

By the time you roll out of here you'll be even happier that you're staying at their five-star accommodations. The true Casanova will reserve the **19 Claiborne House**, the chef's achingly beautiful former cottage. Two stories, several rooms, gorgeous gardens, flatscreen TVs – it's about as good as it gets within a thousand mile radius. Al and Tipper Gore have rested their weary heads here, as have Warren Beatty and Annette Bening. Swingers and penny-pinchers will be glad to know the house sleeps up to four people. The rooms in their actual Inn ain't half bad either.

For those looking to spend a couple hundred less on sleeping accommodations, the **20 Caledonia Farm 1812** is a good option. The flagstone house is on the National Register of Historic Places and sits on big, colorful farmland a few miles up the road from the Inn at Little Washington. Try and stay in the old summer kitchen, which has been converted into a romantic guesthouse. All the suites have working fireplaces and, as a bonus, the owner has an extensive and impressive train collection that he'll be happy to show off. The farm also happens to be the start of a Virginia wildlife and birding trail.

Upon Monday's inevitable arrival, rise early to enjoy the dawn. Eat breakfast in the beautiful morning sun as the light cascades down the crevices of the tree-covered Blue Ridge Mountains. You can't ask for a better start to the workweek, or for more delicious memories of a weekend in love.

David Ozanich

TRIP INFORMATION

GETTING THERE

From Richmond take the I-95 north to the I-66 east into Alexandria. From Washington DC, cross the Potomac River on the I-395 and turn onto the George Washington Pkwy.

DO

Central Coffee Roasters

Find fresh roasted international coffees at the foot of the Blue Ridge Mountains. ☎ 540-987-1006; www.centralcoffee.com; 11836 Lee Hwy, Sperryville; 🕑 10am-5pm Fri-Sun

Crème de la Crème

Gorgeous little baubles, kitchenware, and stationery in the heart of Middleburg. ☎ 540-687-4796; 23 E Washington St, Middleburg; 🕑 10am-5:30pm Mon-Fri, to 6pm Sat, 12-5pm Sun

Glassworks Gallery

An impressive warehouse full of all things glass. ☎ 540-987-8474; www.glassworks gallery.com; 11794 Lee Hwy, Sperryville; 🕑 10:30am-6pm, closed Wed

Glenwood Park

Middleburg's picturesque steeplechase park. Highlights are the spring and fall races. Pretty to visit, even if they aren't racing. www.middleburgspringraces.com; 36800 Glenwood Park Lane off Foxcroft Rd; 🕑 hrs vary according to event; 🚻

Highcliffe Clothiers

The one-and-only Wendy Pepper's dress-shop in historic Middleburg. ☎ 540-687-5633; www.wendypepper.com; 16 S Madison St, Middleburg; 🕑 10am-6pm Mon-Sat, 12-5pm Sun

Old Town Theater

Lovely old vaudeville theater that now shows first-run movies. ☎ 703-683-8888; www.oldtowntheater.com; 815 1/2 King St, Alexandria; 🕑 showtimes vary

EAT & DRINK

Coach Stop

Folksy, low-key restaurant with a full bar on Middleburg's main drag. ☎ 540-687-5515; 9 E Washington St, Middleburg; mains $10-20; 🕑 breakfast, lunch & dinner; 🚻

Home Farm Shop – Traditional Butchers & Graziers

Upscale gourmet shop with a traditional flair. ☎ 540-687-8882; 1 E Washington St, Middleburg; 🕑 10am-6pm

Inn at Little Washington

One of the best restaurants ever – you should sell a kidney and make a reservation. ☎ 540-675-3800; www.theinnatlittlewash ington.com; Middle & Main Sts, Washington; dinner prix fixe $148-165; 🕑 5:30-11pm

Red Fox Inn

Mix fine dining with a historic setting. Chops and fish served fireside in five intimate dining rooms. ☎ 540-687-6301; www.redfox .com; 2 E Washington St, Middleburg

Red Horse Tavern

Cool, friendly sports-bar on the west side of Middleburg, with a great, big patio. ☎ 540-687-6443; 112 W Washington St, Middleburg; 🕑 from noon

Restaurant Eve

A fine meal is guaranteed at this highlight of emerging epicurean Alexandria. ☎ 703-706-0450; www.restauranteve.com; 110 S Pitt St, Alexandria; mains $10-35; 🕑 11:30am-2:30pm & 5:30-11:30pm Mon-Fri, 5:30-11:30pm Sat

Vermilion

Swanky, sexy restaurant and lounge away from the tourists. ☎ 703-684-9669; 1120 King St, Alexandria; www.vermilion restaurant.com; mains $18-30; 🕑 lunch Mon-Fri, dinner Mon-Sat, brunch Sat & Sun

SLEEP

Caledonia Farm 1812

Charming, historic flagstone B&B on farmlands just outside Washington. ☎ 540-675-3693; www.bnb1812.com; 47 Dearing Rd, Flint Hill; r $140-175

Claiborne House

The chef's former "cottage" at the Inn at Little Washington. ☎ 540-675-3800; www .theinnatlittlewashington.com; Middle & Main Sts, Washington; r $1850-2000

Hotel Monaco
Hipster, upmarket bohemian-chic hotel right in the center of Old Town Alexandria. ☎ 703-549-6080; www.monaco-alexandria.com; 480 King St; r $209-500; 🖼 🐾

Morrison House
This stunning boutique hotel is the ultimate Alexandria option for refined elegance. ☎ 703-849-6342; www.morrisonhouse.com; 116 S Alfred St, Alexandria; r $265-600

Red Fox Inn
Dapper little country inn that's been around in one form or another since 1728. ☎ 540-687-6301; www.redfox.com; 2 E Washington St; r $170-300

USEFUL WEBSITES
www.middleburgonline.com
www.town.washington.va.us

LINK YOUR TRIP   www.lonelyplanet.com/trip-planner
TRIP

Virginia Beach: Surf & Turf

WHY GO Though Australia and Hawaii get most of the surf press, Virginia Beach offers the same sea-salty good times – from sipping mai tais at oceanfront bars, to taking dips in the Atlantic. So save the airfare and relax beachside on Virginia's Gold Coast.

Virginia Beach is the state's third largest city and is best known for the sandy spread that abuts the Atlantic just south of Chesapeake Bay. And while its legend may not rival Venice Beach or Miami Beach, it still serves up plenty of fun for those seeking some waterfront action.

The main strip runs for a few miles up and down Atlantic Ave. After the long drive through Hampton Roads, a good place to relax with a drink is ❶ **Catch 31**. Attached to the ubertrendy, if over-priced, seafood restaurant of the same name, Catch 31 is best enjoyed for its outdoor bar, just off the boardwalk. Large fire pits decorate the patio and serve as focal points along with the iron gazebo, where local bands perform. Despite the crowd, perfect martinis are shaken and served.

Now that you've cleared your head with a generous helping of gin, it might be time to check in to your hotel. If you're staying at the ❷ **Hilton**, you're in luck, because Catch 31 is its resident restaurant. If you tend to holiday at W Hotels, you'll probably want to stay here as it's right smack dab in the middle of it all, and is the highest-end resort available.

But Virginia Beach isn't really the most "high-end" place a person could think of, so why push it? A more fun option is the ❸ **Cavalier Hotel**, the Stephen King–style spooky old behemoth of choice for fans of such things. Built in 1927, the beautiful hotel was the first luxury outpost in Virginia Beach. It's getting just a bit ramshackle now, but that serves

TIME
2 days

BEST TIME TO GO
May – Sep

START
Virginia Beach

END
Virginia Beach

ALSO GOOD FOR

FOOD & DRINK

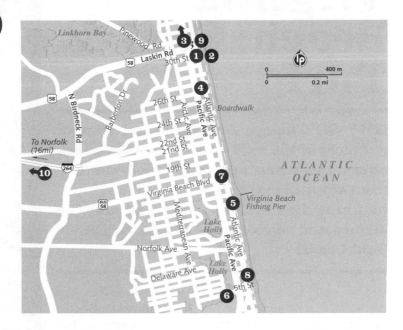

to highlight many of its charms. Of the two sides of this hotel, the Cavalier-on-the-Hill is the one to stay at. The rooms are large and clean, with very fine bathrooms (Crocodile Dundee and the French will be glad to know some rooms offer bidets). Go skinny-dipping in the cavernous indoor poolroom late at night and feel like a jazz-era moll.

"Go skinny-dipping in the cavernous indoor poolroom late at night and feel like a jazz-era moll."

The **4** **Maple Tree Pancake House** is a cheery stop for breakfast. It has strange tiger-art on the walls, along with typical diner decor highlighted by tropical flourishes. The house special, two eggs scrambled with ham chunks and two buttermilk pancakes, though perhaps indelicately described, is a cheap and hearty start to a day of beaching.

The resort strip beaches stretch roughly from 1st St up to 38th St. This is where the boardwalk takes center stage and all of your biking, rollerblading, and saltwater taffy needs can be met. There are several rental outfits to choose from, but the generically named **5** **Bike Rentals** has four locations, including two on the boardwalk at 14th and 18th Sts. This main stretch, which is large and expansive with soft sand, is well looked after by lifeguards and has public amenities. To the south is the Croatan Beach where locals play and all-day surfing is allowed. The North Beaches (above 42nd St) are expansive and less crowded. However, there are no lifeguards and no public parking (save a few street spots) so it's a little less convenient for the casual beachgoer.

If you're looking to get out on the water, try **6** **Rudee Tours**, who offer a few boating options. Hop on the *Rocket* for a high-speed ride, or the more leisurely *Flipper*, for tours up and down Virginia Beach. You can also go deep-sea fishing on the *Angler* year-round. Rudee provides everything you need, from bait and tackle to a fishing license.

If you need to pick up some beach gear, you'll find what you're looking for at the scores of stores up and down Atlantic Ave. One of the most central is **7** **Beach Outfitters** at 17th St. It will satisfy all of your premium surfboard requirements, and offers an ample array of beachwear, sunscreen and other related accoutrements.

DETOUR For something upscale, try the RW Apple–approved **Todd Jurich's Bistro** (www.toddjurichsbistro.com) in nearby Norfolk. Surf options like ahi carpaccio, stuffed jumbo flounder, and sweet-chili-glazed Nova Scotia salmon are on the menu, along with turf selections like rack of lamb or even a vegetable pat tai. A casual elegance imbues the bistro, making it seem a more likely tenant for Tribeca than navy-oriented Norfolk.

The oceanfront is littered with dining options. At the bottom of the Ramada is **8** **Mahi Mah's Seafood & Sushi Saloon**. As you can probably guess, its signature dishes are varieties of sushi, but well-tanned winos will also enjoy wine for 50% off on Wednesday evenings. Mahi Mah's also has a reality-TV connection, as Otto Bursich, from the 2nd season of *Top Chef*, runs the kitchen.

A little more off-the-beaten-boardwalk is the **9** **Surf Club Ocean Grille**, the Wyndham's restaurant, located on North Beach away from the crowds. Patio seating puts you right out on the beach, with nothing to block the view. A local singing duo will likely be playing your favorite pop standards while you sample the surf-and-turf fare.

If you're looking for something a little different as your after-dinner entertainment, check out a drag show at **10** **Klub Ambush**. It's a little ways off the tourist strip, but its fun and friendly and most patrons, regardless of orientation, should feel comfortable here. Food is served, but best to stick to the booze. Just a couple of miles inland, the club is easily found on Lynnhaven Rd, accessible from I-264.

CATCH A WAVE

One of the biggest weekends is when Virginia Beach hosts the **East Coast Surfing Competition** (www.surfecsc.com). It usually takes place mid- to late August and features five days of surfing, volleyball tournaments, and more nouveau sports like skimboarding. You'll also want to keep your eyes peeled for the Miss ECSC swimsuit pageant, naturally.

All in all, despite its ever-growing size, Virginia Beach still manages to welcome visitors with all the low-key frills of an East Coast beach-town – and send them off with plenty of reasons to return next season.

David Ozanich

TRIP INFORMATION

GETTING THERE
From Richmond take the I-64 east to Norfolk. Get on the I-264 to continue east to Virginia Beach.

DO
Beach Outfitters
Come here for surfboards, boogie boards, swimwear and other beach essentials. ☎ 757-422-0880; www.online-sur-shops.com; 17th St & Atlantic Ave; ⏲ 9am-9pm

Bike Rentals
Rent bikes of all sizes, and rollerblades from this place on the boardwalk, inside the Sandcastle Resort. ☎ 757-428-8111; 14th St & Boardwalk; ⏲ 7am-12am; ♿

Rudee Tours
Boat tours of the Virginia Beach waterfront and deep-sea fishing trips. ☎ 757-422-5700; www.rudeetours.com; 200 Winston Salem Ave; ⏲ 8am-7pm; ♿

EAT
Mahi Mah's Seafood & Sushi Saloon
Sushi joint with a great bar, run by a former "Top Chef." ☎ 757-437-8030; www.mahimahs.com; 615 Atlantic Ave; mains $12-25; ⏲ 7am-2am

Maple Tree Pancake House
A top breakfast joint for hungry beach bums. ☎ 757-425-6796; 2608 Atlantic Ave; mains $6-10; ⏲ 6:30am-10pm; ♿

Surf Club Ocean Grille
Casual fine-dining on North Beach, away from the crowds. ☎ 757-425-5699; www.surfclubvabeach.com; 57th St & Atlantic Ave; mains $15-28; ⏲ 6:30am-10pm Sun-Thu, 6am-11pm Fri & Sat

DRINK
Catch 31
The Hilton's restaurant with a fabulous outdoor-patio bar. ☎ 757-213-3472; www.hiltonvb.com; 3001 Atlantic Ave; ⏲ 6:30am-2am

Klub Ambush
This friendly local gay-bar has almost nightly drag performances. ☎ 757-498-4301; www.klubambush.com; 475 S Lynnhaven Rd; ⏲ 5pm-2am

SLEEP
Cavalier Hotel
Ornate old hotel with a 1920s vibe and private beach. Full service and funky. ☎ 757-491-3093; www.cavalierhotel.com; Oceanfront at 42nd St; r $129-300

Hilton
The most top-of-the-line accommodations available on the beach. ☎ 757-213-3000; www.hiltonvb.com; 3001 Atlantic Ave; r $189-500

USEFUL WEBSITES
www.vbfun.com
www.virginiabeach.com

LINK YOUR TRIP

www.lonelyplanet.com/trip-planner

TRIP **46** Historical Eats in Williamsburg opposite

Historical Eats in Williamsburg

WHY GO The sweet smell of American success is nowhere more on display than in the colonial kitchens of Williamsburg. Get in the colonial groove by learning what our forebears really ate and then dine on hearty modern interpretations presented by the chefs of Williamsburg.

TIME
2 days

BEST TIME TO GO
Sep – Dec

START
Williamsburg

END
Williamsburg

ALSO GOOD FOR

HISTORY & CULTURE

You probably went when you were 12. Or maybe you've only heard horrifying rumors of bar wenches in bonnets harassing you while you try to buy an old-timey soda. Yes, this land of carriages and cobblestones reveals Virginia's quirky fetish for a historically accurate costumed interpretation of the past. Yet Colonial Williamsburg is so all-encompassing, so magnificently detailed in its dedication to archeology and anthropology that anyone with even a passing interest in American (and world) history can't help but be fascinated by the goings-on in this Brigadoon from the 18th century.

Fifes and drums. Horses and hounds. Tricorner hats. It's all here, of course, and visitors can indulge any of their particular interests. Especially engaging is the Historic Foodways Department program. The department's employees, led by Frank Clark, spend their time meticulously researching food preparation from period cookbooks like *The Art of Cookery Made Plain and Easy* by Hannah Glasse to help us better understand the ways of yesteryear. You can find them toiling in two primary locations: the Governor's Palace and the Peyton Randolph House.

The main historic building in Colonial Williamsburg is the ❶ **Governor's Palace** at the north end of Palace Green. You can tour the house, which was built for the royal representative and decorated in the lavish and ornate style of the seventh royal governor, the Earl of Dunmore. Outdoors, pop into the freestanding kitchens, near the

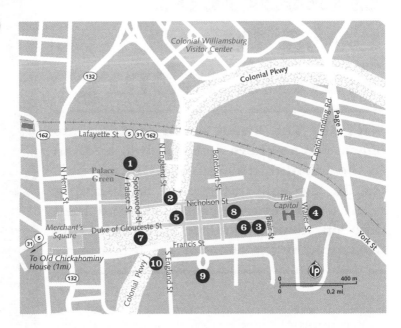

enviable tiered vegetable gardens. Here you can find members of the Food-ways Department preparing dishes for the main meal of the day, traditionally served around 2pm. Several courses will be on display, such as stuffed veal tongue, cabbage cakes and uniquely prepared fowl and beef. The hearths are hot and curators and visitors are likely to sweat from the heat.

The other main kitchen to visit is behind the ❷ **Peyton Randolph House**, the painstakingly restored and furnished home of the first president of the Continental Congress and one of colonial America's most powerful men. In this kitchen, with its complex spit in the massive fireplace, meals are prepared to reflect those of an upper-class family. It must be mentioned how fascinating the folks working behind the tables are. Throw them any question and they'll answer with a friendly authority. One kitchen worker, Barbara, has a wonderfully feisty attitude as she berates her foolish, modern visitors for their silly assumptions about what makes a good meal. She'll tell you more about the fish muddle stews available at taverns for the common man than you ever wanted to imagine – and if you're planning on lunch, you might be better off not knowing just what makes a muddle.

Sadly, due to our more modern health codes, the food they prepare cannot be sampled by visitors. This is not to say that it's inedible, just that they can't be held responsible for any funky rumblings in your stomach after tasting the colonial Jell-o. Among other special events you can attend is the hog slaughter and carving in December, if you're so inclined, or opt instead for chocolate making and beer brewing in the spring and fall.

Those looking to sample the delicacies of yore should make reservations at one of the historic taverns: **3** **Shields Tavern**, **4** **Christiana Campbell's Tavern**, **5** **Josiah Chowning's Tavern**, and **6** **King's Arm Tavern**. The

Carolina fish muddle is available at Christiana Campbell's for seafood lovers. Josiah Chowning's has Welsh rabbit and shepherd's pie. Brave souls can explore the colonial sampler platter at Shields. Meat and potato lovers will prefer the King's Arm Tavern. Listen to the minstrel while dining on Mrs Vobe's Chicken (recommended as fairly historically accurate by the

GARDEN MAZE ALERT

Behind the Governor's Palace is yet another chance to get lost in a **Hedge Maze** in Virginia. This time it's boxwood. Not nearly as difficult as the one in Luray, VA, the Williamsburg maze induces a desire to don wigs and corsets while you wickedly pursue eligible dukes or duchesses. Flirtatious fan waving recommended.

Foodways folk). Those with a hearty appetite will want to try the colonial game pye with venison, rabbit, duck, vegetables and bacon lardoons in a port wine sauce. Dilettantes may prefer the tavern sampler: duck confit pye, peanut soupe, crawfish cake, and biscuits and blueberry jelly.

Eager to take the food home with you, but scared of the queer dishes? Pick up some traditional wassail mix from **7** **Greenhow's Store** on Duke of Gloucester St and go a wassailing. This orange-flavored blend of spices comes with several options for preparation from mild to wild. Most hosts prefer to

make this holiday punch with sherry and apple brandy. Love and joy come to you! And a Merry Christmas, too!

Down the street, kitchenware and baked morsels, along with apple cider, are available at the **8** **Raleigh Tavern Bakery**. It is right behind the Raleigh Tavern proper, which hosted many meetings of colonists planning revolt.

DETOUR Outside of Williamsburg is the **Old Chickahominy House** (www.oldchickahominy.com), open for breakfast and lunch. Besides the delightful name, you will find fabulous traditional Southern fare. Ham and biscuits are a must. Try the Rebel Cocktail, a mix of beer and tomato juice. The place is often busy but you'll find plenty to amuse you in the gift shop while you wait.

Williamsburg is as chock-full of motels as New York coffee is chock-full of nuts. **9** **Williamsburg Inn** is where you'll want to take heads-of-state (Queen Elizabeth II has been in residence twice) or glamorous supermodels. Nearly as enticing is **10** **Williamsburg Lodge**. It's practically adjacent to the Inn, so you can easily make use of the Inn's facilities. Both are Rockefeller approved, and either place will be perfect for laying your weary stomach after a lengthy day of eating historically.

David Ozanich

TRIP INFORMATION

GETTING THERE
Williamsburg is less than an hour's drive from Richmond east on the I-64 to exit 238.

DO
Governor's Palace
The biggest house and main feature of Williamsburg. **Palace Green;** 9am-8pm, kitchen closed Wed;

Greenhow's Store
Kitchenware, ceramics and wassail mix. ☎ 757-229-1000; Duke of Gloucester St near Palace Green; 9:30am-6pm Sun-Thu, to 8pm Fri & Sat

Peyton Randolph House
Upper-class historic home with working kitchen. **Nicholson St at N England St;** 9am-8pm, closed Sun;

Raleigh Tavern Bakery
Kitchenware, cider and baked goods in historic tavern. ☎ 757-229-1000; Duke of Gloucester St near Capitol; 9:30am-6pm;

EAT
Christiana Campbell's Tavern
George Washington's favorite tavern. Seafood oriented. ☎ 757-229-2141; **Waller St at York St;** mains $17-28; 5-10pm;

Josiah Chowning's Tavern
Midday fare in relaxed setting. ☎ 757-229-2141; **Duke of Gloucester at Queen St;** mains $7-18; 11:30am-3pm

King's Arms Tavern
Genteel colonial chophouse with lots of meat pyes. ☎ 757-229-2141; **Duke of Gloucester near Capitol;** mains $20-30; 11:30am-2:30pm & 5-10pm;

Shield's Tavern
Comfort foods and no reservations necessary. ☎ 757-229-2141; **Duke of Gloucester near Capitol;** mains $8-15; 10am-5pm;

SLEEP
Williamsburg Inn
The most glamorous hotel in Williamsburg. ☎ 757-227-7978; 136 E Francis St; r $395-800

Williamsburg Lodge
A fine alternative to the Inn, with bars and restaurants. ☎ 757-227-7978; 310 N England St; r $189-450;

USEFUL WEBSITES
www.colonialwilliamsburg.com
www.visitwilliamsburg.com

SUGGESTED READS
- *The Art of Cookery Made Plain and Easy: Excelling Any Thing of the Kind Ever Yet Published*, Hannah Glasse
- *The Unreal America: Architecture and Illusion*, Ada Louise Huxtable

LINK YOUR TRIP
www.lonelyplanet.com/trip-planner

Richmond Rises from the Ashes

WHY GO Richmond was burned to the ground after the Civil War. Like a Southern phoenix, it has risen from those ashes to become Virginia's grandest city, home to many corporate giants. It's also home to plenty of exciting, urban activities that will satisfy the most hardcore hipsters and fun-seekers.

TIME
2 days

BEST TIME TO GO
Mar – Jun

START
Richmond

END
Richmond

ALSO GOOD FOR

Richmond is most famous for being Virginia's capital city (and the Confederacy's) and as such, it is steeped in historical sites and buildings. But let's get beyond the marble and columns on Monument Ave to find the modern city remaking its image for the 21st century. The downtown districts are gentrifying along with the rest of America's cities, and the results in Richmond are especially pleasing. The two primary areas in the central city where visitors will find the most interesting nonhistorical activities are located on either side of downtown proper.

The first area is the sister-act of ❶ **Shockoe Slip** and ❷ **Shockoe Bottom**. Just north of the James River and east of downtown, the Shockoe is packed full of restaurants, bars, and one of the luxurious hotels in town. The Bottom is to the east of the Slip. The streets are paved in cobblestones and huge, abstract public art is proudly displayed beneath freeway overpasses. Prepare to be delightfully surprised by what is surely some of the strangest, yet most forward-thinking, mixed-use urban planning on the East Coast. Pedestrian-friendly streets and tempting haunts hug freeway onramps and parking lots – somehow all the towering freeways make the area feel intimate. Great old architecture doesn't hurt either, like the burnt-sienna stone facade of Main St Station, which peeks out from behind the I-95.

One of Richmond's favorite after-work gathering spots is the ❸ **Tobacco Company**, This three-story bar and restaurant is in a

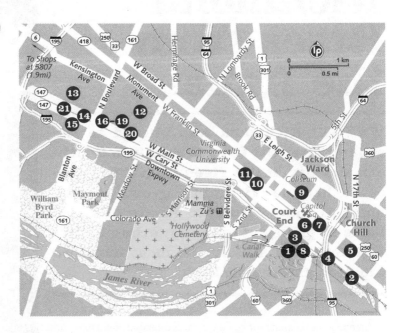

meticulously restored old factory with stained-glass lamps, an open-air elevator, and cigarette girls sashaying about the barroom. Located in the heart of the Slip on cobblestone East Cary St, the Tobacco Company should not be missed. However, the food is mainly standard tavern grub, so grab dinner somewhere else.

DETOUR The locals line up for **Mamma Zu's** (☎ 804-788-4205; 501 N Pine St), an excellent restaurant where the day's fare is hastily scribbled on a blackboard above the bar. You select your own wine from a rack near the bathrooms. It's low-key service in a dark, sultry room. Duck breast with polenta and white beans or the salmon filet make for a satisfying meal. Mamma Zu's is also famous for its tiramisu.

The most rousing place to eat in the Shockoe is incongruously located in the midst of several freeway overpasses and beside elevated train tracks. ❹ **Bottoms Up Pizza** offers the best pizza in Richmond, and probably the best in all of Virginia. Pies come with red or white sauce. Try the Chesapeake with fresh crab meat and sweet onions. Their 2nd-floor outdoor deck hosts local bands like Buttercup whose front woman is a sort of a painted-up Mary-Ann meets Loretta Lynn. And that is meant in only the very best sense. From your seat by the bar you can wave to the conductors of passing trains.

After dinner, try hitting nearby ❺ **Mars Bar** for drinking and dancing with a decidedly '80s vibe. Bust out your Running Man or Roger Rabbit and groove to the sounds of the Pet Shop Boys and Simple Minds.

Right in Shockoe Slip is ⑥ **Berkeley Hotel**, a wonderful boutique hotel. Turn-down service is just one of the many touches that make a stay here feel like you're vacationing in London or Paris. The rooms are big and spacious and have a very tasteful interior design. If you really want to stay in style, reserve the Governor's Suite, which has 30ft-high ceilings and striking views of the Slip and the James River beyond. Downstairs, you can eat at the ⑦ **Dining Room**, among the finest restaurants in Richmond. Dishes like crispy black sea bass on spicy collards are on the dinner menu, but the restaurant is also a perfect locale for breakfast or lunch. Enjoy a tart sidecar with your dinner companions while gossiping about the Richmond society in hushed tones.

After years of losing out to Charlottesville, DC, and Norfolk for great acts, new venues in Richmond have revived the music scene. ⑧ **Toad's Place**, in Shockoe Bottom on the Canal Walk, opened in spring 2007. Built in the old Lady Byrd Hat Factory, this is a state-of-the-art music hall drawing acts like Government Mule, Gogol Bordello, and The New Pornographers. The ⑨ **National** is the second club to have opened recently. Drive By Truckers, Disturbed, Built to Spill, Black Crowes, Amos Lee and others have added Richmond to their tour stops thanks to this 1500 person venue. It's nonsmoking (a rarity in Richmond), parking is easy, and bars abound inside.

DETOUR A little further west are the **Shops at 5807** (www.shops5807.com; 5807 Patterson Ave). A collective of smaller boutiques, 5807 is a bit like walking through the stalls of a summer crafts fair. Scores of vendors are represented with wares like ecofriendly toys and clothes, handmade pillows and great handbags and totes. Particularly enticing is **Openhouse** (www.openhouse-richmond.com) with its motto "seeing the art in the everyday" and a smorgasbord of progressive home furnishings and other delights.

Another place to stay with lots of appeal is the ⑩ **Linden Row Inn**. These renovated townhouses offer huge suites cut from the original parlors. Sofas ideal for swooning are placed just so at the foot of the king-size bed in these fine rooms. Their downtown location is right near the fanciest digs in Richmond, the ⑪ **Jefferson Hotel**. Stay here if you're getting married, getting divorced, or frankly, for any reason you can think of. You can also just wander in for a drink at their bar in the soaring rotunda or for a bite at one of their numerous restaurants and cafés. Fierce!

Across town, on the west side, are the uptown areas known as the ⑫ **Fan** and ⑬ **Carytown**. Both areas are littered with shops and restaurants and have a great communal village amtmosphere that's very urban. The streets swarm with fashionable moms pushing strollers during the day and college kids whooping it up at night. It almost feels like the hip, shop-lined Melrose in Los Angeles.

Along Cary St you'll find the West Coast–inspired **14 Glass and Powder Boardshop**. Skateboarders will enjoy perusing the selection, and those heading east to Virginia Beach can pick up some beachwear along with their board wax. Sad Lily Bart is nowhere to be seen in the rockingly fun **15 World of Mirth** toy store. Need some Elvis glasses? Water-squirting boutonnieres? Strange-looking bike/skateboard/scooter hybrids? They've got it all, plus precious, edgy baby clothes in this big storefront that's like a Christmas stocking stuffed with presents selected by museum curators. A hot shopping spot for sure.

Up on Main St in uptown you'll find **16 Black Swan Books**, which displays a loving and not at all musty dedication to rare books. First editions are up front, but the rows of shelves offer wonderful surprises. You won't need to wade through piles of musty paperbacks by Jackie Collins to find the treasures. Oversized editions of Sherwood Anderson's *Winesburg, Ohio* stand bewitchingly in the afternoon light next to books full of Audubon prints. Black Swan is one of those little finds that makes book-browsing such a fine pastime.

Near the Black Swan on Main St at Robinson are several restaurants clustered around a few cross-streets and often sitting kitty-corner from each other. Have an appetizer at one and dinner at another! First up is the retro-modern **17 Star-lite Diner**. It's as much of a lounge as a diner, with its long interior and high-backed booths, so feel free to just have drinks. Or order from their extensive menu of salads, subs and wraps. A bit sexier is **18 Avalon**, across the street. Intimate and salmon-pink on grey in both decor and mood, Avalon is veggie-friendly with tons of vegetable tapas like watermelon squares with balsamic reduction or asparagus and wild mushroom gratin. Fear not carnivores, for dishes like Asian short ribs and whiskey chicken breast are sure to satisfy as well. It's open until 2am daily so it's great for late-nighters.

> *"With appetizers like chicken fried frog legs, this restaurant came highly recommended by the local construction workers…"*

A more unique offering is the slightly ramshackle but very endearing **19 Helen's**, which has been slinging suppers since 1935. With appetizers like chicken fried frog legs and blue-crab spring rolls, this restaurant came highly recommended by the local construction workers – can you blame them? Bring your appetite and then some when you order Virginia ham-and-Gruyère-stuffed chicken for your entrée. Also popular with the locals is **20 Sticky Rice**, a hip red-and-black Asian (kind of) restaurant. Crowded with youngsters and lanterns, you can smoke by the bar and partake of the unusual menu that offers American mainstays like meat loaf along with sushi and other Asian delicacies. Definitely boisterous, this is a place to come if you like the hustle and bustle of happening eateries.

With a belly full of sticky rice, poke your head into ㉑ **Babe's in Carytown** for a sample of the gay and mostly lesbian scene at this dive bar. Madonna's latest single pulsates on the dance floor while a black-and-white poster of Bette Davis stares coolly at even cooler customers puffing on Marlboros. It's a bit clubby and cliquish, but what local favorite isn't?

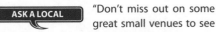

"Don't miss out on some great small venues to see the local music scene. **Alley Katz** and **Canal Club** in the Bottom are still serving up great tunes as well as **Cary Street Cafe** uptown for your hippie fix."

Andy and Katie Howlett, Richmond, VA

On your way back to the hotel, take a cab down Monument Ave. The statues of Civil War heroes are illuminated in the night as are the stately homes lining the grand avenue. Make special note of Arthur Ashe, a recent addition to the sculptural program, who stares in the opposite direction to Lee and Davis and their brethren. No doubt he is gazing at the bright future of Richmond as the South rises again.

David Ozanich

TRIP INFORMATION

GETTING THERE
Richmond is a two hours from DC on I-95.

DO

Black Swan Books
Classy bookstore with first editions, scarce and rare stock. ☎ 804-353-9476; www.blackswanbooks.com; 2601 W Main St; 🕐 11am-6pm Mon-Sat, 1-6pm Sun

Glass and Powder Boardshop
Straight-out-of-Venice-Beach boardshop and skateshop. ☎ 804-355-4441; www.glassandpowder.com; 2934 W Cary St; 🕐 10am-8pm Mon-Sat, noon-6pm Sun

National
New 1500-seat theater with some big acts. ☎ 612-1900; www.thenationalva.com; 708 E Broad St; 🕐 showtimes vary

Toad's Place
Music venue with the Highwater restaurant on the premises and fans in abundance. ☎ 804-648-8623; www.toadsplacerva.com; 140 Virginia St; 🕐 showtimes vary

World of Mirth
Totally the coolest toy store in town. ☎ 804-454-8996; 3005 W Cary St; 🕐 10am-7pm Mon-Sat, noon-6pm Sun

EAT & DRINK

Avalon
Bistro with veggie-friendly options. ☎ 804-353-9709; www.avalonrestaurant.com; 2619 W Main St; mains $16-25; 🕐 5pm-2am

Babe's in Carytown
Lesbian and gay dive/dance bar. ☎ 804-355-9330; 3166 W Cary St; 🕐 6pm-2am

Bottoms Up Pizza
Fun pizza joint with music acts on the deck. ☎ 804-644-4400; 1700 Dock St; mains $7-17; 🕐 from 11am; ♿

Dining Room
Top-notch restaurant at the refined Berkeley Hotel. ☎ 804-225-5105; www.berkeleyhotel.com; 1200 E Cary St; mains $16-30; 🕐 7am-2pm & 5:30-10pm Mon-Sat, 5-9pm Sun

Helen's
Richmond down-home institution. ☎ 804-358-4370; 2527 W Main St; mains $12-20; 🕐 5:30-9:30pm Sun-Mon, to 10:30pm Fri & Sat

Mars Bar
The all '80s restaurant and bar of your dreams. ☎ 804-644-6277; 115 N 18th St; 🕐 11am-2am Mon-Fri, 1pm-2am Sat & Sun

Star-lite Diner
Retro-modern diner and lounge. ☎ 804-254-2667; 2600 W Main St; mains $6-16; 🕐 11am-2am Mon-Fri, lunch Sat & Sun; ♿

Sticky Rice
Features home-style faves and Asian curiosities. ☎ 804-358-7870; 2232 W Main St; mains $5-25; 🕐 lunch Mon-Fri, dinner daily

Tobacco Company
Three-story restaurant and bar with cigarette-girls. ☎ 804-782-9255; www.thetobaccofactory.com; 1201 E Cary St; 🕐 5:30-10pm Sun-Thu, to 2am Thu-Sat

SLEEP

Berkeley Hotel
Refined elegance in the Shockoe Slip. ☎ 804-780-1300; www.berkeleyhotel.com; 1200 E Cary St; r $200-400

Jefferson Hotel
The best in town. ☎ 804-788-8000; 101 W Franklin St; www.jeffersonhotel.com; r $300-800

Linden Row Inn
Old townhouses converted into a charming hotel. ☎ 804-783-7000; www.lindenrowinn.com; 100 E Franklin St; r $100-300

USEFUL WEBSITES
www.visit.richmond.com

LINK YOUR TRIP

www.lonelyplanet.com/trip-planner

HISTORY &
CULTURE

Jefferson's Virginia

WHY GO Blah, blah, blah George Washington. Get inside the head of Virginia's other (and arguably greater) Revolutionary hero on this tour of Thomas Jefferson's homes and architecture in Charlottesville and beyond. He's got it! Yeah, baby, he's got it.

So you've got a thing for the main man, America's favorite colonial raconteur? The ultimate Renaissance man, Thomas Jefferson is responsible for creating America's soul, or at least paraphrasing it, in the Declaration of Independence. Respect must be paid to a man of such mighty influence, and as such, a trip to the Graceland of presidential homes is a must. Do not pass go, proceed directly to ❶ **Monticello**. Home of the illustrious third president of the United States, Monticello is also like Graceland in that it offers tours of just about everything, except that here it's plantations and slave quarters rather than planes and gold records.

The house tour is the main attraction, and rightfully so. It really is the best historical house tour of its sort because Jefferson, a noted architect, is such a cool cat. Each room is rife with his strange inventions and wacky, yet thoughtful, design sense. The guides are quite knowledgeable about his tastes, which will help inform your visits to other sites he designed (especially if you don't bother taking the official tours). The house is full of interesting period furniture, though some guides seem more adept at tactfully answering Sally Hemming questions than indicating which armoires are authentic and which are merely reproductions.

After exploring the house, you are set free to wander about the gardens, back houses, and subterranean features like the wine cellar. Hikers might be interested in the 60-minute Montalto tour that takes you

TIME
2 days

BEST TIME TO GO
**Apr – Jun,
Sep – Nov**

START
**Charlottes-
ville**

END
**Charlottes-
ville**

ALSO GOOD FOR

FOOD &
DRINK

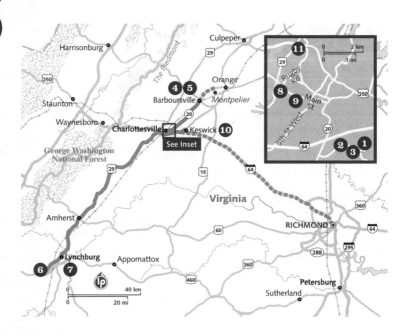

up the mountain for a view of the whole plantation. Another notable site is the still-private Jefferson family cemetery. If you're hungry but just can't bear to stop learning about the past, head down the road to the ❷ **Michie Tavern**. Serving up grub to travelers since the 1780s, the Tavern has costumed staff (a Virginia favorite!) and a bill of fare that includes the likes of "colonial" fried chicken and barbecue pork along with black-eyed peas and baby beets. You can also tour the museum for a taste of the times of yore and stop by the gift shop for all your home tavern needs.

If you drive the other way about a mile or two, you'll hit the ❸ **Jefferson Vineyards**. Jefferson gifted these acres to Italian winemaker Phillip Mazzei, who planted his first grape crop in 1774. Jefferson himself was a famous vintner in Virginia and drank copious amounts of his own wine as well as that of others. You can tour and taste at a modern winery that has set up shop on the site of Jefferson's original vineyards from well over 200 years ago. Come for the history, stay for the booze.

It's all Jefferson all the time on this trip, but that doesn't mean you can't live the high life, just like Mr Jefferson himself. Drive across the Piedmont toward Barboursville to spend the night at the ❹ **1804 Inn**. It sits right next to the ❺ **Barboursville Ruins**, the charred remains of the house Jefferson designed for Governor Barbour. The brick building was damaged by fire on Christmas in 1884, but the Historic Landmark is easily accessible and has such features as the octagonal parlor, which was a favorite of Jefferson's. The inn next door is in the house that replaced the original, though it has no connection to Jefferson per se. Decked out in antiques, this gracious inn with 11ft ceilings has room for only three couples at a time. It's white-glove service through and through. If you really want to get historical, stay in the secluded Vineyard Cottage, an 18th-century building with views of the vineyard and the distant Blue Ridge Mountains.

Had enough of historical homes? For shame! Our man Jefferson was not the type to have just one home, so pack up the babies and grab the old ladies and drive to **6 Poplar Forest**, a country estate for when this dreamer needed to get away from it all. Considering all his responsibilities, you can hardly begrudge him. Jefferson and his wife, Martha Wayles, inherited this land from her father in 1773. He lived here in 1781 for two months to evade the British, but didn't begin a consistent residence until after he had served his two terms in office in 1809. He started building the octagonal house in 1806.

Poplar Forest is a fine counterpoint to Monticello. It's dramatically less crowded due to its outlying location but is just as fascinating as its big brother. The Herculean efforts needed to undertake historic conservation are more on display here, since they don't have the fancy budgets or tourist popularity of Monticello or the University of Virginia. You feel like your admission fee is really going to help something worthy. Take time to explore the grounds under the shade of the majestic poplar trees that have been swaying over the estate since Jefferson's era.

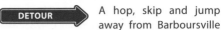

A hop, skip and jump away from Barboursville is **Montpelier** (www.montpelier.org), home to Jefferson chum and historical lion in his own right, James Madison and his wife, Dolly. This estate was bought and restored by the duPonts in 1901. They built two racetracks and started the annual Montpelier Hunt Races, which take place the first Saturday in November. Take a self-guided tour of the house, watch a video documentary about the Madisons and tour the formal garden and arboretum.

The downtown area of the nearby city of Lynchburg is a bit gritty, but the riverfront pocket at its center has some impressive sights, like the ornate hilltop City Hall, and a great spot for lunch, the **7 Depot Grille**. Right off the James River in a spacious old warehouse, this restaurant packs in the crowds. Steak and seafood, barbecued and otherwise, are the order of the day, along with salads and sides like apple sauce. It has a full bar for those needing a brewskie break from all the Jeffersonia.

Back in Charlottesville, you'll want to visit one of the premier Jeffersonian locations, the **8 University of Virginia**. The jewel of Virginia's collegiate crown (don't tell William & Mary), this bastion of southern preppiness will make you want to enroll and stay awhile. Jefferson's work can be seen in the design of the main quad (an idea he pioneered), known as the "academical village." The lovely brick student dorms and "hotels" (larger buildings where students and faculty communed to eat and converse) border the central lawn. The figurehead and focal point of this design is the central rotunda upon which much of the old campus centers. Originally completed in 1826, his original design burned down and was rebuilt in full 19th-century beaux-arts style from a plan by noted New York architect Stanford White. This design remained until 1973, when the building was restored to more accurately reflect Jefferson's original vision.

DETOUR About an hour east of Charlottesville is Richmond, where you can tour one of Jefferson's few public buildings, the **Virginia State Capitol** (www.virginiacapitol.org). Inspired by Roman temples, Jefferson worked on this project from France. Citizens scrambled to save the capitol during the infamous burning of Richmond in 1865. The cornerstone was laid in 1785 and the state congress has met here since 1788. The south portico's columns still encase the original pine-tree center posts.

Enough can't be said about how highly this Unesco World Heritage site campus is regarded. The college literature even boasts that "the American Institute of Architects recognized the Academical Village as the most significant achievement of American architecture in the past two hundred years." So, yeah. Take that in. Regular tours of the rotunda are offered by student guides. Alternatively, you can just pick up the self-guided tour and wander about by yourself, examining the rare books and peering into classrooms that are still in use. You can pay homage to the man himself at the base of his life-size statue in the upper entrance hall.

A cozy spot to play professor is in the **❾ Downtown Grille** on Charlottesville's pedestrian mall along Main St. This chophouse has a clubby, tweedy atmosphere that's very understated yet very upscale. You'll notice students on anniversary dates and UVA faculty members discoursing quietly at the corner tables. Sit in one of the big booths along the back wall and watch the chefs work in the open kitchen. They'll be happy to serve you up a rib eye, New York strip, filet or even cowboy cut with the bone in (vegetarians should keep walking – there's not much for you here). If you're not in a beef mood, try the live Maine lobster or the herb-crusted rack of lamb. Creamed spinach, onion crisps and asparagus with hollandaise sauce are among the many sides. The Grille is also a fine place to pop into for a glass of wine. Sit at the bar up front and look over their expansive wine list, which has a couple of particularly good and highly recommended wines from the Alexander Valley.

> *"You can pay homage to the man himself at the base of his life-size statue..."*

Barboursville might be too far of a drive after such a luxurious meal. You may want to check into one of the nearby resorts, like the exceedingly glam

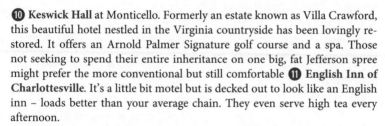 **Keswick Hall** at Monticello. Formerly an estate known as Villa Crawford, this beautiful hotel nestled in the Virginia countryside has been lovingly restored. It offers an Arnold Palmer Signature golf course and a spa. Those not seeking to spend their entire inheritance on one big, fat Jefferson spree might prefer the more conventional but still comfortable **English Inn of Charlottesville**. It's a little bit motel but is decked out to look like an English inn – loads better than your average chain. They even serve high tea every afternoon.

And what more perfect way is there than tea time to remind yourself of how nice it is to have thrown off the shackles of the British Crown? You've seen an awful lot of historical sites so you might want to just skip the tea, uncork some local wine and unwind while gazing at the lush countryside. Thomas Jefferson certainly would have approved.

David Ozanich

TRIP INFORMATION

GETTING THERE
Charlottesville is just over an hour's drive from Richmond, west on the I-64. Lynchburg and Poplar Forest are about an hour south of Charlottesville off Rte 29.

DO

Monticello
Jefferson's home and plantation, which serves as the major historic site of Charlottesville. ☎ 434-984-9822; www.monticello.org; 931 Thomas Jefferson Pkwy, Charlottesville; admission $15; ☺ 8am-5pm Mar-Oct, 9am-4:30pm Nov-Feb; ♿

Jefferson Vineyards
Taste wine from the terra firma Jefferson used on the site of his colonial vineyards. ☎ 434-977-3042; www.jeffersonvineyards.com; 1353 Thomas Jefferson Pkwy, Charlottesville; admission $5; ☺ 10am-6pm

Barboursville Ruins
Historic Landmark ruins of a house Jefferson designed for Governor Barbour. On the site of the Barboursville Vineyards. ☎ 540-832-3824; www.barboursvillewine.com; 17655 Winery Rd, Barboursville

Poplar Forest
Jefferson's country estate in Bedford County near Lynchburg. ☎ 434-525-1806; www.poplarforest.org; 1548 Bateman Bridge Rd (Rte 661), Forest; ☺ 10am-4pm Apr-Nov, closed Tue; ♿

University of Virginia
The Rotunda is the highlight of the Jefferson-designed UVA campus and a Unesco World Heritage site. ☎ 434-924-7969; www.virginia.edu; UVA campus off Main St at Rugby Rd, Charlottesville; ☺ guided tours 10am-4pm or by appointment

EAT

Depot Grille
Popular lunch spot in downtown Lynchburg next to the James River. ☎ 434-846-4464; www.depotgrille.com; 10 Ninth St, Lynchburg; mains $8-18; ☺ 11am-10pm Mon-Thu, to 11pm Fri & Sat, to 9pm Sun

Downtown Grille
Sedate, upscale watering hole and steak house on the Charlottesville downtown mall. ☎ 434-817-7080; www.downtowngrille.com; 201 W Main St, Charlottesville; mains $23-25; ☺ 5-10pm Mon-Thu, to 11pm Fri & Sat, to 9pm Sun

Michie Tavern
A colonial tavern dating from 1784 that serves Southern fare with a historical flourish. ☎ 434-977-1234; www.michietavern.com; 683 Thomas Jefferson Pkwy, Charlottesville; mains $15; ☺ 11:15am-3:30pm Apr-Oct, 11:30am-3pm Nov-Mar

SLEEP

1804 Inn
Very classy and intimate inn on the Barboursville Vineyards estate. ☎ 434-760-2212; www.the1804inn.com; 17655 Winery Rd, Barboursville; r $225-500

English Inn at Charlottesville
Whimsical inn with a heavy Tudor theme. ☎ 434-971-9900; www.englishinncharlottesville.com; 2000 Morton Dr, Charlottesville; r $80-200

Keswick Hall at Monticello
Even classier hotel resort with golf course and spa. ☎ 888-778-2565; www.keswick.com; 701 Club Dr, Keswick; r $395-800

USEFUL WEBSITES
www.monticello.org
www.virginia.ed

LINK YOUR TRIP
www.lonelyplanet.com/trip-planner

Wining & Dining in the Piedmont

WHY GO Virginians have been making American wine long before Northern Californians gained international prominence. Enjoy the region's proud tradition at some premier vineyards while pairing it with the cutting-edge restaurant fare on their thoroughly modern menus.

Virginia's stock and tourist trade is too often unusual meat pyes and other "historic fare" served by women in wench costumes. Not to say this food doesn't have its place, but there is a 21st-century lifestyle in Virginia and it's nowhere more evident than in the kitchens of the Piedmont. Added to this are some highly regarded wineries with vintages fit for the king or queen in everyone.

Like Alexandria, ❶ **Charlottesville** is at the forefront of the state's culinary scene. The mix of college kids and their urbane professors provides a natural audience for an adventurous kitchen. A quaint two-story house just a few blocks off Main St, near the Historic Downtown Mall, is home to ❷ **Bang**. The menu items are a pan-Asian reimagining of dim sum. Classics like pot-stickers and tempura rolls are available along with more unique offerings such as a tasty bacon sushi concoction. Bang has a pretty hip bar for sidling up to and a spacious patio with outdoor seating. Don't miss the black cherry cosmo, which is sweet and packs a mean punch.

Oenophiles with an aversion to cosmos and cocktails will enjoy the expansive ❸ **Siips** wine and champagne bar on Main St, where dozens upon dozens of wines are available by the glass. The service is a little slow, but what's the rush when you're relaxing with a throaty Côte du Rhône or a sweet ice wine? Surprisingly, the selection is a little light on local growers, but it's a good way to compare the regional qualities of French wines. If you stumble upon something you really like, you can buy a bottle from the Siips wine store to take home.

TIME
2 days

DISTANCE
90 miles

BEST TIME TO GO
Apr – Jun, Aug – Nov

START
Charlottes-ville

END
Middleburg

ALSO GOOD FOR

OUTDOORS

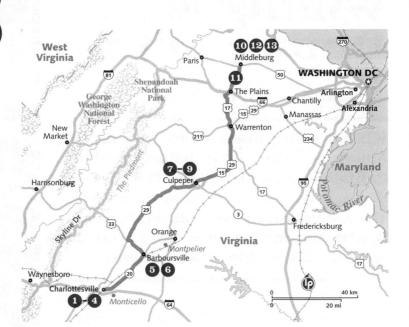

Those with sated stomachs can spend the night at the ④ **Boar's Head Inn**. Built around a reconstructed 1830s gristmill, the Boar's Head sits on massive acreage just outside Charlottesville and has a sports facility, three swimming pools, and a day spa. You can stay in the main building in one of the precious rooms with a historical flair, or retreat to the more modern and spacious rooms in the outlying complexes. Run by the University of Virginia, the inn offers top-notch service – they'll have your newspaper of choice delivered with your breakfast in the morning. And their marquee restaurant, The Old Mill Room, has phenomenal lobster bisque.

About 20 minutes northeast of Charlottesville are the ⑤ **Barboursville Vineyards**. Founded in 1976 by an Italian wine family, the vineyards are off a bucolic highway in farm country, on the site of the historic Barboursville Ruins. The grass creeps up the burned façade of the governor's 18th-century home while grapes glisten in nearby fields. A particular favorite is the Phileo dessert wine, sort of a Moscato, which is available at the impeccable Inn at Little Washington, the region's premiere restaurant.

Part of the Barboursville Vineyards complex is the popular and impressive ⑥ **Palladio** restaurant, where the food is in the tradition of northern Italy. Lunch is a good time to visit since the midday menu is just as interesting as the evening one. The antipasti selections include an heirloom tomato and basil tart with homemade mozzarella. Ravioli of fresh ricotta, peas and lemon zest makes a choice first plate. Rich, thoughtfully prepared second courses include sea scallops with caviar over a cauliflower puree. Naturally, the staff is more than happy to suggest pairings with the house vintages.

Further north on Rte 29 is another vineyard of note: **❼ Prince Michel**. This one gets points for being exceedingly easy to find since it's right off the main road. With the Blue Ridge rising up behind it, the vineyard sits like the king-of-the-foothill overlooking the rolling plains of the Piedmont. These wines have been featured on many a classy menu, such as the Washington "Dinner with Julia Child" event. Their Symbius is an appealing blend of Bordeaux varietals, but even the very affordable cabernet sauvignon is worth taking with you.

If you're looking for an afternoon pick-me-up that doesn't require napping beneath grapevines, check out the **❽ Raven's Nest Coffee House** in Culpeper. This frontier town is home to a couple of unusually groovy outposts. With its hip vibe and high-quality selection, the Raven's Nest would seem a more natural fit for Seattle or San Francisco than tiny farm-centered Culpeper.

> **ASK A LOCAL**
>
> "The busy **Mas Tapas Bar** (☎ 434-979-0990; www .mastapas.com) in the sleepy neighborhood of Belmont runs a wait for tables almost every night and is definitely worth it. Everything on the menu is perfectly prepared and delicious. Stand-out favorites are the grilled lamb-chops, bacon-wrapped dates, potatoes bravos, and the large grilled shrimp. Mas features sangrias and lots of other drinks – I love the blood-orange margaritas. The tapas-sized portions will feed two to three people nicely."
>
> *Janet King, Charlottesville, VA*

Opposite the Raven's Nest, in the heart of Culpeper's Old Town, is one of the best restaurants in Virginia. Discovering **❾ Foti's Restaurant** is like finding El Dorado – you won't believe your good fortune. The owners, chef Frank Maragos and his wife, Sue, worked at the Inn at Little Washington, which sets the local standard for excellence. But they have created a much more accessible restaurant, serving four-course meals with a focus on local produce at prices that won't break the bank. A spectacular main course is barbecue-glazed grilled skirt steak. Succulent Long Island duck breast and prosciutto-wrapped duck confit over lemon-roasted potatoes with a blackberry chardonnay sauce is as elegant a meal as you will find anywhere in the Northeast corridor. The decor is mellow yet refined, the service attentive, and a piano player's tickling of the ivories evokes the ambience of a supper club. Their strawberry bellini is tart and sweet – the finest champagne cocktail in the Piedmont.

Further north on the grape trail is another town full of restaurants and wine cellars. Middleburg's country mystique will win over even the most charm-averse visitor. A good place to bed down for the night is the **❿ Middleburg**

Country Inn. This European-style hotel is in an 1820 three-story brick house and has several large, comfortable rooms, some with Jacuzzis. Though it has certain welcome B&B qualities, like the inviting breakfast of eggs Benedict and waffles served in the dining room, the Country Inn still offers a private, hotel-like feel.

"...a beautiful estate with sprawling vineyards cascading down the hillside like so many Chinese silks."

Just a couple miles south of Middleburg, the popular ⑪ **Piedmont Vineyards and Winery** is a beautiful estate with sprawling vineyards cascading down the hillside like so many Chinese silks. They have several types of chardonnays as well as some intriguing fruit wines like their Little River Peach and Little River Red (made from raspberries and plums).

Sometimes wineries get a bit tiresome, what with their sales pitches and groups of tour-bus riders. If you want all of the wine and none of the brine, try the ⑫ **Tasting Room,** home to the Boxwood Winery. Rather ingeniously they've taken their store and plopped it right in the middle of town where it's much more convenient for the traveling taster. Boxwood is a relatively new winery specializing in fine wines grown with grapes from Bordeaux. Though set inside a small cottage, the Tasting Room remains very modern thanks to plenty of stainless steel and high barstools that give it a cosmopolitan sheen. As a bonus, they don't just sell their own vintages so if your palette needs a quick trip to France they're happy to oblige with a selection of French wines.

Since all things wining and dining ultimately come round to the French in one way or another, you'd best wrap your day up with a trip to the ⑬ **French Hound**, Middleburg's Frenchiest restaurant. The menu is classical – escargot, boeuf bourguignon, with profiteroles and beignets for dessert. The chef's impressive résumé includes work at Thomas Keller's top-notch Bouchon. With warm yellow walls and welcoming fireside bar, it's a very enjoyable château-cum-bistro and perfect for Francophiles who enjoy traditional cuisine.

End the evening with a nightcap, perhaps the Barboursville Phileo that you left chilling back at the Country Inn. Sit on the deck outside your room, staring out past the garden towards the drooping, fat Virginia moon. Discuss the dream kitchen you'll install in that gorgeous country manse you'll buy when you leave it all behind to come out here and ply the wine trade.

David Ozanich

TRIP INFORMATION

GETTING THERE
The I-64 east takes you to Charlottesville from Richmond. Rte 29 takes you north to Culpeper.

DO
Barboursville Vineyards
A top-notch winery and inn with a sterling reputation and a very welcoming complex conveniently located next to historical ruins. ☎ 540-832-3824; www.barboursvillewine .com; junction of Rte 20 and Rte 678, Barboursville; ⊙ 10am-5pm Mon-Sat, 11am-5pm Sun

Piedmont Vineyards and Winery
A popular, pretty estate just a few miles south of Middleburg. Picnickers welcome. A staple of any Virginia wine tour. ☎ 540-687-5528; www.piedmontwines.com; 2546-D Halfway Rd off Rte 626, The Plains; ⊙ 11am-5pm Sat, Sun & Mon holidays, by appointment weekdays

Prince Michel
An easy-to-find vineyard with tasty, democratic vintages that aren't overly persnickety or pricey. ☎ 800-800-WINE; www.prince michel.com; 154 Winery Lane (visible off Rte 29), Leon; ⊙ 10am-6pm daily, to 5pm Mon-Fri in winter

EAT
Bang
A hip restaurant with patio seating that features Asian tapas along with a good, sometimes happening, cocktail bar. Good for large groups. ☎ 434-984-2264; 213 Second St SW, Charlottesville; mains $8-15; ⊙ 5pm-midnight Mon-Sat

Foti's Restaurant
A wonderful, not-to-be-missed, romantic eatery hidden away in Old Town Culpeper. Best food in the Piedmont, hands down. ☎ 540-829-8400; www.fotisrestaurant .com; 219 E Davis St, Culpeper; mains $16-22; ⊙ 11:30am-2pm & 5:30-9:30pm Tue-Fri (closed Wed dinner), 5-9:30pm Sat, noon-8pm Sun

French Hound
A traditional high French restaurant in a lovely Middleburg château. Name-checked by locals as their favorite place. ☎ 540-687-3018; www.thefrenchhound.com; 101 Madison, Middleburg; mains $18-30; ⊙ 5:30-10:30pm Tue-Thu, 11:30am-11pm Fri & Sat

Palladio
An upscale restaurant with Northern Italian fare at the Barboursville Vineyards. Jackets are required for dinner and recommended for lunch. Reservations recommended. ☎ 540-832-7848; www.barboursvillewine.com; junction of Rte 20 & Rte 678, Barboursville; mains $20-30; ⊙ noon-2:30pm Wed-Sun, 6:30-9:30pm Fri & Sat

DRINK
Raven's Nest Coffee House
A surprisingly groovy metropolitan coffeehouse that serves a mean brew in rural Culpeper. A perfect antidote for too much wine! ☎ 540-827-4185; 254 East Davis St, Culpeper; ⊙ 7:30am-5pm Mon-Sat, 9:30am-4pm Sun

Siips
A downtown wine and champagne bar on the Main St pedestrian mall in Charlottesville, with an extensive list of international wines available by the glass as well as for purchase. Open late. ☎ 434-872-0056; www.siips wine.com; 212 East Main St, Charlottesville; ⊙ 11:30am-2am

Tasting Room
A very modern wine-bar inside a cottage on Middleburg's main drag that also serves at the tasting room for Boxwood Vineyards. Offers a large French wine selection. ☎ 540-687-8080; www.boxwoodwinery.com; 16 Washington St, Middleburg; ⊙ 1-9pm Thu-Sun

SLEEP
Boar's Head Inn
A huge resort complex run by the University of Virginia. Has hundreds of rooms in every shape and size, some with patios perfect for star-gazing. ☎ 434-296-2181; www.boars headinn.com; 200 Ednam Dr, Charlottesville; r $139-500; ♿

Middleburg Country Inn

A friendly inn in the heart of Middleburg, offering privacy for travelers who are B&B averse. ☎ 540-687-6082; www.middle burgcountryinn.com; 209 E Washington St, Middleburg; r $150-250

USEFUL WEBSITES

www.middleburgonline.com
www.monticello.org

SUGGESTED READS

• *Culinary Secrets of Great Virginia Chefs: Elegant Dining from Colonial Williamsburg to Historic Richmond*, Martha Hollis Robinson (ed)

• *Patrick O'Connell's Guide to Refined Cuisine: The Inn at Little Washington*, Patrick O'Connell & Tim Turner

• *From Vines to Wines*, Jeff Cox

LINK YOUR TRIP
www.lonelyplanet.com/trip-planner

The Crooked Road: Heritage Music Trail

WHY GO Got the Mule Skinner Blues? Then grab your fiddle and hightail it to western Virginia for a toe tappin', knee slappin' good time at the historic country, bluegrass and "old time" music venues that speckle the landscape between the Blue Ridge and Appalachian mountain ranges.

TIME
2 – 3 days

DISTANCE
145 miles

BEST TIME TO GO
May – Oct

START
Floyd

END
Hiltons

ALSO GOOD FOR

HISTORY &
CULTURE

Down in Appalachia, where Kentucky meets Tennessee meets Virginia, you'll discover a veritable hotbed of country music history. It's here that such legends as the Carter Family began their musical careers. Virginia has done half the work for you, designating a route called the Crooked Road that carves a winding path through the Blue Ridge Mountains and into the Appalachians.

There are a lot of options for where to begin your journey. A good choice is the teeny, tiny town of ❶ **Floyd**. This town is a rather surprising blend of rural conservatives mixed with slightly New Age artisans and coffee lovers. Grab a double espresso from an artsy coffeehouse and then head round the corner to peruse the farm tools on sale in the hardware store.

The musical highlight of this curious town is the jamboree at the ❷ **Floyd Country Store**. Every Friday night, this little store in a clapboard building clears out most of its inventory and lines up rows of chairs around a dance floor. Around 6:30pm the first musicians on the bill start playin' their hearts out on the stage. Pretty soon the room's filled up with locals and visitors hootin' and hollerin' along with the fiddles and banjos. While you listen, you can browse through their extensive selection of music, some of which have endearingly wacky cover portraits. Make your way through the crowd to the deli side of the room and order some ice cream or maybe a root beer float to go with that bag of penny candy from the barrels up front.

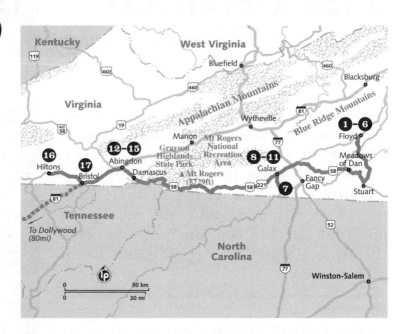

Half the fun of the Friday nights in Floyd is that the music spills out onto the streets. Several jam bands (for want of a better word) twiddle their fiddles in little groups up and down the main road. The listeners cluster round their favorite bands, parking themselves in lawn chairs right on the sidewalk or along the curb. Motorists passing through usually stare at the scene in bewilderment. There's really nothing else like it.

 To get in the old-time music mood, try these on for size:

- "In the Jailhouse Now," Jimmie Rodgers
- "East Virginia Blues," Ralph Stanley & The Clinch Mountain Boys
- "Turkey in the Straw," Dock Boggs
- "Mule Skinner Blues," Dolly Parton
- "Hey, Good Lookin'," Tennessee Ernie Ford
- "Keep on the Sunny Side," Carter Family
- "My Clinch Mountain Home," Carter Family
- "Blue Eyes Crying in the Rain," Willie Nelson

There's also nothing like the hottest fried chicken joint in all of Virginia, which is just a few miles down the highway from the central intersection of Floyd. One taste of the buttermilk biscuits slathered with butter and strawberry jam at the all-you-can-eat **3** **Pine Tavern Restaurant** and your mouth won't stop salivating for the fried chicken and country ham to come. Of course, they also pile on the dumplings, pinto beans, green beans, and mashed potatoes. It's capped by either a fresh fruit or chocolate cobbler. The price for all this? Less than a 12-pack of Bud Light. The restaurant, tucked away between towering pine trees, has been in business since 1927 but new owners have brought their own grandmother's delicious recipes to better serve the traditional Blue Ridge Mountain cuisine. Not to be missed, but prepare to be rolled out at the end.

Floyd has a couple of good options for overnighters. The ❹ **Oak Haven Lodge** is in a fairly new building with big decks and comfortable beds. Some rooms even have a Jacuzzi. Another choice is the aptly named ❺ **Hotel Floyd**, which is also brand new and advertises an "eco-friendly" ethos. Flat-screen TVs with satellite hookups make it easy being green.

In the morning, stop into the old two-story cedar building that houses ❻ **noteBooks and Black Water Loft**. This combination book, art, and music store has a Haight Ashbury–style coffeehouse on the 2nd floor. Browse books by local artists or relax with a vanilla latte on one of the fraying couches as sun streams through the windows.

Once you're on the road again, you'll want to head south toward Hwy 58, which makes up a large portion of the Crooked Road. These roads take you past real working farms, some of which have quite the hardscrabble aesthetic – very different from the estate farms and stables of northern

DOWN TO EARTH EATS

Those who prefer their food organic or their clothes tie-dyed will be pleased with the earthy offerings at **Oddfella's Cantina** (www.oddfellascantina.com; 110 N Locust St, Floyd). Here you'll find a contemporary menu that's more coastal and organic in its influences. Sip wine while you listen to a local musician strumming away on the small stage under twinkling white lights.

Virginia and much of the Shenandoah Valley. When you get to the Blue Ridge Parkway, head south to the ❼ **Blue Ridge Music Center**. This large, grassy outdoor amphitheater offers programming that focuses on local musicians carrying on the traditions of Appalachian music. Performances are mostly on weekends and occasionally during the week. Bring a lawn chair and sit yourself down for an afternoon or evening performance. At night you can watch the fireflies glimmer in the darkness.

Further west is the town of ❽ **Galax,** which is one of the biggest towns and main attractions along the route. In their historic downtown, look for the bright neon marquee of the ❾ **Rex Theater**. This is a big old place, recently restored, with a Friday night show called Blue Ridge Backroads. Even if you can't make it to the theater at 8pm, you can listen to the two-hour show that broadcasts live to the surrounding counties on 89.1 FM.

Galax hosts the Smoke on the Mountain Barbecue Championship (www.smokeonthemountainva.com) on the second weekend in July. Teams from all over crowd the streets of downtown with their tricked-out mobile BBQ units. Judges walk around with signs that read "Silence please. Judging in progress." Booths and games line the streets and live music entertains the crowd. If you aren't lucky enough to be in town for the festival, you can still stop by one of its hosts, the ❿ **Galax Smokehouse**. This popular restaurant has loads of fans and was even called "Best of the Best" by the NBBQN. What's that, you ask? Well, it's the *National Barbecue News*. Did you let your subscription run out? The interior is classic diner/family restaurant and the staff is chipper. No one's puttin' on airs here.

If you think you've got what it takes to play with the boys in the Rex, poke your head into ⓫ **Barr's Fiddle Shop**. This little music shop has got a big selection of homemade and vintage fiddles and banjos along with mandolins, autoharps, and harmonicas. You can get a lesson if you have time to hang around, or just admire the fine instruments which hang all over the walls.

If you ease on down the Crooked Road a little further, you'll come to the gorgeous town of ⓬ **Abingdon**. There, like a watery mirage in the desert, is the best hotel for hundreds of miles in any direction. The ⓭ **Martha Washington Inn** is in a regal, gigantic brick mansion built for General Francis Preston in 1832. Pulling up to this country palace after a long day's drive is like arriving at heaven's gates. You can almost hear the angels sing as you climb the stairs to the huge porch with views framed by columns. The rooms are fabulously appointed and have the most comfortable, impossible-to-leave beds in Virginia.

FIDDLE-DEE-DEE

Every second weekend in August for the last 70-some years, Galax has hosted the **Old Fiddler's Convention** (www.oldfiddlersconvention.com), which now lasts for six days. Hosted by the local Loyal Order of the Moose Lodge, musicians come from all over to compete as well as to play. There's also clog dancing!

The Martha Washington is a full-service resort. Have afternoon tea. Book a massage and a facial in their spa. Relax garden-side in their Jacuzzi the size of a pool. Have a Scotch in the President's Club. Read a back issue of the *New Yorker* in their tony library adorned with a wood-inlay globe and an Algonquin Round Table painting above the mantle. And when you're hungry, slip downstairs to the Dining Room for a sumptuous dinner.

If you can possibly pull yourself away from the Martha, Abingdon has several worthwhile activities. The ⓮ **Barter Theatre**, across the street, is the big man on Main St in its historic red-brick building. This regional theater company puts on its own productions of brand-name plays that run in repertory, and include choices such as *Evita* or *The Who's Tommy*.

Just outside of town is a relic from a more recent age, the ⓯ **MoonLite Drive-In**. Bring some beers or grab a Coke from the concession stand and settle in for a double feature picture show. Smoke cigarettes with the cool kids in their pickup.

Another star attraction on the Crooked Road is about 30 miles from Abingdon in the microscopic town of Hiltons. Here at Clinch Mountain is where you'll find the ⑯ **Carter Family Fold**, which has music every Saturday night. It is overseen by Janette Carter, the youngest daughter of AP and Sara Carter, who, along with sister-in-law Maybelle, formed the core Carter group. (June Carter Cash was Maybelle's daughter.) The music starts at 7:30pm in the big wooden music hall. In the summer there is outdoor seating, too. The hall has replaced the original locale, AP's store, which now houses a museum dedicated to Carter Family history. Also: amateur clog dancing. Be afraid. Be very afraid.

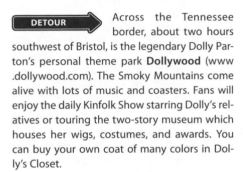

Across the Tennessee border, about two hours southwest of Bristol, is the legendary Dolly Parton's personal theme park **Dollywood** (www .dollywood.com). The Smoky Mountains come alive with lots of music and coasters. Fans will enjoy the daily Kinfolk Show starring Dolly's relatives or touring the two-story museum which houses her wigs, costumes, and awards. You can buy your own coat of many colors in Dolly's Closet.

When you wake up at the Martha, you'll want to take advantage of the very dapper breakfast (included in the price) of waffles, pancakes and omelets made to order in the dining room. Bonus points if you dare to wear your cuddly robe downstairs. In nearby Bristol you can attend the ⑰ **Bristol Motor Speedway**, which runs lots of NASCAR events. If they're not racing, you can still tour the "world's fastest half-mile" and check out the "The Bristol Experience" in the adjacent museum. Oooh.

Ready to head back home? Pop in one of the CDs you picked up along the way and thrill to old-time music one last time as you ease back to modern life, keeping the wistful memories of banjos and bluegrass tucked safely inside your heart so nobody don't break it again.
David Ozanich

TRIP INFORMATION

GETTING THERE
From Richmond, take the I-64 west to the I-81 and head south to the exit for Floyd.

DO

Barr's Fiddle Shop
Real-as-it-gets country music instrument store. ☎ 276-236-2411; www.barrsfiddle shop.com; 105 N Main St, Galax; ☺ 9am-5pm

Barter Theatre
Impressive regional theater in Abingdon. ☎ 276-628-3991; www.bartertheatre.com; 127 W Main St, Abingdon; ☺ showtimes vary, mostly evenings

Blue Ridge Music Center
Outdoor amphitheater on the BR Parkway. ☎ 276-236-5310; www.blueridgemusic center.net; Milepost 213 Blue Ridge Pkwy, Galax; ☺ weekend shows

Bristol Motor Speedway
NASCAR racetrack on the Virginia–Tennessee border. ☎ 423-989-6933; www.bristol motorspeedway.com; 151 Speedway Blvd, Bristol; ☺ showtimes vary

Carter Family Fold
Old-time music at the old Carter Family digs. ☎ 276-386-6054; www.carterfamilyfold .org; 3 miles NE of 709/614 junction on 614, Hiltons; admission $5; ☺ 7:30-11pm Sat, museum from 6pm

Floyd Country Store
Home of the Friday Night Jamboree. ☎ 540-745-6649; www.floydcountrystore.com; 206 N Locust St, Floyd; admission $3; ☺ store 10:30am-5:30pm Tue-Sun, jamboree 7:30pm Fri

Moonlite Drive-In
This fabulous vintage drive-in theater shows new releases. ☎ 276-628-7881; 17555 Lee Hwy, Abingdon; ☺ double feature from 9pm

noteBooks and Black Water Loft
Artsy bookstore with coffeehouse upstairs. ☎ 540-745-3060; www.notebooksandthe loft.com; 117 N Locust St, Floyd; ☺ 8am-6pm, to 8pm Fri & Sat

Rex Theater
Broadcasts the Friday night live bluegrass radio show in historic theater. ☎ 276-236-5309; www.rextheatergalax.com; 113 E Grayson St, Galax; ☺ 8pm-10pm Fri

EAT

Galax Smokehouse
Great barbecue restaurant in the heart of downtown Galax. ☎ 276-236-1000; www .thegalaxsmokehouse.com; 101 W Main St, Galax; mains $6-15; ☺ 11am-9pm Mon-Sat, to 3pm Sun

Pine Tavern Restaurant
Awesomely good fried chicken and traditional mountain cuisine. Go! ☎ 540-745-4482; www.thepinetavern.com; 611 Floyd Hwy N, Floyd; mains $7-12; ☺ 4:30-9:30pm Thu-Sat, 11am-8pm Sun

SLEEP

Hotel Floyd
Green motel in downtown Floyd. ☎ 540-745-6080; www.hotelfloyd.com; 120 Wilson St, Floyd; r $90-150

Martha Washington Inn
Super glamorous hotel in a huge 1832 mansion estate. ☎ 276-628-8885; www .marthawashingtoninn.com; 150 W Main St, Abingdon; r $150-500

Oak Haven Lodge
Comfortable lodge just a few minutes outside downtown Floyd. ☎ 540-745-5716; www .oakhavenlodge.com; 323 Webb's Mill Rd, Floyd; r $65-90

LINK YOUR TRIP

www.lonelyplanet.com/trip-planner

Day Trips from Richmond

Eastern Virginia, along the Chesapeake and James River, has tons of interesting sites and activities for the curious traveler. From epic roller coasters to populist Frank Lloyd Wright architecture, Virginia has many surprises.

FRANK LLOYD WRIGHT'S POPE-LEIGHEY HOUSE

Right near Mount Vernon you will find Pope-Leighey House (www.pope-leighey1940.org), designed by Frank Lloyd Wright. One of his Usonian designs, this tiny yet fascinating house was moved to the Woodlawn Plantation from its original location in Falls Church, VA, in 1964 to protect it from demolition. The comprehensive tours of the simple home run every half-hour. As an added bonus you can wander around Woodlawn's formal gardens or tour the manor, which was a wedding gift to Martha Washington's granddaughter. On your way home, you can stop in Old Town Alexandria for fried Mars bars and fish and chips at Eamonn's Dublin Chipper (www.eamonnsdublinchipper.com). Walk off the calories while you peruse the local shops nestled in centuries-old townhouses. **From Richmond take the I-95 north towards Washington DC and follow the signs to Alexandria and Mount Vernon. Woodlawn is 3 miles past the Mount Vernon estate.**

See also **TRIP 44**

BUSCH GARDENS EUROPE

The 17-years running winner of the award for "Most Beautiful Amusement Park," Busch Gardens (www.buschgardens.com), is not anything like your average Six Flags. Among the greatest beer gardens in the world, Busch Gardens is divided into areas with European country themes. With exchange rates what they are, it's a comparative bargain to visit several countries in the course of an afternoon. Escape from Pompeii in Italy. Ride the Le Scoot log flume in France. Check out the year-round Oktoberfest in Germany. Several roller coasters are real whoppers, like the Alpengeist, which has an inverted loop. When you're tired of lines, relax and drink Budweiser in England or Ireland or ride high above the park in the sky gondolas. They also have a Cirque du Soleil-esque acrobatics show among many others like Animal Shenanigans. **From Richmond take the I-64 east to Williamsburg and exit 242. You won't be able to miss the signs pointing you in the right direction.**

See also **TRIPS 45 & 46**

BERKELEY PLANTATION

Built in 1726 and overlooking the James River, Berkeley Plantation (www .berkeleyplantation.com) was also the site of the first Thanksgiving in 1619. What about the pilgrims? Well, that's for historians to argue. In the meantime, you can explore the brick mansion at the center of the plantation, the home of several important colonial and early-American figures. Benjamin Harrison, the owner, was a signer of the Declaration of Independence. His son, William Henry, was born at Berkeley and became the "Indian fighter" known as "Tippecanoe." He later became the ninth US president. His grandson Benjamin Harrison was the 23rd president of the United States. You can wander about the immaculately restored home crammed with 18th-century antiques and explore the formal terraced boxwood gardens and lawns that extend from the front door to the riverbank. **From Richmond take the I-64 east to exit 211 and head south on Rte 106.**

See also **TRIPS 46 & 47**

CHRYSLER MUSEUM OF ART

Norfolk isn't just a big Navy town. The stunning white palazzo that sits on the Hague Inlet of the Elizabeth River and houses the Chrysler Museum of Art (www.chrysler.org) only hints at the treasures inside. A highlight of the museum is its extensive collection of glass works by Louis Comfort Tiffany and others. They also have extensive collections of African, Asian and Islamic art along with contemporary works by artists such as Roy Lichtenstein. Slip into the Cuisine & Company restaurant for a light lunch of salads and sandwiches. Truly exquisite, the Chrysler is definitely one of the finest museums in Virginia. Nearby you can visit their historic Moses Meyer House, home of Norfolk's first Jew! **From Richmond take the I-64 east to Norfolk.**

See also **TRIP 45**

David Ozanich

Behind the Scenes

THIS BOOK

This guidebook was commissioned in Lonely Planet's Oakland office, and produced by the following:
Product Development Manager Heather Dickson
Commissioning Editor Jennye Garibaldi
Coordinating Editor Laura Crawford
Coordinating Cartographer Corey Hutchison
Coordinating Layout Designer Jacqui Saunders
Managing Editor Sasha Baskett
Managing Cartographer Alison Lyall
Managing Layout Designer Celia Wood
Assisting Editors Carolyn Boicos, Daniel Corbett, Adrienne Costanzo, Carly Hall, Anne Mulvaney
Assisting Cartographers Alissa Baker, Carol Jackson, Sam Sayer
Assisting Layout Designer Wibowo Rusli
Series Designer James Hardy
Cover Designers Gerilyn Attebery, Jennifer Mullins
Project Managers Chris Girdler, Craig Kilburn
Thanks to Jessica Boland, Jay Cooke, Catherine Craddock, Owen Eszeki, Suki Gear, Mark Germanchis, Michelle Glynn, Brice Gosnell, Liz Heynes, Lauren Hunt, Laura Jane, Ali Lemer, John Mazzocchi, Darren O'Connell, Paul Piaia, Julie Sheridan, Glenn van der Knijff

THANKS

Jeff Campbell Jeff has many people to thank: the Quinones clan, Mark Nigara, Daryl Stone, Steve Politi, Sheri & Kip Waide, Carolyn & Lisa, Jen Dickman, Amy Jablon, Terri Scelfo, Jen & Chris, Fred Schmitt, Debbie Taylor. You guys kept me real. Jennye, Adam, David, Ginger: *you guys* rock! Finally, DQ, I owe you big time.

Adam Karlin Thank you: mom and dad for raising me here; my friends, particularly Jessie, Matt, the Brewingthews, the Froveys and the Mussenmeyers, for always making it feel like home; the hometown newspapers that taught me to write and everyone on Bauer Road who helped me love the tidewater.

Ginger Adams Otis Ginger would like to thank her editors Jennye, Heather and Suki for their infinite patience, Brice for chiming in and offering encouragement, and her fellow mid-Atlantic authors, who never seemed to lose focus or get frazzled.

David Ozanich David would especially like to thank Jennye Garibaldi, Buck Drummond, Nate Harris and Chris Tuttle. Research was made immeasurably easier thanks to the input of Scott and June Drummond, Terry and Jerry Bullard, Kate and Andy Howlett, Robin Gibbin, Jim Bradley, Liz Ureneck, Beth Foy and Janet King.

ACKNOWLEDGMENTS

Many thanks to the following for the use of their content:

Internal photographs p8 (bottom) Jim West/Alamy; p14 (bottom) Bora/Alamy; p15 (bottom) Pat & Chuck Blackley/Alamy; p19 (bottom) Vespasian/Alamy; p20 (top) Philip Scalia/Alamy; p23 (bottom) Hemis/Alamy All other photographs by Lonely Planet Images, and by Glenn van der Knijff p5, p13 (bottom), p17; Dan Herrick p6 (bottom), p8 (top), p11 (bottom), p22 (top and middle); Jeff Greenberg p6 (top), p19 (top); Lee Foster p7; Michelle Bennett p9; Richard Cummins p10, p21 (middle); p24 (top); Paul Kennedy p11 (top); Kraig Lieb p12; Jim Wark p13 (top); Margie Politzer p15 (top); Emily Riddell p16; Brent Winebrenner p18; Richard I'Anson p21 (bottom), p24 (bottom).

All images are the copyright of the photographers unless otherwise indicated. Many of the images in this guide are available for licensing from Lonely Planet Images: www.lonelyplanetimages.com.

Index

GreenDex

It seems like everyone's going "green" these days, but how can you know which businesses are actually ecofriendly and which are simply jumping on the bandwagon?

The following have been selected by our authors because they demonstrate an active sustainable-tourism policy. Some are involved in conservation or environmental education, others engage in organic agriculture, and many are locally owned and operated, thereby maintaining and preserving local identity, arts and culture.

For more information about sustainable tourism and Lonely Planet, see **www.lonelyplanet.com /responsibletravel**.

LONELY PLANET OFFICES

USA
150 Linden St, Oakland, CA 94607
☎ 510 250 6400, toll free 800 275 8555
fax 510 893 8572
info@lonelyplanet.com

Australia
Head Office
Locked Bag 1, Footscray, Victoria 3011
☎ 03 8379 8000, fax 03 8379 8111
talk2us@lonelyplanet.com.au

UK
2nd fl, 186 City Rd,
London EC1V 2NT
☎ 020 7106 2100, fax 020 7106 2101
go@lonelyplanet.co.uk

Published by Lonely Planet Publications Pty Ltd
ABN 36 005 607 983